Nietzsche and Irish modernism

Manchester University Press

Nietzsche and Irish modernism

Patrick Bixby

Manchester University Press

Copyright © Patrick Bixby 2022

The right of Patrick Bixby to be identified as the author of this work has been asserted by them in accordance with the Copyright, Designs and Patents Act 1988.

Published by Manchester University Press
Oxford Road, Manchester M13 9PL

www.manchesteruniversitypress.co.uk

British Library Cataloguing-in-Publication Data
A catalogue record for this book is available from the British Library

ISBN 978 1 5261 6321 9 hardback
ISBN 978 1 5261 8263 0 paperback

First published 2022
Paperback published 2025

The publisher has no responsibility for the persistence or accuracy of URLs for any external or third-party internet websites referred to in this book, and does not guarantee that any content on such websites is, or will remain, accurate or appropriate.

EU authorised representative for GPSR:
Easy Access System Europe – Mustamäe tee 50,
10621 Tallinn, Estonia, gpsr.requests@easproject.com

Typeset by
Deanta Global Publishing Services, Chennai, India

In memoriam Carolyn Bixby

Contents

Acknowledgements	*page* viii
Introduction: Nietzsche, Ireland, modernism	1
1 Shaw: 'An English (or Irish) Nietzsche'	42
2 Yeats: 'Proud hard gift giving joyousness'	92
3 Joyce: 'James Overman'	146
4 War: 'The duel between Nietzsche and civilisation'	193
5 Postwar: 'The Forerunner'	235
Index	275

Acknowledgements

> Whoever speaks incurs debt; whoever speaks further, discourses in order to pay back.
>
> Peter Sloterdijk, *Nietzsche Apostle*

This book was written over the course of many years, during which I incurred innumerable debts of gratitude to friends, colleagues, and family members. But let me begin by expressing my appreciation for the institutional support I received from Arizona State University, especially the Provost's Humanities Fellowship that provided a crucial opportunity to concentrate on this project as it began to take shape. The fellowship proved especially valuable due to the feedback and encouragement that I received from the other members of my writing group: Shahla Talebi, Kent Wright, and Juan Gil-Osle. My appreciation also goes to George Justice, Dean of Humanities, for organising the Provost's Humanities Fellows Academy and to Louis Mendoza, Director of the School of Humanities, Arts, and Cultural Studies, for facilitating my research time during the academic year it took place. My colleagues, past and present, in the school have long provided an intellectually enriching environment for my research and I continue to feel fortunate to work amongst them. Those who were particularly supportive of this project include Owen Anderson, Duku Anokye, Christopher Hanlon, Patricia Huntington, Jeffrey Kennedy, Sharon Kirsch, Annika Mann, Miriam Mara, Francine McGregor, Jacob Meders, Eduardo Pagan, Arthur Sabatini, Michael Stancliff, Stefan Stanchev, and Eric Wertheimer. Thank you, all, for your unfailing generosity.

Over the long period that this project developed, I also profited immensely from the support of generous colleagues across the profession. Mostly directly, Gregory Castle, Nadia Louar, and James McNaughton, as well as the anonymous reviewers at Manchester University Press, did me the enormous service of reading and commenting on the manuscript at different stages. Each brought ample talent, considerable care, and generous spirit to the task and the book has benefitted greatly from it (though, of course, any flaws or infelicities that remain belong entirely to me). I should also give credit to the librarians and archivists who assisted me at the National Library of Ireland, University College Dublin, New York Public Library, and Arizona State University, especially Dennis Isbell at ASU's Fletcher library for his friendly support and sage advice in the face of all manner of research conundrums.

Since its initial conception, this book has gained in ways both big and small from my many conversations with colleagues in Irish studies, modernist studies, and adjacent fields. For these felicitous occasions, I would like to voice my gratitude to Douglas Atkinson, Bree Beal, Claire Bracken, Michael D'Arcy, José Francisco Fernández, Matthew Fogarty, Margaret Kelleher, Seán Kennedy, David Lloyd, Emer Nolan, Angus Mitchell, Caoilfhionn Ní Bheacháin, Nels Pearson, and Feargal Whelan. To be sure, chats with this group during the long-drawn-out experience of research and composition continually reminded me to heed the wisdom of Nietzsche's lovely maxim: 'a good writer possesses not only his own spirit but also the spirit of his friends'. In this regard, special thanks should also go to Nicholas Allen for inviting me to speak on Joyce and Nietzsche at the Willson Center for the Humanities and Arts, and to Mark Quigley for inviting me to contribute an essay to a special issue on Ireland and the First World War. Those occasions prompted writing that later became portions of Chapters 3 and 4 of this book, so I would like to recognise the editors of *Modernism/Modernity* and *Modernist Cultures* for allowing me to reprint those materials, which first appeared in their journals.

Of course, my biggest debts of gratitude are owed to members of my family, who offered unwavering encouragement over the lengthy period this book was written. My appreciation goes to my mother-in-law, Jeri Richardson; my aunt, Nancy Foerster; my father, Patrick Bixby; my brother, Brian Bixby; my precious children, Claire and Owen; and my rock, my love, my accomplice in life, Nicole. Sadly, during the writing of this book, I lost my longest-standing supporter, my mother, Carolyn Bixby. How does one account for the debt owed to a beloved parent? She was my first role model as a reader, thinker, sceptic, and cultural wayfarer: an intellectual seeker, whose curiosity knew no bounds; a political interlocutor, with ardent and yet nuanced opinions; an author of op-eds, educational comics, and family recipe collections; a keeper of random customs from traditions around the world; but especially a Francophile who adored the language, treasured the literature, savoured the cuisine, haunted the museums, and rambled the boulevards. She was, for me as for many, a fiercely loyal friend and doting mentor, possessed of the 'gift-giving virtue'. Nothing can repay the debt I owe to you, Mom, but this book is dedicated to your memory.

Introduction

Nietzsche, Ireland, modernism

In the opening pages of *Ulysses*, as the coarse but cultivated Buck Mulligan plays mockingly at the role of a Catholic priest, he scolds Stephen Dedalus for the young man's callous behaviour towards his dying mother: first conceding, 'I'm hyperborean as much as you', he adds, 'but to think of your mother begging you with her last breath to kneel down and pray for her. And you refused'.[1] Evoking Nietzsche's own evocation of the Hyperboreans in the opening pages of *The Antichrist*, Mulligan adopts the paradoxical guise of a heretical cleric who identifies himself and his reluctant acolyte with those mythical people of distant northern climes, casting a cold eye on the moral codes of 'modern man', perhaps even the seemingly unquestionable duty of a son to honour his mother's final wish.[2] Later in the first chapter of Joyce's novel, as Mulligan moves towards the conclusion of his mock mass and prepares to plunge into the sea at the base of the Martello tower, he reasserts his strained kinship with Stephen: 'I'm the *Uebermensch*, Toothless Kinch and I, the supermen'.[3] Now the identification is with the philosopher's notorious figure of self-overcoming, who stands *beyond* the Christian and Platonic values that have defined Western civilisation and stands *for* the potential to forge new values that might transform the modern world. To be sure, coming from a crude young man intent on goading his overly sensitive counterpart, these evocations of Nietzsche's thought can be rather hard to take seriously, but their prominence and insistence in the opening chapter of Joyce's masterpiece are undeniable. What, then, are we to make of these allusions in a novel that has been understood both as the European modernist text *par excellence* and as the first document of Irish cultural and political independence? What significance could the German's philosophy and its evocative terms – the Hyperboreans, the Übermensch, and many others – have for the articulation of new values in an Irish nation on the verge of a new era? What promise could these terms hold for the new modes of speech that Stephen pursues, but struggles to realise, as an exemplar of the modernist will to artistic innovation? What is the relationship between the predicament of modern Irish culture, with its broad recognition and yet marginal status, and the thought of Nietzsche, this 'good European', who conceived himself as the 'dynamite' that might destroy the very foundations of Western civilisation?

It is often remarked that, as *Ulysses* begins, the Martello tower becomes the site of a strategic contest for the future of Irish culture, pitting Stephen against not just Mulligan but their English housemate, Haines, as well. In this sense, the tower forms a metonym for the wider cultural field in Ireland on that fateful day in June 1904, as a number of competing forces converge in this highly politicised space to do battle for the conscience of the nation. Ironically, it is Haines, the Oxford-educated interloper, who represents the cultural nationalist desire to recover folkloric materials and peasant lifeways as repositories of authentic Irishness, though in pursuing his ethnographic efforts he betrays his condescension, and even racism, as a member of the imperial ruling elite. Meanwhile, Mulligan demonstrates a similar condescension towards the Catholic faith and indicates, through his mockery, that it should no longer play a dominant role in Irish cultural and political life as the new century gets underway. To replace it, he facetiously proposes the foundation of a neo-pagan cult in the tower, where the young men could pursue a cultural revolution drawing inspiration from the radical ideas of Nietzsche, as well as the new Hellenism associated with Matthew Arnold, Oscar Wilde, and others. In the midst of all this, Mulligan also launches into a booming recitation of W.B. Yeats's 'Who Goes with Fergus?', a key Revivalist text, based on Irish legend and presented in his controversial verse drama *The Countess Cathleen* – though, in chanting the poem, Mulligan only succeeds in reminding Stephen of the gloomy scene at his mother's deathbed, where the young man had sung Yeats's verse as she wept. No doubt the opening chapter of Joyce's novel is remarkable for the sheer range of cultural positions, engagements, and strategies it tests in this environment, although this does not quite explain why the presence of Nietzsche's thought has garnered so little attention from readers and critics of *Ulysses*. It quickly becomes evident, even in the brief excerpts presented here, that his ideas bear on Stephen's bad conscience, his 'agenbite of inwit', and play an important role in rendering the young man's psychology as a social outsider, daring individualist, and artistic hero, who would become an icon of the modernist movement in its many manifestations.[4] But, as we shall see, it also becomes clear that these provocative ideas bear on what Stephen, at the conclusion of *A Portrait of the Artist as a Young Man*, famously calls the 'uncreated conscience of my race', as he stands poised between a long history of colonial subjugation and a radically uncertain future, just taking shape as Joyce began writing *Ulysses* more than a decade later.[5]

Nietzsche and Irish modernism contends that the thought of the German philosopher played a significant, even decisive, role in the emergence and evolution of a distinctly Irish brand of literary modernism. To understand the intricate cultural dynamics at play in this process the study traces the circulation of Nietzsche's ideas through the work of major Irish writers, including George Bernard Shaw, W.B. Yeats, and, of course, James Joyce – and, more broadly, through the Irish cultural field between 1893 and 1925, as his thought emerged in this arena and exerted its greatest impact. This book is concerned, then, not only with canonical works of literature such as *Ulysses*, but also with the movement of these ideas through minor works of literature, scholarly essays, magazine articles, newspaper debates, public lectures, and private correspondence – in order to mark their transference, translation, and transformation in particular social and political circumstances. To be sure, Nietzsche's writing provides a case study in how the cultures of modernism circulated through Europe and beyond, generating book-length studies of its reception in a variety of national settings, including England, France, Germany, Spain, Russia, and the United States.[6] But, even as the study of Irish modernism has developed in recent years, literary and cultural historians have largely neglected to examine the significance of Nietzsche's thought against the backdrop of Irish history during the tumultuous years of cultural revival, Home Rule agitation, world war, revolution, civil war, and state building.[7] In books such as *Thus Spake Zarathustra*, *A Genealogy of Morals*, *Twilight of the Idols*, and *The Antichrist*, Nietzsche articulated a host of ideas that threatened some of the most dearly held values of Western culture, with his challenges to Judeo-Christian morality, Enlightenment rationality, and the spirit of democracy – ideas embodied, if rather ambiguously, in the figure of the Übermensch (translated into English variously as 'beyond-man', 'overman', and 'superman'). At the same time, Nietzsche was recognised as an acute psychologist who had developed a vocabulary – including terms such as bad conscience, decadence, nihilism, and *ressentiment* – for diagnosing the ills of the modern mind and the troubles of the modern age, a vocabulary that in due course would spread through a variety of discourses and national traditions. For many early commentators, as for many more recent critics and scholars, Nietzsche's writing (despite or perhaps because of its metaphorical and elusive qualities) seemed to articulate the shared preoccupations of the new cultural movements that came to be referred to collectively as 'modernism'. At the turn of the twentieth century, on the geographical and economic margins of Europe, a new variety of cultural capital began to circulate, giving the likes of Buck Mulligan and Stephen Dedalus access to a resource that might well be valuable for native forms of cultural production. Irish writers soon started to adopt Nietzschean ideas and adapt them to different historical circumstances in order to address the problems of metrocolonial modernity and a specifically Irish variety of cultural crisis, including anxieties about autonomy, masculinity, and communal values in the context of British rule. To trace the movement of Nietzsche's ideas in relation to these circumstances is thus to work towards a more complete and refined understanding of Irish modernism, which views the field of cultural production in Ireland as a site of convergence and contestation, defined by a complex negotiation between native concerns and foreign perspectives.

This is not to return to outworn notions of international modernism or cosmopolitan detachment, but rather to view Irish modernism as an indigenous literary and artistic movement linked to both local historical conditions and transnational cultural currents. Nor, in arguing that Nietzsche's thought played an important role in the emergence and development of Irish modernism, does this study claim that modernism was in some sense imposed on or imported to Ireland; instead, it sets out to investigate the dynamic interaction between native cultural movements and the flow of ideas, images, and forms across national boundaries. When Buck Mulligan concludes his jocular mass by travestying and transvaluing Proverbs 19:7 – 'He who stealeth from the Poor lendeth to the Lord. Thus spake Zarathustra' – he seems to contradict his earlier rebuke of Stephen's lack of Christian pity and to advocate instead for selfishness, licentiousness, and callousness, while slyly ridiculing the young man's impoverished condition.[8] Most evidently, as the cultural contest that plays out in the chapter comes to an end, the mock quotation works to denigrate the authority of sermonic speech, as it facetiously inverts the values expressed in the scripture and defies their power to forever define the conscience of the Irish people. But, playing at the role of a Nietzschean priest, Mulligan also undermines his own authority: in his mouth, the refrain that follows the parodic scripture has lost its authority, attaching itself to a bit of playful heresy and calling attention to its diminishing force, with each repetition, in the pages of *Thus Spake Zarathustra*. The words thus tell us something about the speaker himself: his irreverent attitude, his access to international cultural capital, and even his proneness to being taken in by intellectual fashions, at the expense of the kind of deep reflection valued by his counterpart, Stephen. But the words also tell us something about the modernist aspiration to create new values that might overcome the feelings of antipathy, of ressentiment and bad conscience, which have weighed so heavily on the young man, as well as on his fellow Catholics and compatriots. All this suggests that the opening chapter of *Ulysses* is not just the site of a dialogue between different social languages, but of a stirring encounter between Nietzschean thought and national tradition (and the many discourses that contribute to the latter, from early folkloric stories and medieval Irish sagas to those found in contemporary newspapers and ethnographic studies), an encounter that marks their powerful influence even as it cunningly resists the authority of any single discourse to define the values of the Irish people. A particular strain of modernism, then, can be seen as growing directly out of this encounter, this synchronicity, between the incursion of images and ideas from abroad and the revival of indigenous cultural traditions at home.

In recent years, critics have become increasingly willing to speak of a distinctly Irish variety of modernism – to acknowledge the native investments of writers like Joyce as aligned with, rather than contrary to, their participation in a broader literary movement that pursued both new forms of expression and a revaluation of received cultural norms and traditions.[9] It is under the heading of 'Irish modernism' that we can best account for his enduring preoccupation with both the national conscience of the Irish people and the transnational resources available to reinvent that conscience. But Joyce, long perceived as an exile and cosmopolitan, is not the only writer to be reconsidered in this way over the last two decades: Yeats, often considered something of an anomaly in the modernist canon given his early commitments to revivalism, cultural nationalism, and the renewed importance of indigenous mythology and local folklore, has recently been at the centre of critical debates that seek to renovate the field of modernist studies by addressing these very commitments. Joe Cleary, for instance, has suggested that we need not view modernism in Ireland as a repudiation of revivalism, but as an extension of it; nor do we need to conceive of revivalism as merely a reaction against an imposed imperial culture.[10] The history of colonialism in Ireland, with its deprivations, oppressions, and other motives for emigration, helps to explain why these writers spent large portions of their careers abroad in European capitals and so often encountered foreign ideas and artistic movements. But it is no longer necessary to see modernism, given its orientation towards contemporaneity and futurity, as incompatible with revivalism, given its concern for history and tradition, since the temporality of each has been recognised as much more elastic than these terms indicate. Nor is it necessary to conceive of modernism, even in its earliest phase, as strictly a Continental and Anglo-American affair, taking place in Paris or Berlin or London or New York, since its emergence was always dependent upon exchanges (of ideas and individuals) between these capitals and the province, the colony, the so-called peripheries. Conceived in this way, Irish modernism is a category that, despite their differences, Joyce and Yeats can coinhabit more comfortably than other literary-historical configurations. It also provides room for a number of other figures who have been marginalised or simply excluded from discussions of both Irish and modernist literature, most notably those Irish expatriates in late Victorian England, Oscar Wilde and George Bernard Shaw. The accommodation of these writers suggests just how crucial the category is, even as it reminds us of how unlikely it might have once seemed that Ireland, with its reputedly delayed or compromised modernity, should have engendered writers who occupy such a vast territory on the literary landscape of the period.

Egerton and the transvaluation of all values

George Egerton (Mary Chavelita Dunne) has emerged as another key figure in the category of Irish modernism: in recent years, she has finally been recognised not just as a vital contributor to the emergence of this unique brand of literary modernism, but also as an early propagator of Nietzschean images and ideas in the English-speaking world. Although her radical social and political views, along with her experiments in stream-of-consciousness narrative, have led critics to acknowledge Egerton as a forerunner to Joyce, she should be viewed as an important innovator of the modernist short story in her own right, as well as a writer exemplary of the transnational dimensions of Irish modernism.[11] Her early interest in Nietzsche, moreover, makes Egerton a crucial figure for the cultural history set out in this study. Born in 1859 to an Irish father and Welsh mother, she spent her early years in Australia, New Zealand, and Chile before receiving a Catholic education in Ireland and spending a year in a Catholic convent school in Germany, where she learned the German language. Despite her restless movements around the globe, Egerton considered herself 'intensely Irish' because she spent many of her formative early years in Dublin and its environs.[12] In the 1880s, she went on to live in London, New York, and then Christiana (now Oslo), as she became immersed in the work of Scandinavian modernists, including Henrik Ibsen, August Strindberg, Ola Hansson, and Knut Hamsun. It was in Norway that she was introduced to Nietzsche's work, which was quickly gaining attention across Scandinavia thanks to a widely publicised series of lectures by the influential Danish critic Georg Brandes in the spring of 1888. Provocatively, Brandes identified Nietzsche as an 'Aristocratic Radical', who sought to achieve distinction by combating the conventions of 'religion, morality and literature', as well as 'marriage, the family, the community and the State'– and by beginning to create 'new tables of values', independent of the decadent institutions that had come to define European modernity.[13] Due to her rather unusual background and her timely arrival in Norway, Egerton was well positioned not only to witness the emergence of the philosopher's public image, but to read his work in the original German and to discuss it with other enthusiasts such as Hansson and Hamsun. In her early short story collections, *Keynotes* (1893) and *Discords* (1894), she draws on elements of Nietzsche's thought to interrogate the bourgeois institutions and values that Brandes's essay enumerates, as well as the idealised images of traditional femininity that became an object of critique for the 'New Woman' writing of the 1880s and 1890s.

This is not to say that Egerton's stories uncritically assimilate Nietzsche's ideas. To enlist the philosopher in the feminist cause might seem contradictory or even absurd, given the caustic statements about womanhood to be found in his oeuvre. But it is very much in keeping with the way his broader critiques of conventional morality and European civilisation were soon to be adapted to new circumstances, with novel social and political implications. In 'A Cross Line', the opening story of *Keynotes*, Egerton depicts an extramarital relationship between the 'Fisherwoman' and an outdoorsman, whom she encounters near a country estate that she shares with her loving but rather dull husband in Millstreet, County Cork. In the midst of her narrative, the Fisherwoman considers whether the other women she has known share her 'thirst for excitement, for change, this restless craving for sun and love and motion'.[14] This reflection then leads her to laugh because, she ponders,

> [men] have all overlooked the eternal wildness, the untamed primitive savage temperament that lurks in the mildest, best woman ... And when a Strindberg or a Nietzche [*sic*] arises and peers into the recesses of her nature and dissects her ruthlessly, the men shriek out louder than the women, because the truth is at all times unpalatable, and the gods they have set up are dear to them.[15]

Although, as Daniel Brown notes, this depiction of Strindberg and Nietzsche heralds the reputation that they would soon garner as 'the great misogynists of their age', it also evinces Egerton recruiting them as 'influential allies for her brand of feminism', insofar as they upset the conventional notions of meek and mild femininity that predominated in fin-de-siècle society.[16] In the response to these notions, Egerton asserts a vision of womanhood that, as other critics have pointed out, adopts an essentialising perspective.[17] But this is a perspective that nonetheless contradicts the restrictive images of femininity that had been imposed on women by a range of social institutions, practices, and norms that sought to 'tame' or 'improve' them for the benefit of their male counterparts. That women, despite all of this, are still capable of deep affection is the 'crowning disability' of their sex, according to the Fisherwoman, who chafes against this compulsion: 'if it were not for that, we women would master the world'.[18] It is women, in other words, who are closer to realising the promise of the Übermensch, for whom the 'elaborately reasoned codes for controlling morals or man do not weigh a jot ... against an impulse, an instinct'. It is men, on the contrary, who have become 'tamed, amenable animals' just as Nietzsche had asserted, even as he failed to value sufficiently 'this untameableness of ours' that the Fisherwoman proclaims for her gender: the qualities that 'go to make a

Napoleon – superstition, want of honour, disregard for opinion and the eternal I', she tells her lover, 'are oftener found in a woman than a man'.[19]

If Nietzsche's thought thus becomes a resource for Egerton's critique of the gender norms that prevailed in modern European society, then his name also becomes a byword for dissent from all conventions (as Brandes's lectures would have it) 'with respect to marriage, the family, the community and the State'. In the autobiographical story 'Now Spring Has Come', based on her brief but intense relationship with Hamsun, Egerton has her two protagonists discuss ideas drawn from a range of fashionable iconoclasts – Tolstoy's doctrine of celibacy, Ibsen's exposé of neurosis in *Hedda Gabler*, and Strindberg's harsh view of 'the female animal' – before agreeing that 'Friedrich Nietzche [*sic*]' appeals to them 'immensely'. With this litany of scandalous topics, punctuated by the name of the German philosopher, the lovers demonstrate themselves to be the members of a cultural elite at odds with both the vulgarities of popular taste and the restrictions of bourgeois morality. The next story in the collection, 'The Spell of the White Elf', centres on an independent and imaginative woman, a writer who describes how she became enthralled with the idea of motherhood after encountering the young child of a distant relative. Such is the enchantment cast over the woman that she spends her money on pretty clothes for the 'white elf', instead of buying 'a pragtbind of Nietzsche', which 'must wait'. It has been suggested that Nietzsche is used here 'as an indicator of social and intellectual sophistication', which surely he is insofar as the 'pragtbind' or 'deluxe edition' of his work is marked as a valuable piece of cultural capital.[20] But it becomes increasingly evident that what Nietzsche offers is a new illicit variety of cultural capital, which places its possessor in opposition to those Brandes calls 'Culture-Philistines', who still believe in the value of the reigning 'conventions with respect to religion, morality and literature'. The conflict between the protagonist's maternal yearnings and her desire for the book is thus indicative of the divergence between a feminine impulse reinforced by social expectations and the radically dissenting views to be found in Nietzsche's writings. The conflict faced by Egerton's protagonist is one that permeates her fiction, which repeatedly marks the disjuncture between the 'affection' and 'softness' of her female characters, on the one hand, and the 'wild' and 'untamed' elements of their nature, on the other.[21]

It is only with 'The Regeneration of Two', the final story in *Discords*, that Egerton mends this disjuncture, at least provisionally. As the story begins, the protagonist, an Englishwoman in Norway referred to simply as 'Fruen' (or 'mistress'), confesses that she has considered 'having a mission' like many of her fellow countrywomen, who 'go in for suffrage, social reform, politics, all sorts of fatiguing things', but she has dismissed any such undertaking because 'it would last just as long as it was a new sensation'.[22] A chance encounter with an indigent writer, however, soon introduces her to a Nietzschean perspective on the affairs of her fellow men and women:

> Close your eyes, Fruen, and look down over all the cities of the world – look with your inner eyes, try to pierce the soul of things; what do you see? Shall I tell you what *I* see? A great crowd of human beings. Take all these men, male and female, fashion them into one colossal man, study him, and what will you find in him? Tainted blood; a brain with the parasites of a thousand systems sucking at its base and warping it; a heart robbed of all healthy feelings by false conceptions, bad conscience, and a futile code of morality – a code that makes the natural workings of sex a vile thing to be ashamed of; the healthy delight in the cultivation of one's body as the beautiful perfect sheath of one's soul and spirit, with no shame in any part of it, all alike being clean, a sin of the flesh, a carnal conception to be opposed by asceticism.[23]

By way of conclusion, he adds that 'salvation lies with the women and the new race they are to mother'.[24] Although the writer and Fruen soon part, this stunning vision lingers with her and works to shape her 'mission' over the succeeding years, largely because it has 'stung' her to look more closely at herself: 'to see what was under the form into which custom had fashioned me, of what pith I was made, what spirit, if any, lay under the outer woman'.[25] This process of self-inspection eventually leads her to transform her country estate into a kind of utopian community, where unwed mothers and their children, once outcast by society, can make their own livings, their own rules, their own educational programmes. In this way, Fruen begins to actualise a Nietzschean vision in the domestic sphere that Mulligan can only play at with his evocations of a masculinist cult of 'new paganism' to be founded in the Martello tower. Reunited with the long-absent writer in this new environment, Fruen draws on Nietzsche as she explains her efforts to produce 'a feminine "Umwerthung aller Werthe" [transvaluation of all values] a new standard of woman's worth', which urges each member of her sex to 'worthen herself by all-seeing knowledge' rather than to 'cheapen herself body and soul through ignorant innocence'.[26] For Nietzsche, the proper response to the 'morality of *taming*' was to expose its values as mere fictions, which should be revised in a manner that embraces human instincts in more candid and life-affirming ways.[27] Although the philosopher occasionally acknowledged the fictions imposed on women, Egerton extends the imperative to transvalue all values in a direction that Nietzsche never did – that is, to contest the role that morality has played in arresting women in the image of chaste, naive, and weak creatures unsuited of deep psychological insights or strong sexual passions. Her rebellious vision of the 'New Woman' issues from such transvaluations.

Nietzsche's influence and modernist studies

Egerton must be duly credited with being not just the first writer in English to integrate Nietzsche's thought into her fiction, but the first to do so in critical and creative ways that helped to shape both her writing and the nascent modernist movement in Ireland. As we will see in Chapter 4, she was not the only Irish woman to adapt Nietzsche's ideas to her cause, though very few would follow her lead. Rather, it was primarily her male counterparts in Great Britain and Ireland, including her friend and sometimes antagonist, Shaw, who would be most receptive to the inducements of Nietzsche's thought. Even so, it would be difficult to overstate Nietzsche's impact on the cultures of modernism across Europe and North America. In the late 1890s, as his writings were translated and republished, his name quickly became associated with a strident dissent from modern decadence, mass politics, and the traditions of nineteenth-century Western culture and society in general. During the course of the next quarter-century, his ideas were taken up by a broad array of artists, intellectuals, and writers, from D.H. Lawrence and Wyndham Lewis in England, to André Gide and André Malraux in France, to Rainer Maria Rilke and Thomas Mann in Austria and Germany. Viewing these literary figures and others like them through the critical paradigm of international modernism, a series of major Anglophone studies written in the 1980s retrospectively consolidated the sense that Nietzsche's influence was nearly unavoidable, even as each deployed very different conceptions of what amounts to 'influence'. In *Heirs to Dionysus* (1981), for instance, John Burt Foster Jr. announces a vague consensus among literary scholars when he claims that the philosopher became 'a commanding presence for the modernists because he expressed some of their deepest impulses so fully and so pointedly'.[28] The use of experimental forms to conduct a radical questioning of established orthodoxies, Foster suggests, enabled Nietzsche to become not just an intellectual force but a literary one. This is not to say that his 'heirs' fully acknowledged their debt to him, but that traces of his thought – his emphasis on polaristic thinking, his psychology of creativity, his conception of the tragic, his reflections on instinct, his sense of cultural crisis, and his vision of cultural renewal – were woven into the very fabric of literary modernism. Keith May's *Nietzsche and Modern Literature* (1988) also affirms the broad influence of Nietzsche's writing, but focuses on four writers he regards as 'the most considerable of those who have faced their world somewhat "Nietzscheanly"' – W.B. Yeats, Rainer Rilke, Thomas Mann, and D.H. Lawrence. This is not a conventional study of influence so much as an attempt to read images in Yeats or settings in Mann side by side with metaphors and concepts in Nietzsche. The result is an examination of the affinities between the 'thinking' of these writers and the complex, perspectival views held by the philosopher, affinities that, according to May, bring his philosophy into a more definitive 'shape'.[29]

It becomes evident in these studies that, precisely due to its extensive breadth and force, Nietzsche's legacy provided an important testing ground for new theories of influence and intertextuality during this period of modernist scholarship, itself deeply indebted to poststructuralist theory and criticism. Margot Norris's *Beasts of the Modern Imagination* (1985), another significant example of this effort, explores what the critic calls the 'biocentric tradition' in modern thought and literature: that is, the critique of anthropocentrism that arises from Darwin's theory of evolution but exerts its influence through Nietzsche's reading of those ideas.[30] The philosopher is seen as a kind of conduit through which the radical Darwinian view of the human being as bestial, irrational, and vitalistic is passed on to artists and writers such as Franz Kafka, Max Ernst, and D.H. Lawrence. Similarly, Kathryn Lindberg's *Reading Pound Reading: Modernism after Nietzsche* (1987) focuses on various theories and practices of interpretation that Ezra Pound borrowed from Nietzsche and other philosophers, scientists, critics, and poets and then incorporated into his own efforts to foment, and later defend, his modernist 'revolution of the word'.[31] Nietzsche is key to this critical narrative not due to any particular idea or perspective he provides to Pound, but because he modelled innovative rhetorical strategies that assisted the poet in his polemical and pedagogical writings. Revising the history of modernism in the aftermath of these studies, Michael Bell has claimed that Nietzsche served 'not as an influence' so much as a forerunner who 'articulated discursively and in advance the complex of themes and the composite worldview that can be deduced from a large part of modernist writing'.[32] In this regard, the philosopher has been an aide more to modernist critics than to modernist artists and writers themselves. For, according to Bell, although many key figures in the modernist movement were quite familiar with the Nietzsche's writing, it is not the case that his views on women or education or power helped to shape modernism, but that his 'diagnostic and deconstructive critique of cultural forms' parallels that found in much modernist writing.[33] Nonetheless, Bell does provide an overview of the various ways that Nietzsche's ideas on the nature of power, the constitution of human values, and the damaging influence of democracy took hold in certain artistic circles. In the final analysis, however, it is the philosopher who owes something to modernist novelists and poets, since his 'most radical claims for the metaphysical significance of the aesthetic might not be comprehensible without the examples of such writers as Joyce and Yeats'.[34]

Focusing on the scene of Irish modernism, the present study seeks instead to track the ways that a particular group of writers took up Nietzsche's ideas as a means not only to diagnose cultural ills or expose the perverse character of dominant values, but also to begin forging new values that might replace the discredited ones. In this sense, Irish modernism refers to a specific variety of what Robert Gooding-Williams calls 'novelty-engendering interruptions of received practices and traditions', in the context of a subjugated society and a tumultuous epoch, which presented the possibility of radically divergent futures.[35] If these terms broadly describe the circumstances from which modernism emerged, they take on particular inflection in Ireland, which since the Act of Union in 1800 had no longer been a discrete geopolitical domain but rather that anomalous and paradoxical thing: a metropolitan colony. To put this in other terms, the island nation was something of an exception in Europe, because, as Terry Eagleton has persuasively argued, it had not 'as a whole ... leapt at a bound from tradition to modernity. Instead, it presented an exemplary case of what Marx has dubbed combined and uneven development'.[36] If Ireland had undergone modernisation in sectors such as public administration, centralised education, and parliamentary politics, it could be said to fall behind in areas such as industrial manufacturing, income growth, and urban development. This state of affairs has been attributed to the arrival of modernity to Ireland by other means: that is, by the work of colonisation in the form of British influence rather than by industrialisation in the form of broad-scale development through internal economic reorganisation. It also suggests the persistent danger that Irish nationalism, in its effort to designate native values, might succumb to colonial resentments. Meanwhile, the powerful influence of the Catholic Church meant that, while the rest of Europe was adopting steadily more secular customs and beliefs, Ireland remained, in the eyes of many, devoutly religious, socially conservative, and sexually repressed. The trouble with this historical narrative is precisely that it fails to account for indigenous forms of modernisation in both Irish art and society. Nonetheless, by the end of the nineteenth century, a sustained intrusion on native traditions, coupled with the broad distribution of outside influences, was provoking insistent questions regarding the role that Irish culture should serve in understanding a shared past, meeting the present needs of the national community, and realising a collective future. It appears certain in hindsight that this confrontation between the modern and the traditional in Ireland generated conditions favourable to a vibrant modernist culture.

What is most significant about Nietzsche, at least in relation to Irish modernism, is that he is a writer who initiates the potential for new modes of speech to address the predicaments of modernity. Previous writers and thinkers had challenged the prevailing conventions of Christian morality and bourgeois society; previous writers had sought to diagnose the decadence of modern man and his social institutions; previous writers had claimed to understand the psychology of persistent guilt, rancour, or abstinence;

previous writers had dedicated themselves to the improvement or perfection of humanity. But Nietzsche, questioning the very value of values, was the first to make the creation of new values a central philosophical problem whereby 'the text' or 'language' itself could be seen as establishing the possibility of asserting innovative moral or ethical perspectives.[37] Nietzsche's 'diagnostic and deconstructive critique of cultural forms' reveals the crisis of values at the heart of modernity as it sheds light on the deceptions of not just morality or religion, but gender, nationality, and a multitude of other concerns.[38] It follows, however, that this critique is valuable only insofar as it opens the way to the creation of new values: it is here that the critical and the creative, the ethical and the aesthetic, intersect. Nietzsche attributes to art a central role in the generation of values, so that whatever new ideals come into being do so as a result of the creative force of 'the will to power', no longer restrained by the sense of what had been considered 'given' or 'necessary' or 'transcendent' under the established moral codes. The figure of the Übermensch is perhaps best understood as the embodiment of this potentiality. *Thus Spake Zarathustra*, in this regard, aspires to found a new myth, one that would redirect the modern world from its descent into nihilism by providing it with a new aspiration, the starting point for a new culture. But it is just as significant that Nietzsche is largely reticent about the precise characteristics of the Übermensch and the specific values that he represents, so that any call for the emergence of such a figure maintains a provocative openness to the future. At the same time, such a call generates an 'economic paradox', because there is no guarantee that the immense cost to be paid in the forfeiture of our sustaining illusions – regarding morality or religion, gender or nationality, and so on – will be adequately compensated by the deployment of creative energies.[39]

This paradox speaks directly to the value of Nietzsche for Irish modernism. For Peter Sloterdijk, the 'Nietzsche-event' should be viewed as 'a catastrophe in the history of language', because his intervention as 'a literary new-evangelist' challenges the modes of understanding that have predominated in Western culture.[40] According to this argument, Nietzsche's distinctive use of language challenges the Judeo-Christian understanding of 'the Word' as a medium for God's perpetual self-praise by emphasising the narcissistic self-regard inherent in all discourse. Nietzsche's break from the evangelic tradition marks the end of a certain discursive potential: that is, the possibility for the messenger of such glad tidings to take up the Word to his advantage; instead, his 'dis-evangel', *Thus Spake Zarathustra*, secures a profit precisely through the parodic subversion of earlier modes of value assertion or legitimation, which had long since lost credit in the modern era. It could be added, however, that Nietzsche's writing also works to get 'beyond' the dominant modes of discourse in Western philosophical tradition not by directly denouncing them, but by writing in relation to them – in a parodic and stylised manner that renders them merely conventional or even absurd. Nietzsche's form of critical inquiry, then, is not conducted in the conventional manner of philosophical investigation, but instead through a series of what Paul de Man calls 'value-seductions': 'pragmatic and demagogical value-oppositions [such] as weakness and strength, disease and health, herd and the "happy few"'.[41] He cannot demonstrate the correctness of his revised hierarchies through some non-tautological analysis of value. He can only affirm what is high or noble or aristocratic through the force of his rhetorical appeals, which often assert these values as a matter of personal taste and individual style, against the presumed gravity of theological and philosophical discourse.

Like Sloterdijk, but in a more direct and sustained manner, I draw on the sociology of culture developed by Pierre Bourdieu to examine Nietzsche's writing as a strategic intervention in the field of cultural production that resists previous modes of legitimation to the degree that they impose certain norms and sanctions on artists and thinkers.[42] The field of cultural production thus becomes a symbolic space of struggle over contending regimes of value and over the cultural authority or influence necessary to participate in a new regime. There is good reason for scepticism regarding the success of such novel efforts, about the possibility of 'overcoming' or 'transvaluing' the regimes of value that have defined Western culture, even if it is a scepticism that Nietzsche himself shares at certain moments. For a modernist writer to cite his philosophy is to adopt a strategy, however risky and uncertain, designed to outflank or displace the 'Culture-Philistines' in a contest that leads to the revolution in taste and value called 'modernism'. With the rise of this cultural fashion, often associated with the new, the provocative, the shocking, a dramatic restructuring of the cultural field commenced in the final years of the nineteenth century.[43] At stake in the redeployment of Nietzsche's language is the redefinition of cultural distinction, as a broad range of writers borrow on what could be called its black-market cultural capital – derived from his dangerous and dissident reputation – to establish their own position in the emergent field of modernist cultural production.

The present study is thus concerned not so much with affinities or echoes or influence, certainly not influence in the anxious sense associated with Harold Bloom, but rather with the possibility of tracking the figure of Nietzsche and a number of his trademark ideas through the archive of modern Irish culture. This is not to suggest that these units of philosophical thought somehow retain their originary value, which continues to exercise a mystifying power even after they are detached from the corpus of Nietzschean philosophy. Nor is it to assign a discursive priority to philosophy over and against literature, which becomes merely an exemplification or narration of its rational claims. Rather it is to acknowledge, with Jacques Derrida, that each unit of philosophical thought issues from a network of tropes or figures and should be understood as a trope itself, which can be transplanted, grafted, cut and pasted, into a new textual system – *and*, I want to add, a new socio-political context – even if a trace of its originary identity always remains.[44] Nietzsche's writing, as de Man reminds us, is particularly prone to this kind of treatment because it is largely comprised of 'discontinuous, aphoristic formulations', which can be freely detached from their original contexts and also readily classified as so many suggestive tropes, amounting to an extended demonstration of the literary quality of philosophical discourse.[45] The Übermensch is again a case in point: announced directly enough within the rhetorical frameworks constructed by Nietzsche in *The Joyful Wisdom* and *Thus Spake Zarathustra*, but, as Bell puts it, 'retain[ing] a teasing indeterminacy at the level of any imagined instantiation'.[46] Such a figure might be found in a young man who overcomes his provincial upbringing to become an artist, in a 'busy minded' woman who establishes a new community on radical social ideals, in some future race that leaves behind the restrictions of human society altogether, or in any number of other persons as long as they depart from the legacy of Western culture that has defined 'man'. In this regard, Nietzsche's philosophy has enjoyed a remarkable success, fostered by its ability to evade definitive interpretation, even if that success has made his ideas attractive to those who would cut and paste them into the propaganda of social and political causes that he either denounced or could not foresee. It is for this reason, moreover, that Nietzsche's writing has generated such a varied and voluminous reception history, albeit one that has not fully accounted for his accommodation by Irish modernists. The present effort to trace out the circulation of these units of thought necessarily involves marking their transference, translation, and transformation in new texts and contexts (as well as the reciprocal transformation of those texts and contexts) in order to demonstrate their value for modern Irish culture.

Nordau on Nietzsche and degeneration

At the turn of the twentieth century, Nietzsche's emerging reputation as a leading emissary of 'the modern' in European culture owed much to Max Nordau's scandal-making screed, *Entartung* (1892, translated into English as *Degeneration*, 1895). With the pretence of objectivity, the physician-turned-cultural-critic employed a medico-scientific model of cultural pathology to diagnose what he viewed as the many ills of fin-de-siècle decadence, including the immoral, irrational, and anti-social nature of 'ego-maniacs' such as Ibsen, Verlaine, Wagner, Baudelaire, Wilde, and Nietzsche. Nordau opposes the 'snobs' – who praise the work of these degenerate writers and thus 'affect to have the same taste as the select and exclusive minority' – to 'the great majority of the middle and lower classes' – 'the Philistine or the Proletarian' who 'still finds undiluted satisfaction in the old and oldest forms of art and poetry'.[47] But while *Degeneration* itself was soon dismissed as symptomatic of bourgeois moralism and misguided positivism, the book nonetheless became required reading in the final decade of the nineteenth century for anyone interested in the emerging cultural trends that would come to be known retrospectively as 'modernism' – in fact, quickly translated and republished across the Continent, the massive tome capitalised on the rising interest in these trends to became one of the ten bestselling books in Europe as the century drew to a close. *Degeneration* duly made its mark on cultural history by pathologising modernism at its very inception. Echoes of its basic thesis can be heard not just in National Socialist propaganda, which proclaimed that 'degenerate art' was an affront to the German spirit, but in the strident claims of critics such as György Lukács, who dismissed much of modernism, including the philosophy of Nietzsche and the fiction of Joyce, as symptomatic of cultural crisis and biological decline, rather than as exemplary of a welcome emergence of the new from received practices and traditions.[48]

Nordau derived the term 'degeneration' from the famed psychiatrist Benedict Morel who had postulated that mental deficiency and psychological aberration were the outcomes of physiological deterioration across generations, largely brought on by the rapid industrialisation and urbanisation of the modern world. According to Nordau, however, 'degenerates are not always criminals, prostitutes, anarchists, and pronounced lunatics; they are often authors and artists'.[49] Such individuals were seen as nothing less than threats to the health of the entire population. Looking out at the cultural field of the fin de siècle, he develops his own taxonomy of degeneration and catalogues his own collection of degenerates, attempting in the process to delegitimise their modes of cultural production: Nietzsche, like his fellow egomaniacs, is labelled as an 'invalid who does not see things as they are, does not understand the world, and cannot take up a right attitude towards it' because he gives entirely too much attention to the self and its internal processes.[50] In his lengthy chapter dedicated to the philosopher, Nordau displays particular scorn for this variety of individualism, announcing that 'as in Ibsen ego-mania has found its poet, so in Nietzsche it has found its philosopher', who supplies the theory, or something that proclaims itself as such, 'of the person who "wills", is "free", and more "wholly himself"'.[51] For Sloterdijk, looking back on the reception history of the philosopher, Nietzsche can best be understood as a 'brand name' associated with strident individualism, first advertised by his self-eulogistic assertions about the value of his work and his status as an author.[52] This was later promoted by the selective compilation of his work, beginning with the dubious editorial efforts of his sister, Elisabeth Förster-Nietzsche, as well as the polemical commentary of sympathetic pundits like Brandes and vehement critics such as Nordau, who assembles a troubling case file on Nietzsche from scraps and shards of his philosophy detached from their original contexts.

With his diagnosis of the philosopher, Nordau forcefully declared the terms, if not exactly the tone, that would largely define Nietzsche's early reception in Europe and North America. The primary basis for his dire assessment is found in Nietzsche's singular style, with its continuous 'tumult of phrases', which were not indicative of literary achievement, but something far less impressive: when properly interpreted, according to Nordau's pathologising and *ad hominem* emphasis, this tumult can be seen as merely a distraction from the philosopher's unfailingly hackneyed ideas and his underlying psychological disorders. Once the reader 'has acquired some practice in discerning the actual theme among the drums-and-fifes of this ear splitting, merry-go-round music, and, in the hailstorm of rattling words, that render clear vision almost impossible, has learned to perceive the fundamental thought, he at once observes that Nietzsche's assertions are either commonplaces ... or bellowing insanity'.[53] As evidence of this, Nordau proceeds to quote passage after passage, full of 'obviously insane assertions or expressions', from *Thus Spake Zarathustra*, *The Joyful Wisdom*, and *Beyond Good and Evil*, lifting them out of their original contexts and attributing them directly to Nietzsche and his lamentable condition, rather than to his fictional prophet or his rhetorical flair.[54] To be sure, the philosopher has been notoriously prone to this sort of treatment at the hands of both his champions and detractors. More than anything else, what Nordau succeeds in demonstrating by appealing to these foreshortened and distorted fragments is simply that Nietzsche is not a 'systematic' philosopher of the sort prescribed by the German tradition. As we shall see, however, the critic does attribute to the philosopher an unequivocal doctrine that he believes is a direct threat to his most cherished values: liberalism, positivism, scientific progressivism, and, above all, bourgeois respectability. In the process, Nordau also contributes in a substantial way to a remarkable inversion – what might be called the 'modernist inversion' – whereby Nietzsche and many of his fellow degenerates amassed cultural prestige according to the measure of their dissent from prevailing social and political norms, as well as their aesthetic analogues.[55] Paradoxically, then, Nordau's effort to demonstrate the pathological qualities of Nietzsche's writing, which the critic carries out in his own prolix manner, helped nonetheless (or all the more) to attract new disciples to the extraordinary 'madman' through a prurient interest in his ravings. The effort, that is, succeeded in introducing Nordau's audience to much of what early readers found so compelling in Nietzsche's philosophy, especially in his style, at a time when his works were not yet widely translated and available.[56]

Nordau does more to give Nietzsche the appeal of scandal, of danger, by emphasising the moral and ethical dimensions of his thought, which become the object of much derision from the critic, even as they are quite evidently the object of much fascination. Early in the chapter, the critic lays out the key elements of 'Nietzsche's doctrine', which 'promulgated as orthodoxy by his disciples, criticises the foundation of ethics, investigates the genesis of the concept of good and evil, examines the value of that which is called virtue and vice, both for the individual and for society, explains the origins of conscience, and seeks to give an idea of the end of the evolution of the race, and, consequently, of man's ideal – the "over man" (*Uebermensch*)'. A sympathetic commentator could not do much better in adumbrating the basic features of this 'doctrine', as Nordau attempts to 'condense [them] as closely as possible ... but without the cackle of ... mazy digressions or useless phrases' to be found in their original rendering.[57] The critic also introduces readers to his own greatly condensed version of Nietzsche's *Zur Geneaologie der Moral* (*A Genealogy of Morals*): noble races 'of blond beasts' subjugating less noble races at the beginnings of civilisation; the noble races creating a master-morality that associates 'evil with vulgar' and 'good' with their own 'severity, cruelty, pride, courage, contempt of danger, joy in risk'; subjugated races opposing these values with their own slave-morality, which 'distinguished and glorified' those qualities that 'served to ameliorate the existence of sufferers', including 'compassion ... patience, humility'; and then this slave-morality overthrowing master-morality and the 'new valuation of all moral concepts. (In his insane gibberish Nietzsche names this "transvaluation of values" – *Umwerthung der Werthe*.) That which, under master-morals, had passed for good was now esteemed bad, and *vice versa*'.[58] In this genealogical narrative, Nordau recognises a kind of mirror image to his own theory of degeneration, since Nietzsche claims that, in the aftermath of the slave revolt in morality, 'man is becoming dwarfed, enfeebled, vulgarized, and gradually degenerate'.[59] But for Nietzsche, crucially, 'the fundamental instinct of the healthy man is not unselfishness and pity, but selfishness and cruelty'.[60] This 'new morality', which permits anything to the sovereign individual as it liberates him from all bonds of custom, will reach its apotheosis in the figure of the 'over-man'.[61]

For Nordau, then, the trouble with Nietzsche is precisely that, at the end of the nineteenth century, he had called for another 'transvaluation of values' that might free humanity from a morality of custom that was essentially at odds with what the philosopher viewed as the instincts of strong and vigorous individuals. In presenting the stakes of Nietzsche's philosophy in this way, Nordau's argument also aims to take the high ground in a cultural contest that maps moral distinctions onto the divide between middle-brow culture and the avant-garde of European arts and letters. In this way, moreover, *Degeneration* could engage in a kind of symbolic aggression, backed by the authority of science, against the forms of cultural production it labelled degenerate because they failed not just to inspire the appropriate moral feelings, but to subordinate themselves to science, to society, to virtue. Nordau's attention to Nietzsche's style – and to his 'philosophy' alongside the work of painters, poets, novelists, composers, but not other 'philosophers' – is all the more significant in this light, because it enables the critic to merge aesthetic and moral judgement. Locating the root cause of these transgressions in the philosopher's '"individualism", *i.e.*, his insane ego-mania',[62] Nordau quickly dismisses the most radical implications of this individualism for a new 'transvaluation of values': that 'the intellectually free man must stand "beyond good and evil"; these concepts do not exist for him; he tests his impulses and deeds by their value for himself'.[63] He also dismisses the implications of this 'ego-mania' for modern political life, because they only 'attract those who instinctively feel that at the present day the State encroaches too deeply and too violently on the rights of the individual'.[64] All this is anathema to Nordau's sense of social propriety and political conservatism, so it is deemed vulgar to his sense of aesthetic taste. But in attaching Nietzsche and his most notorious intellectual product, the Übermensch, to a mounting individualist vogue, *Degeneration* also helped to promote the philosopher as the mastermind, albeit a deranged mastermind, of this disruptive new cultural trend and to advertise his work as the quintessence of its aesthetic and moral attributes.

Shaw on Nordau and Nietzsche

George Bernard Shaw was among the first reviewers to respond to the English translation of *Degeneration*, with a long essay initially published as 'A Degenerate's View of Nordau' in the July 1895 issue of *Liberty*, an American periodical edited by the 'philosophic Anarchist' Benjamin Tucker.[65] In his characteristically caustic manner, Shaw defends his fellow 'degenerates' against the moral traditionalism of Nordau and his adherents: 'any development in our moral views', he suggests, 'must appear insane and blasphemous to people who are satisfied with the current morality'. Shaw's defence of modern artists and writers against Nordau's attacks is also an argument in favour of the transvaluation of values, so that artistic success is equated with a kind of cultural power – to transform not just aesthetic but moral standards. But whereas 'heterodoxy in art is at worst rated as eccentricity or folly', 'heterodoxy in morals is at once rated as scoundrelism, and, what is worse, propagandistic scoundrelism, which must, if successful, undermine society and bring us back to barbarism'.[66] What is really at stake in *Degeneration*, then, is the maintenance of the values of an established ideology, which sought to secure the continued ascendency of these norms by diminishing the cultural capital of these upstart movements. The critic had scored an initial victory in this conflict insofar as he had become a cultural sensation himself: 'In Easter of 1895 ... Nordau was the master of the field, and newspaper champions of modern Literature and Art were on their knees before him, weeping and protesting their innocence'.[67] But Shaw blithely dismisses the book as not particularly threatening because it merely collects 'all the exploded bogey-criticisms of the last half-century into a huge volume'.[68] Promoting his earlier foray into this arena, *The Quintessence of Ibsenism* (1891), Shaw asserts that the Norwegian playwright was received with horror for the same reason that Nordau responds to Nietzsche with such dread: 'every step in morals is made by challenging the validity of existing conception of perfect propriety of conduct'.[69] Over and over, Shaw demonstrates that Nordau is not the progressivist he claims to be, but rather a squeamish 'reactionist' who consistently conflates 'freedom' with 'wickedness', and a 'modern scientific Rationalist' who nonetheless 'shrieks' about 'moral corruption and decay'.[70] *Degeneration* is best understood as an extended gripe, propped up with dubious claims and rhetorical bluster, ultimately offering little more than a long litany of everything that offends the middle-brow taste of its author, from new fashions and hairstyles to innovative art and literature. Ultimately, the overheated rhetoric of fear and loathing that characterises *Degeneration* becomes the most damning evidence against the arguments it advances, and so Shaw repeatedly quotes from its most ferocious *ad hominem* attacks: 'Nietzsche "belongs, body and soul, to the flock of the mangy sheep"; Ibsen is "a malignant, anti-social simpleton"; and so on'.[71]

Nordau's extended screed nonetheless drew the battle lines that would demarcate the early phases of the modernist revolution. Shaw's review had sought to defend not just Ibsen and Nietzsche, but Wilde, who was addressed in Nordau's chapter on the German philosopher: 'whenever Nietzsche extols the "I", its rights, and claims', the critic hears echoes of the Irish playwright and other egomaniacs, who share in his biochemical derangement.[72] Their resistance to common opinion is not a matter of philosophical disagreement or cultural innovation, but their mutual defiance of healthy-minded positivism and right-thinking consensualism. Nordau sets out to 'prove' his medico-scientific claims with reference to the textual evidence: for instance, in Nietzsche's assertion that 'all science is at present busied in talking man out of the self-respect he has hitherto possessed'; in Wilde's complaint that nature 'is so indifferent' to him that he 'is no more to [it] than the cattle that browse on the slope'; and in Nietzsche's praise of art, because 'in it the lie sanctifies itself, and the will to deceive has a quiet conscience on its side', which might be derived, the critic suggests, directly from Wilde's own 'The Decay of Lying'.[73] Nordau thus concludes that 'the similarity, or rather identity, is not explained by plagiarism, it is explained by the identity of mental qualities in Nietzsche and other egomaniacal degenerates'.[74] If *Degeneration* brought Nietzsche to the attention of readers in England, Ireland, and the United States for the first time, then the original German edition, *Entartung*, could be said to have had a similar promotional effect for Wilde, since it was the first book in the language to provide an account of his life and work – and, as the book sent shockwaves across Europe, it also gained Wilde a reputation as one of the important early exponents of modernism.[75] Unfortunately for the Irish playwright, those shockwaves reached England at exactly the wrong moment: the publication of Nordau's book took place just a month prior to Wilde's arrest in London on charges of committing 'acts of gross indecency with another male person' and by the time his damning second trial had commenced on 26 April 1895, *Degeneration* had already entered its fifth printing in English. In reporting on the trial, which received extensive coverage in the British press, Nordau was repeatedly invoked as a kind of expert witness for the prosecution while Wilde was tried and convicted in the court of public opinion.

The fame of the book meant that it was often conjured in the popular press to frame derogatory accounts of new developments taking place in the arts and literature. Hugh Stutfield's infamous essay, 'Tommyrotics', appearing in the June 1985 issue of *Blackwood's Edinburgh Magazine*, praises Nordau as 'a new prophet' who had 'arisen to point out some of the dangers which lie in the path of modern civilisation', especially the 'absurd claim [of some] to form ... [an] artistic aristocracy apart from the common herd'.[76] According to Stutfield, 'recent events, which shall remain nameless', had no doubt 'opened the eyes even of those who have hitherto been blind to the true inwardness of modern aesthetic Hellenism'.[77] By the final paragraph of the essay, however, he is pleased enough to apply a name to those events as he proclaims 'it was Oscar Wilde who infected us with our dread of the conventional, with the silly straining after originality characteristic of a society that desires above all things to be thought intellectually smart'.[78] Between these two dismissals, Stutfield repeatedly casts scorn on 'a somewhat similar, and scarcely less unlovely, offspring of hysteria and foreign "degenerate" influence': the 'neurotic and repulsive fiction', like 'Miss George Egerton's "Discords" ... which some critics are trying to make us believe is very high-class literature'.[79] Stutfield also links Egerton's writing to Nietzsche's via a particularly nasty claim. Earlier in the year, Egerton had published her translations of Hansson's prose poems, *Young Ofeg's Ditties*, which she introduced as 'an exposition of Friedrich Nietzche's [*sic*] triumphant doctrine of the ego'.[80] Provoked by this phrase, Stutfield attacks both the German philosopher and the Irish writer: 'By the way, the "triumphant doctrine of the ego", which Miss George Egerton finds so comforting, appears to be the theory of a German imbecile who, after several temporary detentions, was permanently confined in a lunatic asylum'.[81] In the end, however, these new figures in the cultural field fail to threaten the status quo: 'the Philistine' can 'take heart', claims Stutfield, because 'he is not alone in his fight for common-sense and common decency'; instead he is accompanied by 'that large number of really cultivated people whose instincts are still sound and healthy, who disbelieve in "moral autonomy", but cling to the old ideas of discipline and duty, of manliness and self-reliance in men, and womanliness in women'.[82]

Always up for a fight, Shaw became an important agent in the circulation of Nietzsche's new ideas in Great Britain and Ireland during the final years of the nineteenth century and into the early decades of the twentieth century – a role that he would also play for Ibsen, Wagner, and Schopenhauer during the same period. Within a year of publishing 'A Degenerate's View of Nordau', Shaw wrote a review of the first volume of Nietzsche's collected works to be published in English – including *The Case of Wagner*, *Nietzsche contra Wagner*, *Twilight of the Idols*, and *The Antichrist* – under the editorship of Alexander Tille, a lecturer in German Language and Literature at the University of Glasgow. Appearing in the 11 April 1896 issue of the *Saturday Review* (the London-based weekly edited by Galway-born Frank Harris, who had recently brought Shaw on as a drama critic and book reviewer), the article extends the argument made in his response to Nordau, by defending the value of this new volume – 'And such a volume, too!' – which contains 'everything that [Nietzsche] wrote just before he reached the point at which Germany made up its mind that he was mad, and shut him up, both figuratively and actually'. Directing his wit at what he sees as the philistinism of his British audience, Shaw continues: 'whilst I am still at large, I may as well explain that Nietzsche is a philosopher – that is to say, something unintelligible to an Englishman. To make my readers realise what a philosopher is, I can only say, *I* am a philosopher'. The identification is clear. In a rather sly effort to heighten his own stature (detailed in Chapter 1 of this study), Shaw associates himself with both Nietzsche's persecuted status and his vocation as a philosopher, albeit a philosopher according to Shaw's rather idiosyncratic definition. The philosopher, for Shaw, is not a sequestered thinker who spends his or her days in idle contemplation, among books or *objets d'art*, but rather an engaged participant in 'intercourse with men and women': 'you must transact business, wirepull politics, discuss religion, give and receive hate, love and friendship with all sorts of people before you can acquire the sense of humanity. If you are to acquire the sense sufficiently to be a philosopher, you must do these things unconditionally'. Although Nietzsche avoided the arenas of business dealings and practical politics, Shaw already saw an opportunity to harness some of his most controversial ideas, as well as his increasingly scandalous reputation. What is most important for Shaw in this first encounter with the writings of Nietzsche is the sense that, at the end of the nineteenth century, the philosophical vocation should not be limited by class affiliations, virtuous illusions, moral convictions, or what the reviewer saw as other forms of prudishness. This means that the philosopher must operate beyond the conventional moral categories of good and evil – that, indeed, if he cannot be a 'good man' in the conventional sense, he might nonetheless aspire to be a 'great man'. Shaw urges his readers to forgive these 'venial irregularities': 'it is the price of progress; and, after all, it is the philosopher, and not you, who will burn for it'.

In this regard, Nietzsche is not so much a role model as an inimitable pioneer of sorts, whose caustic style and corrosive criticism make him unique in the world of letters: 'Nietzsche is worse than shocking', claims Shaw, 'he is simply awful: his epigrams are written with phosphorous and brimstone'. Shaw is nonetheless reluctant to give him too much credit – Nietzsche has become a great *succès de scandale* with his penetrating wit, which is, very much counter to Shaw's Fabian socialism, often put in the service 'of privilege, of power, of inequality'. If the playwright's work had already been mistakenly identified as falling under the philosopher's influence, his commentary in *The Quintessence of Ibsenism* did share something important with Nietzsche's critique of philosophical idealism and Christian morality: 'his pungency; his power of putting the merest platitudes of his position in rousing, startling paradoxes; his way of getting underneath the moral precepts that are so unquestionable to us that common decency seems to compel unhesitating assent to them, and upsetting this with a scornful laugh ... So far I am on common ground with Nietzsche'.[83] In the remainder of the review, however, Shaw is at pains to distance himself from Nietzsche the critic, taking issue with his taste in music, his account of human history, and his understanding of politics. Still, his sympathy with Nietzsche's ethics – and with the style in which he delivers his insights – is such that the review repeatedly emphasises their significance to his readers. In this regard, now that Nietzsche's work was available in English, Shaw's review helped to initiate a more thoughtful and even sympathetic response to his work, which was soon greatly extended in a series of three articles by Havelock Ellis published in *Savoy* through the summer of 1896. The renowned sexologist and Shaw's fellow Fabian socialist, who had been familiar with Nietzsche's writing for more than a decade, not only treated his mental illness with more compassion, he countered Nordau's claims by attributing to the philosopher 'a sane and democratic individualism'.[84] The articles would soon be reprinted in the November 1898 numbers of *The Eagle and the Serpent*, a new British journal 'dedicated to the Philosophy of Life Enunciated by Nietzsche' and a number of his fellow freethinkers, and advertised as a propaganda organ for the cause of 'social justice', which promoted 'egoism' over 'altruism' as a means of freeing humanity from the bondage of international capitalism.

As the century neared its end, Nietzsche and his brand of individualism were quickly being co-opted for an array of social and political agendas across the English-speaking world, though the circulation of his ideas was never a consistent or predictable matter. Still, there could be little doubt that he was emerging as a cultural force, as his new disciples attempted to wed his philosophical dissidence with their various plans and programs. But if his ideas were attracting the attention of engaged intellectuals such as Shaw and Ellis, they nonetheless remained something of a curiosity, derived from the realm of an artistic and philosophical avant-garde at a considerable remove from the cultural mainstream in Great Britain and Ireland. For now, Irish readers would have to rely on British publications for information on this dangerous new thinker. The first account of Nietzsche's philosophy in an Irish periodical, the 6 October 1897 issue of *The Cork Examiner*, is a brief summation of an essay originally published in *Blackwood's*, which dismisses his theories as 'preposterous', though 'his conclusions and steps by which he reaches them form an instructive chapter in the history of ideas'.[85] Shaw continued his commentary on Nietzsche in *The Eagle and the Serpent*, though when he came to review the latest volumes of the collected works in English – *A Genealogy of Morals* and *Thus Spake Zarathustra* – for the *Saturday Review* in May 1899, he felt compelled to begin by recounting the problematic history of their publication. The effort had begun under the auspices of Henry and Co. and its impresario director John T. Grein, who had endeavoured in 1891 to 'explod[e] a performance of Ibsen's "Ghosts" on an unprepared London' under the auspices of his Independent Theatre Society. A year later, the company had also produced Shaw's first play, *Widowers' Houses*. All three undertakings had been audacious and the latest one, at least, had resulted in abject failure, with the press forced to sell off its remainders and settle its accounts, while passing along responsibility for the publication of the collected works to 'the respectable hands of Mr. Fisher Unwin' – who, after 1899, managed to produce only one more volume, *The Dawn of Day* (1903). Nietzsche, the great iconoclast, was not or not yet a bestseller and publication of the collected works in English would not be completed until 1911.

In 1899, however, on the strength of *A Genealogy of Morals* and *Thus Spake Zarathustra*, Shaw was prepared to counter again the influential evaluation of Nordau and to confer upon Nietzsche, as upon Ibsen and himself, the honorific title of 'a Devil's Advocate of the modern type'. According to Shaw, Ibsen was the first to drag 'duty, selflessness, idealism, sacrifice, and the rest of the antidiabolic scheme to the bar at which it had indicted so many excellent Diabolians. In his plays, the movement at last became influential by challenging the prevailing assumption about what constitutes the good, the good man, and whose interests these ideals serve'. Following on the dramatist came the philosopher – or, rather, philosophers – of this modern movement: 'In England, G.B.S.: in Germany, Nietzsche'. Once the latter had 'tasted the joys of iconoclasm', he 'became an epigrammatic Diabolian; took his stand "on the other side of good and evil", "transvalued" our moral valuations; and generally strove to rescue mankind from rulers who are utterly without conscience in their pursuit of righteousness'.[86] This emergent variety of modernism is opposed on virtually every matter to the reigning religious and political conservatism that focuses moral indignation on any perceived departure from received standards of valuation, including aesthetic valuation. Shaw claimed for his kind the status of heroic contrarians who possessed a variety of cultural power that allowed them somehow to circumvent the authority of the dominant class (even as, in many cases, they belonged to a dominated minority within that class) and, in their radical artistic and intellectual practice, to resist the established order instead of falling into blind subservience. With his plays, as will be elaborated later in this study, the rabble-rousing Irish writer would also attempt to combine intellectual avant-gardism with political interventionism in his adopted English home. Here is the image of Nietzsche that Shaw would have his audience recognise in himself: the agitator, who is relentless, and relentlessly witty, in his attack on the aesthetic and moral standards of a conformist, conservative, and mostly Christian middle class.

Literary Ideals in Ireland

At the very moment that Nietzsche was emerging onto the field of cultural production as a prominent representative of the new movement in the arts and letters, various forces in Ireland were facing off over the relative value of national traditions and cosmopolitan movements for the future of Irish culture. If, as Yeats famously postulated, the cultural field had taken on increasing prominence in Ireland after the fall of Charles Stewart Parnell and the ensuing crisis in the Home Rule movement, Irish writers and intellectuals were reluctant to reach a consensus on the values or ideals they should pursue as their nation entered the new century. The contests that play out in *Ulysses* – first in the Martello tower, as the young combatants, Dedalus, Mulligan, and Haines, offer up their opposing views, and then again in the National Library, as the more established voices of John Eglinton (William Kirkpatrick Magee) and Æ (George Russell) enter the fray – were only the fictional reprisals of a relentless debate that took place in such face-to-face encounters, as well as in a range of print media. Such dialogical tensions are nowhere more clearly evinced than in the celebrated exchange among Yeats, Eglinton, and Russell that transpired in successive Saturday editions of the Unionist *Daily Express* in the fall of 1898 (indeed, the debate, which Yeats manufactured 'to keep people awake' as he developed plans for his nascent theatre project, was deemed 'so illustrative of the new movement of ideas which is observable in contemporary Ireland, that is was felt it would be interesting to bring them together in volume form, if only as furnishing a possible chapter of Irish literary history' and the contributions were duly published as *Literary Ideals in Ireland* the following spring).[87] The previous summer, Yeats and his collaborators, Augusta Gregory and Edward Martyn, had drawn up a manifesto for 'The Celtic Theatre', which declared their objective to found a national theatre that would 'bring upon the stage the deeper thoughts and emotions of Ireland'.[88] Quickly becoming an important critical voice in Ireland after the publication of his *Two Essays on the Remnant* (1896), Eglinton initiated the exchange in the *Daily Express* with an essay whose very title served as a shot over the bow of the new theatre company: 'What Should Be the Subjects of National Drama?' The essay begins to address this question by running through a litany of themes that had already become conventional for the Revivalist movement – Irish legend, peasant life, local folklore, national history – before suggesting the answer that Eglinton plainly seeks – 'life at large as reflected in [the writer's] own consciousness'.[89] This emerging modernist mode of expression finds fertile ground in Ireland, he suggests, precisely because it is 'a quiet country' on the peripheries of Europe, where neither a well-established literary tradition nor a well-established civil society will impede innovation. In this regard, Ireland's diminished Home Rule prospects in the aftermath of the Parnell affair could well serve as a cultural asset: 'no one can say that political feebleness or stagnation might not be actually favourable to some original manifestation in the world of ideas'.[90]

What Eglinton portends here is precisely what Pascale Casanova a century later would designate the 'Irish Miracle'. Calling on Bourdieu and his understanding of the cultural field, her influential thesis is that, although Ireland was seen as a 'literarily destitute country under colonial rule'[91] at the end of the nineteenth century, it had accumulated enough linguistic and cultural capital from its proximity to London, one of the centres of 'the world republic of letters', to stage a rebellion against (and inversion of) 'the literary order'. This rebellion eventually resulted in some of the greatest achievements of the modernist period in the works of Wilde, Shaw, Yeats, Joyce, and Beckett.[92] Mapping the 'world literary space', Casanova details an 'uneven distribution'[93] of cultural resources according to established hierarchies and relations of dependency: the great national literary spaces, including England, Germany, and especially France, have accumulated the greatest stores of cultural capital over the course of their traditions, while those nations long under external political control or comprehensive colonial domination have only recently begun to accumulate their capital and remain poor by comparison. 'The distinctive quality of the Irish case', according to Casanova, 'resides in the fact that over a fairly short period a literary space emerged and a literary heritage was created in an exemplary way' – exemplary, that is, of 'the strange and complex links between aesthetics and politics' in 'small literatures'.[94] This emergence can be observed in the fact that what might have been seen as a local literary skirmish between competing parochial figures in the pages of the *Dublin Daily Express* was soon printed by the major London publishing house of T. Fisher Unwin (just then publishing the latest translation of Nietzsche's work). For Casanova, this rise was due to the symbolic struggle not just between Irish writers and English cultural authorities, but among the key contributors to Irish modernism themselves, with each taking up a strategic position in the field of cultural production: Yeats, for whom 'England was the Philistine', sought to elevate indigenous folklore and legend to the status of high literature through ennobling forms of poetry and drama;[95] Joyce, drawing on a range of international materials (including the English language and literary tradition), sought to invent a form of cultural autonomy liberated from political influence, whether nationalist or imperialist; Shaw, 'placing himself at an equal distance from his two countrymen', between folkloristic irrationalism and iconoclastic ambition, 'sought to subvert English norms, only by rejecting Irish national (and nationalist) values'.[96] In this way, with its rapid invention of new cultural positions, the Irish case provides a 'compact history of the revolt against the literary order' established in the cultural capitals of Europe, especially in London, which continued to exercise a certain amount of authority over the periphery insofar as they continued to depend on resources and recognition from the centre.[97]

Organised according to this strict binary relationship between centre and periphery, the comprehensive literary-historical schema elaborated by Casanova in *The World Republic of Letters* tends to elide many of the finer social and political complexities that structure the cultural field in 'small nations' on the edge of the 'world-system'. In particular, her account of the 'Irish paradigm', with its exemplary status for all small literatures, has been criticised for offering little more than a familiar and 'formulaic image of Irish literature' that opposes the linguistic and literary nationalism emerging in the nineteenth century to the 'autonomy of literature' pursued by modernist writers in the twentieth.[98] Indeed, to the degree that this paradigmatic approach downplays the specific histories of the Irish literary space, Casanova consistently overstates the extent to which contributors to the Irish Literary Revival, ranging from Yeats and Russell to George Moore and James Stephens, shared a commitment to 'Irish popular genius',[99] just as she can be accused of exaggerating the extent to which Joyce achieves independence ('an almost absolute autonomy') from the 'highly politicised space' of Irish culture and society.[100]

Nonetheless, because Casanova lays out the broad outlines of the cultural field so visibly, and in the process identifies the stakes of Irish modernism so plainly, her schema provides an opportune starting point for a more nuanced and dialectical account of this crucial period of cultural history, an account that would register not only the mobile positioning of various players on that field, but also their relationships and quarrels, their agreements and disagreements. Eglinton, for instance, emerges at the end of the nineteenth century as a figure already intent on accelerating the entrance of Irish literature into international space by urging Irish writers to produce a national literature from a humanist, rather than nationalist, perspective, in order to avoid severing ties with the rest of European civilisation or with what is most urgent in their own culture. If Irish writers are content with retelling the old stories, revising the old themes, they will produce nothing more than a *belle lettrist* literature, which fails to 'raise people above themselves', Eglinton argues, because they rely on the expression of 'latent ideals': 'Ireland must exchange the patriotism which looks back for the patriotism which looks forward'.[101] Yeats, on the other hand, responds to this perceived slight to the burgeoning Revivalist movement in a manner that asserts both his patriotic spirit and his international outlook. In 'A Note on National Drama', he argues that the contributions made to 'national literature' by such modern masterpieces (rather than symptoms of 'degeneration') as Ibsen's 'Peer Gynt' in Norway and Wagner's dramas in Germany demonstrate that '"these subjects" (ancient legends)', do *not* 'obstinately refuse to be taken out of their old environment and be implanted into the world of modern sympathies'.[102] Gazing outward as much as inward, Yeats argues that because Irish legends are more numerous and every bit as beautiful as Norse or German legends, they 'alone among great European lands have the beauty and wonder of altogether new things': 'May one not say, then, without saying anything improbable, that they will have a predominant influence in the coming century, and that their influence will pass through many countries?'[103] This argument could be read, per Casanova, as part of a concerted effort to attain the 'consecration' of the centre for a literature of ennobled legends and popular narratives, though at the same time it suggests a redeployment of these materials in ways that do not look backwards but forward, providing new ways of conceiving Irish temporality, Irish identity, Irish values.

It is possible, then, to see Irish modernism as emerging from the dialectical tension between such competing points of view, rather than from the transcendence of Yeats's 'nationalism' and its invented tradition by Eglinton's – or later, Joyce's – 'cosmopolitanism' and its ambition to achieve a form of literary autonomy. In his next contribution to the debate, 'National Drama and Contemporary Life', Eglinton acknowledges that 'Yeats's own dramatic poems seemed to open up the possibility of a drama with a distinctive note'[104] in Ireland and he even welcomes the reappearance of legendary figures such as Finn MacCool and Cuchulain in Irish literature – though he advises that, if they are to be relevant to contemporary readers, they must be imbued with 'something of the weariness and fret of our age'. In the work of Ibsen and Wagner, he suggests, such legendary characters 'become entirely new creations by virtue of the new spirit and import' instilled in them by artists who have 'the power to make them live again in a new way'.[105] It is in this manner that the writer can speak to 'his age', while at the same time maintaining the integrity of the self, of the individual artist, in the face of both national tradition and the recent demands for patriotic propaganda. Yeats, noting Eglinton's concession that ancient legends may have a place in modern literature, takes issue with his continued insistence that the best writing must form 'an expression of its age' and insistently address 'the facts of life', phrases which bind poetry to 'all the lusts of the marketplace'.[106] He asserts, on the contrary, that 'the renewal of belief' in 'old faiths, myths, dreams',[107] which is 'the great movement of our time, will more and more liberate the arts from "their age" and from life',[108] and thus defy the demand for 'popular literature'.[109] Yeats concludes, nonetheless, with something of a concession himself, which places the focus again squarely on the talent and commitment of the individual artist: 'I believe, too, that the difference between good and bad poetry is not in its preference for legendary, or for unlegendary subjects, or for a modern or for an archaic treatment, but in the volume and intensity of its passion for beauty, and in the perfection of its workmanship'.[110]

It still remained, however, to settle the question of what ideals and values should be pursued in Irish writing. Here Russell, 'as one of those who believe that the literature of a country is for ever creating a new soul among its people', entered the fray in the hope of reconciling the remaining differences between Eglinton and Yeats and thus moving Irish writers towards a consensus regarding the ideals they should adopt, though his means of doing this is largely to assert that Eglinton has misunderstood Yeats.[111] Modern literature, for Russell, 'grows more subjective year after year', though this does not mean that it becomes detached from cultural traditions but rather that it ranges over the collective memory in search of whatever might 'express lofty things to the soul'.[112] This, he suggests, is something with which both Yeats and Eglinton would agree – literature, the best literature, seeks after ideals – even if they differ on the question of where these ideals are to be sought. Concluding the debate with his essay, 'Nationalism and Cosmopolitanism in Literature', Russell acknowledges that the modern literature of Europe increasingly manifests a 'cosmopolitan spirit', so that writers like Ibsen and Tolstoy have abandoned 'what is distinctly national' as 'less valuable' and instead draw on 'an immense wealth of universal ideals' as they address a broadly European audience.[113]

Yet here Russell also begins to make a case for Irish exceptionalism. Adopting a position reminiscent of Nordau, he suggests that while 'art in the decadence of our times', especially the work of figures like Rossetti in England, must deal with 'the psychic maladies which attack all races when their civilisation grows old', Ireland is 'not yet sick with this sickness', by virtue, it would seem, of its peripheral positioning and delayed modernity.[114] Instead, as the century draws to a close, it is a vibrant nation possessed of 'a number of men who have a common aim in building up an overwhelming ideal – who create, in a sense, a soul for their country' and who share a 'profound conviction that its peculiar ideal is nobler than that which the cosmopolitan spirit suggests'.[115] For Russell, the dedicated theosophist, this conviction derived from his sense that a 'spiritual force' was at work in Ireland, but also from his view that 'much in the creation of the Ireland in the mind is already done, and only needs retelling by the new writers'.[116] The most celebrated rebuttal to this view can be found in those closing lines of *A Portrait of the Artist as a Young Man*, as Stephen embarks on his self-imposed Continental exile in order 'to forge in the smithy of my soul the uncreated conscience of my race'. In this crucial moment, the young man asserts his openness to a wider cosmopolitan perspective, the vital role of his own subjectivity in crafting collective values, and his intention to draw on 'the reality of experience' rather than some well-established archive of national tradition in order to fulfil his artistic ambition.[117]

Nietzsche comes to Ireland

That Yeats and Eglinton, along with Joyce and Shaw, would all soon turn to Nietzsche in their efforts to articulate their literary ideals attests to the importance of the philosopher for modern Irish culture. It is undeniably remarkable that, even as Yeats strove to establish a national theatre in Ireland, an institution that might serve to disseminate a national literature and define the values of the Irish people, he was also engaging intensely with Nietzschean ideas regarding aesthetics, morality, modernity, and other matters. If he had assigned himself the task of reviving an 'ancient national and popular patrimony', he would also appeal to the most innovative and outrageous of Continental thinkers in order to contest what he saw as already outmoded in modernity, including crass commercialism, mass politics, and democratic principles.[118] By 1904, in his essay titled 'First Principles', Yeats was advocating for a more cosmopolitan perspective against what he saw as the 'propagandists' and provincials of the Revival, even as he continued to advocate for a strict focus on indigenous topics, especially 'Irish kings and Irish legends and Irish-men':

> If Ireland is about to produce a literature that is important to her, it must be the result of the influences that flow in upon the mind of an educated Irishman to-day, and, in a greater degree, of what came into the world with himself. Gaelic can hardly fail to do a portion of the work, but one cannot say whether it may not be some French or German writer who will do most to make him an articulate man.[119]

In the same year, Eglinton co-founded a short-lived periodical titled *Dana: An Irish Magazine of Independent Thought*, which sought to promote 'a spirit of intellectual freedom, and a recognition of the supremacy of the humanity'[120] in opposition to what the editors saw as the patriotic zeal of the Irish Literary Revival, with its presumed reliance on 'traditional methods and traditional themes' and the dogmatic influence of the Catholic faith.[121] In the October 1904 issue, Eglinton published an essay titled 'A Way of Understanding Nietzsche', which contributed to this larger project by asking the Irish people to open their minds to a thinker considered to be on the leading edge of European modernism. Yet Nietzsche is worth understanding, according to Eglinton, not for reasons of idle cosmopolitanism or intellectual curiosity, but because he speaks to native concerns, to the Irish mind and its desperate need for 'independent thought'. In her account of Irish exceptionalism, Casanova argues that in opposition to the Revival, 'which, [Joyce] said in *Ulysses*, threatened to become "all too Irish"', the novelist managed to 'establish an autonomous, purely literary pole, thus helping to obtain recognition for the whole of Irish literature by liberating it to some extent from political domination'.[122] But she does not observe that this key phrase, uttered by Stephen in 1904 to describe his own father, draws playfully on the Nietzschean formula made famous by *Human, All Too Human: A Book for Free Spirits* (*Menschlich, allzumenschliches*) in order to intimate his desire to overcome both his patrimony and what he considers the merely national or parochial, even as it evokes the more sweeping project of overcoming what humanity has been made into by Western civilisation.

The early chapters of the present study consider how Nietzsche's ideas bore on the reconceptualisation of the role of the Irish artist and the development of new forms of Irish writing during the first decade of the twentieth century. Chapter 1 examines Shaw in the guise of a self-styled 'artist-philosopher', who sought to provoke his London audience – so concerned with profit making, social class, and late Victorian respectability – into recognising its own short-sightedness, as he worked to remake the national conscience of both England and Ireland. In doing so, the chapter provides the first comprehensive reading of Shaw's *Man and Superman* (1903) in terms of Nietzsche's philosophy. Capitalising on the philosopher's growing reputation, and appropriating his most infamous idea, the Übermensch, Shaw's text develops a sprawling, contradictory, dialectical new form of drama in order to promote something that Nietzsche's oeuvre did not offer: a cogent political philosophy. Like his German counterpart, the Irish playwright pursued a position both within and without traditional philosophical discourse and its field of cultural production, where he could enjoy both the benefits of membership and the returns on transgression. His first 'drama of ideas' mingled Nietzschean philosophy, Fabian socialism, and Lamarckian evolutionary theory, along with a parodic comedy of manners, a surreal tableau called 'Don Juan in Hell', and an appended 'Revolutionist's Handbook', which collectively strain against the traditional form of the well-made play and shatter the rhetorical conventions of philosophical discourse. But this new 'modernist' form of drama nonetheless served to advance a Shavian vision of human enhancement and political transformation. A real revolution, whether in England or Ireland, would only be brought about by changing the 'raw material' of the citizenry – the physiological basis of their moral sensibility and collective conscience – in order to raise the national community to heights previously associated with the singular Übermensch. The title of Shaw's play linked his own reputation to the reception of Nietzsche's writing, and also allowed critics to write off his 'drama of ideas' as recycled German philosophy, though the play itself ultimately offered a type of political philosophy – and worrying propaganda – like nothing before seen on the page or stage in England or Ireland.

Shortly after the publication of *Man and Superman*, Shaw was invited to contribute a play to the Irish National Dramatic Society by Yeats, who was in the first flush of his own life-long enchantment with Nietzsche. The coincidence is a telling one. Chapter 2 turns to Yeats and his newly founded theatre company to examine the ethos of a 'proud hard gift giving joyousness', which the poet and developing playwright derived from the German philosopher and placed in the service of a native cultural revival. Like Shaw, Yeats conceived the theatre as an arena where the conscience of a nation might be defined or redefined, but as he sought to impart his ideas of artistic value, cultural continuity, and noble generosity, he encountered an unreceptive audience that he came to refer as the 'mob' or 'crowd'. His work as a playwright during the first decade of the century is best understood as a sustained attempt to appeal to the tastes and values of Irish theatre-goers without condoning what he viewed as their lower instincts. Throughout this period, Nietzsche's writings were a constant companion and perhaps Yeats's greatest resource, providing him with the means to reconceive the roles of both the individual artist and the dramatic arts in pursuing his communal project. As demonstrated by the multiplying drafts of his plays and his extensive correspondence with collaborators, Yeats strove persistently to realise a Nietzschean conception of generosity: beginning with his revisions to *Where There Is Nothing* and continuing through his composition of *The King's Threshold*, he imagined heroes with a kind of haughty intensity, coupled with an overflowing fullness, who encounter audiences not yet ready to receive their messages. As he continued to read Nietzsche with great enthusiasm, Yeats went on to write – and repeatedly revise – two plays featuring the mythological hero, Cuchulain, as the exemplar of a renewed communal spirit, both proud and generous, hard and joyous. With the decade drawing to a close, however, he came to consider his efforts a failure, though the ambition remained to fashion a national conscience in the form of an aristocratic ethos suitable to his vision of the Irish people and their destiny.

Chapter 3 examines the concentrated attention that other Irish writers gave to Nietzschean thought during the first decade of the twentieth century, making legible the conflicts within and around the Revival movement, especially the tensions among Irish Catholicism, cultural nationalism, and international modernism. To be sure, Joyce's writing made use of some of Nietzsche's most famous tropes in articulating a response to these conflicts, a response embodied in the figure of an artist-hero, whose radically new ethical and aesthetic disposition might have a broad communal significance for his people. In July 1904, not long after he had commenced his first attempt to write a novel, the young man signed a lettercard to a friend with the alias, 'James Overman', evincing the importance of the Übermensch for Joyce and other members of his circle, including John Eglinton and Thomas Kettle, who looked to Nietzsche in their own efforts to promote an 'efflorescence of art and culture' in modern Ireland. In *Stephen Hero*, Joyce calls directly on a number of Nietzsche's ideas – not just the Übermensch, but slave morality, noble values, and the death of God – to depict the emergence of a heroic artistic consciousness, struggling to overcome nationalist ressentiment and religious authority. This struggle reaches a critical point in the final lines of *A Portrait of the Artist as a Young Man*, where Stephen proclaims his desire to produce something radically new, a conscience beyond bad conscience, which would break from the manners and mores that govern his compatriots. Revisiting the 'Telemachus episode' – written in 1914, a decade after Joyce's noteworthy lettercard – the chapter provides a full account of Stephen's return to Ireland, the reemergence of his bad conscience, and Buck Mulligan's playing at Zarathustrian prophecy, all as signs that the modernist project of creating new values is necessarily a vexed one, especially in the chastening context of Irish history. At the very outset of *Ulysses*, Nietzschean allusions cast doubt on the heroic creator of values who emerges in *A Portrait*, but these references nonetheless offer an important point of departure for understanding the project of cultural transformation undertaken by Joyce's art and the ethics of Irish modernism negotiated in the pages of his masterpiece.

An important aim throughout *Nietzsche and Irish modernism* is to reexamine the relationship between literature and philosophy by rigorously historicising their encounter in modern Irish culture. After the outbreak of the First World War in August 1914, Nietzsche's name quickly became prominent in Irish (and English) newspapers as shorthand for a 'Gospel of the Devil', associated with German militarism and its perceived threat to Christian civilisation. Chapter 4 documents the emergence of this strain of propaganda in the writings of Thomas Kettle, who wrote an introduction to Daniel Halévy's *The Life of Friedrich Nietzsche* (1911), which expounds on 'the duel between Nietzsche and civilisation', even as it dismisses his philosophy as nothing more than a rather vivid form of poetry. Three years later, on a gun-running mission for the Irish Republic Brotherhood, Kettle witnessed the so-called Rape of Belgium and immediately wrote a series of articles for the *Daily News*, attributing the rapid escalation of German belligerence to Nietzsche's destructive influence. Within a few short weeks, a host of Irish clerics reaffirmed the connection, as they negotiated their difficult position between the Home Rule cause and the British war effort by arguing in the popular press that Ireland and England must stand together against the 'poison doctrines' of the German philosopher. By November 1914, Yeats could rather mischievously evoke Nietzsche's name in Kettle's presence at a nationalist celebration, drawing rousing applause from the Dublin audience for this now explicitly anti-British (if also anti-Christian) figure. During the course of the war, the Nietzsche controversy raged on in newspapers across the Allied powers, while Yeats remained largely silent about the conflict and its catastrophic impact on Western civilisation. But, in January 1919, only days after the armistice was signed, he would return to some of Nietzsche's most provocative tropes in a series of allusions in 'The Second Coming', a poem that famously responds to the trauma of the war years by transforming the imagery of Christian faith into a nightmarish vision of the Antichrist. The final section of the chapter focuses on Yeats's poem in the context of the Nietzsche controversy in order to read it in terms of the philosopher's radical transvaluation of its values, which suggests a daunting future for both postwar Europe and postcolonial Ireland.

Just a few years later, during the Irish Civil War, the philosopher's name would be evoked on the floor of the Dáil Éireann (lower house of parliament) to pose the relationship between the values of the Irish people and the draconian measures of their new government as 'a case of Christianity vs. Nietzscheanism'. Drawing on an opposition made familiar by Kettle and Allied propagandists, the remark addresses, in the bluntest terms, the issues at stake for the national conscience as Ireland entered the era of independence. Chapter 5 demonstrates that Nietzsche, despite his drubbing in the public sphere, remained an important point of reference for the foremost Irish writers as they looked beyond the tumultuous intensity of the period and embraced prophetic modes of discourse. With a peculiar admixture of mythology, cosmology, eccentric historiography, and Nietzschean ideas, Yeats sought in *A Vision* (1925) to offer a systematic, if highly idiosyncratic, account of the patterns of human history that might reveal something about the future. Meanwhile, in his five-part play, *Back to Methuselah* (1921), Shaw attempted to translate the tenets of his philosophy of Creative Evolution into the legends of a new religion of human enhancement: legends that revise the story of the Garden of Eden, comment directly on the political failings of the present, and project a posthuman future some 30,000 years hence. After the war, like many of their contemporaries, Yeats and Shaw became increasingly enamoured with the potential of eugenics to overcome the counter-selective effects of the recent conflict and to breed the human race into a fitter political animal. Joyce, for his part, demonstrates considerable scepticism about such a potential, but he was nonetheless preoccupied with human breeding and the question of futurity in the 'Oxen of the Sun' episode of *Ulysses*. Among the many competing discourses that addressed these issues in Ireland and beyond, Nietzschean philosophy is again crucial, precisely because it remains open to multiple interpretations, multiple potentialities for the future of humanity, or rather a future beyond humanity, when at least certain individuals will live according to new codes, new values, and new ideals. One of the great achievements of Irish modernism, as we shall see throughout this study, is that its leading writers accommodated these provocations to their own array of provocative images, metaphors, and myths, which repeatedly crossed the borders between art and society, aesthetics and politics.

Notes

1 James Joyce, *Ulysses* (London: Egoist, 1922), p. 5.
2 Friedrich Nietzsche, *The Case of Wagner; Nietzsche Contra Wagner; The Twilight of the Idols; The Antichrist*, Thomas Common (trans.) (London: H. Henry, 1896), p. 241.
3 Joyce, *Ulysses*, p. 35.
4 Ibid., p. 16.
5 James Joyce, *A Portrait of the Artist as a Young Man* (New York: Huebsch, 1916), p. 299.
6 Carol Diethe provides the closest thing to a comprehensive overview of the reception of Nietzsche's works in her *Historical Dictionary of Nietzscheanism* (New York: Scarecrow, 2013). Monographs such as R. Hinton Thomas's *Nietzsche in German Politics and Society, 1890–1918* (Manchester: Manchester University Press, 1983) and Steven E. Aschheim's *The Nietzsche Legacy in Germany, 1890–1990* (Berkeley: University of California Press, 1994) have aimed to analyse the impact of Nietzsche's philosophy in more circumscribed temporal, geographical, and cultural domains. Alan Shrift's *Nietzsche's French Legacy: A Genealogy of Poststructuralism* (New York: Routledge, 1995) and James Brusseau's *Decadence of the French Nietzsche* (New York: Lexington, 2006) describe the enthusiastic reception of Nietzsche's work in Parisian intellectual circles, while demonstrating the diversity of interpretations among his French readers. More recently, Jennifer Ratner-Rosen's *American Nietzsche: A History of an Icon and His Ideas* (Chicago: Chicago University Press, 2012) has chronicled the response to the German philosopher in the United States in order to explain his surprising, even paradoxical, impact on his transatlantic readership. Essay collections such as Manfred Pütz's *Nietzsche in American Literature and Thought* (Rochester: Camden House, 1995) and Bernice Glatzer Rosenthal's *Nietzsche and Soviet Culture: Ally and Adversary* (Cambridge: Cambridge University Press, 1994) have surveyed a variety of perspectives on reception of the philosopher's work in particular national contexts. In each case, these volumes demonstrate how Nietzsche's readers engaged in cultural production precisely by thinking with and against the German philosopher.
7 This is not to say that Nietzsche has been entirely ignored in relation to Irish writing, but that the attention given to this relationship has been far narrower in scope than what the present study offers. Single-author studies tracking the affinities between the philosopher and select Irish writers began in the 1980s with Otto Bohlmann's *Yeats and Nietzsche: An Exploration of Major Nietzschean Echoes in the Writings of William Butler Yeats* (London: Macmillan, 1982) and Frances Nesbitt Oppel's *Mask and Tragedy: Yeats and Nietzsche, 1902–10* (Charlottesville: University of Virginia Press, 1987), resuming again with Sam Slote's *Joyce's Nietzschean Ethics* (New York: Palgrave, 2013). These books are addressed in the relevant chapters of this study. The first attempt to account for the broader impact of the philosopher in this context is Jean-Michel Rabaté's invaluable chapter 'The Birth of Irish Modernism

from the Spirit of Nietzscheanism', in his *The Pathos of Distance: Affects of the Moderns* (London: Bloomsbury, 2016), pp. 51–68.
8 Joyce, *Ulysses*, p. 22.
9 See, for instance, Edwina Keown and Carol Taafe (eds), *Irish Modernism: Origins, Contexts, Publics* (Bern: Peter Lang, 2009); Joe Cleary (ed.), *The Cambridge Companion to Irish Modernism* (Cambridge: Cambridge University Press, 2014); Gregory Castle and Patrick Bixby (eds), *A History of Irish Modernism* (Cambridge: Cambridge University Press, 2019); Kathryn Conrad, Cóilín Parsons, and Julie McCormick Weng (eds), *Science, Technology, and Irish Modernism* (Syracuse: Syracuse University Press, 2019); Maud Ellmann, Siân White, and Vicki Mahaffey (eds), *The Edinburgh Companion to Irish Modernism* (Edinburgh: Edinburgh University Press, 2021); and Paul Fagan, John Greaney, and Tamara Radak (eds), *Irish Modernisms: Gaps, Conjectures, Possibilities* (London: Bloomsbury, 2021).
10 Joe Cleary, 'Introduction', in Cleary (ed.), *The Cambridge Companion to Irish Modernism*, pp. 12–13.
11 On the connections between Egerton and Joyce, see Whitney Standlee, 'George Egerton, James Joyce and the Irish Künstlerroman', *Irish Studies Review* 18:4 (November 2010), 439–52; Ann Fogarty, 'Women and Modernism', in Cleary (ed.), *The Cambridge Companion to Irish Modernism*, p. 150; Paul March-Russell, 'Introduction', *New Woman Fiction, 1881–1889, Vol. 8: George Egerton*, The Wheel of God *(1898)* (New York: Routledge, 2016), pp. xxiii–xxxv.
12 Qtd in Maureen O'Connor, '"I'm Meat for No Butcher!": The Female and the Species in Irish Women's Writing', in Elke D'hoker and Raphaël Ingelbien (eds), *Irish Women Writers: New Critical Perspectives* (New York: Peter Lang, 2010), p. 140.
13 George Brandes, *An Essay on the Aristocratic Radicalism of Friedrich Nietzsche*, A.G. Chater (trans.) (Girard: Haldeman-Julius, 1910), pp. 6, 19.
14 George Egerton, *Keynotes* (London: Mathews and Lane, 1893), p. 21.
15 Ibid., p. 23.
16 Daniel Brown, 'George Egerton's *Keynotes*: Nietzschean Feminism and *Fin-de-Siècle* Fetishism', *Victorian Literature and Culture* 39:1 (March 2011), 143.
17 Iveta Jusová, 'George Egerton and the Project of British Colonialism', *Tulsa Studies in Women's Literature* 19:1 (Spring 2000), 34–36.
18 Egerton, *Keynotes*, p. 27.
19 Ibid., p. 28.
20 David Kornhaber, *The Birth of Theater from the Spirit of Philosophy: Nietzsche in Modern Drama* (Chicago: Northwestern University Press, 2016), p. 199.
21 In doing so, as Elke D'hoker argues, the 'stories explicitly stage some of the paradoxes of Nietzsche's philosophy, in particular the conflict between selfish individualism and a concern or love for others'. '"Half-Man" or "Half-Doll": George Egerton's Response to Friedrich Nietzsche', *Women's Writing* 18:4 (November 2011), 539.
22 George Egerton, *Discords* (London: John Lane, 1894), p. 166.

23 Ibid., pp. 189–90.
24 Ibid., p. 192.
25 Ibid., p. 242.
26 Ibid., p. 241.
27 Friedrich Nietzsche, *Twilight of the Idols*, Thomas Common (trans.) (London: H. Henry, 1896), p. 152.
28 John Burt Foster Jr., *Heirs to Dionysus: A Nietzschean Current in Literary Modernism* (Princeton: Princeton University Press, 1981), p. 5.
29 Keith M. May, *Nietzsche and Modern Literature: Themes in Yeats, Rilke, Mann and Lawrence* (London: Macmillan, 1988), p. 4.
30 Margot Norris, *Beasts of Modern Imagination: Darwin, Nietzsche, Kafka, Ernst and Lawrence* (Baltimore: Johns Hopkins University Press, 1985), p. 3.
31 Kathryne V. Lindberg, *Reading Pound Reading: Modernism and Nietzsche* (Oxford: Oxford University Press, 1987).
32 Michael Bell, 'Nietzscheanism: "The Superman and the All-Too-Human"', in David Bradshaw (ed.), *A Concise Companion to Modernism* (Oxford: Blackwell, 2003), p. 57.
33 Ibid., p. 58.
34 Ibid., p. 64.
35 Robert Gooding-Williams, *Zarathustra's Dionysian Modernism* (Palo Alto: Stanford University Press, 2001), p. 3. In this regard, moreover, Nietzsche's language provides Irish modernism with a key source of what Maud Ellmann, Siân White, and Vicky Mahaffey call its 'heresies', that is, 'its trademark modes of resistance to orthodoxy and tradition' ('Introduction', in Ellmann, White, and Mahaffey (eds), *The Edinburgh Companion to Irish Modernism*, p. 1.
36 Terry Eagleton, *Heathcliff and the Great Hunger: Studies in Irish Culture* (London and New York: Verso, 1995), p. 274.
37 For more on modernism as a 'philosophical problem' for Nietzsche, see Gooding-Williams, *Zarathustra's Dionysian Modernism*, pp. 3–14.
38 Bell, 'Nietzscheanism', p. 58.
39 Peter Sloterdijk, *Nietzsche Apostle*, Steven Corcoran (trans.) (Los Angeles: Semiotext(e), 2013), p. 41.
40 Ibid., p. 8.
41 Paul de Man, *Allegories of Reading: Figural Language in Rousseau, Nietzsche, Rilke, and Proust* (New Haven: Yale University Press, 1979), p. 119.
42 My analysis is particularly indebted to Bourdieu's essay 'The Field of Cultural Production, or: The Economic World Reversed', in Randal Johnson (ed.), *The Field of Cultural Production* (New York: Columbia University Press, 1993), pp. 29–73, and his detailed study of taste and cultural capital, *Distinction* (New York: Routledge, 1986).
43 See James F. English, 'Cultural Capital and the Revolutions of Literary Modernity, from Bourdieu to Casanova', in Jean-Michel Rabaté (ed.), *A Handbook of Modernism Studies* (West Sussex: Wiley-Blackwell, 2013), pp. 363–73.

44 See Jacques Derrida, 'Tympan', in Peggy Kamuf (ed.), *A Derrida Reader: Between the Blinds* (New York: Columbia University Press, 1991), pp. 146–71.
45 de Man, *Allegories of Reading*, p. 101.
46 Michael Bell, *Open Secrets: Literature, Education, and Authority from J-J. Rousseau to J. M. Coetzee* (Oxford: Oxford University Press, 2007), p. 155.
47 Max Nordau, *Degeneration* (New York: Appleton, 1895), p. 7.
48 See, for instance, György Lukács, 'The Ideology of Modernism', in his *The Meaning of Contemporary Realism*, John and Necke Mander (trans.) (London: Merlin Press, 1963), pp. 17–46.
49 Nordau, *Degeneration*, p. vii.
50 Ibid., p. 243.
51 Ibid., pp. 415–16.
52 Sloterdijk, *Nietzsche*, p. 68.
53 Nordau, *Degeneration*, p. 417.
54 Ibid., p. 419.
55 For further discussion of this 'upside down cultural logic', see English, 'Cultural Capital and the Revolutions of Literary Modernity', pp. 366–69.
56 Nordau, *Degeneration*, p. 416.
57 Ibid., p. 420–21.
58 Ibid., p. 422.
59 Ibid., pp. 423–24.
60 Ibid., p. 424.
61 Ibid., p. 426.
62 Ibid., p. 417.
63 Ibid., pp. 425–26.
64 Ibid., p. 471.
65 Later republished in book form as Bernard Shaw, *The Sanity of Art* (New York: Tucker, 1908), p. 10.
66 Ibid., p. 44.
67 Ibid., p. 10.
68 Ibid. p. 22.
69 Ibid., p. 44.
70 Ibid., p. 69.
71 Ibid., p. 102.
72 Nordau, *Degeneration*, p. 442.
73 Ibid., p. 443.
74 Ibid., p. 444.
75 See Stephano Evangelista, 'Introduction: Oscar Wilde: European by Sympathy', in Stephano Evangelista (ed.), *The Reception of Oscar Wilde in Europe* (London: Bloomsbury, 2010), p. 4.
76 Hugh Stutfield, 'Tommyrotics', *Blackwood's Edinburgh Magazine* 157 (June 1895), 838.
77 Ibid., 835.
78 Ibid., 845.
79 Ibid., 835.

80 Ola Hansson, *Young Ofeg's Ditties*, George Egerton (trans.) (London: John Lane, 1895), p. 5.
81 Stutfield, 'Tommyrotics', 838.
82 Ibid., 845.
83 G.B. Shaw, 'Nietzsche in English', *Saturday Review* (11 April 1896), 373.
84 Havelock Ellis, 'Friedrich Nietzsche', *The Savoy* 1 (January 1896), 88.
85 'October Magazines', *The Cork Examiner* (6 October 1897), 3.
86 G. Bernard Shaw, 'Giving the Devil His Due', *Saturday Review* (13 May 1899), iii.
87 William Kirkpatrick Magee, 'Editor's Note', in William Kirkpatrick Magee (ed.), *Literary Ideals in Ireland* (London: Fisher Unwin, 1899), p. 5.
88 Qtd in Paige Reynolds, *Modernism, Drama, and the Audience of Irish Spectacle* (Cambridge: Cambridge University Press, 2007), p. 41.
89 John Eglinton, 'What Should Be the Subjects of National Drama?', in Kirkpatrick Magee (ed.), *Literary Ideals in Ireland*, p. 9.
90 Ibid., p. 10.
91 Pascale Casanova, *The World Republic of Letters*, M.B. DeBevoise (trans.) (Cambridge: Harvard University Press, 2004), p. 84.
92 Ibid., p. 305.
93 Ibid., p. 83.
94 Ibid., p. 304.
95 Ibid., p. 303.
96 Ibid., p. 313.
97 Ibid., p. 304.
98 Michael Malouf, 'Problems with Paradigms: Irish Comparativism and Casanova's *World Republic of Letters*', *New Hibernia Review* 17:1 (Spring 2013), 45.
99 Casanova, *World Republic*, p. 226.
100 Ibid., p. 315.
101 Eglinton, 'What Should Be the Subjects', p. 12.
102 W.B. Yeats, 'A Note on National Drama', in Kirkpatrick Magee (ed.), *Literary Ideals in Ireland*, p. 17.
103 Ibid., p. 19.
104 John Eglinton, 'National Drama and Contemporary Life', in Kirkpatrick Magee (ed.), *Literary Ideals in Ireland*, p. 23.
105 Ibid., p. 24.
106 W.B. Yeats, 'John Eglinton and Spiritual Art', in Kirkpatrick Magee (ed.), *Literary Ideals in Ireland*, p. 35.
107 Ibid., p. 33.
108 Ibid., p. 36.
109 Ibid., p. 33.
110 Ibid., p. 37.
111 A.E., 'Nationality and Cosmopolitan in Literature', in Kirkpatrick Magee (ed.), *Literary Ideals in Ireland*, p. 79.

112 A.E., 'Literary Ideals in Ireland', in Kirkpatrick Magee (ed.), *Literary Ideals in Ireland*, p. 52.
113 A.E., 'Nationality and Cosmopolitan in Literature', p. 82.
114 Ibid., p. 80.
115 Ibid., p. 82.
116 Ibid., p. 85.
117 Joyce, *A Portrait*, p. 299.
118 Casanova, *World Republic*, p. 305.
119 W.B. Yeats, 'First Principles', in Mary FitzGerald and Richard J. Finneran (eds), *The Collected Works of W.B. Yeats, Volume VIII: The Irish Dramatic Movement* (New York: Scribner, 2003), p. 63.
120 Frederick Ryan, 'Political and Intellectual Freedom', *Dana: A Magazine of Independent Thought* 1 (May 1904), 31.
121 John Eglinton and Frederick Ryan, 'Introductory', *Dana: A Magazine of Independent Thought* 1 (May 1904), 1.
122 Casanova, *World Republic*, p. 315.

1

Shaw: 'An English (or Irish) Nietzsche'

On 26 December 1902, shortly after completing the manuscript of *Man and Superman*, George Bernard Shaw wrote to his recently hired German translator, Siegfried Trebitsch: 'I want the Germans to know me as a philosopher', he claimed only half-jokingly, 'an English (or Irish) Nietzsche (only ten times cleverer)'.[1] The playful, boastful comment is typical of Shaw's response to Nietzsche and, for that matter, to many of the playwright's most significant predecessors in that it acknowledges a certain affiliation, even identification, and then seeks to establish a safe distance in the next breath. In his most generous moments, Shaw had attributed to Nietzsche 'the really new idea of challenging the validity of idealism and duty, and bringing Individualism round again to a higher plane', aligned with Shaw's own socialist views; and, even more important, he had acknowledged that the German's philosophy 'shewed signs of being able to rally to it men beneath the rank of the geniuses who had been feeling their way towards it for centuries', thus reaching a much broader audience with his radical views. Nietzsche was, in short, a new sort of philosopher, the likes of which England (or Ireland) had never before seen. In his emerging reputation, Shaw had seen his own opportunity and, with his 1896 review of *The Case of Wagner* and three other texts (collected in a single volume), he had begun to conceive his vocation and had advertised himself to his readers in precisely these terms. In the review, as we have seen, Shaw had conjured the title of philosopher in part to provoke his English audience – with what he presumed to be its prosaic, utilitarian, and generally parochial sensibilities – into recognising its own short-sightedness.

This provocation was integral to his agenda as a Fabian socialist, which Shaw had been articulating for nearly two decades in essays and articles that sought to bring about the gradual transformation of British society by changing the way it thought about land ownership and industrial capital. By 1898, he could claim in *The Eagle and the Serpent* that, in taking up these social and economic issues, 'the Fabian Society has exercised a great influence, and has attained, perhaps, the maximum success possible to such organizations'. But he also felt that its partner organisation, the New Life Fellowship, which numbered Nietzsche aficionados Havelock Ellis and John Davidson among its members, had failed in the related 'ethical and philosophical' effort to 'free personal ideals and duties from superstition' and had, in fact, 'laid even greater stress on sacredness of the ideals and duties than the comparatively easy-going superstitious people did'. These assertions came in response to Thomas Common's suggestion in the previous issue of the journal that the time had come for the foundation of a Nietzsche Society in England, a suggestion that Shaw thought 'may possibly prove fruitful' because the new organisation 'might hit the target that the Fellows of the New Life missed, and might repeat on the ethical plane the success of the Fabian Society on the political one'. Ultimately, plans for the society were never realised, leaving the aspiring philosopher alone (as he no doubt preferred) to take on the challenge of responding to 'the political and economic side of the social question', along with the 'ethical and philosophical side', which he soon did in *Man and Superman*.[2]

In a sense, Nietzsche's brand of philosophy was the perfect one for Shaw's play to emulate.[3] The German philosopher had repeatedly criticised English political and intellectual life, perhaps most famously in the opening lines of Book I of *A Genealogy of Morals*, which chastise the attempts of 'these English psychologists' to explain morality in strictly utilitarian terms and to support a politics that would aim to secure the greatest happiness for the greatest number.[4] Although carried out with stolid intellectual labour, these attempts suffered from a lack of historical sense, according to Nietzsche, because they were too much indebted to the decadent, bourgeois, and Christian morality of their own time. They were, moreover, oriented towards a teleological evolutionary narrative, which the philosopher also identifies in the history of morality proposed by his friend Paul Ree, tracing an arc from the 'Darwinian beast' to 'the most modern and modest morality-tenderling, who "no longer bites"'.[5] For Shaw, who had reviewed *A Genealogy* in 1899, the English too had failed to fully engage with the pressing questions about mankind and morality that preoccupied the fin de siècle, so concerned were they with profit-making, social class, and late-Victorian respectability. Shaw's efforts at launching his own brand of philosophy in England and Germany and elsewhere, which often harnessed Nietzsche's growing reputation without necessarily endorsing his ideas, proceeded precisely by denigrating these established values and conventional modes of thought. To be a 'philosopher', according to his definition, could not mean to be someone engaged in thinking as an aloof academic routine, speculating idly about ethics, aesthetics, or politics, much less logic, metaphysics, or epistemology; it could not mean to participate in the rarefied pursuit of grand abstractions or the construction of comprehensive schemas in exchange with only canonical philosophical texts. Such bookish pursuits would merely lead one to hide away in the library and 'having pieced an illusory humanity and art out of the effects produced by his library on his imagination, build some silly systematization of his worthless ideas over the abyss of his own nescience'.[6] Instead, adopting the role of a particularly savvy propagandist, the Shavian philosopher should participate in a vigorous competition with the various forces of the outside world, promoting those that embody what he values, what he desires, in a manner that defies what he saw as the intellectual conformity and political detachment of academic philosophy.

In his introduction to the 1896 edition of *The Case of Wagner*, Alexander Tille addresses the state of philosophy in England at the end of the nineteenth century, as the nation unwittingly readies to receive the first English translations of Nietzsche's work. During this period, Tille was instrumental in disseminating the German philosopher's ideas in Great Britain and Ireland, and in laying the groundwork for his initial reception – a task that Tille, another regular contributor to *The Eagle and the Serpent*, took to with his own rather pitiless social Darwinist agenda. Much like Shaw, he laments the survival of 'intellectual cobwebspinning in the mode of Spinoza or Hegel' and declares that 'the continuation of speculative tradition is no longer regarded as the test of a philosopher of significance'.[7] First and foremost, the task of philosophy in both Germany and England is to come to terms with new discoveries in the natural sciences, especially the emerging conception of man derived from evolutionary theory. Unfortunately, according to Tille, English philosophy had discredited itself not only by being slow to adequately address these new discoveries, but by being unwilling to acknowledge what he sees as the chief implication of Darwinian theory – 'the selection of the fit and the elimination of the unfit' for the 'progress of civilisation'.[8] Instead, thinkers such as Sir Francis Galton, William Bateson, and, most notably, Herbert Spencer had resorted to Lamarckian ideas about the heredity of acquired characteristics to explain human existence, as well as the existence of certain human values and social institutions (in this regard, his association with social Darwinism and the phrase 'survival of the fittest' was entirely misguided). Along with many of his peers, Spencer had attempted to separate zoological or physiological transformation from the processes of psychological and social change in order to 'naturalise' the Judeo-Christian values of mildness and altruism. Man was regarded as 'higher' based on neither his greater physical ability, including reproductive ability, nor his 'general intellectual qualities', but on 'the extent of his subjection to the traditional restrictions of action called morality'.[9] Tille argues that such a view, coloured by 'traditional prejudices', fails to ask, much less answer, 'the question whether such a "general improvement of the race" can, under the circumstances, rightly be called an improvement at all'.[10] Seeking to give

Nietzsche the credit he deserves, Tille identifies him as the first philosopher with enough intellectual courage to challenge the traditional prejudices that underlay these judgements and to undertake his famous 'transvaluation of all values' in response. For both Tille and Shaw, however, English philosophy had failed to follow suit and address the difficult, uncomfortable, and increasingly urgent concerns regarding the status of moral ideas and the measure of superior humanity, as well as the need to help nature along with the new science of eugenics.

Shavian political philosophy

It is clear that if Shaw wanted his audience to know him as a philosopher, it was neither in the outmoded fashion of Spinoza or Hegel nor in the discredited manner of his English contemporaries, but rather in a new mode that challenged intellectual detachment, rhetorical conventionality, and moral conservatism. Like Nietzsche, he sought a position both within and outside traditional philosophical discourse and its field of production, where he could enjoy both the benefits of membership and the returns on transgression by writing in a way that participated in its discursive norms only to expose their assumptions. As Shaw advocates in his 1896 review, the philosopher should shun abstract or disinterested contemplation and instead pursue direct engagement with works of art, with music, with men, as the means to producing novel insights, expressed in novel terms. His 'drama of ideas', a phrase that Shaw uses in the opening stage directions of *Man and Superman*, offered him a new set of possibilities for appealing to his audience and articulating his vision of racial improvement and political transformation, which set out to challenge what he saw as the glaring failures of English (and Irish) society. His pretence to be a philosopher, and not merely a playwright or propagandist, can be seen as a marketing strategy to ensure the triumph of this vision above and beyond any commercial or critical success in the theatre, but it relies on the objectification and even destruction of philosophy as an established discursive practice, at a time when the hope of a radical reconstruction of the discourse seemed to be fading, at least in England.

Perhaps most important to his sense of the vocation is his professed openness, or at least lack of squeamishness, when it comes to the affairs of the world – the philosopher, that is, must suspend the categories of good and evil as he or she participates in and closely observes these affairs. It is exactly this ability, Shaw suggests, that the English lack, with their strict concern for class hierarchies, social propriety, conventional morality; in his characteristically mischievous manner, he begs pardon for the 'venial irregularities' of his philosopher, which demand the dismantling of all varieties of conventionality: for, as we noted earlier, this is simply the 'price of progress' as he views it.[11] Here we can clearly see his modernist ambitions at work. Like Nietzsche, Shaw places great emphasis on the antagonistic relationship between the philosopher and the prevailing values of his age, including the value of 'progress' itself, and the attendant sense that the philosopher accrues credit precisely by subverting those values and saying something new. With this antagonism, however, also comes the sense that the philosopher is responsible in some important way for investing his words in the future of humanity – or, at least, the portion of humanity that is his audience – in order to cultivate new and higher modes of life that would overcome present biological and political limitations.

In this sense, moreover, Shaw might well wish to be known not strictly as an English philosopher but as an 'English (or Irish)' philosopher. It is true that Shaw had been living in England for more than a quarter-century by the time he wrote to Trebitsch in 1902. It is also true that he often proclaimed his distaste for what he saw as the backward or parochial qualities of Irish life, which he sought to escape in order to make his way, as he said, to 'the forefront of the age', defined in his characteristic self-defensive and self-promoting fashion as 'the period of Ibsen, Nietzsche, the Fabian Society, the motor-car, and my own writings'.[12] Shaw was no doubt scarred by the humiliation of his upbringing in a Protestant Ascendancy family that, due to the improvidence of his father, never rose above a kind of 'genteel poverty'. His biographer, Michael Holroyd, has detailed his deep ambivalence about Ireland, which led Shaw to defend Home Rule, but attack nationalism; oppose the compulsory teaching of Gaelic in schools, but encourage the spread of Gaelic literature; and later attempt to discount Sinn Féin, but defend the courage and sincerity of its members.[13] Yet, like his compatriot Oscar Wilde, Shaw also found himself something of an outsider in Victorian and later Edwardian England, where he was at odds with nearly the entire social and political establishment. Since the mid-1880s, he had been an important force behind the Fabian society, leading the rhetorical efforts of the anti-revolutionary socialist organisation, which aimed to fundamentally remake English society through the steady reform of its political and intellectual life. Recent scholarship has begun to demonstrate just how important his writings also were for those involved in both cultural revival and radical politics in Ireland.[14] He used his journalism, his reviews, and later his plays to attack the 'artificialities and hypocrisies' of English culture, on the one hand, and to question the clichés and covenants of Irish culture, on the other.[15] Shaw was, in an important sense, an internationalist, who strongly criticised both imperialism and nationalism, as Pascale Casanova emphasises in her account of his positioning in relation to the 'British literary space', where the playwright enjoyed a certain amount of 'aesthetic freedom and critical tolerance'.[16] But Shaw was also, in his idiosyncratic way, an Irishman concerned with the oppression of the Irish people. When he wrote to Trebitsch, he was already making plans for his most 'Irish' play, *John Bull's Other Island*, which took on both the abuses of British imperialism and the 'whole spirit of the Neo-Gaelic movement', with what he saw as its provincialism and misguided patriotism. To these issues, he brought a mind steeped in Fabian socialist rhetoric, experienced in the intrigues of local politics, and committed to Lamarckian evolutionary theory, as well as sharpened by years of writing about art, music, and theatre in the imperial metropole.

It was on these grounds that he could stake his claim to being 'ten times cleverer' than his German counterpart. This bit of braggadocio is, of course, quintessentially Shavian, though it is also very much aligned with the Nietzschean boasts to be found, for example, in the autobiographical *Ecce Homo*, which contains chapters with titles such as 'Why I Am So Clever' ('Warum Ich so Klug bin') along with other immodest, and not simply ironic, titles such as 'Why I Am So Wise', 'Why I Write Such Good Books', and 'Why I Am a Destiny'.[17] In adopting these titles, Nietzsche was (much like Shaw in his 1896 review) courting controversy, even as he sought to hinder future critics (such as Shaw in the same review) from making partial or distorted judgements of his work. His grandiloquence is demonstrative of his view that language is self-affirming by its very nature and that this capacity should be harnessed to elevate rather than denigrate or belittle the individual. He was, moreover, initiating what Peter Sloterdijk calls 'the discursive event which bears the name Nietzsche', which pertains to the very nature of modern authorship and literary discourse insofar as his extravagant self-praise 'posits the text for himself'.[18] For both Nietzsche and Shaw, writing is necessarily affirmative of the self, even in the face of democratic notions of human equality and traditional notions of authorial decorum. Nietzsche's writing, in this sense, sponsors Shaw's own self-celebration. He offers his readers the possibility of achieving distinction, of becoming noble, so that they may escape the debilitating effects of resentment and bad conscience that plague the modern world. If they take up this offer, his readers are not so much acquiring a debt but rather benefiting from a generosity to the future in the form of a pluralism, a multiplicity of possibilities, that will not be contained in any new unity or coherence. In other words, the philosopher after Nietzsche is freed to imagine new modes of moral valuation and new forms of human striving – to imagine new and higher forms of existence, including new types of individuals or races of people.

Certainly, Nietzsche and Shaw were largely in sympathy regarding the vocation of philosophy, which each took to be corrupted by overriding solipsism and mere bookishness, even if the malleability of Nietzschean individualism would allow it to be transmuted into an almost unrecognisable form in Shavian socialism. If he was quick to deny any influence from Nietzsche's *Beyond Good and Evil* on his *Quintessence of Ibsenism*, Shaw did acknowledge that 'in fact Nietzsche's criticism of morality and idealism is essentially demonstrated in my book as at the bottom of Ibsen's plays'. He admired and even identified with Nietzsche's 'pungency; his power of putting the merest platitudes of his position in rousing, startling paradoxes; his way of getting underneath the moral precepts which are so unquestionable to us that common decency seems to compel unhesitating assent to them, and upsetting them with a scornful laugh'. To be sure, Shaw's reviews of Nietzsche's writing are primarily exercises in self-reflection, if not outright self-celebration, as he seeks to construct a persona, a clever or witty philosophical persona, for his readers and his growing theatre audience.

What elevates Shaw over Nietzsche in these terms, according to the playwright, is precisely that the German philosopher suffers from the same solipsism and bookishness he criticises, which prevent him from properly engaging with the world beyond the self: 'never was there', according to the playwright, 'a deafer, blinder, socially and politically inepter academician' than the German. Shaw avers that, for all of his learning, Nietzsche has failed in his efforts to develop an acute understanding of modern political institutions and their precursors in the ancient world. His principal sin is precisely his seclusion or sequestration, which has led him to blunder over 'politics, social organization, and administration', as someone with no experience in the realm of men and action. But, even worse, his detachment from these matters has led Nietzsche to become a conspiracy theorist of the highest order: 'To him modern democracy, Pauline Christianity, Socialism, and so on are deliberate plots hatched by malignant philosophers to frustrate the evolution of the human race and mass the stupidity and brute force of the many weak against the beneficial tyranny of the few strong'.[19] For Shaw, as for many since, Nietzsche is a disastrous political theorist – an anti-political philosopher of culture and value at best, an anti-democratic thinker of aristocratic hierarchies at worst. In his own estimation, on the other hand, Shaw had developed a far more refined sense of historical agency, derived through his research into historical materialism and his work with the Fabian Society, as well as his firsthand experience in municipal politics. His Fabianism did not stress theoretical sophistication so much as pragmatic action, albeit action founded on argument and persuasion, in its efforts to 'cultivate leaders and the best brains of both parties (or of none) ... to accept the need for basic reform and a new structure for the economy and society'.[20] But, as *Man and Superman* demonstrates, Shaw became increasingly preoccupied with a grand biopolitical project that might enforce technocratic authority on human beings precisely as a biological species in order to bring forth nothing less than a superior race suited to the demands of socialism.

The seeming lack of a coherent political philosophy in Nietzsche authorised Shaw to adopt and adapt the Übermensch, that figure of heroic individualism, for his socialist programme, even though the philosopher had explicitly cautioned against such efforts. The playwright, nonetheless, cuts out this most provocative trope, this most dangerous fragment, and pastes it into his 'philosophy', which distorts or ignores some of the most radical ethical and spiritual implications of the original. To be sure, Shaw was not entirely alone in this project: the previous decade, as Steven Aschheim has demonstrated, 'marked the beginning of a project amongst European socialist theoreticians and activists to fashionably synthesize Nietzsche and Marx', most often by reconciling 'the imperatives of community and selfhood, the free development of the individual with the just society'.[21] But the playwright was quite solitary in his effort to integrate the figure of the Übermensch with the principles of Fabian socialism and to do so in a way that might overcome the moral and conceptual limitations of the English philosophical tradition, as he understood them. In this way, Shaw takes up what could be considered the political implications of Nietzsche's most provocative idea and attempts to develop them, with the guidance of his own political agenda, into something approaching a cogent political philosophy. In this way, furthermore, he addresses what Daniel Conway calls in his work on the philosopher 'a calamitous, and previously unapproachable, question of political legislation: *what ought mankind to become?*' (original emphasis).[22] Nietzsche and Shaw both insist that this question (which Conway deems the founding question of politics) had rarely been considered in previous eras, but in doing so, they also gave comfort and inspiration to a new generation of eugenicist thinkers across Europe. The Übermensch, as an aspiration for mankind, takes precedence over the rights of individuals, their duties to one another, and even the state as a compulsory organisation of individuals. But we might also say that Shaw's play misappropriates Nietzsche's gift. His cleverest drama of ideas accepts the philosophical inducement of the Übermensch and flirts with an insidious eugenicist programme, making the 'quality' of the population a political problem, at the same time as it promotes utopian possibilities – or necessities – for governing socialist societies in England, Ireland, and elsewhere.

Titles, genres, and artist-philosophers

Shaw's title, *Man and Superman*, couples the generic term for a human being with an idiosyncratic English translation of Nietzsche's famous concept to provide a name for the complex set of texts that comprise the 1903 tome. As an allusion, the title taps into an escalating vogue in England and Ireland (and on the Continent, as well) around Nietzsche's philosophy and especially the concept of the Übermensch – and thus promotes the play and its companion pieces as contributions to the avant-garde of European literature and thought. As early as 1896, acknowledging the social and cultural, if not intellectual, capital accumulating around the name of philosopher, Shaw had quipped that the 'only excuse for reading' the German philosopher 'is that before long you must be prepared either to talk about Nietzsche or else retire from society, especially from aristocratically minded society'. If Nietzsche 'had a great *succès de scandale* to advertise his penetrating wit', Shaw was not averse to harnessing that ill-gotten fame for his own purposes:[23] drawing on the notoriety of a name brand, his allusion to its most famous product, the Übermensch, in the hope of riding a market wave and carrying his work to triumph. To be sure, he was well aware that his title functioned in this way and later wrote in the preface to *Back to Methuselah* (1921) that he had 'put all [his] intellectual goods in the shop window under the sign of *Man and Superman*', happily acknowledging 'that part of [his] design succeeded', even if the success appeared to be fleeting.[24] The title announces Shaw to his English (or Irish) audience, that is, as an English (or Irish) Nietzsche, whatever reservations he might have harboured about that identification. But it is worth noting that Shaw opted for his own coinage, 'Superman', as he had done in 'A Degenerate's View of Nordau' in 1895, rather than the more common 'over-man', which had been used in the translation of *Degeneration* that year, or 'beyond-man', which Tille had used in his translation of *Thus Spake Zarathustra* in 1896. The pairing of the terms 'man' and 'Superman' also announces the content of his play in a programmatic way, by suggesting a movement – whether ethical, biological, or political – from man to Superman, from our present state to some future telos. But the conjunction leaves an open question as to whether the Superman represents the fulfilment of some potential within man (the highest type of humanity) or the achievement of something radically different (a complete break from humanity).

Man and Superman also possesses a binary subtitle, *A Comedy and a Philosophy*, which advertises the divided generic commitments of Shaw's play, even as it throws into question the relationship between these commitments, and raises the issue of just how his readers should approach such a text. It is presented as a tome organised in terms of this basic opposition, between discourses, between classifications, which addresses itself to gaiety, lightness, and wit, on the one hand, and to the ostensible solemnity, however pretentious, of intellectual inquiry, on the other. From the very outset, then, the volume poses a puzzling contradiction for its reception, much as

Nietzsche's subtitle for *Thus Spake Zarathustra* had: *A Book for All and None*. Like that book, *Man and Superman* seems to make a vulgar appeal to a mass audience, which is immediately undercut by its claims to distinction or exclusivity. The more conventional elements of Shaw's book – the play that unfolds in Acts I, II, and IV – call to mind a comedy of manners or light Victorian theatre, even his earlier plays, as they satirise the behaviour of the British bourgeoisie, with a collection of stock characters: the stodgy patriarch, the young rebel, the dreamy poet, and the eligible young woman, and so on. Nonetheless, as Shaw indicated to Trebitsch in 1902, he wanted to be known as 'a philosopher ... and *not* as a mere *carpenter of farces* like *Helden* [the German title of *Arms and the Man*] and nursery plays like *Candida*' (emphasis added). Many of his contemporaries – and, indeed, many later critics – recognised Shaw primarily as a satirist, if not an outright controversialist, prone to crude characterisations and implausible assertions, which disqualified him from consideration as a purposeful thinker. But *Man and Superman*, as its subtitle suggests, would put comedy in service of philosophy, an approach that might make his audience more amenable to his increasingly radical and often arcane views. Shaw felt, as he also acknowledged in 1921, that the 'sweet-shop view of theatre', by then out of fashion, compelled him to sugar-coat the pill of philosophy with his rollicking comedy and thus to deliver his polemical message without resorting to a stultifying lecture or treatise.

But the conjunction in Shaw's subtitle also suggests an intimacy between the comedic and the philosophical, which might well compromise the seriousness of a message that bore on the very future of the human race. The playwright came to believe that the 'philosophical' elements of the text – the surreal dream sequence of Act III, known as 'Don Juan in Hell', along with the long-winded preface, called the 'Epistle Dedicatory to Arthur Bingham Walkley' (composed as if to his friend and fellow critic), and the appended 'Revolutionist's Handbook and Pocket Companion', which contains its own preface and appended 'Maxims for Revolutionists' – were all but swallowed up by its comedic features in 'the intellectual whirlpool' that was *Man and Superman* in its entirety. Shaw had attempted to turn light Victorian theatre, with its bourgeois platitudes and clichés, against itself with the aid of a brash avant-garde philosophy.[25] If he had erred in the direction of comedy, he did so because he had succumbed to the influence of middle-class tastemakers: 'the worst convention of the criticism of the theatre current at that time was that intellectual seriousness is out of place on stage; that the theatre is a place for shallow amusement'.[26] But he also acknowledged that the triumph of the comedy on stage led to the text being 'a good deal discussed'. His philosophy became a species or, at least, a close relative of comedy, and vice versa, so that the reader must consider them together as possessing performative and cognitive dimensions, and never as being simply playful or serious, trivial or significant, reckless or responsible. While some early readers of the play, from Sidney and Beatrice Webb to H.L. Mencken, were enthusiastic about this new form, it may not be surprising that many other critics were far less so, condemning Shaw for abandoning organic plot development, realistic dialogue, and even his vocation of a dramatist, in favour of the 'exhibition of ideas'.[27] This chapter contends, against a very long critical trend, that the text should be taken quite seriously precisely as a comedy *and* a philosophy – and that the effort to combine these modes in an expansive new dramatic form made an important contribution to the emergence of Irish modernism, at 'the forefront of the age'. In any case, it seems wise to abandon the assumption that Shaw penned a comedy in any conventional sense.[28] Rather, he had written something entirely new, which Harold Bloom rather disparagingly called a 'comedy of ideas', but which might be called more favourably an eminently modern 'drama', perhaps even the first modernist 'play' of the twentieth century.

As we have observed, Shaw preferred to call the text his 'drama of ideas', a label that acknowledged a certain debt not just to Nietzsche, but to what the playwright identified as a tradition of 'artist-philosophers', who combined their talents for literary or artistic style and close scrutiny of human behaviour with a concern for fundamental political, ethical, and even metaphysical questions. If Shaw was often compelled to fend off the charge of being derivative, especially when it came to his relationship with Nietzsche, he readily acknowledged his relationship with this idiosyncratic genealogy of painters, writers, composers, and thinkers, if only due to their idiosyncrasy. In the 'Epistle Dedicatory', Shaw thus offers a long list of his artistic and intellectual forebears: 'Bunyan, Blake, Hogarth and Turner (these four apart and above all English classics), Goethe, Shelley, Schopenhauer, Wagner, Ibsen, Tolstoy, and Nietzsche are among the writers whose peculiar sense of the world I recognise as more or less akin to my own. Mark the word peculiar'.[29] Shaw makes a claim to cultural capital according to his membership in this eccentric canon, which acquires its status by virtue of distinction from both traditional or systematic philosophy, on the one hand, and the leading raconteurs of the English literary tradition, on the other. According to the playwright, the members of his canon are quite different from the likes of Dickens and Shakespeare, whose 'pregnant observations and demonstrations of life are not coordinated into any philosophy or religion'.[30] Artist-philosophers, however, are not concerned with diversities of human experience and behaviour, but with underlying unities that give them their moral and even metaphysical significance. According to Shaw, they are granted a kind of ahistorical status, which ensures the universality of their claims (but which also risks emulating precisely what the playwright had condemned in 'academic' philosophers). He acknowledges that 'it may seem a long step from Bunyan to Nietzsche; but', he claims, 'the difference between their conclusions is purely formal'. What Bunyan expressed about righteousness and morality 'in the terms of a tinker's theology' – i.e. Christian allegory – 'is what Nietzsche has expressed in terms of post-Darwinian, post-Schopenhauerian philosophy ... Nothing is new in these matters except their novelties'. No doubt this is a gross misprision, which threatens to defuse what is most radical, most consequential, in Nietzsche's thought, even more so if we take the claim as attributing a stable underlying basis to the philosopher's moral and political views. But it gives, or attempts to give, a kind of lasting legitimacy to Shaw's efforts to get 'underneath moral precepts' of his own time and place in order to reach some universal bedrock – it attempts, that is, a philosophical justification of his comedy.[31] The details of his comedy of manners may be trifling, and the machinations of the young people who inhabit his play may be trivial, but they seek to reflect on fundamental questions regarding our ethical and political lives in a manner as penetrating as any academic or systematic philosophy.

While Shaw takes on the role of the artist-philosopher in order to further the 'attack on morality and respectability', he insists on an objectivity that means his 'plain statement of a fundamental constitution of London society' should not be understood by his English audience as 'an Irishman's reproach to your nation'.[32] Yet the Irishman's play most certainly includes an attack on what passes for morality and respectability, social norms and class hierarchies, in the English capital, albeit an attack that Shaw attempts to launch from a strategic position of distance and detachment, rather than of some unyielding national resentment. In the 'Epistle Dedicatory', Shaw explains that *Man and Superman* began as a Don Juan play and places it in a long line of dramas featuring this figure as one who 'whilst gaining the ardent sympathy of our rebellious instincts ... finds himself in mortal conflict with existing institutions'.[33] His protagonist, John Tanner, is based on the familiar figure, though he is very much a modern man who finds himself in conflict with 'those forces of middle class public opinion, which hardly existed for a Spanish nobleman in the days of the first Don Juan'.[34] *Man and Superman*, in all its unwieldy and contradictory complexity, is directed at an effort to overturn these opinions, to transvalue these values, and in the process it contributes to the emergence of Irish modernism, a movement that here shuns Irish cultural nationalism *and* the pretences of British society. In the comedy of manners that makes up the bulk of the play, Tanner inhabits the role of a political agitator, social critic, and confirmed bachelor, who persistently questions the norms of late-Victorian and Edwardian social life, especially the privileged status granted to the middle and upper classes and the social expectations that compel men and women to enter into marriage.

Shaw warns in his preface that his readers should prepare themselves 'to face a trumpery story of modern London life, a life in which, as you know, the ordinary man's business is to get means to keep up the position and habits of a gentleman, and the ordinary women's business is to get married'.[35] His new Don Juan is no longer 'victor in the duel of sexes' and he has too much 'prudence and good manners' to actually assault the conscience of his times.[36] But, rather unexpectedly, he has discovered 'a moral in his immorality'. 'Instead of pretending to read Ovid he does actually read Schopenhaur [sic] and Nietzsche, studies Westermarck, and is concerned for the future of the race instead of for the freedom of his own instincts'.[37] 'By launching him as a modern Englishman into a modern English environment', then, Shaw has transformed Don Juan into something very different: Donjuanism is now understood as a variety of moral scepticism and eugenicist speculation rather than 'mere Casanovism'.[38]

In this guise, the new Don Juan provides Shaw with a means to criticise the 'modern English environment', as well as the tradition of British radicalism that he had long thought ideologically suspect, but now found utterly rigidified into a set of outmoded moral doctrines and retrograde political positions. Before any of his characters even speak a word in his text, the playwright indicates his position with a key piece of set decoration – a bust of 'Mr Herbert Spencer', an item of philosophical kitsch that occupies a prominent place in the study of Roebuck Ramsden and looms over the action of the entire first act.[39] As we soon learn, Ramsden claims to be an 'advanced thinker' who 'stood for equality and liberty of conscience while [others] were truckling to the Church and to the aristocracy', but who is presently denounced by Tanner as 'an old man with obsolete ideas'.[40] Spencer, who died in December 1903 shortly after the publication of Shaw's play, was widely recognised as the father of social Darwinism and the most prominent English philosopher of the late nineteenth century. Advocating utilitarian ideals and *laissez-faire* economics, Spencer proposed a teleological vision for the future of mankind, progressing towards higher and higher forms of altruism through the parallel action of biological and social development. But, by the turn of the century, his efforts to develop a 'synthetic philosophy', which combined evolutionary principles with biological, sociological, psychological, and broadly moral concerns, were falling increasingly out of favour.[41] Nietzsche, as we have seen, targeted the philosopher and his English colleagues in the opening pages of *A Genealogy of Morals* for what he viewed as their misguided attempts to explain the origins of morality in utilitarian terms; in *Twilight of the Idols*, he would go on to claim with a rather cruel irony that, like both latter-day Christians and socialists, Spencer was 'a decadent', precisely because 'he sees something desirable in the triumph of altruism'.[42] As Tille acknowledges in his introduction and many subsequent critics affirm, Nietzsche thus opposed prevailing teleological assumptions that evolution would lead to the gradual emergence of a morality already inherent in the natural order. A similar consensus has developed around the opinion that Spencer failed to produce a 'truly radical break with traditional morality', and instead succeeded in merely naturalising the very same values that the British middle class had long sought to validate with reference to Christian theology.[43]

Shaw's brand of philosophy joins this attack on Spencer's ideology as a means of advocating his own socio-political positions, which draw on Nietzsche's ireful example but for very different ends. Reviewing *A Genealogy of Morals* in 1899, Shaw acknowledged that Spencerian thought, with its unconcealed agnosticism, had long had a corrosive effect on religious faith in England, but that it continued to exalt the values of 'duty, morality, law, and altruism'.[44] Like Nietzsche, Shaw recognised that 'synthetic philosophy', despite its claims to strict materialism, was permeated by the misguided assumption that evolution was a developmental process leading to moral ends. But Shaw, as a socialist, took notice of the ways that this assumption worked as an ethical and biological justification for free enterprise; as a socialist of the Fabian variety, he gave particular attention to the anarchic qualities of Spencerian thought, which suggested that the unrestricted forces of the market would and should eventually supplant the coercive structures of the state. As early as 1884, Spencer had come to oppose all forms of social welfare as the inauspicious precursors to the socialisation of the means of production and the emergence of socialist or communist regimes, which he warned against as 'the coming slavery'.[45] Five years later, in his contribution to *Fabian Essays in Socialism* (1889), Shaw had directly challenged Spencer and other 'modern anarchists' for their belief 'that a right and just social order was not an artificial and painfully maintained legal edifice, but a spontaneous outcome of the free play of the forces of Nature'. In *You Can Never Tell*, first performed in 1894, he went on to mock this brand of social and political thought with the figure of McComas, a solicitor who claims, much like Ramsden, that he is 'a Philosophic Radical, standing for liberty and the rights of the individual, as I learnt to do from my master Herbert Spencer. Am I howled at? No: I'm indulged as a fogey. I'm out of everything, because I've refused to bow the knee to Socialism'.[46] Spencer's advocacy of laissez-faire capitalism, as the highest form of social organisation yet achieved by mankind, stemmed from his belief it would spur the weak to greater efforts and allow the strong to work towards collective happiness. Conveniently, then, his philosophy postulated evolution as an intrinsically progressive process, a postulate that allowed it to 'negotiate between the claims of the individual and those of the species, to overcome the conflict between egoism and altruism', not in the figure of an Übermensch or Superman, but in what Spencer called the 'ideally moral man'.[47]

The bust of Spencer thus sets the stage (quite literally) for Shaw to explore the titular dyad of man and Superman. That Spencerian thought seemed to promise this eventual perfection of mankind, brought about by the inevitable process of social and biological development, became one of its principal attractions at the height of its fashion. According to the English philosopher, 'the members of this future race will exist in a state of perfect equilibrium', balancing the needs of the individual with the demands of the community in a complex, symbiotic relationship.[48] Unlike Darwin, then, Spencer viewed evolution as a fundamentally goal-driven or teleological process guided by Lamarckian use-inheritance, with each generation striving toward a physical and mental improvement and passing its small achievements along to the next. In the social realm, as in the biological realm, this process moved from 'simple, undifferentiated homogeneity' to the 'higher evolution' of 'complex, differentiated heterogeneity', which would ultimately result in the ideal society of the future, characterised by universal freedom, harmonious cooperation, and lasting peace, thanks to a population made up of his moral exemplars.[49] Nietzsche directly and repeatedly challenged this account of moral evolution, though it appears to have played an important role in the development of his alternative notion of human perfectibility. In *Nietzsche, Biology, and Metaphor*, Gregory Moore details the German philosopher's rejection of Spencer's 'ideally moral man', who seemed to embody the very principles of herd consciousness and slave morality that were deemed decadent or degenerate. Like Spencer, Nietzsche can be seen to understand evolution primarily in moral terms, recognising moral and biological development as intertwined processes that move towards a superior type of human being. But crucially, for Nietzsche, this process entails a 'transvaluation of all values' as it advances 'from the "herd egoism" of animals and modern humans to the higher egoism of the *Übermensch*'.[50] Nietzschean philosophy, viewed from this angle, effectively reverses the direction of Spencerian evolution, no longer leading to the inevitable development of a communal and altruistic form of consciousness, but rather to the refinement of egoistic impulses in an authentic form of individuality.

In setting out to articulate his own vision of the Superman, Shaw allies with Nietzsche in a general assault on the 'British perspective', which had passed for a form of radical or advanced thought in the latter half of the nineteenth century. In his 'Epistle Dedicatory', the playwright complains of the view, based on Darwinian theory, that 'progress can do nothing but make the most of us all as we are, and that most would clearly not be enough even if those who are already raised out of the lowest abysses would allow the others a chance'. There is, for Shaw, no hope for improving the race if the evolutionary process proceeds by blind chance because any improvements attained by one generation cannot, with any certainty, be passed along to the next. Nor is there any sense in relying, as Spencer does, on the processes of biological and social evolution to lead, through the 'survival of the fittest', to higher and higher levels of individual altruism and communal cooperation. According to Shaw,

> Promiscuous breeding has produced a weakness of character that is too timid to face the full stringency of a thoroughly competitive struggle for existence and too lazy and petty to organise the commonwealth co-operatively. Being cowards, we defeat natural selection under cover of philanthropy: being sluggards, we neglect artificial selection under cover of delicacy and morality.

This defeat and neglect are the misdeeds of the previous generation of thinkers such as Ramsden, who classes himself as an 'advanced man' for championing the twin notions of biological evolution and laissez-faire economics, but who, in doing so, merely justifies the interests of an emerging class of bourgeois entrepreneurs. By the time the play opens, the radical tradition of Spencer had come to look decidedly conservative in its adherence to a progressive view of human society and its reliance on a laissez-faire approach to *both* economics and evolution. In this light, *Man and Superman* can be seen as putting comedy and philosophy into the service of biopolitical propaganda, directed against the status quo in Great Britain and Ireland and designed to transform middle-class opinion across the United Kingdom. 'We must', Shaw implores, 'either breed political capacity or be ruined by Democracy, which was forced on us by the failure of older alternatives'; the time has come, he would have his readers believe, to acknowledge the true lessons of evolutionary theory and embark on a eugenicist project.[51]

Comedy of manners, comedy of morals

The comedy of manners that unfolds in Act I serves this project by chipping away at the 'delicacy and morality' that have shaped the relations between the sexes and, therefore, the progress of the human species up to the present time. What most clearly reveals Ramsden's 'advanced' thinking as fundamentally conservative are his attitudes towards sex and sexuality, which remain stereotypically Victorian. Already in a huff about the scandalous implications of Tanner's 'Revolutionist's Handbook', Ramsden begins to seethe about the younger man's relationship with Ann Whitfield, whom the older man sees as far too accommodating. As he speaks with the dreamy poet, Octavius, Ramsden 'fumes down to Herbert Spencer': 'there are limits to social toleration. You know that I am not a bigoted or prejudiced man

... But I draw the line at Anarchism and Free Love and that sort of thing'.[52] To be sure, there are strict bounds on Ramsden's moral vision, which relies heavily on the very values that Spencer's philosophy sought to naturalise and legitimise with reference to evolutionary principles. But Shaw's comedy is corrosive. Later in the act, as Ann, Octavius, and Jack discuss the illegitimate pregnancy of another young woman, Violet, the generational divide between the young and old radicals is accentuated:

> RAMSDEN: [*facing Tanner impressively*] And Morality, sir? What is to become of that?
> TANNER: Meaning a weeping Magdalen and an innocent child branded with her shame. Not in our circle, thank you. Morality can go to its father the devil.
> RAMSDEN: I thought so, sir. Morality sent to the devil to please our libertines, male and female. That is to be the future of England, is it?
> TANNER: Oh, England will survive your disapproval. Meanwhile, I understand that you agree with me as to the practical course we are to take?
> RAMSDEN: Not in your spirit, sir. Not for your reasons.
> TANNER: You can explain that if anybody calls you to account, here or hereafter. [*He turns away, and plants himself in front of Mr Herbert Spencer, at whom he stares gloomily*].[53]

The radical tradition may have denied any transcendental source of values, but at least in the figure of Ramsden, it continues to adhere to Christian morality in all matters relating to sexuality and procreation. Nietzsche was a strident critic of just this strain of thought, which he identified in examples of the British mind from Spencer to George Eliot, and which provided an important foil for his own position on conventional morality. In *Twilight of the Idols* (reviewed by Shaw in 1896), the philosopher claims that 'they have got rid of Christian God, and now think themselves obliged to cling firmer than ever to Christian morality: that is *English* consistency ... In England for every little emancipation from divinity, people have to reacquire respectability by becoming moral fanatics in an awe-inspiring manner' (original emphasis).[54] For both Nietzsche and Shaw, the English – at least, the generation of Ramsden and Spencer – are an all too conventional and 'consistent' people, mired in decadent ideas about right and wrong, good and evil, regardless of claims to the contrary made by these outmoded 'advanced' men.

Shaw provides an intellectual antagonist for Ramsden and his contemporaries in the figure of Tanner, the young revolutionary and modern-day Don Juan who, as we know from the 'Epistle Dedicatory', has read 'Schopenhauer and Nietzsche, studied Westermarck'. He is, in other words, a thinker who has steeped himself in fashionable philosophical, sociological, and anthropological accounts of the relations between the sexes, the history of marriage institutions, the emergence of superior individuals, and the 'will' or 'force' or 'energy' that generates these phenomena. This is to say that he is not a mere libertine: he is, after all, 'concerned for the future of the race instead of for the freedom of his own instincts'. But, 'more Hamlet than Don Juan', he may not turn his concerns into action, into political engagement or revolutionary struggle, much less into some eugenicist breeding programme of his own design.[55] Rather, in the end, he may be all talk. Indeed, from the outset of the play, we may well doubt the value of his philosophy as contained in the 'Revolutionist's Handbook', which presents itself as a guide to action of sorts, but which Ramsden discards violently in the waste paper basket during their first encounter on stage. Tanner is very much the brash, boisterous, armchair radical, as concerned with pursuing the latest intellectual fashions and antagonising the older generation as he is with translating his ideas into social or political practice. He is, in other words, an object of satire much like Ramsden. But, significantly for the 'philosophy' of the play, he is also a stand-in for Shaw himself, as evinced in Harley Granville-Barker's attempt to impersonate the playwright, complete with his exaggerated beard, when he played Tanner in the first production of the play. What is clear is that, as a thinker, Tanner shares with his creator a 'moral passion', which he describes to Ann in a conversation about a childhood intrigue between them: that passion dignified his juvenile 'greedinesses and cruelties, curiosities and fancies, habits and superstitions ... gave them conscience and meaning, found them a mob of appetites and organised them into an army of purposes and principles'.[56] He has turned the destructive tendencies of his youth towards the construction of a new morality that may be yet more destructive – of the restrictive morals and Victorian hypocrisies represented by Ramsden – though the question remains whether or not Tanner has produced a mode of thought that is more restrictive than the ones he battles against with the philosophical weapons provided by the likes of Schopenhauer, Nietzsche, and Westermarck. The question remains, moreover, of how seriously he should be taken as a philosopher. In this ambivalent guise, as will be elaborated below, the character allows Shaw to garrulously voice perspectives, argue claims, and proclaim principles that have touched his own moral passion, without having to take full responsibility for them.

The Shavian comedy of manners thus serves both as means to critique British society – especially as it was represented in late-Victorian and Edwardian theatre – and to explore new ideas regarding courtship, marriage, and sexuality, ideas that might ultimately lead to an understanding of the vitalistic forces that drive men and women into the arms of one another. Ramsden, the keeper of conventional morality, has been tasked with serving as guardian to the wilful and precocious Ann after the loss of her father;

unfortunately for him, he is compelled to share this duty with the wilful and unconventional Tanner, who resists the commission because he fears he will never be able to control the young woman (we glimpse an image of the Shavian 'New Woman' in her). Both guardians, at least initially, favour a match between Ann and Octavius, who has been blinded to the young woman's defiant character by his own naïve attraction to her. Into this love story, as mentioned above, comes the 'terrible news' that Violet is soon to become an unmarried mother. Of course, Ramsden, Octavius, and even Ann are scandalised by this moral transgression, but Tanner sees things differently: the report is to be celebrated because a young woman has turned away from the idle pastimes of her class and gender and towards 'the fulfilment of her highest purpose and greatest function – to increase, multiply and replenish the earth'.[57] These contrasting narratives are complicated further when we learn that there is an ongoing attraction between Ann and Tanner, through which the young woman seeks conquest and from which the young man seeks escape. In Act II, the complications only multiply: Tanner offers solace to Octavius after Ann has rejected the latter's proposal, the entire group becomes swept up in plans to travel to the Continent, and a young American, Hector Malone, enters the scene. We soon learn that this new character, so outwardly chivalrous, is not only the father of Violet's unborn child, but he is also her husband. Their affair has been secreted because it threatens to result in the disapproval of Hector's billionaire father, who wants his son to marry into the British aristocracy. While plot points like these, however preposterous, were familiar enough on the Victorian stage, they provide the opportunity for Shaw (through his mouthpiece, Tanner) to offer up some rather unusual views on love and marriage, which he sees merely as a means to some higher, evolutionary purpose. This is a play not about romance or sentiment so much as procreation. The comedy, that is, offers an opportunity for the playwright to reflect – in the mode of an 'artist-philosopher' – on the underlying motives that drive these actions, motives that influence not just the happiness of those involved or the stability of their society, but the future of the entire human race.

'Don Juan in Hell' and Shavio-Socratic dialogue

This reflection becomes the focus of the play as the scene shifts in Act III to the dream sequence known as 'Don Juan in Hell' – and Shaw takes up the role of a modern artist-philosopher, pursuing a kind of avant-gardist distinction by imbuing this surrealist form with elements of Lamarckian theory and Nietzschean philosophy. With strains of 'Mozartian' music rising, Don Juan enters a subterranean space where moments before there had been '*nothing;*

omnipresent nothing ... no sound, no time nor space, utter void' (original italics for stage directions).[58] The famous lover is familiar to the audience because his features and his name – Don Juan Tenario – both suggest the protagonist of the first two acts – John Tanner. He is soon joined on stage by a woman whose features recall Ann Whitfield, but whose plaintive conversation with Don Juan reveals her to be his former lover, Dona Ana, much aged since their last encounter. They are eventually joined by 'the Statue', a figure of white marble come to life whose voice much resembles that of Roebuck Ramsden, and later, with another flourish of Mozartian music, by 'the Devil' himself. Critics have often noted the innovative elements of 'Don Juan in Hell', which anticipates aspects of surrealism and metatheatre as it unfolds on an overtly theatricalised stage, but what most plainly defines the act is its lengthy excursion into philosophical debate. In the 'Epistle Dedicatory', endeavouring to market his message, Shaw trademarks the scene as a piece of 'Shavio-Socratic dialogue', which pits the 'angelic' Life Force philosophy of Don Juan against the 'diabolic' pessimism of the Devil, who refuses to be converted to the optimistic view of human progress announced by his interlocutor.[59] The act, in this way, also enters into a dialectical mode of reflection on the idea of the Superman, which is not merely adopted from Nietzsche, but rather amended, distorted, and extended in a variety of ways. Provisionally titled 'The Superman, or Don Juan's Great Grandson's Grandson', the act was later described by Shaw as 'a careful attempt to write a new Book of Genesis for the Bible of Evolution', one that he trusted would not require the redaction of its miraculous or simply foolish stories by philosophers, scientists, and historians, 'however fantastic its legendary framework may appear'. To be sure, the act enters into wider debates regarding the social, moral, and biological significance of evolutionary theory, which Shaw was implicitly conducting with Darwinians such as Spencer, T.H. Huxley, and H.G. Wells. But 'Don Juan in Hell' is much more closely engaged with Nietzsche and the volumes of his philosophy familiar to Shaw – including the text that the German philosopher referred to as a 'new "holy book"' and a 'fifth Gospel', *Thus Spake Zarathustra* – than critics have acknowledged. The dialectical mode of the act allows Shaw to playfully entertain both sides of the optimistic/pessimistic divide: to promote his alternative faith while acknowledging, at least in passing, the potential criticisms that it might provoke and even heading them off in the process. It is, in this sense, exemplary of his particular mode of philosophical ideation.

Yet despite its idiosyncrasies, Shaw's philosophy is still reminiscent of a general neo-Lamarckian trend in evolutionary thinking, particularly in England, at the turn of the twentieth century. Indeed, for all his own posturing as an 'advanced' thinker, Shaw himself might well be classed with those English philosophers whom Tille condemns for denying the most far-reaching consequences of Darwin's *Origin of Species* and, instead, attempting 'to show that sexual and natural selection and elimination cannot possibly account for what, since the middle of the last century, has been called "human progress"'.[60] For Shaw sought to rescue the idea of 'human progress', albeit in his own distinctive form, with the neo-Lamarckian conception of what his Don Juan calls 'Life: the force that ever strives to attain greater power of contemplating itself ... Not merely the need to do, but the need to know what I do'.[61] According to this brand of Shavian vitalism, evolution proceeds by a 'continual effort not only to maintain itself, but to achieve higher and higher organization and completer self-consciousness'.[62] The lover-turned-philosopher admits that, so far, evolution has waged 'a doubtful campaign between its forces and those of Death and Degeneration', but he maintains faith in the purpose and potential of this vital energy, the 'Life Force'. If the theory of natural selection produced fears that life was characterised by nothing more than nightmarish struggle and senseless accident, the philosophy-cum-religion of the Life Force responds with an assertion of this natural creativity. Like Samuel Butler and other neo-Lamarckian thinkers, whose evolutionary writings Shaw consistently praised, the playwright sought to identify a vital motive energy behind the workings of evolution that might provide them with a moral, if not exactly divine, purpose. He later celebrated Butler's foresight in recognising 'how the Darwinians, in their revolt against crude Bible worship, would empty the baby out with the bath and degrade the whole conception of Evolution by levelling it down to Natural Selection, which though a potent method of adaptation, is not true Evolution at all'.[63] But, in holding fast to a teleological view of evolution, Shavian Life Force philosophy only succeeded in repeating many of the same cognitive blunders that had prevented Spencer from making a radical break from moral orthodoxies and led Nietzsche to condemn him and his fellow English philosophers. This brand of vitalism, that is, resorts to a quasi-religious justification of the beliefs and values that it postulates as correct by dictating that those beliefs and values must lead to a particular end.

The basic assumption of Shaw's philosophy is clearly that evolution is working towards the purpose or goal of the Superman. What is amiss with mere 'man' is quite evident to Don Juan: 'Here is the highest miracle of organization yet attained by life, the most intensely alive thing that exists, the most conscious of all the organisms; and yet, how wretched are his brains!'[64] If his interlocutors are 'agreed that Life is a force which has made innumerable experiments in organizing itself', from the mouse to the man, they will likewise agree, he argues, that these are 'all more or less successful attempts to build up that raw force into higher and higher individuals, the ideal individual being omnipotent, omniscient, infallible, and withal completely unilludedly self-conscious: in short, a god'.[65] The evolutionary process, driven by the 'incessant aspiration' of the Shavian Life Force, is thus eminently purposeful, rather than the blind and random process described by Darwinian evolutionary theory. Shaw largely adopted this perspective from Butler, whom he called 'the founder of the religion of evolution', and whose arguments for teleology in works such as *Evolution, Old and New* and *Luck or Cunning?* (reviewed by Shaw for the *Pall Mall Gazette* in 1887) retained a metaphysical, even theological, quality in making what amounted to a case for design.[66] Rather than directly creating species, this principle worked in neo-Lamarckian fashion through the instinctual striving of individuals that led eventually to new physiological structures. If Darwinian theory was 'supposed to be fatal to a purposive view of animal and vegetable organs', Butler sees 'signs in the structure of animals and plants, of something which carries with it the idea of contrivance so strongly that it is impossible for us to think of the structure, without at the same time thinking of contrivance, or design, in connection with it'.[67] Butler gave particular attention to the brains and mental lives of animals, but unlike Shaw 'he did not regard consciousness as the highest form of this activity'. Instead, he 'argued that instinct was the most fully developed kind of mental activity' and even suggested (much as Nietzsche had, in fact) that 'man himself would be much happier if he could eliminate all conscious thought and reduce his life to instinctive activity'.[68]

The form of the Shavio-Socratic dialogue allows the playwright, through a shrewd calculation, to make his case for his own 'religion of evolution', while in some measure deflecting criticism from himself for adopting Butler's neo-Lamarckian position. Shaw's Don Juan argues stridently that the universe has been aiming at the evolution of the Superman in the form of 'the philosophic man', who is capable of understanding the 'inner will of the world' so that nature will finally arrive at a mode of self-understanding, a comprehension of the evolutionary process beneath or behind its outward appearance. But the Devil, a proper 'Diabolian', as Shaw had envisioned in his 1899 review of Nietzsche, is there to rebut the assumptions on which this argument rests:[69] 'You think', he tells Don Juan, 'because you have a purpose, Nature must have one. You might as well expect it to have fingers and toes because you have them': his position, in other words, is nothing more than facile anthropomorphism, a kind of pathetic fallacy that extends to the entirety of the universe. Of course, Don Juan has his neo-Lamarckian response: 'I should not have them if they served no purpose. And I, my friend, am as much a part of Nature as my own finger is a part of me. If my finger is the organ by which I grasp the sword and the mandoline, my brain is the organ by which Nature strives to understand itself'.[70] And so on for more than twenty pages. Throughout their long exchange, Don Juan plays the role of the optimist, with his theory of the Life Force, while the Devil is the pessimist or rather sceptic who raises objections that are, rather surprisingly given the source, almost uniformly of a moral kind, calling attention to the hedonistic, egoistic, and ultimately destructive qualities of mankind. Much like Nietzsche, the Devil in *Man and Superman* subjects modernity to a thorough critique, which denigrates the violence and destruction enabled by technology, the greed and sloth enabled by industrialisation, the hatred and resentment enabled by religion, and the hypocrisy and exploitation enabled by morality. He challenges, in short, the entire ideology of human progress. But in each case Don Juan refuses to see the evidence as damning: instead, he blithely, and often wittily, subordinates each of these objections to nature's grand plan. He would appear to be the victor in the extended back and forth between the two, but the contradictions in the Shavio-Socratic dialogue are never finally resolved; firm conclusions are never finally reached, indicating the unremitting tensions within Shavian Life Force philosophy itself. Indeed, this lack of resolution puts the 'Shavio-' in 'Shavio-Socratic' dialogue.

Like Shaw's Devil, his Diabolian philosopher, Nietzsche is sceptical of redemptive teleological narratives that might justify the notions of progress and development by explaining away the ills of the modern world. But, if he expresses profound doubts about such goal-directed thinking, he also, like Shaw's Don Juan, seeks some goal that might nonetheless fulfil his desire for perfection and give human life lasting significance – and this goal he gives the name of Übermensch. Zarathustra takes it as his personal aim to teach the Übermensch to his fellow men and, from the outset, his lesson is rendered in evolutionary terms:

> Man is a something that shall be surpassed ... All beings hitherto have created something beyond themselves: and are ye going to be the ebb of this great tide and rather revert to the animal than surpass man? What with man is the ape? A joke or a sore shame. Man shall be the same for beyond-man, a joke or a sore shame. Ye have made your way from worm to man, and much within you is still worm. Once ye were apes, even now man is ape in a higher degree than any ape.[71]

The future of man is to give birth to the Übermensch. Although he returns over and over to this lesson, Zarathustra does very little to specify the characteristics of this evolutionary telos, this being-to-come; indeed, the details of this teaching remain rather sketchy in all of Nietzsche's writings, so that the Übermensch remains a rather perplexing goal, an unstable signifier, a metaphorical vehicle with no certain tenor. Shaw even has a bit of fun with this fact, which is the condition of possibility for his own project: when the Statue asks 'And who the deuce is the Superman?', the Devil quips 'Oh, the latest fashion among the Life Force fanatics. Did you not meet in Heaven, among the new arrivals, that German Polish madman – what was his name? Nietzsche?'[72] To be sure, it could be claimed that what is most important to Nietzsche's thought is precisely his conception of life as 'will to power', which inflects his understanding of politics, morality, science, and so on. But it seems that, while the Statue finds the Superman to be a nice slogan, a rallying call, as far as the Devil is concerned it is hardly a new idea, but rather an idea 'as old as Prometheus' that is merely the 'newest of the old crazes'. This admixture of comedy and philosophy allows Shaw to trade on the name of Nietzsche and his once 'latest fashion', while seeking to elevate his own philosophical perspective to the status of the very latest fashion, opposed to that of a philosopher who has (so we learn) run off to heaven after a quarrel with Wagner. The Devil and Zarathustra agree, nonetheless, that the Superman is 'not yet created' or 'never yet … existed': he remains an unrealised, perhaps unrealisable, goal; moreover, they acknowledge that the precise form he would take remains indeterminate, even if his general contours can be glimpsed from time to time.[73]

On this point, there is still a crucial distinction between Shaw's philosopher, Don Juan, and Nietzsche, who harshly criticises teleological thinking in many of his writings and even suggests in several places that Übermenschen have already existed, if only by some fortunate chance. To redact these elements of his writing is to fail to see Nietzsche as an 'advanced' thinker and instead to open his writing to all manner of propagandistic appropriation. In the opening passages of *The Antichrist*, among the very first of his volumes published in English, the German philosopher writes quite directly that 'this more valuable type has often enough existed already: but as a happy accident, as an exception, never *willed*' (original emphasis). Rather,

> the reverse type has been willed, cultivated, *attained*; the domestic animal, the herding animal, the sickly animal man, the – Christian … Mankind does not manifest a development to the better, the stronger, or the higher, in the manner in which it is at present believed. 'Progress' is merely a modern idea, i.e., a false idea.[74]
>
> The European of the present is, in worth, far below the European of the Renaissance; onward development is by *no* means, by any necessity, elevating, enhancing, strengthening. In another sense, there is a continuous success of single cases in the most different parts of earth, and from the most different civilisations, in which, in fact, a *higher type* manifests itself: something which, in relation to collective mankind, is a sort of beyond-man. (original emphasis)

Nietzsche offers us a very different picture of the evolutionary process here. Instead of emerging through the slow accumulation of traits, the Übermensch leaps out from the development of the species as a chance occurrence. For Nietzsche, as he writes later in the same book, the traits of cunning, forbearance, and the aptitude for imitation necessary for survival have been harnessed by Christianity to wage '*deadly war* against the higher type of man' in taking the side of 'the weak, the low, the ill-constituted' (original emphasis). It has made a virtue of these traits in members of the so-called herd, who value nothing more than conformity and devote their intellects to its pursuit. In doing so, Christianity has branded the 'strong man as the typical reprobate, as "out-cast man"' and 'made an ideal out of the *antagonism* to the preservative instincts of strong life; it has ruined the reason even of the intellectually strongest natures, in that it taught men to regard the highest values of intellectuality as sinful, as misleading, as *temptations*' (original emphasis).[75] For Nietzsche, the Übermensch is a creature of instincts, but the right instincts. Modern man, on the other hand, has fallen into an overreliance on his intellect, on his consciousness, that has drawn him away from the crucial regulation of drives or impulses offered by his better instincts. This is precisely the condition that the philosopher consistently refers to as decadence.

Nietzsche provides his most penetrating critique of evolutionary teleology, and its implication with decadent values, in a well-known passage from the 'Second Essay' of *A Genealogy of Morals*. There is no better example of practising the vocation of the philosopher, as Nietzsche conceives it. He challenges the timeworn assumption that the 'cause of the origin of a thing and its ultimate utility, its actual application and linking into a system of purpose' are connected in some necessary and irrevocable way. In doing so, he critiques the persistence of a conviction, an article of faith, that has taken on the guise of truth by virtue of its tenacious ability to avoid our close consideration. 'It is customary to think that by understanding the demonstrable purpose, the utility of a thing (or form, or institution) the reason for its origin was also understood'. To be sure, Shaw continued to think in this way about the very examples that Nietzsche provides: 'the eye being explained as having been made for the purpose of seeing, the hand for the purpose of seizing'. But Nietzsche defies this orthodoxy by claiming that the purpose of a thing is continually transformed by 'some will to power', capable of redefining that purpose, so that any origin will be obscured or elided altogether. He claims that:

> The entire history of a 'thing', an organ, a custom may, in this way be one unbroken sign-series of constantly changing interpretations and adjustments, the causes of which need not even be connected among themselves, but may, according to circumstances, follow upon, and replace one another quite at random. By no means, therefore, is the 'evolution' of a thing (or a custom or an organ) its *progressus* towards a goal, still less a *progressus logicus* advancing in a straight line and with the least expenditure of power and pains, – but rather a series of more or less important, more or less independent, processes of over-powering.[76]

Such is the force of the will to power in both cultural and biological, both moral and physiological, evolution. The form of a thing or a custom or an organ is always mobile and mutable, 'but the sense is still more so'. This logic extends to the constitution of each individual or society: 'every essential growth of the whole will cause the '"sense" of the individual organs shifts. According to circumstances the partial destruction of these organs, their diminution in number ... may be sign of growing power and perfection'.[77] Nietzsche argues that Darwinian theory, with its reliance on 'the absolute fortuitousness and even mechanistical nonsensicalness', fails to recognise this logic and, as a consequence, it has mistakenly emphasised adaptation as the key to the evolutionary process. Evolutionary thinkers (and here Nietzsche again singles out Spencer) have come to define life by this 'second rate activity, in fact, a mere reactivity', but this is to overlook the 'true nature and function of life' – those 'spontaneous, aggressive, transgressive, new-interpretive and new-directive forces', which he sums up as the will to power. It is also to overlook what Nietzsche calls the 'conditions of true progress', which require a greater power to be enforced at the expense of a large number of lesser powers. In a phrase that has long drawn shocked attention, Nietzsche exemplifies this dynamic in the human realm: 'mankind *en masse* sacrificed in order to insure the growth of a single, *stronger* species of man – that *would be* progress' (original emphasis).[78]

Both Nietzsche and Shaw, through their mouthpieces, Zarathustra and Don Juan, explore the idea of pursuing moral and political progress through the 'breeding' of exemplary human beings: 'My will clingeth round man', Zarathustra exhorts, 'with chains I bind myself unto man because I am torn upwards unto beyond-man. For thither mine other will is longing'.[79] Similarly, Don Juan tells us 'that as long as I can conceive something better than myself I cannot be easy unless I am striving to bring it into existence or clearing the way for it'.[80] Responding to the zeal of both Zarathustra and Don Juan (and ironically commenting on the efforts of his author to create a 'Book of Genesis' for the 'Bible of Evolution'), the Devil objects that 'all your philosophizing has been nothing but a mask for proselytizing!' and in his mounting fear, the Devil warns: 'Do not listen to their gospel ...: it is dangerous. Beware of the pursuit of the Superhuman: it leads to an indiscriminate contempt for the Human'.[81] The characterisation of this discourse as proselytising or gospel would take hold during the first decade of the twentieth century and the warnings about the ethical dangers of the Superman idea would echo through its entire duration. But this does not deter Don Juan from his aim: 'The great central purpose of breeding the race, ay, breeding it to heights now deemed superhuman'. In the view of the legendary lover, this must also become the central purpose of marriage, which has been so long 'hidden in a mephitic cloud of love and romance and prudery and fastidiousness'.[82] Here the relationship between the Shavio-Socratic dialogue and the comedy of manners that frames it is clearly announced; and here too Don Juan parrots Zarathustra, who offers a critique of the traditional purpose of marriage as a social institution. 'Though shalt build beyond thyself .... Though shalt not only propagate thyself but propagate thyself upwards! Therefore the garden of marriage may help thee!'[83] Marriage should not be conceived as the unification of souls, a heavenly blessing, or even a sympathetic bond, for 'even your best love is but an enraptured parable and a painful heat'. Instead, this pain should be seen as a prompt to pursue a greater objective: 'Bitterness is in the cup even of the best love: thus it bringeth longing for beyond-man: thus it bringeth thirst unto thee, the creator! Thirst unto the creator, an arrow and longing for beyond-man'.[84] Both Don Juan and Zarathustra take it as their task to encourage, in eugenicist fashion, the breeding of a new kind of humanity, even if they have very different ideas about what his enhancement amounts to and what kind of society would result from it.

No doubt there are the beginnings of a frightful politics – or more precisely, biopolitics – in all this. Shaw's play is articulating a case, however ironically, for the active management of 'life' by some form of institutional authority that would address itself not just to the body of the individual but to man as a species. In *Breeding Supermen: Nietzsche, Race and Eugenics in Edwardian and Interwar Britain*, Dan Stone details how early interpreters of Nietzsche's writing made sense of it with reference to both Darwinian evolutionary theory and a burgeoning interest in eugenics, which sought to apply recent ideas about biology to social and political affairs. Indeed, Tille's work was instrumental in disseminating this understanding of the German's philosophy through commentaries that return over and over to the new biology and link it with earlier ideas about human perfection. For instance, in his introduction to *Thus Spake Zarathustra*, he reviews ideas about human perfection and breeding from Goethe, Prince Pickler-Muskau, Darwin, and Wilhelm Jordan, before claiming that Nietzsche 'had taken up the idea and made it almost the leading motive of his Zarathustra' and, with this text, finally allowed the idea to 'impress itself upon large circles of the educated youth'.[85] Many latter-day commentators have sought to absolve Nietzsche's work of the charge that it was 'advocating some program of breeding a supposedly superior race';[86] but others, such as Conway, have seen in Nietzsche's attention to these concerns his 'general answer to the founding question of politics: "we" should undertake to breed a type of individual whose pursuit of self-perfection contributes to the enhancement of humankind and thereby justifies our own existence'.[87]

If there is a tension in Nietzsche's philosophy between the project of species-overcoming, which would require the creation of new forms of institutional organisation, and self-overcoming, which calls for the individual to transform what existing institutions have made him, then Shaw's philosophy decidedly shifts its emphasis to the former. What is most significant for *Man and Superman* is that Shaw takes up Nietzsche, and the association between the philosopher and the eugenics movement, in a manner calculated to extend the reach of his own political message. At the end of Act III, Shaw plays on this association with a bit of sly sloganeering, when Dona Ana discovers that the Superman has not yet been created: 'Then my work is not yet done. [*Crossing herself devoutly*] I believe in the Life to Come. [*Crying to the universe*] A father – a father for the Superman!'[88] Critics, perhaps taking Shaw a bit too literally, have seen in the Don Juan in Hell scene 'nothing more than an idiot's Lamarckianism', which turns poorly understood science and philosophy into utterly misguided politics.[89] But this is to fail to see Shaw's philosophical comedy at its best: Ana's ecstatic cry is both a sign of devotion to the new religion of evolution and a mating call of sorts, which returns the text to its concern with romantic intrigues.

The search for a Superman

When the 'Don Juan in Hell' dream sequence ends, Dona Ana's cry continues to resonate, evoking comparisons between the figure of the Superman and the many characters, from across the social and ideological spectrum, who inhabit the outer play: the world of history and politics and comedy. To be sure, the final act of the play can be read as offering a series of ironic answers to the vexing question of just what type of person the Superman is to be. As the hellish figures vanish into the void, Tanner appears on a stage that has now come to resemble the Sierra Nevada Mountains in southern Spain, where he and his travelling companions have been waylaid by a gang of brigands. Their leader, Mendoza, bears a striking resemblance to the Devil, with the same 'Mephistophelean affectation', but here he serves as 'President of the League of the Sierra', a roaming band of anarchists and thieves. He promises the possibility of revolution and denies the influence of ideology, claiming that 'I am not a slave to any superstition. I have swallowed all the formulas, even that of Socialism; though, in a sense, once a Socialist, always a Socialist'.[90] In this guise, he is a man of action, holding up motorcars and stealing from the rich in order to 'secure a more equitable distribution of wealth'. But he is not possessed of the consciousness of the Superman: 'common sense is good enough for [the ordinary man]; and in our business affairs common sense is good enough for me'. Nor does the play's other socialist exemplar, Henry 'Enry' Straker, possess an expansive mind. The cockney chauffeur and 'motor engineer' is what Shaw calls 'the New Man', whose strong will and technological competence make him superior in many ways to his employer, Tanner. This member of 'the efficient engineering class' may help to 'sweep the jabberers out of the way of civilisation', but his mind is ultimately limited.[91] For, as Shaw emphasises, he is strictly a materialist: he is a socialist, but 'a scientific one'; he is an adept, but a mechanical one. In the cases of both Mendoza and Straker, socialism is a heroic undertaking, promising armed revolution or technological know-how that will ultimately do away with the unequal distribution of wealth and the exploitation of the labouring class. But it is also wanting in 'philosophy'.

Perhaps a stronger candidate for the role of Superman is to be found in Hector Malone's father, the elder Mr Malone, 'one of the master spirits of the age', who has accumulated vast wealth through the sheer force of his will.[92] Driven from Ireland as a child by the Great Famine, he arrived in the United States entirely destitute and yet he managed to make himself into a billionaire. For all his success, however, Mr Malone has become a monster of *ressentiment*. Telling his life story 'with smouldering passion', he insists that the Irish Famine was no famine at all, but a 'starvation': 'When a country is full of food, and exporting it, there can be no famine. My father was starved dead; and I was starved out to America in my mother's arms. English rule drove me and mine out of Ireland'.[93] Now, with his wealth secured, he seeks to exact his revenge on England not by building up Ireland, but along with others like him, 'coming back to buy England; and we'll buy the best of it'. He will take over the country estates of a decadent British aristocracy, who nonetheless remain the standard-bearers for nobility and civilisation. '*Withal*', the stage directions tell us, he is '*a man to be rather pitied when he is not to be feared; for there is something pathetic about him at times, as if the huge commercial machine which has worked him into his frock coat had allowed him very little of his own way and left his affections hungry and baffled*' (original italics for stage directions).[94] His project is a failed one from the outset. In 1901, Shaw had published a satirical tract titled *Socialism for Millionaires*, which called on his readers to remember that the 'plight' of the wealthy man is 'getting worse and worse with the advance of civilisation', because he suffers from the problem of having too much money to spend solely on himself.[95] The essay suggests further that, in Ireland, the absentee landlord is 'bitterly reproached' for being 'a pure parasite upon the industry of the country'.[96] Mr Malone seems to have overcome the problem of the rich man precisely by concocting his absentee landlord revenge scheme. But he is no Superman, for he is dominated by what Nietzsche calls 'those instincts of reaction and resentment', which undermine all noble ideals; he is, instead, one of 'these bearers of prostrating and vengeance-craving instincts, the progeny of all European and non-European serfdom', who 'represent the *decline* of mankind!' (original emphasis).[97]

In the figure of Malone, that is, Shaw suggests that the Irish will never be fully emancipated, never fully overcome their history, until they abandon their nationalist ressentiment, as well as the capitalist ethos of their imperial masters. Although he has gotten only scant attention in the critical literature on *Man and Superman*, Mr Malone is thus a figure of crucial importance to the politics of the play. His Irishness, announced clearly through a 'native intonation' that has '*clung to him through many changes of place and rank*' sets him against '*Straker, as a very obvious cockney*', who '*inspires him with implacable contempt*'. The billionaire regards the driver as '*a stupid Englishman who cannot even speak his own language properly*', while Straker '*regards the old gentleman's accent as a joke thoughtfully provided by Providence expressly for the amusement of the British race*'. These prejudices prompt Malone to tease and torment Straker, while it encourages the Englishman to treat the Irishman '*with the indulgence due to an inferior and unlucky species*', despite his superior wealth and social standing (original italics for stage directions).[98] Race, nationality, and class, that is, become markers of ascendancy in this battle: the wealthy Irishman can look down on the working-class Englishman – and vice versa. These resentments also form an obstacle to the romantic relationship between Hector Malone Jr and Violet Robinson, because Malone Sr refuses to allow his son to marry someone without a title. The father's revenge plot requires the son's selection of a proper spouse to confirm his elevated social position in England: 'Let him raise himself socially with my money or raise somebody else: so long as there is a social profit somewhere, I'll regard my expenditure as justified. But there must be a profit for someone'.[99] This is his all-too-traditional idea of marriage: exchanging financial capital for social capital. But, in true comedic fashion, this principle is soon undone by the charms of the young woman, who manages to secure her husband and the estate of her choice – an abbey, no less – at her father-in-law's expense.

Tanner, as the most 'philosophic' of Shaw's characters, may well be the best candidate to father the Superman, if not to be one himself; and yet, as a man of intellectual ambition, he is also a confirmed bachelor. Here, again, is the corrosive potency of Shaw's comedy. Witnessing Hector Malone Jr's affections for Violet, he proclaims, 'Another madman! These men in love should be locked up' – although, with this proclamation, he becomes the object of comedy, because he has failed to recognise what the audience already knows: that Hector and Violet are already betrothed.[100] Tanner, the audience also knows, tends to speak before (and more than) he thinks. He is a man of many words and few actions: a soapbox socialist, a rabble-rouser, a chaser after intellectual fashions. He attempts to abstract general lessons about the relations between the sexes, the relations between the classes, and the relations between the individual and the collective, from his experience of British upper-class life. To his mind, the philosopher must resist the distractions of love and marriage, for they only inhibit his efforts to understand workings of nature, of the evolutionary process, behind the outward appearance of the world. But, in the end, he cannot be taken seriously as a thinker: despite his protestations about romance and marriage, despite his claims that Ann is a liar and a hypocrite, he finds it impossible to extricate himself from her charms. Rather than comprehending the Life Force, he becomes its victim, its tool, its means: seizing Ann in his arms, he proclaims 'The Life Force enchants me: I have the whole world in my arms when I clasp you. But I am fighting for my freedom, for my honour, for my self, one and indivisible'.[101] In the very last line of the play, all his philosophy is reduced to mere 'talking' while the Life Force has worked through Ann to overmaster his intellectual ambitions. In this sense, it is Ann, a woman, who is the Superman: for she is the conduit of the Life Force, as it strives to replace mere man with a creature capable of contemplating this process, while the hapless male 'philosopher' is deprived of his free will.

The 'Revolutionist's Handbook' and a eugenicist's programme

This is all part of Shaw's ironic and often incongruous positioning of philosophical perspectives within the many conjoined texts that make up *Man and Superman*. The play's conclusion serves to further compromise Tanner's credibility as a philosopher ahead of the book's addendum, its notorious 'Revolutionist's Handbook and Pocket Companion': not only does the play proper ridicule him as one overflowing with idle talk, the title page of the handbook identifies him as a John Tanner, MIRC (Member of the Idle Rich Class). It is clear, as we have already noted, that Tanner is meant to serve as a mouthpiece for many of the views that Shaw himself sought to disseminate, though he is also a figure of self-mockery or, at least, persistent irony, very much an English philosopher, with all the foibles and failings that the title implies for Shaw. In the preface to his handbook, Tanner defines the revolutionist as 'one who desires to discard the existing social order and try another'. But, he also suggests that advocating revolution is a perfectly respectable occupation for an Englishman, because it comes in the form of a popular election 'every seven years'.[102] In this sense, in addition to being an English philosopher, Tanner is also very much the Fabian revolutionary, content (or resigned) to pursue socialist ends through gradualist and reformist means undertaken within existing democratic frameworks. 'And yet', he continues, 'revolutions have never lightened the burden of tyranny: they have only shifted it to another shoulder'. What is the necessity of this 'handbook', then? It offers itself as a collection of instructions on the subject of revolution, *and yet* it undercuts the value of revolution; it proposes a political philosophy, *and yet* it does so under the authorship of a philosophical windbag. It does nonetheless offer Shaw the opportunity to announce a series of propositions – some of them as controversial as the establishment of a 'State Department of Evolution', and a 'private society or a chartered company for the improvement of human live stock' – while at least partially sidestepping responsibility for their dire ethical implications.[103] To be sure, contemporary reviewers of *Man and Superman* found the policies advocated in the handbook hard to take seriously and even posited that Shaw was 'perfectly aware of the farcical absurdity of his proposal for breeding a race of such men on an artificial system', *and yet* the book contributed to an emerging market for those ideas.[104]

At the centre of the dubious philosophy articulated in the 'Revolutionist's Handbook' is again the figure of the Superman. But, departing from the metaphysical claims made by his counterpart, Don Juan, Tanner tells us that, 'the need for the Superman is, in its most imperative aspect, a political one'.[105] The 'Proletarian Democracy' that has taken hold in Great Britain and elsewhere owes its success not to any of its inherent qualities, but only to the 'failure of alternative systems'. In the absence of Supermen, government by consent of the governed has emerged by default, since it requires only the mediocrity of 'human nature' in its current form to function effectively. The English people, led by their disappointing philosophers and even more disappointing politicians, may claim to believe in a 'progressive moral evolution operating visibly from grandfather to grandson' but not even 'the most confident of Whig meliorists, can produce any such evidence that will bear cross-examination'.[106] Meanwhile, the complications of governance continue to multiply apace. In his writings for the Fabian Society, Shaw had returned over and over to the challenges represented by the 'growth of the social organism', as well as 'the rise of foreign trade and Capitalism', which continually outstripped the control, 'not merely of the individual, but of the village, the guild, the municipality, and even the central government'.[107] Now, he has Tanner suggest that the way to avoid the repeated catastrophes of history, and to address the increasing difficulties of domestic governance and international relations, is to create a 'Democracy of Supermen' of sufficient talent and insight to govern in a complex world. Only in this way can the future of socialism be assured, because only in this way can a revolution be brought about and 'net progress' be assured.[108] This might be viewed as an ironic rejection of the very possibility of adducing an egalitarian political philosophy from Nietzsche's concept of the Übermensch, which would require the improbable, if not paradoxical, circumstance of every citizen attaining the status of a Superman.[109] But Tanner duly sketches his biopolitical programme with characteristic verbosity, claiming that the need to breed the Superman will override the established institutions of property and marriage, which stand in the way of social equality and thus impede 'sexual selection with irrelevant conditions'.[110] New governmental institutions and social policies – including state agencies, domestic subsidies, and even 'a joint stock human stud farm (piously disguised as a reformed Foundling Hospital or something of that sort)' – will be necessary to assist women in the proper selection of fathers and nourishment of themselves to produce the desired outcome.[111]

By the turn of the century, Nietzsche's thought and particularly the idea of the Superman had already been appropriated by not just socialists, but anarchists, feminists, German imperialists, advanced capitalists, and many others for their own political ends – despite the philosopher's outspoken criticism of each of these schools of thought as so many signs of modern decadence. In that sense, Shaw's use of the Superman was just another instance in a long history of misappropriations, which would notoriously continue with Nazi efforts to provide an ideological justification for their illiberal agenda by selecting out just those images, ideas, and passages that served their political ends. The Superman served Shaw's comedic, philosophic, and propagandistic ends not simply as a productive concept, but as a cultural phenomenon that had gathered large amounts of attention with its provocative, even shocking, implications. In appropriating the idea, Shaw's spokesman, Tanner, claims a kind of public domain – 'cry for the Superman did not begin with Nietzsche nor will it end with his vogue' – but he nonetheless capitalises on that fashion to promote his own programme.[112] No doubt the details provided by Nietzsche are too sparse to authorise a particular image of the figure, even if we can be assured of its capacity to renew certain dimensions of individual and social life. But Shaw nonetheless found sanction in his philosophy to advance a connection between eugenics and democracy that was not an uncommon one at the turn of the century, when socialists, liberals, and other reformers on the left advocated eugenicist schemes along with plans for public education and hygiene.

Perhaps most important, Shaw (through Tanner) attempts more directly than Nietzsche to answer the question of just what type of person the Superman is to be. In addressing this question, the 'Revolutionist's Handbook' produces his most potent admixture of philosophy and comedy, which results in its odd variety of propaganda – promoting controversial social and political ideas in one breath and risibly undermining them in the next. This is the way, in short, that the play repackages Nietzsche's philosophy for Shaw's purposes. Tanner begins by postulating – in the manner often, though erroneously, attributed to Nietzsche – 'some sort of good-looking philosopher-athlete, with a handsome healthy woman for his mate, perhaps'. However vague this conception may be, it represents 'a great advance on the popular demand for a perfect gentleman and a perfect lady', a demand that merely reflects conventional notions of value and morality. But, for all his certainty, or at least desire for certainty, Shaw's philosopher is obliged to admit that 'the proof of the Superman will be in the living; and we shall find out how to produce him by the old method of trial and error, and not by waiting for a completely convincing prescription of his ingredients'.[113] Still, intervention in the evolutionary process is necessary if it is to result in the goal of a 'Democracy of Supermen'. Tanner claims, counter to the position of most of his peers in Great Britain, that there have been no permanent advances toward virtue and civilisation over the course of human history. 'The existence of a progressive moral evolution ... is very acceptable to Englishmen, who always lean sincerely to virtue's side as long as it costs them nothing';[114] but the fact of the matter, according to him, is that the few 'accidental supermen' who have populated history, 'our Shakespears, Goethes, Shelleys' have lived precariously, if aloofly, in relation to the enduring barbarism of mankind.[115]

Another key example of the accidental Superman offered by Tanner is the American religious philosopher and utopian socialist, John Humphrey Noyes, who founded the Oneida Community of Perfectionists in Madison County, New York, in 1848. The project undertaken by Noyes, which had recently been commemorated in Allan Estlake's *The Oneida Community: A Record of an Attempt to Carry Out the Principles of Christian Unselfishness and Scientific Race-Improvement* (1900), is significant for Tanner because it was 'a highly selected community' that, given the presence of its founder, 'simplified the breeding problem for the Communists, the question as to what sort of man they should strive to breed being settled at once by the obvious desirability of breeding another Noyes'.[116] But the Oneida Community is also crucial to Shaw's philosopher because it demonstrates the key problem that necessitates the formulation of his own brand of utopian socialism: that such a community will not succeed until it can call on a collective of Supermen.

> If Noyes had had to organise, not a few dozen Perfectionists, but the whole United States, America would have beaten him as completely as England beat Oliver Cromwell, France Napoleon, or Rome Julius Caesar. Cromwell learnt by bitter experience that God himself cannot raise a people above its own level, and that even though you stir a nation to sacrifice all its appetites to its conscience, the result will still depend wholly on the sort of conscience the nation has got.[117]

Socialism will not, cannot, prevail until it achieves a normative consensus, in the form of the national conscience, which will support it as a form of political life in the absence of religious authority or state coercion. This represents the abandonment of Fabian gradualism, with its pragmatic emphasis on the slow transformation of political attitudes and institutional structures, for another kind of gradualism on an even longer timeline – that is, an evolutionary gradualism assisted by selective breeding. Like so much else in Shaw, then, this is a joke that should be taken seriously. For nearly two decades, he had argued that the process of getting socialism into 'working order' would be undertaken with a 'humdrum program' of popularising already accepted ideas regarding private property and social justice, and would 'at no point … involve guillotining, declaring the Rights of Man, swearing on the altar of the country'.[118] But, by the time he came to write *Man and Superman*, he had grown increasingly impatient with this ethos and had taken to wryly rejecting it. The tinkering of parliaments and congresses may create some small advances in the distribution of wealth or the management of conflict, 'but all this is mere readjustment and reformation'.[119] Real revolution, however slow, would only be brought about by changing the 'raw material' of the citizenry, the physiological basis of their conscience or moral sensibility, and raising the collective to the heights hitherto only reached by solitary individuals: 'The only fundamental and possible Socialism', Tanner concludes, 'is the socialization of the selective breeding of Man'.[120]

This programme, however, presents the fundamental problem of how to achieve an effective consensus in society at large; this problem, in turn, generates many of the creative tensions and troubling contradictions that characterise Shaw's comedic efforts to frame a political philosophy. Nietzsche's philosophy, as recent criticism has demonstrated, can be seen as a form of political scepticism insofar as it is concerned with the rise of the state, which requires normative consensus to legitimise its authority, even as the process of secularisation throws the possibility of producing such agreement into doubt.[121] His Zarathustra had famously claimed that 'the state is called the coldest of all cold monsters', because it 'is a liar in all tongues of good and evil; whatever it saith, it lieth, whatever it hath, it hath stolen'.[122] It is an institution, in other words, that may have the ideological and propagandistic means to generate a consensus but for Nietzsche, as this recent criticism has emphasised, it provides no guarantees that it should 'converge around the right (as opposed to merely politically expedient) norms' or normative beliefs.[123] He sees that modern states cannot rule just through direct coercion, but must be viewed by their subjects as conforming to correct norms in order to sustain their political legitimacy. Shaw points to an analogous ideological need in his proposed socialist utopia, which must appeal to the 'conscience of the nation', its sense of what is right and wrong, good and evil, in order to organise the citizens around a shared communal enterprise: to compel its populace 'to sacrifice all its appetites' in order to 'raise a people above its own level'.[124] As early as 1889, while professing his faith in the 'inevitable' progress of 'social evolution' in 'The Transition to Social Democracy', he also recognised that continued progress would require both the transformation of 'ordinary middle-class opinion' regarding socialism and the establishment of new confidence in the 'State' to serve as 'the representative and trustee of the people'.[125] Social democracy, according to Shaw, promised to bring about these transformations by effectively and efficiently gathering 'the raw material of Socialism – otherwise the Proletarian man' into the democratic state machinery, so that it could be trusted with 'all the sources of production ... which are now abandoned to the cupidity of irresponsible private individuals'.[126]

But by 1903, despite his reservations that 'God himself' could not accomplish this collective task, Shaw could claim – or, at least, have Tanner claim – that there is a means to generate the necessary consensus: namely, a religion of socialist evolution, constructed around the figure of the Superman. How else might, say, a 'State Department of Evolution' be established? How else could his biopolitical programme be fulfilled? Shaw dismissed the ideas of natural selection and Darwinian evolution, so consequential to Spencer and his peers, as having no utility for revolutionary purposes because they provided no common goal or purpose for mankind and thus encouraged men to look out only for themselves. On the other hand, he embraced the notions of the Superman and the Life Force, because to his mind they affirmed a purpose in the universe, which would allow men to identify their own purpose with it and to make the fulfilment of that purpose, as Shaw would later write, 'an act, not of self-sacrifice for himself, but of self-realization'. If, for Nietzsche, the primary object of interest is individual freedom rather than political structures, he would seem to be far more concerned with the critiquing those ideologies, those forms of bad conscience and ressentiment, that stand in the way of human flourishing – at least for the privileged few. He seemed to have little faith that the problem of legitimacy was one that could be solved in the modern state, even if certain individuals were able to ascend to the status of Supermen, precisely because in his conception the values of such an individual would be, by definition, non-normative. As Tanner recognises, when it comes to actualising his political vision, the relationship between the individual and the collective is seemingly an intractable one: 'Until there is an England in which every man is a Cromwell, a France in which every man is a Napoleon, a Rome in which every man is a Caesar, a Germany in which every man is a Luther plus a Goethe, the world will be no more improved by its heroes than a Brixton villa is improved by the pyramid of Cheops'.[127] Shaw is thus motivated, over and over, to merge religious and evolutionary perspectives in order to develop structures through which truth claims collapse into value claims – and might thus come to exercise influence on the conscience of an entire nation.

The figure of the Superman, in this sense, becomes an essential, indeed *the* essential, article of the new Shavian faith. Here, it is wise to recall Gareth Griffith's cautionary remarks regarding this faith: that 'it would be wrong to discount Shaw's evolutionary righteousness simply as the disturbing hyperbole employed by a controversialist ... The controversialist was also a moralist and self-appointed arbiter of the right to life with a commitment to social and spiritual progress'.[128] Tanner's historical examples of the Superman – Napoleon, Caesar, Goethe, and (interestingly, given that the memory of his talents as a general and statesman mixes with that of his brutal reconquest of Ireland) Cromwell – failed in his opinion precisely because they were all unable to create or recreate a national conscience, to transvalue national values in line with their political, military, and cultural aims. A few years earlier, in the preface to his play on Napoleon, *The Man of Destiny*, Shaw had mischievously confessed that he found it 'impossible to live in England without sometimes feeling how much that country had lost in not being conquered' by Napoleon as well as Caesar. In 1902, writing under his own name in *The Eagle and the Serpent*, Shaw claimed that his two heroes had both suffered from 'the efforts of the average respectable man to destroy [them]': 'Napoleon's military system finally reduced itself to absurdity, and forced the dufferdom of Europe to combine and destroy him. Caesar, with immense social talents and moral gifts in addition to moral capacity, bribed the masses into tolerating him, but was killed by a conspiracy of "good" men who killed him on principle as a protest of right against might'.[129] Each Superman, in other words, was brought down by forces of slave morality and ressentiment, which conspired to crush the superior individual. For Nietzsche, as he claims in *A Genealogy of Morals*, the appearance of Napoleon in the midst of the French Revolution and 'the popular resentment instincts' that initiated it was 'the most unexpected thing': it asserted the antique ideal – 'the privilege of the fewest' – which 'appeared *bodily* and with unheard-of splendour before [the] eyes and conscience of humanity' just when 'the old, false battle-cry of resentment about the *right of the most*' was resounding through France (original emphasis).[130] But, for Shaw, the subsequent demise of Napoleon indicates that 'under the rule of a standard Morality evolution is limited by the fact that at a certain point of development the individual in whom the advance is manifested (say the Superman) is attacked and destroyed in the name of Right by the other less developed individuals'.[131]

What is needed, then, is a radically new brand of egalitarianism, which would somehow raise the entire population to the level of the Superman. To the extent that a positive politics can be attributed to Nietzsche, it centres on the figure of an exemplary individual who extends the scope of human perfectibility, as Napoleon, Caesar, and Goethe each did in his estimation. But he does not view these exemplary individuals as political figures nor does he seek to define the future of the Übermensch in political terms; he does not view the Superman as a means to a more perfect democracy, much less a more successful socialism, but as an end in himself, albeit one that would represent the overcoming of the decadence and nihilism characteristic of modernity. To be sure, Nietzsche saw liberal institutions, once established, as a threat to the emergence of great individuals because, as he argued in *Twilight of the Idols*, their easily granted freedoms 'make people small, cowardly, and voluptuous, – with them the herding animal always triumphs'.[132] In the same passage, he cites Caesar as 'the highest type of free men' since he had overcome 'the highest resistance' in the form of his own tyrannical and pitiless instincts, which called forth 'the maximum of authority and discipline'.[133] Great individuals, according to this thesis, are 'explosive materials' that accumulate force over extended periods, even epochs, only to be touched off by 'the most accidental stimulus'. His exemplar of this process is Napoleon who was not a beneficiary of the French Revolution, but rather 'the heir of a stronger, more enduring and older civilisation than that which vanished into the vapour and fragments in France'. He was crucially, necessarily, 'a different type', antithetical to his age, who demonstrated that the superior individual was most likely to emerge precisely when the social order was defined by contradictory values.[134] For Shaw, despite the seeming impossibility of his 'every man' a 'Superman' schema, there is nothing contradictory about it at all; nor is there anything contradictory in the aims of the singular Superman and the aims of a socialist collective. What is required (and what his philosophy as propaganda encourages) is a transformation in the collective conscience so that it might overcome the influence of slave morality, including its dictates regarding marriage and procreation, and align itself with the higher purpose of following the Life Force and fulfilling its evolutionary telos. Here, then, is a radical biopolitics that would fundamentally alter the relationship of the individual and society by gradually, but deliberately, overturning existing social and political institutions and introducing a new form of communal organisation inhabited by a new form of political animal. But despite the distressing possibility of selectively breeding human beings, this is a political philosophy that would promote the creation of a race of Supermen conforming to the generally mild economic and political demands of Fabian socialism.

Ireland, national conscience, and the drama of ideas

The concern with national conscience marks an important connection, if not exactly continuity, between *Man and Superman* and Shaw's next play, his most Irish play, *John Bull's Other Island*. To be sure, Tanner's eugenicist thinking extends beyond England to encompass, at the very least, the United Kingdom of Great Britain and Ireland: for instance, in considering the means to enable a young woman to breed superior offspring, Tanner suggests that she might 'financed by herself, or by her father, or by a speculative capitalist, or by a new department of, say, the Royal Dublin Society', that august organisation founded in 1731 to 'to promote and develop agriculture, arts, industry, and science in Ireland'.[135] In December 1902, as Shaw was writing *Man and Superman*, W.B. Yeats mentioned in a letter to his collaborator Frank Fay that the playwright had offered to compose a piece for their new theatre company, which would soon become the Irish National Theatre Society at the Abbey Theatre. And, in June 1903, shortly before the publication of *Man and Superman*, Shaw wrote to Yeats again, reminding him that he had it 'quite seriously in [his] head to write an Irish play', but that it would be 'frightfully modern – no banshees or leprechauns'.[136] Shaw did not actually begin drafting *John Bull's Other Island* until June of the following year (17 June 1904, one day following Bloom's Day, to be exact), after he had seen the Irish National Theatre Society's first performances in London at the Royal Theatre. Eventually, he scripted a very long play set in a contemporary, and altogether unromantic, Ireland, a play that demonstrated an intense and sustained interest in questions regarding Irish national character, self-determination, and Home Rule. Unfortunately, when Yeats read the play in October 1904, he expressed disappointment that the opening acts (if not others) dealt too much with the 'difference between English and Irish character, or whatever else it was all about', though he did compliment Shaw's 'wonderful knowledge of the country', which surprised him a bit due to the playwright's long absence from his homeland.[137] But despite his fondness for certain aspects of the play, Yeats went on to enumerate the many practical problems it represented for effective staging and casting, as well as to recommend many cuts and alterations that ultimately scuttled any plans for an Abbey production. In this preface to the play, however, Shaw cites 'another reason for changing the destination of John Bull's Other Island': 'It was uncongenial to the whole spirit of the neo-Gaelic movement, which is bent on creating a new Ireland after its own ideal, whereas my play is a very uncompromising presentment of the real old Ireland'.[138]

The preface also addresses itself to the 'curse of Nationalism' and the 'tyranny of the Church' that have plagued Ireland as a Catholic country under foreign rule and kept Shaw's countrymen from 'the light of the world'.[139] For the playwright, a 'healthy nation' is 'unconscious' of its nationality, but a nation like Ireland, suffering from a 'broken' nationality, develops an unhealthy obsession with making itself whole again. The 'neo-Gaelic movement', for instance, has harnessed this obsession to make 'an attack on the native language of the Irish people' – that is, for Shaw, English – because it is also the language of their English rulers.[140] The diagnosis is a Nietzschean one: Irish nationalism has been defined by ressentiment, the feeling of envy or animosity that is a defensive reaction against the values of the powerful, arising from a largely unacknowledged sense of weakness or subordination. The national conscience, in this way, has long been arrested in this binary relationship between Ireland (good) and England (evil). Irish politics, in turn, have been completely debased by this reactionary mindset according to Shaw:

> Every election is fought on nationalist grounds; every appointment is made on nationalist grounds; every judge is a partisan in the nationalist conflict; every speech is a recapitulation of nationalist twaddle; every lecture is a corruption of history to flatter nationalism or defame it; every school is a recruiting station; every church is a barrack; and every Irishman is unspeakably tired of the whole miserable business, which nevertheless is, and perforce must remain his first business until Home Rule makes an end of it, and sweeps the nationalist and the garrison hack together into the dustbin.

Home Rule is a necessity if only to bring this unhealthy obsession to an end and eventually to insert Ireland to its 'place in the world's march', along with other members of the commonwealth of nations.[141] But the Catholic Church, Shaw claims, 'naturally fosters his submissiveness. The British Government and the Vatican may differ very vehemently as to whose subject the Irishman is to be; but they are quite agreed as to the propriety of his being a subject'. Indeed, in many ways the Church is more restrictive than the government: it denies him any voice in selecting its leadership, it limits his educational opportunities, and it aims 'to make him and keep him a submissive Conservative'. It is only the external force of 'economic oppression and religious persecution' from the British government that produced and maintain the conflicted, resentful conscience of the Irish, 'this unnatural combination of political revolution and Papal reaction, and of hardy individualism and independence with despotism and subjugation'.[142]

In these details, there is a striking coincidence between the diagnosis offered by Shaw in *John Bull's Other Island* and that offered by Joyce in *A Portrait of the Artist as a Young Man*. Both are sceptical of the language movement, critical of nationalist myopia, and disparaging of the role of the Catholic Church in serving the interests of the Irish people. Nevertheless, both also recognise their own implication in the ressentiment evoked by British rule in Ireland: 'I am hampered, as an Irishman', Shaw reflects, 'by my implacable hostility' to English domination.[143] And yet both dedicate their art, albeit in very different ways, to the possibility of remaking the conscience of the Irish people and, as I will discuss in subsequent chapters, their thinking on the matter owes more than a little to the promptings of Nietzsche and his notion of the Superman. The correlation is indeed a remarkable one: in *A Portrait*, Stephen Dedalus makes his declarations about the conscience of the Irish on 27 April 1903, nearly the same moment that Shaw was finishing *Man and Superman*, with its 'Revolutionist's Handbook', and commencing work on *John Bull's Other Island*. We will return to *A Portrait* in greater detail in Chapter 3. For now, it can suffice to say that when Stephen announces his intention to 'forge the uncreated conscience of my race', he announces a desire to overcome the influence of Irish nationalism and the Catholic Church, but also to transvalue national values, to produce a communal conscience independent of submissiveness and ressentiment.[144] In doing so, as Pericles Lewis has pointed out, Stephen 'shares many of the crucial assumptions of Irish nationalists whose overt political and cultural agenda he opposes. In particular, he rejects political activism in favour of cultural renewal and associates this cultural renewal with expressing the essence of the Irish race'.[145] But his project of cultural renewal contains a crucial biological or racial component, 'accepting the idea of a biological essence of the nation, as opposed to the purely legal or political notions of membership in the community implied, for example, by the term "citizenship"'.[146] Despite his stated preference for aesthetics over eugenics, Stephen wonders earlier in the novel how his art might 'hit' the 'conscience' of the Irish patrician class 'or how cast his shadow over the imaginations of their daughters, before their squires begat upon them, that they might breed a race less ignoble than their own'.[147] The problems of race and breeding, on the one hand, and nation and conscience, on the other, are thoroughly intertwined in the consideration of a future for Ireland.

Throughout *John Bull's Other Island*, Shaw is at pains to overturn the very idea of an Irish race and to challenge the common stereotypes associated with the concept. But he still advocates altering the basic conditions of the Irish people. Taking himself as an example, he acknowledges in a playfully paradoxical fashion that his 'extraction is the extraction of most Englishmen': that is, he has 'no trace' in him of 'the commercially imported North Spanish strain which passes for aboriginal Irish'; he is, rather, 'a genuine typical Irishman of the Danish, Norman, Cromwellian, and (of course) Scotch invasions'. What is more, even though he is staunchly Protestant according to his family tradition, he will not offer his allegiance to the English government. The genuine Irishman, that is, is a thoroughly hybrid creature. Indeed, if Shaw has a claim to being Irish, it is primarily based on the fact that 'I was born in Ireland, and that my native language is the English of Swift and not the unspeakable jargon of mid-XIX century London newspapers'.[148] He goes so far as to say 'there is no Irish race any more than there is English race or a Yankee race', only an amalgam of people living in the same geographic location and economic climate.[149] Like Joyce, he mocks those 'Irish gentlemen' of the patrician class who are convinced of their superiority based not on their own qualities so much as on their ability to trace a 'pedigree to the conquest or one of the invasions', as if that made each of them 'a genuine true blue heir' to English superiority.[150]

At every turn, then, Shaw is concerned to upset the national stereotypes that Matthew Arnold had labelled so indelibly in the evolutionary ethnological argument of *The Study of Celtic Literature* (1867) as a series of inherited racial traits: the 'poor, slovenly, and half-barbarous' Celtic people, whose 'sentimental talents' were nonetheless a corrective to the rationality and good sense of the Anglo-Saxon temperament.[151] Shaw claims that:

> when I see Irishman everywhere standing clearheaded, sane, hardily callous to the boyish sentimentalities, susceptibilities, and credulities that make the Englishman the dupe of every charlatan and the idolater of every numbskull, I perceive that Ireland is the only spot on earth which still produces the ideal Englishman of history.[152]

Shaw personifies this reversal in the characters who feature in the play that follows: the Englishman, Tom Broadbent, who is a 'romantic duffer' caught up in the sentimental attraction of the neo-Gaelic movement and the Irishman, Larry Doyle, who is a 'cynical realist', well-adapted to his role as a civil engineer in London. As Declan Kiberd describes the arrangement, 'the English have enjoyed a scale of wealth so great that it allows them to indulge their victims with expansively sentimental gestures', while 'the Irish have become fact-facers through harsh poverty'.[153] Still, Broadbent remains an efficient man of commerce, who seeks to develop an estate in Rosscullen in order to capitalise on what he sees as the rustic charms of the place and its people. Despite his challenges to racial stereotypes, Shaw fears that the Catholic peasants who remain in Ireland, while so many others have boarded the emigrant ships, may be too 'docile' and 'reverent' to protect their country from exploitation: 'the Irish love their priests ... They love their landlords too ... They love the English, as every Englishman who travels in Ireland can testify. Please do not suppose that I speak satirically: the world is full of authentic examples of the concurrence of human kindliness with political rancour. Slaves and schoolboys often love their masters'.[154] As Doyle repeatedly claims, the Irish peasant is all too ready to be exploited, to be overworked, to be underpaid. In the context of *Man and Superman*, the nature of the situation is entirely evident, if only implicit: the Irish, even more urgently than the English, await the transformation of their national conscience and the slow transition to a 'Democracy of Supermen', who will ensure the socialisation of the sources of production by the expropriation of private property, as well as the transfer of that wealth to the entire nation.

By the time Shaw came to write his next play, *Major Barbara* (1905), which could be considered his third instalment in a trilogy on political philosophy, he felt it necessary to distance himself from Nietzsche and some of the other artist-philosophers whom he had identified as his kindred spirits in the 'Epistle Dedicatory' to *Man and Superman*. The new play, as David Kornhaber has argued, represented an attempt to further extend the form of the 'drama of ideas' in 'the direction that properly thoughtful and intellectually active drama should take' and thus to answer the question of 'how the theater should be best calibrated to encompass intellectual concerns'.[155] Beginning in the opening paragraph of the Preface, which Shaw wryly titled 'First Aid to Critics', he seeks to set the stage for this project by inveighing against an 'unpatriotic habit into which many critics have fallen' – that is, to identify the most radical elements of his art with the abiding influence of 'Schopenhauer, Nietzsche, Ibsen, Strindberg, Tolstoy, or some other heresiarch in northern or Eastern Europe'. In what might seem to be a curious reversal of his earlier attacks, he asks his critics 'why if they must give the credit of my plays to a philosopher, they do not give it to an English philosopher'.[156] Shaw does not have in mind the likes of Galton, Bateson, or Spencer, but his own canon of British thinkers, including Samuel Butler and Belfort Bax. To be sure, Bax himself studied philosophy in Germany, edited the works of Kant, and wrote extensively on the history of philosophy, though Shaw identifies him here as 'an English Socialist and philosophic essayist' renowned as a 'ruthless critic' of not only 'feminist sentiment', but also 'current morality'.[157]

Sensitive to his own rising status as an English (or Irish) philosopher, both a socialist and an immoralist, Shaw was concerned to disclaim any long-term attachment to Nietzsche in particular and to demonstrate that the German philosopher, despite all his claims to originality, was hardly the first thinker to challenge 'our mercanto-Christian morality'. But, ever the controversialist, Shaw also saw fit to defend Nietzsche from his detractors and even to publicly, if provisionally, cast his lot with the philosopher, who was, thanks largely to the influence of Max Nordau, 'the victim in England of a single much quoted sentence containing the phrase "big blonde beast"'. 'On the strength of this alliteration', Shaw claimed,

> it is assumed that Nietzsche gained his European reputation by a senseless glorification of selfish bullying as the rule of life, just as it is assumed, on the strength of the single word Superman (Übermensch) borrowed by me from Nietzsche, that I look for the salvation of society to the despotism of a single Napoleonic Superman, in spite of careful demonstration of the folly of that outworn infatuation.[158]

This may be a bit of revisionism on the part of the playwright, perpetrated to deflect some of the harsher criticisms away from his own brand of political philosophy. But it should not obscure the fact that Nietzsche and Shaw also sought to understand the development of moral behaviour and political possibility in terms provided by evolutionary biology: both were preoccupied with what the future might hold for humanity or its successor. Shaw understood that the success of his efforts depended on entering into the marketplace of ideas by the means at his disposal and then carving out a market share for his new hybrid variety of socialist thought, however ironic that effort might be. The critical response to the *Man and Superman*, as much as its title, had inextricably linked Shaw's reputation with the reception of Nietzsche's ideas, and also allowed detractors to write off elements of his drama as recycled German philosophy, which could be 'picked up at any bookstall'.[159] But this dismissal represented a narrow view of both the implications of Nietzschean philosophy and the innovations of Shavian drama, which had grown into an expansive, contradictory, dialectical form like nothing before seen on the page or stage in England or Ireland. In this regard, long before such major achievements as Joyce's *Ulysses* or Yeats's *A Vision*, *Man and Superman* contributed to the rise of Irish modernism by developing a sprawling new aesthetic form capable of accommodating a broad range of discourses and ideologies, all of which bore on the exigencies of the modern world.[160] It played at philosophy, it worked at propaganda, and it ultimately succeeded as theatre, if a very unconventional sort, which used comedy as a means to convey a very serious, and often very troubling, message – one that, as we shall see in Chapter 5, Shaw expanded to even greater dimensions, with even greater fervency, some two decades later in *Back to Methuselah*.

Notes

1 George Bernard Shaw, *Collected Letters 1898–1910*, Dan H. Laurence (ed.) (London: Bodley Head, 1972), p. 298.
2 George Bernard Shaw, 'Leading Opinions Concerning Nietzsche', *The Eagle and the Serpent* (November 1, 1898), 77.
3 Given the obvious significance of Nietzsche for Shaw, it is surprising how little criticism has been dedicated to the two. Much of what there is dates to the 1960s and 1970s, when scholars first began to calculate the importance of the philosopher for English literature. See, for instance, Margery M. Morgan, 'Shaw, Yeats, Nietzsche, and the Religion of Art', *Komos* (1967), 24–34; Carl Levine, 'Social Criticism in Shaw and Nietzsche', *Shaw Review* 10 (1967), 9–17; and David S. Thatcher, *Nietzsche in England, 1890–1914: The Growth of a Reputation* (Toronto: University of Toronto Press, 1970). More recent contributions to the scholarship include Michael Solomonson, 'Man and Superman: The Shavianizing of Friedrich Nietzsche', *Independent Shavian*

34:3 (1996), 54–59; David Kornhaber, *The Birth of Theater from the Spirit of Philosophy: Nietzsche and Modern Drama* (Chicago: Northwestern University Press, 2016), pp. 117–36; Reinhard G. Mueller, 'The "Breeding of Humanity": Nietzsche and Shaw's *Man and Superman*', *SHAW: The Journal of Bernard Shaw Studies* 39:2 (2019), 182–98.
4 Friedrich Nietzsche, *A Genealogy of Morals*, William A. Haussmann (trans.) (New York: Macmillan, 1897), p. 17.
5 Ibid., p. 11.
6 George Bernard Shaw, 'Nietzsche in English', *Saturday Review* (April 11, 1896), 373.
7 Alexander Tille, 'Introduction by the Editor', in Friedrich Nietzsche, *The Case of Wagner, Nietzsche Contra Wagner, Twilight of the Idols, The Antichrist*, Alexander Tille (ed.), Thomas Common (trans.) (London: H. Henry, 1896), p. ix.
8 Ibid., p. x.
9 Ibid., p. xiii.
10 Ibid., p. x.
11 Shaw, 'Nietzsche in English', 373.
12 Bernard Shaw, 'Science and Common Sense', *Current Literature* 29:1 (1900), 196.
13 See Michael Holroyd, *Bernard Shaw* (New York: Random House, 1998).
14 See, for instance, Gearóid O'Flaherty, 'George Bernard Shaw and Ireland', in Shaun Richards (ed.), *The Cambridge Companion to Twentieth-Century Irish Drama* (Cambridge: Cambridge University Press, 2004), pp. 122–35; Christopher Innes, 'Defining Irishness: Bernard Shaw and the Irish Connection on the English Stage', in Julia Wright (ed.), *A Companion to Irish Literature, Volume Two* (Oxford: Wiley-Blackwell, 2010), pp. 35–49; Anthony Roche, *The Irish Dramatic Revival, 1899–1939* (London: Bloomsbury, 2015), pp. 79–98.
15 Stanley Weintraub, 'Introduction', in Stanley Weintraub (ed.), *The Portable Bernard Shaw* (New York: Viking, 1977), p. 6.
16 Pascale Casanova, *The World Republic of Letters* (Cambridge, MA: Harvard, 2004), p. 314.
17 Shaw would have been unaware of all this in 1896 and still in 1902, since Nietzsche's book, though written in 1888, was not published in Germany until 1908 and not translated into English until 1911.
18 Peter Sloterdijk, *Nietzsche Apostle*, Steven Corcoran (trans.) (Los Angeles: Semiotext(e), 2013), p. 51.
19 Shaw, 'Nietzsche in English', 374.
20 T.F. Evans, 'Introduction: The Political Shaw', in T.F. Evans (ed.), *Shaw and Politics* (University Park: Penn State University Press, 1991), p. 5.
21 Steven E. Ascheim, *The Nietzsche Legacy in Germany: 1890–1990* (Berkeley: University of California Press, 1994), p. 178.
22 Daniel Conway, *Nietzsche and the Political* (New York: Routledge, 2005), p. 3.

23 Shaw, 'Nietzsche in English', 373.
24 Bernard Shaw, 'Preface: The Infidel Half Century', in Bernard Shaw, *Back to Methuselah: A Metabiological Pentateuch* (New York: Brentano's, 1921), p. c.
25 Ibid., p. xcix.
26 Ibid., p. c.
27 Arthur Bingham Walkley, *Drama and Life* (London: Methuen, 1907), p. 224. 'It is a three-ring circus', Mencken mused, 'with Ibsen doing running high jumps; Schopenhauer paying the calliope and Nietzsche selling peanuts in the reserved seats'. Henry Louis Mencken, *George Bernard Shaw: His Plays* (Boston: J.W. Luce, 1905), p. 70.
28 As Christopher Innes points out, critics 'who support Shaw as a modernist do so on a primarily intellectual basis, as representing a mode of though specific to the period of social transition leading up to the European cataclysm of World War I, while those who deny him the modernist label do so on the basis of style' ('Modernism', in Brad Kent (ed.), *George Bernard Shaw in Context* (Cambridge: Cambridge University Press), p. 152). But this binary does not hold for *Man and Superman* insofar as the text integrates its radical political philosophy into a decidedly innovative dramatic form.
29 Bernard Shaw, 'Epistle Dedicatory to Arthur Bingham Walkley', in Bernard Shaw, *Man and Superman: A Comedy and a Philosophy* (New York: Brentano's, 1905), p. xxviii.
30 Ibid., pp. xxviii–xxix.
31 Ibid., p. xxxii.
32 Ibid., p. xv.
33 Ibid., p. ix.
34 Ibid., p. xii.
35 Ibid., p. xiv.
36 Ibid., p. xii.
37 Ibid., p. xiii.
38 Ibid., p. xiv.
39 Shaw, *Man and Superman*, p. 2.
40 Ibid., pp. 7, 9.
41 For instance, he became a target of the *The Eagle and the Serpent*, where the 'famous altruist' was mocked for the 'extraordinary degree of egoism' he had derived from his work. 'The Mask of Pity, or a World-Damning Delusion', *The Eagle and the Serpent* (15 June 1898), 36.
42 Friedrich Nietzsche, *The Case of Wagner, Nietzsche Contra Wagner, Twilight of the Idols, The Antichrist*, Thomas Common (trans.) (London: H. Henry, 1896), p. 202.
43 Gregory Moore, *Nietzsche, Biology and Metaphor* (Cambridge: Cambridge University Press, 2002), p. 70.
44 G. Bernard Shaw, 'Giving the Devil His Due', *The Saturday Review* (13 May 1899), 111.
45 Herbert Spencer, *The Man Versus the State* (New York: D. Appleton, 1885), p. 18.

46 Bernard Shaw, *You Can Never Tell: A Pleasant Play* (New York: Brentano's, 1908), p. 40.
47 Moore, *Nietzsche*, p. 71.
48 Ibid., p. 64.
49 Peter J. Richerson and Morten H. Christiansen, 'Introduction', in Peter J. Richerson and Morten H. Christiansen (eds), *Cultural Evolution: Society, Technology, Language, and Religion* (Cambridge: MIT Press, 2013), p. 8.
50 Moore, *Nietzsche*, p. 73.
51 Shaw, 'Epistle Dedicatory', p. xxiv.
52 Shaw, *Man and Superman*, pp. 6–7.
53 Ibid., pp. 29–30.
54 Nietzsche, *Case of Wagner*, p. 167.
55 Shaw, 'Epistle Dedicatory', p. xiii.
56 Shaw, *Man and Superman*, p. 35.
57 Ibid., p. 25.
58 Ibid., p. 87.
59 Shaw, 'Epistle Dedicatory', p. xiv.
60 Tille, 'Introduction', p. ix.
61 Shaw, *Man and Superman*, p. 105.
62 Ibid., p. 112.
63 Bernard Shaw, 'Mr. Gilbert Cannan on Samuel Butler', in Brian Tyson (ed.), *Bernard Shaw's Book Reviews, Volume Two: 1884–1950* (University Park: Pennsylvania State University Press, 1996), p. 303.
64 Shaw, *Man and Superman*, p. 105.
65 Ibid., p. 114.
66 Bernard Shaw, 'Hyndman', in Tyson (ed.), *Bernard Shaw's Book Reviews, Volume Two*, p. 266.
67 Samuel Butler, *Evolution, Old and New* (London: Hardwicke and Bogue, 1879), p. 1.
68 Peter Bowler, *Evolution: The History of an Idea* (Berkeley: University of California Press, 2003), p. 239.
69 Shaw, 'Giving the Devil His Due', 111.
70 Shaw, *Man and Superman*, p. 133.
71 Friedrich Nietzsche, *Thus Spake Zarathustra: A Book for All and None*, Alexander Tille (trans.) (New York: Macmillan, 1896), p. 5.
72 Shaw, *Man and Superman*, p. 136.
73 Ibid., p. 137.
74 Nietzsche, *Case of Wagner*, p. 243.
75 Ibid., p. 244.
76 Nietzsche, *A Genealogy*, pp. 94–95.
77 Ibid., p. 95.
78 Ibid., p. 96.
79 Nietzsche, *Zarathustra*, p. 204.
80 Shaw, *Man and Superman*, p. 129.
81 Ibid., p. 136.

82 Ibid., p. 125.
83 Nietzsche, *Zarathustra*, p. 94.
84 Ibid., p. 96.
85 Alexander Tille, 'Introduction by the Editor', in Nietzsche, *Zarathustra*, p. xxii.
86 Robin Small, 'Nietzsche's Evolutionary Ethics', in Gudrun Von Tevenar (ed.), *Nietzsche and Ethics* (New York: Peter Lang, 2007), p. 119.
87 Conway, *Nietzsche*, p. 26.
88 Shaw, *Man and Superman*, p. 138.
89 James Alexander, *Shaw's Controversial Socialism* (Gainesville: University of Florida Press, 2009), p. 178.
90 Shaw, *Man and Superman*, p. 76.
91 Shaw, 'Epistle Dedicatory', p. xxvii.
92 Shaw, *Man and Superman*, p. 157.
93 Ibid., p. 150.
94 Ibid., p. 145.
95 Bernard Shaw, *Socialism for Millionaires* (London: Fabian Society, 1901), p. 4.
96 Ibid., p. 171.
97 Nietzsche, *A Genealogy*, p. 43.
98 Shaw, *Man and Superman*, p. 145.
99 Ibid., p. 149.
100 Ibid., p. 154.
101 Ibid., p. 172.
102 Ibid., p. 179.
103 Ibid., p. 180.
104 'Books of the Week: Man and Superman', *Irish Times* (19 September 1903), 3.
105 Ibid., p. 196.
106 Ibid., p. 216.
107 Bernard Shaw, 'Transition to Social Democracy', in Bernard Shaw (ed.), *Fabian Essays in Socialism* (Boston: Ball, 1911), p. 159.
108 Shaw, *Man and Superman*, p. 191.
109 Drawing evidence from *Human All Too Human* (not published in English until 1909), Mueller claims in 'The Breeding of Humanity' that, 'similar to Tanner's *Handbook*, Nietzsche expected that politicians have to acquire greater competencies in a more complex modern society to make decisions on a global scale' (192). But for the German philosopher, these greater competencies will not be developed through eugenic breeding, but rather through what Mueller calls 'philosophical breeding', that is, a 'more competent, truthful, and autonomous orientation' cultivated by routines of thinking and acting in daily life (186).
110 Shaw, *Man and Superman*, p. 191.
111 Ibid., p. 221.
112 Ibid., p. 182.
113 Ibid., p. 182.
114 Ibid., p. 216.
115 Ibid., p. 215.
116 Ibid., p. 191.

117 Ibid., p. 192.
118 Shaw, 'Transition', p. 182.
119 Shaw, *Man and Superman*, p. 193.
120 Ibid., p. 219.
121 See Tamsin Shaw, *Nietzsche's Political Skepticism* (Princeton: Princeton University Press, 2007).
122 Nietzsche, *Zarathustra*, pp. 62–63.
123 Shaw, *Nietzsche's Political Skepticism*, p. 3.
124 Shaw, *Man and Superman*, p. 192.
125 Shaw, 'Transition', p. 164.
126 Ibid., pp. 165, 171.
127 Shaw, *Man and Superman*, p. 193.
128 Gareth Griffith, *Socialism and Superior Brains: The Political Thought of George Bernard Shaw* (New York: Routledge, 2002), p. 59.
129 'Not the Pope but Mr. G. Bernard Shaw', *The Eagle and the Serpent* 18 (1902), 69.
130 Nietzsche, *A Genealogy*, p. 58.
131 'Not the Pope', 69.
132 Nietzsche, *Case of Wagner*, p. 202.
133 Ibid., p. 203.
134 Ibid., p. 211.
135 Shaw, *Man and Superman*, p. 221.
136 Qtd in Michael Holroyd, *Bernard Shaw: 1898–1918, The Pursuit of Power* (New York: Random House, 1988), p. 81.
137 Shaw, *Collected Letters*, p. 453.
138 Bernard Shaw, 'Preface for Politicians', in Bernard Shaw, *John Bull's Other Island and Major Barbara* (New York: Brentano's, 1907), p. v.
139 Ibid., p. xxxv.
140 Ibid., p. xxxvi.
141 Ibid., p. xxxvii.
142 Ibid., p. xxi.
143 Ibid., p. lxi.
144 James Joyce, *A Portrait of the Artist as a Young Man* (London: Egoist, 1916), p. 299.
145 Pericles Lewis, *Nationalism and the Novel* (Cambridge: Cambridge University Press, 2000), p. 38.
146 Ibid., p. 36.
147 Joyce, *A Portrait*, p. 38.
148 Shaw, 'Preface for Politicians', p. viii.
149 Ibid., p. xi.
150 Ibid., p. x.
151 Matthew Arnold, *On the Study of Celtic Literature* (London: Smith, Elder and Co., 1867), p. 105.
152 Shaw, 'Preface for Politicians', p. viii.
153 Declan Kiberd, *Inventing Ireland* (Cambridge: Harvard University Press, 1997), p. 52.

154 Shaw, 'Preface for Politicians', p. xxii.
155 Kornhaber, *The Birth of Theater from the Spirit of Philosophy*, p. 118. Kornhaber goes on to argue that, despite all disclaimers, 'Nietzsche haunts the three acts of *Major Barbara*. Certainly this is true in a diegetic and thematic sense – Andrew Undershaft [the play's protagonist] may be the most exuberant and outspoken fictional advocate of the Nietzschean revaluation of values since Zarathustra himself. Nietzsche's shadow is, in fact, so dark across Undershaft's anti-moral proclamations that Shaw would devote nearly a third of his preface to disclaiming any influence whatsoever from the German philosopher'. Kornhaber, however, is not concerned with the articulation of Nietzschean ideas in *Major Barbara* so much as its 'self-conscious counterpoint to Nietzsche's own very different conceptualization [in *The Birth of Tragedy*] of how the historically fraught relationship between theatre and philosophy might finally be resolved' (119).
156 Bernard Shaw, 'Preface to *Major Barbara*', in Shaw, *John Bull's Other Island and Major Barbara*, p. 147.
157 Ibid., p. 151.
158 Ibid., p. 152.
159 William Archer, 'Notice, World', in T.F. Evans (ed.), *George Bernard Shaw* (New York: Routledge, 2013), p. 116.
160 In this sense, the play also anticipates the Irish modernism exemplified by *Back to Methuselah* (1921), which Nicholas Allen ('Material Modernism: An Irish Case, circa 1921', in Gregory Castle and Patrick Bixby (eds), *A History of Irish Modernism* (Cambridge: Cambridge University Press, 2019), pp. 191–206) has associated with aesthetic forms 'that allow the contradictions and complexities of [intellectual] practices and histories to become visible to the reader, even as the meaning of these disjunctions may still be unclear at the time of writing' (200).

2

Yeats: 'Proud hard gift giving joyousness'

On 26 December 1902, the very day that Shaw had written to Siegfried Trebitsch regarding his desire to be known as an 'English (or Irish) Nietzsche', W.B. Yeats wrote to his 'dear friend' and patroness, Augusta Gregory, that she had 'a rival in Nietzsche, that strong enchanter'. That fall, Yeats had received several volumes of the philosopher's work from his new associate and patron in America, John Quinn, and he had been reading them with such intensity in the intervening weeks that he made his 'eyes bad again', just as they had seemed to be improving. The attraction immediately placed Nietzsche in his personal pantheon of artistic and intellectual heroes. In the previous decade, Yeats had often used the word 'enchanter' to describe the role of the poet as he envisioned it; now, he suggested that his enchantment was due in part to a sense that 'Nietzsche completes Blake',[1] the poet that he perhaps admired most because, as Yeats wrote in 1897, his verse had 'announced a religion of art'.[2] 'I have not read anything with so much excitement', he continued in his missive to Gregory, 'since I got to love Morris's stories which have the same curious astringent joy'. The comparison with William Morris – the English designer, writer, socialist, and friend to both Yeats and Shaw – is even more surprising, though the near oxymoron 'astringent joy' neatly captures the quality of Nietzsche's prose that had appealed to many early commentators, who admired the philosopher's combination of severity – his harsh criticism of reigning orthodoxies – and the apparent delight he took in meting it out. In the rest of the letter, Yeats informs Gregory that his new play, *Where There Is Nothing*, had been readied at last for both the press and the stage after much revision, and that he had written 'a very severe letter' to Frank Fay rejecting the production of James Cousins's latest farce, *Sold*, which he dismisses as 'rubbish & vulgar rubbish'.[3] These additional details offer a reminder that, as he was experiencing his initial enchantment with Nietzsche, Yeats was also deeply involved in shaping the agenda of the Irish National Dramatic Society and seeking to distinguish the theatre company by the distinctions it would make between the tasteful and the vulgar, artistic value and mere rubbish. It was self-evident to him that, through its value-assessing and value-imposing functions, the theatre should work to shape the disposition of its audience towards a legitimate *national* culture. During the decade that followed, as Yeats struggled to realise his vision for a national theatre, Nietzsche was a frequent companion and one of his greatest benefactors, providing him with a means to reconceive the roles of both the individual artist and the dramatic arts in fulfilling this communal charge.

By the end of 1902, the national theatre movement in Ireland had already experienced a well-documented series of failures and triumphs. From the beginning, when Yeats sat down with Edward Martyn and Gregory to draft a manifesto for 'The Celtic Theatre' in 1897, the founders of the movement had recognised the tension between their efforts to foster artistic freedom – over and often against political agendas and cultural orthodoxies – and the expectations placed on a national theatre as a cultural institution. The project nonetheless managed to gather support from a long list of prominent backers, including many Anglo-Irish Protestants and even some staunch Unionists with an interest in the arts, who signed on as guarantors of a theatre that would perform Irish plays by Irish authors. In the spring of 1899, the Irish Literary Theatre staged its inaugural production at the Ancient Concert Rooms, Dublin, where audiences from across the Irish social and political spectrum (and London critics such as Max Beerbohm and Arthur Symons) assembled to see the first public performance of Yeats's blank verse drama *The Countess Cathleen* (performed by English actors). But, despite these rather auspicious circumstances, the play immediately provoked controversy among critics, and raucous Catholic university students, who took offence at what they viewed as the portrayal of an Irish peasantry too ready to sell their souls and commit all manner of other sacrileges. Like Shaw, Yeats conceived the theatre as an arena where the conscience of a nation might be defined or redefined, but in the Antient Concert Rooms he had encountered an unreceptive audience that he would come to refer to as a 'crowd' and a 'mob'. He also came to see more clearly the essential function that competing forms of cultural nationalism played in confirming certain social and political differences: 'I think', he wrote in 1900, 'that our Irish movements have always interested me in part, because I see in them the quarrel of two traditions of life, one old and noble, one new and ignoble. One undying because it satisfies our conscience though it seemed dying and one about to die because it is hateful to our conscience, though it seems triumphant throughout the world'.[4] As this chapter will demonstrate, Yeats's work as a playwright over the ten years that followed can be understood best as a sustained attempt to both shape and satisfy 'our conscience', but in this effort he faced the conundrum of how to appeal to the tastes of the theatre-going public without condoning what he viewed as their lower instincts – to address his audience as a proud people rather than a resentful mob.

Despite Yeats's early efforts to garner cultural capital in the name of an 'old and noble' tradition, and to exchange this capital for a more general form of social influence, the Irish Literary Theatre collapsed in 1901 for want of financial resources. When the project was revived the following year as the Irish National Dramatic Society, with the assistance of Frank and William Fay, Yeats experienced his greatest theatrical triumph with *Cathleen ni Houlihan* and its standard nationalist themes drawn from the 1798 rebellion. Nonetheless, as Marjorie Howes concisely phrases it, he continued to feel 'ambivalence about popular Irish nationalism' due largely to 'the fact that it involved crowds, that it was, inescapably, mass politics':[5] his work for the theatre, that is, represented an attempt to come to terms with the mass character of Irish nationalism and to generate another kind of collective ethos among the Irish people. One possible move in this cultural contest – a move that sought to capitalise on the authority of the Gospel in Irish society – can be found in Yeats's next play, *The Hour-Glass*, which he described in April 1902 as 'a little religious [sic] play in one act with quite as striking a plot as Kathleen – it cannot offend anybody and may propitiate Holy Church'.[6]

A very different move – a move that sought to generate another kind of authority altogether – can be found in *The King's Threshold*, a play dedicated to the theme of artistic freedom, which implicitly argued that 'Irish dramatists must be allowed complete artistic independence and not be expected or exhorted by political or religious leaders, or their audience, to serve a particular cause'.[7] Even if the theatre addressed itself to a gathered collective, it should not drag art into the realm of nationalist propaganda. The play, which was conceived just a few weeks after Yeats wrote to Gregory regarding Nietzsche, provides a clear indication of his shifting preoccupations as he read the philosopher for the first time. Among other things, Nietzsche offered Yeats a radical alternative to liberal political theory for thinking about social hierarchies and national collectives, one that rivalled anything he might have found in the occult doctrines and practices that had preoccupied him for years and had given him, according to Howes, 'a way for him to negotiate his ambivalences about Irish nationalism as mass politics'.[8] Increasingly, as the new century got underway, his sense of modernist cultural distinction mixed with notions of aristocracy and Anglo-Irish Ascendancy, so that he shied away from anything that could be considered 'popular' in either aesthetic or political senses. He sought, instead, to resuscitate certain ideas of artistic value, cultural continuity, moral autonomy, and individual heroism that he associated with the 'old and noble', whether or not they were grounded in any verifiable history and demonstrable tradition. Success in the theatre would mean redefining the conscience of his audience, so that the Irish people might become more receptive to his message and aspire to something like Nietzschean nobility, liberated from the enervating influence of the ruling political and religious orthodoxies. But his drive for success also lead Yeats to a point of artistic and political crisis as his repeated gestures of communal generosity also aroused an egotism that eventually threatened his efforts at artistic and political collaboration.

Reading Nietzsche, revising *Where There Is Nothing*

On 6 February 1903, when Yeats finally wrote back to Quinn in order to thank him for the gift of 'the three volumes of Nietzsche', he confessed, or rather averred, that he had not read the German philosopher before receiving the books, but that, as he now discovered, he and Nietzsche 'had come to the same conclusions on several cardinal matters'. With the three extant volumes of *The Works of Friedrich Nietzsche* in his possession (adding *The Case of Wagner* volume and *A Genealogy of Morals* to the copy of *Thus Spake Zarathustra* he had received the previous fall), Yeats now clearly recognised his affinity with the philosopher and he repeated his insights about the kinship between Nietzsche and two of his artistic and intellectual heroes: 'In some ways he completes or rather modernises the doctrine that I learned from Blake, and I dont [sic] find him apart from certain stray petulances incompatible with the kind of socialism I learned from William Morris'. In Nietzsche, that is, the poet had discovered a thinker whose ideas complemented those notions of artistic reverence and political radicalism that he had learned from the idols of his youth. More important, even if Yeats did have certain reservations about the tone of the philosopher's pronouncements, he was ready to acknowledge the vital contribution that Nietzsche's writings might make to his artistic project: 'He is exaggerated and violent but has helped me very greatly to build up in my mind an imagination of the heroic life. His books have come at exactly the right moment, for I have planned out a series of plays which are all intended to be an expression of that life which seem[s] to me a kind of proud hard gift giving joyousness'.[9] Indeed, as Yeats wrote to Quinn, he had already begun revisions to *On Baile's Strand*, the first of three plays he would write in the decade featuring the Irish mythological hero, Cuchulain, as the exemplar of a renewed national ethos for the Irish people.[10] A few weeks earlier, writing to Gregory about the need for the play to have a few 'new passages here & there', he had assured her that she 'need not be troubled about my poetic faculty. I was never so full of new thoughts for verse though all thoughts quite unlike old ones'. With plenty of evidence from the letters during this period, critics have often attributed the arrival of this inspiration precisely to Yeats's reading of Nietzsche's philosophy, the 'astringent joy' of which had led to a new phase of creative output:[11] 'My work', he told Gregory in the same letter, 'has got [sic] far more masculine. It has more salt in it'.[12] But the same critics who have noted this shift have seldom given any extended attention to how the provocation of Nietzsche's gift – cultural capital in the form of images, aphorisms, and ideas – helped make possible not just Yeats's more vigorous style, but also his distinctive ethical bequest to the Irish people.[13] As we will see below, this renewed sense of nobility was implicated in Yeats's developing formal or aesthetic concerns in the early years of the century, as well as in his evolving ideas regarding race, class, and nation, ideas drawing heavily on the Nietzschean sources that he read and discussed with great intensity during the period.

Quinn had sent Yeats his copy of *Thus Spake Zarathustra* in the fall of 1902 because, as he said in the letter that followed on 27 September, Nietzsche's 'wonderful epigrammatic style' had reminded him of the dialogue of Yeats's new play, *Where There Is Nothing*, which Quinn had received in typescript just a few days earlier.[14] Despite Quinn's praise for Nietzsche's style, the gift also came with a rather firm disclaimer: 'I don't know whether you are acquainted with Nietzsche's writings or not ... his so-called philosophy is utterly abhorrent to me – the philosophy of the "blond beast", of the exaltation of brutality'.[15] Such repudiations were common enough during this early period of Nietzsche's reception in the English-speaking world, but Yeats's opinion was not swayed. On 22 October, he wrote back to Quinn thanking him for the book: 'I have long desired to have it. I bought a pamphlet with that name upon it in London but found it only contained about three chapters'.

Here is thus a clear indication of Yeats's interest in Nietzsche's writing, and *Thus Spake Zarathustra* in particular, even if he had not read much past the table of contents before receiving the full-length volume from Quinn. And, like Quinn, he recognised a certain resonance between the proud, lofty, prophetic speech of Nietzsche's protagonist and that of Yeats's own recently minted hero: 'Before I knew why you had sent it', he told Quinn, 'I read out one or two bits to Lady Gregory, and said it sounded to me like Paul's talk'.[16] Gregory, who was pleased with the 'splendid' play, was also 'glad', as she had already written to Quinn on 9 October, that Yeats 'had finished it before your Niedsche [sic] (for which he is very grateful) came, for it is the more original'.[17] No doubt this was the case. But, as was his habit, especially when writing for the theatre, Yeats did not settle with the initial published version of the text, which had prompted Quinn to send along his copy of *Thus Spake Zarathustra*. The first editions of the play were published almost simultaneously in Ireland (in the *United Irishman*) and the United States (in a small private edition by John Lane) in early November. But, Yeats leads off his 6 February letter to Quinn (the same letter that expressed his deep gratitude for the three volumes of Nietzsche) with a description of the revisions he and Gregory had recently made to *Where There Is Nothing*, which had repeatedly been on the verge of completion over the intervening months. During that period, as the extant drafts and his correspondence demonstrate, Yeats had continually amended the play, sometimes with Gregory and sometimes on his own, revising every act, but dedicating most of his attention to the final two.

Some, if not indeed most, of this restlessness can be attributed to his enchantment with Nietzsche, which was increasingly felt as the still-inexperienced playwright attempted to actualise his vision for the play. To be sure, with its iconoclastic hero, the first version of the play already revealed a number of shared preoccupations with *Thus Spake Zarathustra*: namely, an antipathy towards 'newspaper ethics', herd thinking, Christian dogma, and strictly codified moral systems in general. Both Paul and Zarathustra are sermonisers who, after long periods of absence, wander the world of men to decry various forms of false authority, even as the prophetic figures promote their finer sentiments. In November 1902 and again in February 1903, as he revised the play repeatedly and read Nietzsche raptly, Yeats wrote of his desire to make Paul a 'more loveable' character than the one who, with something less than generosity, had 'ram[med] his ideas down people's throats' in the earlier version of the play.[18] The playwright did not want to 'give him any new opinions, but ... was anxious to get him for a little while away from opinions that [he] might make him more emotional, more merely emotional ... I have tried to show Paul's magnetic quality'.[19] This effort entailed attributing to the hero of *Where There Is Nothing* a number of attitudes and attributes to be found in the protagonist of *Thus Spake Zarathustra*. Paul's passion is particularly evident in the sermon, much amended and revised, that he delivers in Act IV, Scene II of the new version of the play, where he exalts in a breaking of 'the walls' of civilisation that portends a return to 'the joy of the green earth'.[20] At least momentarily, Paul delights in the material world and sensual life, which once possessed a kind of divinity because they preceded the attempts of men to impose moral laws and rational order on their environment. This much Yeats's prophet shares with Nietzsche's Zarathustra, who implores his listeners, as he introduces his teaching of the 'beyond-man', to '*remain faithful to the earth*' (original emphasis) because it maintains a higher significance than the 'superterrestrial hopes' and divine imaginings of mere men.[21] The lesson, which he elaborates throughout the course of the text, is the highest of his 'gifts to men': that it might provoke his listeners to engage in new self-affirming and world-affirming ways of being.[22]

As we know, Yeats wrote to Quinn that Nietzsche had 'helped me very greatly to build up in my mind an imagination of the heroic life' and that the books he received had assisted his plans for 'a series of plays which are all intended to be an expression of that life which seem[s] to me a kind of proud hard gift giving joyousness'. But it is clear that, with the volumes in hand, the playwright was already working towards an expression of this sort in his revisions to *Where There Is Nothing*. To be sure, Zarathustra's 'Introductory Speech', which takes the form of a conversation with an old man referred to as 'the saint', vividly exemplifies this particular species of generosity: the prophet denies any love for men and their imperfections, but descends into the world below in order to bestow them with the wisdom and insight he has garnered during long years alone in his mountaintop home. Predictably, when he enters the marketplace of the town on the plain and attempts to deliver his message to the assembled multitude, he finds an uncomprehending audience: '"There they are standing", he said unto his heart, "there they are laughing: they do not understand me"'.[23] Similarly, when Paul senses that the decisive hour has come and leaves the monastery to bring his message to the world, he encounters a perplexed crowd: as his follower, Aloysius, comments in the revised version of the play, 'He is too far above them; they have not education to understand him'.[24] Yeats claims, in his letter to Quinn, that nonetheless 'people love Paul because they find in him a certain strength, a certain abundance', which 'comes from him in the first three acts with a kind of hard passion'. 'But', he continues, 'his five years in the monastery as I understand him fills him with dreams, mad reverie, and detaches him from the things about which men are passionate'.[25] The attempt to address the mass of men on their own level, to adjust himself or his doctrine downward to speak to them of commerce or politics, is of little interest to Paul. Like Zarathustra, that is, he brings with him a kind of haughty intensity, which is coupled with a superfluity or overflowing fullness, but he encounters a public not yet ready – perhaps never to be ready – to receive what he offers.

There is an evident analogy between the activity of these two figures and the role of the artist that Yeats was conceiving for himself during this period, a role that put him increasingly at odds with the penchants of the 'mob' or 'crowd'. 'We could march on the towns', Paul claims near the end of the revised play, 'and we could break up all settled order, we could bring back the old joyful, dangerous, individual life'.[26] The 'old joyful, dangerous, individual life', as embodied in the figure of the Übermensch, is precisely what Zarathustra advocates in the face of the bemused crowd and its modern decadence, and he repeatedly deploys these very terms – joyful, dangerous, individual – in his speeches. This is the gift that he offers his listeners: a provocation to the *vita activa*, the generation of deeds, thoughts, and affects grounded in an affirmative will to power. Both prophets challenge the contentment of their listeners so that members of the gathered multitudes might recognise their own poverty and accept the gifts the prophets have to offer. Both represent a danger to the modern crowds they address because they offer gifts that threaten to demolish the status quo and even transform mankind itself. In the end, the mob in the marketplace rejects their offerings: Zarathustra will have to abandon the multitude for a small band of disciples who are willing to listen to his message; Paul will meet a far worse fate, as the crowd swarms and slays him in the closing moments of the play.

It should be made clear here that, in the final analysis, Paul is hardly a Nietzschean hero: for all his 'astringent joy', he remains wedded to the 'Will of God' and the promise of eternal life, rather than acknowledging or promoting the 'will to power'. His surrender to the violence of the mob is indicative of the very kind of world-weariness that Zarathustra warns against: a 'weariness which, with one jump, with a jump of death, wanteth to reach the last, a poor ignorant weariness is not even willing any more to will'. This is the kind of weariness that, according to the prophet, has 'created all Gods and all back-worlds'.[27] To be sure, as Robert Gooding-Williams indicates, Zarathustra's descent from the mountaintop means a renewed embrace of the human condition as Christianity has constituted it, an enervated condition that threatens to ruin his creative enterprise and deplete his greatest gift.[28] But if Zarathustra seeks to sweep away the life-denying values of Christianity to make room for his life-affirming ideals – that is, to announce the death of God so that the beyond-man might live – then Paul declares that 'we must destroy everything that has Law and Number, for where there is nothing there is God'.[29] With this dramatic declaration – which, of course, gives the play its title – Yeats's hero announces himself as a nihilist in Nietzsche's conception: he calls for the destruction of our value systems even as he affirms God as an absence, vacating the moral doctrines that provide a means to assess or confer value. This may explain why the play, despite its devout Christian protagonist, could be denounced as an example of 'godless cosmopolitanism'.[30] At least initially, Yeats had attempted to appease an Irish audience already suspicious of his heretical tendencies, though the play did very little to help his cause. It is evident that his encounter with Nietzsche did not help much either, as it provoked the playwright to create a new kind of dramatic hero and to pursue a new ethical imperative for his art, one that made demands on his audience that it was not yet willing to accept. But it is also evident that the consequences of this provocation were still to be fully explored.

'The Bestowing Virtue', *The King's Threshold*, and bardic tradition

The notion of a 'proud hard gift giving joyousness' that Yeats derived from his reading of *Thus Spake Zarathustra* is indeed one of the predominant themes of the text, especially its first volume. As we have seen, Zarathustra's first speech, made shortly after his decent from the mountaintop, announces his 'gift' to mankind – the glad tidings of the Übermensch and the transvaluation of all values – which he will attempt to impart to his fellow men in the face of all resistance. He seeks to overcome human deficiency with the overflowing of his own spirit, but he must first persuade his listeners of their need: his gift is not, or not only, a positive doctrine, but a destructive one that will sweep away existing values, with the announcement of the death of God, before the creation of anything new can begin in the form of the Übermensch. And yet this doctrine is not measured or calculated. Instead, it issues from an exuberant overabundance of the will to power that holds nothing back as it seeks, through persuasive speech alone, to impose on its recipients a sense of their own poverty of spirit. Only in this way can the giver of gifts create recipients worthy of what he has to offer, his gifts of spirit. Peter Sloterdijk, in one of the most significant commentaries yet on the theme of generosity in Nietzsche, emphasises that his approach to 'sponsorship' exceeds 'the common discourse of gifts and poisons', because it outstrips the 'base economy' that associates the enhancement of the giver with an offence to the receiver.[31] Crucially, the gift comes in the form of a provocation that would have the receiver cease to passively accept values from outside, from authorities of one sort or another, and instead begin asserting his or her own active force in opening up a future defined by new values: to leave behind slavish values in favour of the cultivation of 'free souls'. It is in this sense that Nietzsche's philosophy is almost obsessively focused on the notion of generosity, of restoring his readers to themselves, by presenting them with an understanding of their existence that had previously been obscured by Christian moral virtues, bourgeois social norms, and decadent modern manners. It is in this sense, moreover, that Gilles Deleuze can claim that '*the will to power is essentially creative and giving*: it does not aspire, it does not seek, it does not desire, above all it does not desire power. It *gives*: power is something inexpressible in the will (something mobile, variable, plastic); power is in the will as "the bestowing virtue" [*Die schenkende Tugend*] through power the will itself bestows sense and value' (original emphasis).[32]

Yeats's interest in Nietzsche centres on 'the bestowing virtue', which is embodied in the Übermensch and remains significant throughout the philosopher's later thought. The poet and playwright's work in the first decade of the twentieth century represents an ongoing negotiation between the 'proud hard' elements of this virtue and its joyous or beneficent features, as he seeks to create a receptive audience for his work in the theatre. This was, to put matters in different terms, the dilemma of how to realise a vision of heroic Nietzschean selfhood while also addressing the hopes and dreams of an independent Irish nation. Part I of *Thus Spake Zarathustra* ends with a section titled, in Tille's translation, 'Of Giving Virtue' (later translated as 'On the Gift-Giving Virtue' and 'The Bestowing Virtue') which provides a detailed account of this quality, growing from Zarathustra's own passions: his disdain for mankind and his desire for the Übermensch lead the prophet to explore a particular kind of generosity that elevates the giver as he seeks to express his will to power in relation to others. But, as Richard White has argued, the 'gift-giving virtue' may be understood in terms of a spiritual generosity that leads to '"sovereignty" as an outcome', which he takes to mean something like 'self-determination' and 'openness to the inspiring possibilities of life'.[33] Like Sloterdijk and Deleuze, then, White suggests that generosity 'is a spring of pluralism leading beyond all expectations of unity', that it aims 'to generate dissensus, which is to say competition', and that 'it would consider itself to have failed were it to be said it had obtained a monopoly'.[34] Yeats sought 'sovereignty' for the Irish people in the sense of freeing them from the submission to slavish values, but his desire to impose his idea of a unified, hierarchical, and at times atavistic culture put limitations on his generosity. Nonetheless, as he negotiated the role of the artist in Irish society, the poet and playwright pursued the creation of challenging gifts that might cultivate renewed aesthetic, ethical, and political sensibilities, while provoking his audience to initiate a more promising future for the Irish nation.

The first of the works Yeats planned with the intention to express 'that life which seem[s] to me a kind of proud hard gift giving joyousness' was *The King's Threshold*, mentioned in a letter to Gregory on 14 January 1903, before he dictated the majority of the first draft to her in late March and early April of that year. The hero of the play, Seanchan, is a poet – in fact, he takes his name from the Irish *seanchaí*, the storytellers of indigenous oral tradition – and provides Yeats with an opportunity to announce the nature and status of that vocation as he came to see them in the early years of the century. As the play opens, Seanchan is lying on the stairs before the royal palace in Gort, where he has commenced a hunger strike in protest of King Guaire's mandate that the poet take a place at a lower table, away from the bishops, soldiers, and lawmakers who sit at the high table. Deeply concerned, the poet's pupils have gathered to convince him to relent, but Seanchan defiantly asserts the value of his art:

What was it that the poets promised you
If it was not their sorrow?
...

> And I would have all know that when all falls
> In ruin, poetry calls out in joy,
> Being the scattering hand, the bursting pod,
> The victim's joy among the holy flame,
> God's laughter at the shattering of the world
> And now that joy laughs out and weeps and burns
> On these bare steps.[35]

Creativity and generosity mingle in the expression of the poet's will to power, which alone can bestow sense and value on human experience, whatever devastation and suffering that experience may include. Richard Ellmann, Frances Nesbitt Oppel, Adrian Frazier, and many others have acknowledged the 'enthusiasm for Nietzsche' that colours *The King's Threshold* and the 'proto-Nietzschean speeches' that its protagonist delivers.[36] The connection appears to be most direct between the assertions made by Seanchan and the 'intoxicating joy' that Zarathustra associates with the creative process in his speech on the 'Back-Worlds-Men', which prepares the way for his teaching of the Übermensch. Returning to the theme in 'On the Blissful Islands', Zarathustra proclaims that 'creating ... is the great salvation from suffering, and an alleviation of life. But for the existence of the creator pain and much transformation are necessary. Yea, much bitter death must be in your life, ye creators!'[37] This is the task of the Übermensch for Nietzsche: through creating, he finds redemption from the anguish of the human condition, but he must also endure his own heartache to do so. This is also the dual vocation of the poet for Yeats: bringing joy and laughter from conflagration, destruction, and sorrow. Poetic creation is figured as both a scattering hand, inseminating the world with his transformative vision, and a bursting pod, ruptured by the overflowing of its abundant gifts.

Seanchan's assertions also insist on the poet's importance in relation to his society's structures of power and authority. Critics have often identified parallels between his situation and Yeats's own as the poet turned to the theatre and sought a larger role in Irish public life for his visionary literary art. Frazier points out, for instance, that Yeats wrote *The King's Threshold* when the Irish National Theatre Society, the recent replacement of the Irish National Dramatic Society, was having what he later called 'a hard fight for the recognition of pure art in a community of which one half was buried in the practical public affairs of life, and the other half in politics and a propagandist patriotism'.[38] His response at the time might well be considered its own variety of propaganda in service of the artistic vocation. In the play, Yeats asserts the independence of the artist to break free from the demands of political leaders, religious authorities, and even of an audience that would have him write in the service of a national movement or any collective cause. As he articulated the case for artistic independence, he was drawing on and seeking to reassert what Seanchan calls 'the ancient right of poets' as evinced in the Irish bardic tradition.[39] In fact, Yeats had recently read Jane Wilde's *Ancient Legends of Ireland*, which includes chapters on Seanchan and 'The Bards', and proclaims that the poet in early Ireland was 'esteemed not only as the highest of all men for his learning and intellect, but also as being the true revealer of the supreme wisdom'.[40] But, as Frazier suggests, Yeats's Seanchan makes increasingly exaggerated claims for the role of the poet, 'passing from powerful assertion through hyperbole to delirious megalomania',[41] in a manner, it might be added, that parallels what Sloterdijk calls Nietzsche's progressively more 'conspicuous statements about himself'.[42] Both writers participate in a self-eulogistic discourse that not only contradicts the 'traditional morality of self-dispossession' in a most aggressive manner, but asserts the *a priori* value of his text for himself in anticipation of its *a posterioi* legitimation at the level of culture.[43]

The extent to which Nietzsche's philosophy played a role in Yeats's conception of the artistic vocation – and, more specifically, in his conception of the Irish Literary Revival – can be observed in his review of Gregory's *Poets and Dreamers*, 'A Canonical Book', published in *The Bookman* of May 1903. In late April, the poet and playwright had posted a letter to his patroness and collaborator promising to 'write about Nietzsche' and noting his efforts to placate critics such as Richard Best, who had raised concerns about the pagan tendencies of her volume on Cuchulain.[44] No surviving correspondence fulfils his promise, but Yeats clearly had the philosopher on his mind when he drafted his review, which attempts to establish the importance of Gregory's efforts to revive the bardic history of Ireland and its noble values. He had claimed in 1902 that *Cuchulain of Muirtheme* and 'this new book of hers' demonstrate 'the same spirit coming down to our own time in the verses of Gaelic poets and in the stories of the country people'.[45] But many critics, especially 'before the modern feeling for folk-thought on the one hand, and for certain schools of esoteric poetry on the other hand, had brought a greater trust in the imagination', failed to appreciate the kind of poetry presented in the volume and 'would probably call it vague and absurd'.[46]

All too often, according to Yeats, the modern critic ignores 'the hidden life of the soul' in favour of some spurious lesson in morality: 'he could hardly come to understand that the poet was too full of life to concern himself with that wisdom, which Nietzsche has called the infirmary for bad poets'.[47] The allusion derives from the final paragraphs of the eighth section of the second part of *Thus Spake Zarathustra*, 'Of the Famous Wise Men', where the prophet chastises modern philosophers who pose as freethinkers or authentic 'free spirits' in search of an elusive 'truth' but do little more than reinforce 'the superstition of the folk' in order to make a comfortable living. These philosophers risk nothing, for they have neither courage nor passion: they 'have frequently made out of wisdom an alms-house and infirmary for bad poets', because they have offered teachings that derive from their own meekness and caution, their own conformism and conventionality. They work merely in the service of the people, nation, race, or worse, those possessed of political power, maintaining the status quo rather than attempting to tell the difficult truths revealed in nature or to raise mankind to new heights of creative overcoming. They know the will to power and its manifestation as spirit, but they are unable to harness it, to transform it into real knowledge, virtuous activity, aesthetic achievement or anything that reaches beyond man in his present state. Their facile wisdom may offer a place of respite for bad poets, equipping them with palliative clichés and moral platitudes designed to appease their audiences, but it cannot provide nourishment to the passions or offer passage to that 'hidden life of the soul'. Great poetry, of the sort that Seanchan praises, must seek out harder truths that surpass this understanding of knowledge altogether. 'I would send any man who wants to be cured of wisdom', Yeats claims, to the books under review: 'the end of wisdom is sometimes the beginning of heroism, and Lady Gregory's country poets have kept alive the way of thinking of the old heroic poets that did not constrain nature into any plan of civic virtue, but saw man as he is in himself'. At stake is the very definition of cultural value.

There is also evidence here that Nietzsche's thought played an important role in Yeats's developing social and cultural taxonomy, especially in the crucial distinction between the folk or people and the mob or crowd. In 'A Canonical Book', and in many of his writings from the 1890s and onward into the new century, Yeats praises what he calls 'folk-thought', which is synonymous with a rude, and therefore unfettered, imagination inspired by close contact with nature and freed from 'our modern logic, a child of parliaments and law courts'. Yeats was among the first generation of antiquarians and scholars to adopt this new sense of the term 'folk', and its various compounds, as pertaining to the mass of common people whose culture is transmitted through oral tradition. Here we should recall that, although Yeats had little interest in the 'scientific' study of folklore at the time, his early reputation was built to a large extent on his work as a folklorist in books such as *Fairy and Folk Tales of the Irish Peasantry* (1888) and *The Celtic Twilight* (1893). In 'The Celtic Element in Literature' (1897), he explains his interest in these materials by advocating for the value of 'all folk literature, and all literature that keeps the folk tradition', because they delight in 'unbounded and immortal things'. But there was always something more in this interest than the widely held nationalist assumption that the Irish peasantry should be represented as the authentic personification of the nation. By the end of the century, Yeats was also one of the most prominent advocates for adapting folk songs and stories in the creation of a modern literature full of what he saw as the beauty and spontaneity of an earlier age. There is clearly an element of primitivism in his attitude, and yet it is not simply an atavistic celebration of the peasant or the pagan. His brand of cultural nationalism, that is, depended on a complex, almost paradoxical relationship between the traditions of the Irish people and that of the bards, the great poets past and present – Yeats, of course, included – who helped to revive those communal traditions with their visionary talents.

In *Thus Spake Zarathustra*, responding partly to the *völkisch* movement in Germany, Nietzsche had emphasised another aspect of the folk as a social and cultural collective. Yeats's interest in folklore, as Donald Childs and others have suggested, inherited a sense of the nation as 'a human community sharing a common essence' from a definition fashioned under the auspices of German Romanticism in the early years of the nineteenth century.[48] But during the course of the century, a variety of German groups interested in local folklore, national history, and rural populism combined in a loosely affiliated movement that also came to embrace xenophobic and antisemitic sentiments. As it grew and evolved, the *völkisch* movement responded to the effects of modernisation and industrialisation by promoting an idyllic mode of communal life conducted in an almost mystical relationship with the national soil. In short, the movement contributed to the new age of mass politics, founded on sentiment, symbolism, and chauvinism. Nietzsche asserts that 'the superstition of the folk' is a corrupting force precisely because it holds 'the famous wise men' in its thrall (and, in doing so, generates a wisdom for bad poets) because they do not have the nerve to transgress the values and beliefs of the folk and instead spend their energies in merely serving its prejudices.[49] The two sections that lead up to 'Of the Famous Wisemen' – 'On the Rabble' and 'Of Tarantulae' – establish the existence of a kind of spiritual underclass and articulate a disparaging view of the modern state and mass politics, especially the doctrine of social equality. If Yeats shared this perspective on mass politics, he nonetheless desired to rescue the 'folk-thought' of Ireland from what he viewed as the corrupting forces of modernity and particularly the influence of the mob or crowd.

What is at stake for the poet and playwright is the claim to cultural nobility and the struggle between different groups within Ireland regarding the very idea of culture and the appropriate relation to tradition. Massification, with its corrupting 'modern logic', was increasingly seen as a threat to national tradition, which must be saved from the collective will expressed in the negative responses to *The Countess Cathleen* and later *The Playboy of the Western World*. Elizabeth Cullingford, Adrian Frazier, and Marjorie Howes have all written incisively about Yeats's increasing tendency during these years, in part due to Nietzsche's influence, to deploy the term 'mob' to describe those elements of Irish public life that he found disturbing, especially what he saw as the cultural impoverishment of the Catholic middle class.[50] Like Nietzsche, Yeats came to believe that in order to bestow gifts one would need the right mode of communication and the right sort of recipients, which would be prepared to grasp his message: 'Zarathustra is not to speak unto the folk, but unto companions! Zarathustra is not to be the herdsman and the dog of a herd!'[51] The poet and playwright would seek to create a literature drawing on the folk traditions of the Irish people, which he continued to see as an invaluable resource, even as he addressed his art more insistently to an audience – or, at least, an idea – of the aristocratic minority, which in time might be enlarged into a noble majority.

Yeats's concerns regarding the mob thus found a solution of sorts in the identification of what Nietzsche's philosophy calls 'noble races', which do not succumb to the kind of petty ressentiment that had led audiences to reject his *The Countess Cathleen*. Rather, they would be capable of pursuing loftier values. To be sure, commentators on *The King's Threshold* have often cited the final lines of Yeats's play as evidence that he was under Nietzsche's influence as he wrote, though these critics have not drawn any distinct parallels with the philosopher's work.[52] As the king at last accepts the authority of the poet, he kneels before Seanchan and offers his crown to the noble bard, who responds:

> O crown, O crown,
> It is but right if hands that made the crown
> In the old time should give it when they will.
> O silver trumpets, be you lifted up
> [He lays the crown on the King's head]
> And cry to the great race that is to come
> Long-throated swans upon the waves of time
> Sing loudly, for beyond the wall of the world
> That race may hear our music and awake.[53]

With this 'Nietzschean invocation', Seanchan confirms the power of the poet to bestow the gift of his poetic vision, not just on the king, but on an entire people.[54] It is the poet, with his artistic imagination, who first envisioned the crown as an emblem of the power, legitimacy, and nobility of the monarch and then disseminated this vision to the subjects of the kingdom. What is more, it is the poet, not the king, who is capable of summoning 'the great race that is to come' with his art, so that the Irish people might be elevated to something better, something stronger, something nobler. Seanchan calls on the trumpets to announce not a royal progress or triumphal entry, but the joyous emergence of a new people; he calls on the majestic swans, which would become one of Yeats's obsessive many-sided symbols of the soul, of uplift, of power, to rouse the spirit of his fellow Irish men and women out of some metaphysical slumber so that they might wake to their historical destiny.

In this way, then, Seanchan offers nothing short of a prophecy for the Irish people, a prophecy that can only be fulfilled through the transformative – even evolutionary or eugenic – force of his imaginative gift. His sponsorship of the Irish people emanates from the assumption that, over the course of their long racial history, they have not known true nobility, except perhaps in a handful of heroic figures who have been the subject of bardic celebration. Earlier in the play, speaking dreamily to his sweetheart, Fedelm, of the proper time for marriage and childrearing, Seanchan describes a hunger-provoked vision of the race to come:

> I lay awake,
> There had come a frenzy into the light of the stars
> And they were coming nearer and I knew
> All in a minute they were about to marry
> Clods out upon the plough-lands, to beget
> A mightier race than any that has been ...
> The stars had come so near me that I caught
> Their singing; it was praise of that great race
> That would be haughty, mirthful, and white-bodied
> With a high head, and open hand, and how
> Laughing, it would take the mastery of the world.[55]

He envisions not a singular Übermensch, but a race of Übermenschen, who are proud ('high head'), generous ('open hand'), and joyous ('laughing'). This is the ultimate act of creative annihilation, for it invites an end to the Irish people as they are in favour of a superior race to come: what can be loved in the present generation, as Zarathustra says of his own contemporaries, is that they are 'a *transition* and a *destruction*' (original emphasis).[56] But the 'open hand' is not Yeats's modification of Nietzsche's specifications, as Conor Cruise O'Brien would have it, so much as their tailoring to Yeats's own mythos of the artist-hero (with his own grand vision of racial self-overcoming).[57]

Moreover, it is clear that Yeats's passage is implicitly addressing the prominent imperial discourses that had proclaimed 'the British race [as] the greatest governing race that the world ha[d] ever seen', while relegating the Irish to a fixed place in the lower orders of a racial hierarchy.[58] He had addressed these claims directly in 'The Celtic Element in Literature', where he sought (much like Shaw during this period) to challenge the version of this hierarchy erected by Matthew Arnold in *On the Study of Celtic*

Literature, which depicts an English people characterised by rationality and manly genius as superior to a Celtic people portrayed as not just unkempt and uncivilised, but sentimental and feminised. As O'Brien argues, however, the poet and playwright can also be read as calling for the propagation of a particular strain of aristocratic Irish men and women, who would one day become a 'haughty, mirthful, and white-bodied' race. To be sure, Yeats was not alone among his Revivalist contemporaries in intermingling the narrative of Irish national identity with emergent eugenic notions regarding the breeding of a superior form of humanity.[59] At the very least, we already see glimpses of what would later become his fascination with these ideas. The poet in his conception, more than any king or conqueror, contributes to the cultivation of an environment where the emergence of such a race is possible, precisely because he teaches his people how to exalt in the face of a history of cruelty, destruction, and oppression. He foresees a race of men and women who do not resent, but who rejoice – like the masters described by Nietzsche, who are capable or will be capable of 'that eccentric suddenness of anger, love, reverence, gratitude and revenge by which noble souls at all times have recognised themselves as such'.[60]

Race, class, and the Anglo-Irish Ascendancy

Yeats would have found direct support for his assertions about the Celtic race in the anthropological ruminations presented in *A Genealogy of Morals*, where Nietzsche enters into a speculative analysis of 'the etymological signification of the names coined by different languages for denoting what is "good"'.[61] According to his findings, these names always indicate the same 'shifting of concepts': 'that "superior", "noble" in its caste sense, was in every instance the fundamental concept from which "good" in the sense of "superior in sentiment", noble in the sense of "with lofty sentiment" "privileged in sentiment" necessarily developed'.[62] It is often the case, according to Nietzsche, that those of higher rank will just give themselves names that accord with their superior power or some emblem of their superiority. He identifies this logic in 'the Iranian and Slavic languages', in ancient Greek, and in Latin, which indicates in the term *malus* 'the dark-complexioned, especially the black-haired man' whose colour distinguished him from 'the prevailing, to wit, the Aryan conquering race'; Gaelic, Nietzsche claims, furnishes him with a 'precisely analogous case': '*Fin* (for instance, in the name *Fin-Gal*), the word characterising nobility, denoting ultimately the good, the noble, the pure, originally the flaxen-haired man in contradistinction to the dark, black-haired aborigines. The Celts, it may be observed here, were throughout a blond race'.[63] With this conjecture, Nietzsche elevates the Celts to a position of superiority among European stock. Indeed, he challenges the tendency in the late nineteenth century to assign to them categories such as 'blackness': 'We do wrong if, as is still done by Virchow, we connect those streaks of an essentially dark-haired population, noticeable on the more carefully prepared ethnographical maps of Germany, with some doubtful Celtic origin and blood-admixture. On the contrary, it is the *pre-Aryan* population which makes itself felt in such places' (original emphasis).[64] Nietzsche does not deny the merger of multiple ethnic or 'racial' strains in Ireland and elsewhere, but he does single out the Celts as an exceptional group.

These ideas support Yeats's increasingly racialised thinking and supply evidence, however historically dubious and ideologically vexed, that the Irish people belong to a masterful and mastering bloodline. Yet the temporality of his invocations exemplifies the curious time of revival: some extended process has come to a culmination as Seanchan, a representative of the long tradition of bardic poetry stretching back to 'the old time', exercises his right to bestow the crown to the king. And some new process has begun that will result in 'the great race that is to come'. But just when will this process culminate? When will the 'long-throated swans upon the waves of time' finally alight? Will it be in Yeats's own time, many years after the action of the play, when the Irish achieve cultural, if not political, independence? Or in some future yet to come? Nietzsche's position, as we noted in the previous chapter, was famously coy: '"progress" is merely a modern, i.e., a false idea', and the emergence of the beyond-man, of 'even entire races, tribes, and nations', of higher types results from 'a good hit'.[65] In 'The Irish Literary Theatre, 1900', as Yeats announced the aims of his new dramatic company, he had taken up a strikingly similar position:

> New Races [of which he numbered the Irish] understand instinctively, because the future cries in their ears, that the old revelations are insufficient, and that all life is revelation beginning in miracle and enthusiasm, and dying out as it unfolds itself in what we have mistaken for progress. It is one of our illusions, as I think, that education, the softening of manners, the perfecting of law – countless images of a fading light – can create nobleness and beauty, and that life moves slowly and evenly towards some perfection. Progress is miracle, and it is sudden, because miracles are the work of an all-powerful energy, and nature in herself has no power except to die and to forget.[66]

A good hit, a miracle: both represent the emergence of some unpredictable advance that cannot be explained away by the familiar modern idea of 'progress'. The attainments of civilisation are not cumulative or linear, moving from lower states of barbarism and backwardness to the achievement of nobleness and beauty. Rather, as Yeats would come to believe, they are constantly in danger of biological degeneration, which threatens to overwhelm the noble or aristocratic classes and suppress the emergence of superior individuals from the general population. Like Nietzsche, then, he deprecates the nineteenth-century obsession with progress, especially progress as a kind of moral and material attainment towards which history moves. The imposition of modern mores, along with the force of technocratic manipulation or colonial administration, have only thwarted the enhancement of mankind. Such enhancement is far more mysterious than these enterprises would suggest, because it evinces the eruption of 'an all-powerful' energy, a will to power, which is not cultivated or imposed so much as envisioned and celebrated. Thus arises the ethical imperative of his art. The emergence of a 'great race that is to come' is a matter for poets, not politicians or the people themselves, even if they understand that 'the old revelations are insufficient, and that all life is revelation beginning in miracle and enthusiasm'.[67] But the greatness of a people, and its revival, is also somehow inherent in their collective genius: 'as poets and musicians see the whole work in its first impulse, so races prophesy at their awakening whatever the generations are to prolong their traditions shall accomplish in detail'.[68] Whether Ireland will achieve a great literature in the new century is not certain in this initial statement from Yeats in 1900, but the moral sensibilities of the people have been 'aroused by political sacrifices' and the nation, in his estimation, is now ready to be 'moved by profound thoughts that are part of the unfolding of herself', the fulfilment of some life-affirming racial destiny.[69]

The notion of race, mingled with ideas of class and tradition, would become central to Yeats's particular brand of cultural nationalism as it developed in his theatrical proposals and practices over the course of the decade – and the influence of Nietzsche's philosophy on his thinking soon became evident to those around him. On 4 May 1903, he read out *The King's Threshold*, which he was still referring to as 'Sencan', in his apartment on Woburn Walk, London to a group that contained, among other friends and acquaintances, Annie Horniman and Harry Granville-Barker, who would soon star as John Tanner in *Man and Superman*; earlier in the day, Yeats had received a visit from Maude Gonne who was increasingly distressed by her recent marriage to John MacBride, though she was finding some solace in her simultaneous conversion to Catholicism. It is clear from his correspondence during this period that Yeats adopted a condescending attitude towards his estranged muse, but he also took the opportunity of their meeting to read from his latest revisions to the rites of the Celtic Mystical Order. Gonne had collaborated with Yeats on earlier efforts, but she was not pleased with his newest version, as she told him quite clearly in a letter dated 7 May:

> I have been thinking over the Celtic rite you read to me & away from the glamour of the musical words I see some defects which I think I should [?signal] to you. As I said at the time it is far too much influenced by Neiche [Nietzsche], not only as to expression but as to fundamental thought, *for Neiche is not Celtic*, though his intense individualism & his rushing fiery paradox & his impatience & his contempt for *banalité* & smallness of the many useless ones, appeal to us – Neiche's central thought seems to be to do away with the Gods, & to reverence & to recognise nothing greater than himself, this is most contrary to Celtic thought.[70]

This version of Yeats's occultism had become, in short, far too Nietzschean for Gonne's taste. Although it grew out of his association with the Golden Dawn, Yeats's work on the Celtic rites accompanied his efforts in the theatre as two components of his larger project to revitalise the cultural life of the Irish people. Drawing on an eclectic mix of occult sources, including the symbols of the sword, stone, cauldron, and spear, these ceremonial performances were meant to purify the initiate and unite them with natural beauty, ancient divinities, and the spirit of the Celtic race. Roy Foster suggests that Yeats had 'manipulat[ed] the Celtic Rites to express his repugnance at [Gonne's] conversion to Catholicism', though, in doing so, he had also adopted a vision of the Celtic race that owed something to the heresy and aristocratic hauteur of Nietzschean thought.[71] At the same time, however, he was also lending this hauteur to his developing mythos of the Anglo-Irish Protestant Ascendancy tradition, as an antidote to the mob mentality he increasingly associated with the Catholic Church in Ireland. In the strident claims of the letter, it is possible to discern both a sense of Yeats's precarious position in Gonne's personal affections and a more general anxiety about the declining status of the Ascendancy in Ireland's social hierarchy as the new century was getting underway. He could not fail to recognise that the political hegemony once enjoyed by the Protestant minority in Ireland had slowly succumbed to the overwhelming influence of the Catholic majority in its millions. But, at the same time, Yeats came to believe that he could convert his leadership of a cultural aristocracy into a form of political influence that might reverse these trends by defining the distinction between high and low, noble and ignoble, as part of the natural order of Irish society.

There can be little doubt that Yeats's reading of Nietzsche's philosophy was helping to shape his view of the divisions within Irish society, as well as his understanding of how he should respond to these schisms. On 10 February 1903, just a few days after Yeats had written to Quinn thanking him for the latest volumes of Nietzsche and just a week before Gonne was received into the Catholic Church, he wrote to her with an appeal to continue their work together for the Irish nation:

> For all who undertake such tasks there comes a moment of extreme peril. I know now that you have come to your moment of peril. If you carry out your purpose you will fall into a lower order & do great injury to the religeon [sic] of [pure] free souls that is growing up in Ireland, it may be to enlighten the whole world. A man said to me last night having seen the announcements in the papers 'The priests will [all triumph over for you] exult over us [us for generations] us all for generations because of this'. There are people (& these are the greater number) who need the priests or some other master but [there] are a few bid me write this letter. You possess your influence in Ireland very largely because you come to the people from above. You represent a superior class, a class whose people are more independent, have a more beautiful life, a more refined life ... It was our work to teach a few strong aristocratic spirits that to believe the soul was immortal & that one prospered hereafter *if one laid upon oneself* an heroic discipline in living & [?to] send them to uplift the nation.[72]

Drawing on vocabulary from *A Genealogy of Morals* and *The Antichrist*, Yeats contrasts the Catholic church, with its domineering priests and slavish morality, to the 'religeon [sic] of [pure] free souls' emerging in Ireland at that very moment. Like the 'free spirits' Nietzsche describes, the 'free souls' that Yeats evokes have declared their independence from clerical authority in order to devote themselves to another calling, a higher calling. And like these free spirits, they risk being outcast from a society that fails to understand their vocation, because that society remains mired in the resentful feelings and slavish morals of the Christian faith. Foster suggests that Yeats is railing against the priests who had 'truckled under the government over the Act of Union and had betrayed the Fenians'.[73] But, in a more general sense, the priests described by both Yeats and Nietzsche exercise their will to power over followers who learn from them only the decadent, life-denying values of the 'mob' or 'herd'. The heroic calling of the artist is to take up another task: 'to teach a few strong aristocratic ... spirits' to 'uplift the nation'. Yeats and Gonne are fit for this task, in his estimation, precisely because they too belong to the ranks of the 'free souls', the 'aristocratic spirits', who are capable of creating their own valuations and sharing them with other noble individuals.

Yeats lays these Nietzschean distinctions over the pre-existing divide between the Anglo-Irish Protestant Ascendancy – to which both he and Gonne could claim membership, however tenuous – and the majority of Irish Catholics, despite his professed admiration for an indigenous peasant population so closely identified with the Church. As Marjorie Howes succinctly puts it, 'he imagined the Anglo-Irish as a noble and worthwhile tradition, one capable of providing Ireland with the cultural continuity, political leadership and artistic integrity that he thought middle-class Catholic Ireland lacked'.[74] Although he maintained a faith in Gaelic-speaking peasant culture, Yeats came to believe that revival would be impossible in Ireland if it were not for the 'self-sacrifice of a few' like himself and Gonne who had managed to sustain 'the understanding of the arts and of high thinking'. His sense of class propriety treats their taste – their sense of 'a more beautiful life, a more refined life' – as an indication of their ability to sustain a cultural aristocracy, despite the rather precarious social and economic standing of Yeats and the Anglo-Irish Ascendancy as a whole. According to the anxious argument in his letter, to acquiesce to the Catholic faith is to give up this elevated status and to 'fall into a lower order'; instead, Yeats would have her maintain what Nietzsche famously calls the 'pathos of distance': 'the noble, the powerful, the higher-situated, the high-minded felt and regarded themselves and their acting as of first rank, in contradistinction to everything low, low-minded, mean and vulgar'.[75] A short time later, Gonne wrote back to Yeats with a conciliatory letter, which nonetheless must have stung him to the quick; for it sought to explain her conversion to Catholicism, not as a momentary slip in her allegiance to 'the few', but as evidence of her enduring populist sentiments: 'I have always told you I am the voice, the soul of the *crowd*' (original emphasis).[76]

In his 1904 essay, 'First Principles', which adumbrates his evolving beliefs about the role of the theatre in Ireland, Yeats seems to confirm that, at least for the purposes of his art, this superior class or 'race' had already arrived:

> I do not think it a national prejudice that makes me believe we are a harder, a more masterful race than the comfortable English of our time, and that this comes from an essential nearness to reality of those few scattered people who have the right to call themselves the Irish race. It is only in the exceptions, in the few minds, where the flame has burnt as it were pure, that one can see the permanent character of a race.

The great men, 'who have dominated Ireland for the last hundred and fifty years', are characterised by a singular 'strength of personality', which makes them the perfect symbols for his art because this quality 'stirs Irish imagination most deeply in the end'.[77] In emphasising the qualities of the exceptional few, Yeats does not escape the inclination to define the Irish in relation to their English counterparts, though he does offer a transvaluation that figures the Irish people as a 'more masterful race'. It bears remembering that Arnold's proto-anthropological work had coincided with the circulation of dehumanising images of Irish simians in periodicals such as *Punch* and *Harper's Weekly*, which had harnessed mounting fears about the implications of Darwinian evolutionary theory; and it had been followed in the 1890s by projects such as the Anthropological Institute of Great Britain and Ireland's anthropometric survey, which set out to 'unravel the tangled skein of the so-called "Irish Race"' by gathering data on the cranial size, limb length, and 'nigrescence' of the peasant population.[78] Yet, as Michael North points out, Yeats's response suggests 'an odd brand of racialism, in which the race is epitomised precisely by those who do not fit comfortably into it'.[79] It is only those who live with a certain Paterian intensity that can rightly call themselves members of the race, for only they evince what is essentially Irish, which Yeatsian art might serve to restore and enhance.

As in his letter to Gonne, Yeats promotes a hierarchical and honorific, if not strictly biological or genetic, distinction to be made between those who merely inhabit the island and those characterised, as Nietzsche would have it, by 'the good, the noble, the pure'.[80] Such claims demonstrate the increasingly strained concept of cultural nationalism that Yeats was advocating by the middle of the decade, as his notion of the spiritual unity of the Irish people confronted his advocacy of 'a few strong aristocratic ... spirits'. In the face of this contradiction, as North suggests, Yeats really had only one option: 'he had to invent a minority that could serve to represent the whole'.[81] With the help of Nietzsche, he does so by looking back at the heroes of recent Irish history, with their 'strength of personality', and transforming them into powerful symbols of racial superiority. To be sure, a great many, if not most, of these heroes – Swift, Parnell, and Synge, among others – were members of the Anglo-Irish Protestant Ascendency, rather than of a peasant or Catholic majority in Ireland, and thus for Yeats they asserted a kind of intellectual independence even as they contributed to the traditions of Irish culture. These heroic figures, that is, offered examples that could teach his contemporaries to attain their own courage. But Yeats's most important heroic figure was one Standish O'Grady's two-volume *History of Ireland* (1878–1880) had resurrected to offer the Ascendancy its own model of valiant leadership, Cuchulain. Because he was drawn from Gaelic antiquity, this legendary figure offered different potentialities for unifying the Irish people: he belonged to a chivalric pre-sectarian era of Irish history and embodied noble virtues that preceded the emergence of Christian morality.[82] In drawing on Irish mythology for his hero, moreover, Yeats sought to fulfil the promise of the bardic tradition to serve an important national or racial function by providing his audience with an image of man unrestrained by decadent modern values.

On Baile's Strand, generosity, and tragedy

Cuchulain would become Yeats's most enduring symbol of heroic independence because the ancient warrior, as he wrote, 'was creative joy separated from fear'.[83] The warrior had played an important role in the symbology of the Celtic Mystical Order, where he was envisioned as 'the risen national hero', 'standing in a chariot drawn by two bright steeds ... his hair was as the sun's rays & he was clad in a white tunic with golden mail'.[84] In his first play featuring Cuchulain, *On Baile's Strand*, Yeats develops the hero into a personification of what Paul had called in *The King's Threshold* 'the old joyful, dangerous, individual life', at odds with the careful and conservative King Conchubar. This image owed something not just to O'Grady's histories but to Gregory's *Cuchulain of Muirtheme*, though many critics[85] have suggested that Yeats's treatment of Cuchulain as a 'great man' or 'noble type', who possessed a 'sense of allegiance to a self that is superior not only to contemporary mores but also his own failures', was probably drawn out of an admiration for Nietzsche's philosophy.[86] Yet these claims do not necessarily account for the chronology of Yeats's reading and writing: he wrote on 25 July 1901 that he had started 'on a little play about Cuchullin' and he continued to work on the play in fits and starts through the rest of the year and into the spring and summer of 1902, all before his first enchantment with Nietzsche. He would continue to revise the play repeatedly through several publications and performances until printing what amounts to the final version in October 1906. Great care must be taken, then, in tracking the evolution of the manuscript against Yeats's reading of Nietzsche's philosophy in order to clearly understand the role of the philosopher's ideas in the development of the playwright's hero.[87]

It is clear from the initial drafts of the play, for instance, that Yeats was already preoccupied with the theme of generosity before receiving the volumes of Nietzsche sent to him by Quinn. When the young champion challenges him to do battle, Cuchulain responds not with anger or threats but with curiosity and gifts: 'He takes th circle fro his hand & th [?armor] fro / [?the] arm & [?lays] thes to [?down] by it [?soft] / There I give you gifts – Is go back-/ [[inserted: Your shield for my great [?stave], let th [?is/em] signify [?here] I]] / t your own country, & boast there if you wish / that Cuchu feared to fight you'.[88] The warrior is openhanded with his possessions and with his reputation, as he encourages the young man to take credit for having frightened the great champion and to seize his armour or his weapon as evidence of this. The gathered kings, however, will not allow the outsider to 'go unfought' and, one after another, they threaten to take up the challenge that Cuchulain has, at least initially, refused. The contrast is evident: where the kings will let no slight go unanswered, Cuchulain possesses an easy confidence, a true nobility, which allows him to meet such occasions with relative equanimity, even with a kind of joy for their enlivening or entertaining qualities. He is renowned for triumphing in battle after battle, but he will not be provoked by his enemies nor will he bow to the wishes of his supposed friends and allies: 'The women are always egging me to fight / But I will not fight with boys I will send out / And call him to my house & give him gifts'.[89] What we observe here is a tribal warrior ethos that exemplifies certain aspects of what Nietzsche had identified in other noble cultures and castes.

In the version of the play published in 1903, which Yeats was revising that January as he was in the first throes of his enchantment with the philosopher, this passage is expanded with additional details and weighted with additional significance:

> *Cuchullain.* I'll give you gifts, but I'll have something too,
> An arm ring or the like, and if you will
> We'll fight it out when you are older boy.
> *An Old King.* Aoife will make some story out of this.
> *Cuchullain.* Well well, what matter, I'll have that arm ring boy
> *The Young Man.* There is no man I'd sooner have my friend
> Than you whose name has gone about the world
> As if it had been the wind, but Aoifed say
> I had turned coward.
> *Cuchullain.* I will give you gifts
> That Aoife'll know and all her people know
> To have been my gifts. Mannanan, son of the sea,
> Gave me this heavy purple cloak. Nine Queens
> Of the Land Under Wave had woven it
> Out of the fleeces of the sea. O tell her
> I was afraid, or tell her what you will –
> No tell her that I heard a raven croak
> On the north side of the house, and was afraid.
> *An Old King.* Some witch of the air has troubled Cuchullain's mind.

The extra details serve to highlight the hero's 'proud hard gift giving joyousness', which cannot be comprehended by the Old King who comments on the exchange between Cuchulain and the young man, but the aged man's comments suggest his lack of true nobility as he frets over the possibility that 'Aoife will make some story out of this'.[90] He would not have Cuchulain act on his desire to make an offering, to exercise his instinct, but instead to react to the authority of another – therefore, he can only attribute the hero's behaviour to some kind of witch's spell. Indeed, his response suggests that Cuchulain's generosity to the young man might be taken as a sign of weakness or effeminacy by the powerful warrior-queen; that the fiercely confident hero is unconcerned by this possible gender dissonance can be seen as 'strangely coextensive with his adherence to a primordial style of masculinity'. It is also a key feature of Yeatsian revivalism. For Joseph Valente, this paradoxical situation allows Yeats to both 'put more masculine "salt" into his work' and 'to critique the cramped sexual traditionalism of his nationalist compeers as a corruption of the aboriginal Irish warrior culture'.[91]

In his self-possessed generosity, Cuchulain offers up a gift that is not only closely associated with his own power and status, but one that provides the possibility of recognition and reward for the young man when he returns home. This largesse of spirit, this superabundance of life, is on display in the speech that leads up to his offer:

> *Cuchullain.* You'll stop with us
> And we will hunt the deer and the wild bulls,
> And, when we have grown weary light our fires
> In sandy places where the wool white foam
> Is murmuring & breaking & it may be
> That long haired women will come out of the dunes
> To dance in the yellow fire light. You hang your head,
> Young man as if it was not a good life
> And yet whats better than to hurl the spear
> And hear the long-remembering harp & dance
> Friendship grows the [?chest] in that murmuring dark.[92]

Cuchulain, that is, displays the 'spontaneous manifestation and ardent ebullition of highest rank-regulating and rank-differentiating valuations' that Nietzsche associates with aristocratic or noble morality. There is no 'arithmetical prudence' or 'utilitarian calculation' in his actions, which instead emerge from an overflowing of life-affirming virtues.[93] The hero's munificence is a particular kind of generosity that, unlike Christian charity, derives from 'selfishness' and elevates the giver as he seeks to express his will to power in relation to others – not in relation to the recipient of the gift, but in relation to the prudence and prudery of the Old King and the ancien régime of stolid values that he represents. It represents a direct threat to the status quo, including the reigning standards of gender normativity. But Cuchulain does so not in the name of modern virtues, but rather in that of a still more primaeval ethos associated with his warrior culture, which resists both caution and careful reckoning. Read as an allegory of colonialism, the play suggests that Cuchulain's resistance is that of a primitive but noble Celtic past that refuses to embrace the imperial narrative of progress and move into a future defined by 'civilisation' and 'rationality'.

The tragic quality of *On Baile's Strand* stems directly from Cuchulain's abandonment of his natural impulse towards gift-giving and taking up arms against the youthful champion – who, of course, turns out to be his own son. The tragedy is all the more poignant because, in slaying the young man, Cuchulain not only brings an end to the life of his child, but as what Valente calls the 'main avatar of native Celtic ways' in the play, he brings an end to a lineage that may have resulted in 'the great race that is to come'. Critics have long struggled to explain Cuchulain's sudden change of heart, which seems to lack any credible psychological motivation. To be sure, Yeats himself had difficulty in understanding the hero of his play for he believed that 'when one creates a character one does it out of instinct & may be wrong when on analyses the instinct afterwards'. Nevertheless, as he began revising the play yet again in January 1904, Yeats wrote to Frank Fay that he had:

> to make the refusal of the sons affection tragic by suggesting in Cuchullains [sic] character a shadow of something a little proud, barren & restless as if out of shere [sic] strength of heart or from accident he had put affection away. He lives among young men but has himself outlived the illusions of youth ... Probably his very strength of character made him put off illusions & dreams (that make young men a womans [sic] servant) & made him become quite early in life a deliberate lover, a man of pleasure who can never really surrender himself. He is a little hard, & leaves the people about him a little repelled – perhaps this young mans [sic] affection is what he had most need of. Without this thought the play had not had any deep tragedy.[94]

According to this oft-cited description, it appears that Yeats attempted to create his Cuchulain very much in the mould of an Aristotelian hero, whose *hamartia* or 'tragic flaw' is precisely that part of himself that is 'proud, barren & restless'. Pride or hubris, as the poet and playwright well knew, is the archetypal form of hamartia, found again and again in Greek tragedies as the overweening self-confidence of the protagonist leads to a disastrous conclusion. Aristotle contended that the cathartic effect of such a story is more powerful if the hero is an elevated figure of superior moral worth who, like Cuchulain, is possessed of a certain 'strength of character'. But he also suggested that the tragic hero who will evoke the most fear and pity in the audience is the one who is neither wholly good nor wholly bad, but possessed of both traits in nearly equal measure. If a 'shadow' of hamartia hangs over Cuchulain – if he is 'a little proud' and 'a little hard', an admixture of masculine traits which have led him to 'put affection away' and 'leaves the people about him a little repelled' – he is still possessed of the 'gift giving joyousness' that is expressed in his encounter with the young champion. He expects nothing more in return, it seems, than 'this young mans [sic] affection', but his tragic flaw prevents him from winning what he most desires. His generosity depleted, he has become 'barren'. To put this another way, the tragedy of *On Baile's Strand* results from the 'proud' and 'hard' elements of his character outstripping the 'gift giving joyousness' that accompanies and complements them.

But Yeats's letter suggests a dimension of Cuchulain's character that is not so easily accounted for by Aristotle's schema – and here Nietzsche's philosophy is again significant. After acknowledging his difficulty in analysing his own protagonist, Yeats immediately goes on to develop an evaluation: 'The touch of something hard, repellent yet alluring, self assertive yet self immolating is not all but it must be there. He is the fool – wandering passion, houseless & all but loveless. Concobar is reason that is blind because it can only reason because it is cold'.[95] Together, that is, Cuchulain and Conchubar seem to embody the two opposing forces or drives that Nietzsche famously defines as the sources of the tragic in *The Birth of Tragedy*. Cuchulain is the Dionysian who, allied with music and dance, represents a condition of excess and expressiveness that assaults distinctions and limitations; Conchubar is the Apollonian who represents the norms of civic order, temperance, and restraint that respect boundaries and limits.[96] This distinction is accentuated in Yeats's revisions for the 1906 version of the play when, for instance, the two discuss the arrival of the young champion:

Conchubar: He came to land
While you were somewhere out of sight and hearing;
Hunting or dancing with your wild companions.
Cuchulain: He can be driven out. I'll not be bound.
I'll dance or hunt, or quarrel or make love,
Wherever and whenever I've a mind to.
If time had not put water in your blood
You never would have thought it.[97]

For Nietzsche, the value of tragedy is found precisely in the harmony of opposites that allowed the Greeks to recognise clearly the original intensity, chaos, and amorality of existence, which is here championed by and embodied in Cuchulain. This recognition, according to the philosopher, provided the Greeks with a profound understanding of the human condition. For Yeats, the significance of Cuchulain lay precisely in his providing a symbol of this kind of unrestrained passion and vitality in an age that had become entirely too restrained by calculation, industrialisation, commercialisation, and bureaucratisation. Rob Doggett suggests, moreover, that 'it is Cuchulain alone who has remained true to his Celtic roots' for his 'wandering passion' flies in the face of the Saxon 'reason' of Conchubar.[98] In this way, the play transvalues the racial distinctions that Arnold had applied to the Irish and English people. But, in this way, the play also delivers a Nietzschean message to Yeats's contemporaries and compatriots who lived in a culture that no longer recognised the inhuman chaos of existence but focused instead on a host of rational concepts and moral norms.

The Birth of Tragedy and the genius of Irish culture

Critics have often speculated on the role that *The Birth of Tragedy* may have played in Yeats's developing theory of dramatic art and the contribution the theatre could make to the revival of Irish culture. Michael

Valdez Moses, for instance, has suggested that Nietzsche influenced Yeats in his attempt 'to effect a rebirth of premodern, ritualised, and aristocratic tragedy within the apparently uncongenial confines of contemporary Irish politics'.[99] Moses traces this connection all the way back to Yeats's 1897 essay, 'The Celtic Element in Literature', which much like Nietzsche's early study of the tragic impulse, 'praises Wagner and the composer's use of the ancient myths of Scandinavia' as an example of the recuperation of ancient myth as a repudiation of decadent modern values.[100] But there is no substantial evidence of Yeats's exposure to the philosopher's ideas on the matter until late August 1902, when his friend and frequent interlocutor, Arthur Symons, published a brief review of the French translation of *Die Geburt der Tragödie aus dem Geiste der Musik* titled 'Nietzsche on Tragedy'. It is more than likely, given his expressed interest in Nietzsche later in the year, that Yeats had discussed the book with Symons in London during their encounters in the city between 1902 and 1903 – indeed, few other sources were available at the time, as Symons had produced one of the first English-language responses to the book, which would not appear in translation as *The Birth of Tragedy* until 1910.[101] In the review, he outlines 'the conflict of the two creative spirits, symbolised by the Greeks in the two gods, Apollo and Dionysus', that give rise to the arts. He goes on to explain that, according to Nietzsche, the origin of tragedy is to be found in the chorus, which itself 'arose out of the hymns to Dionysus'. Tragedy comes to an end as a cultural form, according to Symons, when these 'Dionysiac' elements are suppressed by 'Apollonic' forces in the dramas of Euripides, 'as he substitutes pathos for action, thought for contemplation, and passionate sentiments for the primitive ecstasy'.[102]

Yeats makes no direct mention of these categories and concepts until mid-May 1903, shortly before the publication of *On Baile's Strand*; but when he does reference them, they take on an important role in his evolving conception of his work in the theatre and its relation to Irish cultural traditions. For instance, in a lecture given at Clifford's Inn in London on 12 May (reported on by H.W. Nevinson in the *Daily Chronicle*), Yeats defines the difference between folk and heroic literature by

> follow[ing] out the distinction which Nietzsche drew between the Dionysic and Apollonic moods of poetry, which went to make up the perfection of the Greek drama. The folk poetry, corresponding to some extent to the Greek chorus, is the extravagant cry, the utterance of the greatest emotions possible, the heartfelt lyric of an ancient people's soul. With the heroic poetry comes the sense of form, the dramatic or epic portion of the work of art, the heroic-discipline, which, of course, has no relation to morality as generally understood or to service to the State and mankind.[103]

There is very little of Nietzsche's thesis here that Yeats could not have gleaned from Symons's review (which, like Yeats's lecture and letters, favoured 'Dionysiac' or 'Dionysic', over the more common 'Dionysian') but what he does with it is entirely his own undertaking: he attempts, through reference to Nietzsche's categories, to recount the origin story of Irish culture. As we know from 'The Celtic Element in Literature', Yeats had long praised the passion and spontaneity of folk poetry – of the type produced by the wandering ballad singers of Gaelic Ireland – because it was uncorrupted by any abstraction or artifice that would debase its imaginative and emotive force. In the lecture, likening the folk poetry of ancient Ireland to the choral singing of ancient Greece, he attributes to these songs and poems an ecstatic quality that fuses a race or people in a state of primordial unity, prior to any subjective individuation or conceptual distinctions. The development of heroic poetry, however, brings Apollonian order and restraint, imposing limits on Dionysian excess and passion with the implementation of beautiful forms and ordering symbols. Moreover, Irish heroic literature, like Greek epic poetry, exalts individuality by depicting pleasing images of singular heroes, particular places, and distinct events. These representations do not find their justification in any kind of ethical or political utility, but rather in their aesthetic superiority, in a world where art is still assimilated into the daily life of the people and still considered to be of fundamental importance to their existence. According to Yeats, this heroic literature manages to achieve something that Nietzsche had attributed to Greek tragedy – that is, an essentially non-moral vision of human life, which manages to address the lust for political power, sexual conquest, and physical violence, without judging them according to normative moral standards.

It is little wonder that Yeats was drawn to this version of cultural history: it has important consequences for his conception of the Irish past, the project of cultural revival, and the place of his theatre work in that project. Like many other eighteenth- and nineteenth-century accounts of Western civilisation, *The Birth of Tragedy* locates the pinnacle of human culture in ancient Greece, though Nietzsche isolates the most advanced expression of that culture not in its contributions to science and philosophy, but in fifth-century Attic tragedy, with its perfect resolution of the strife between Dionysian and Apollonian forces. If the Dionysian state, with its access to what is most primordial in human nature and most destructive in nature itself, revealed the essential chaos and meaninglessness of existence, the Apollonian state helped to redeem this chaos by giving it shape, by providing it with aesthetically pleasing forms that make existence less threatening, less dire, more beautiful, more joyful. Together, Nietzsche tells us, 'the Dionysian and the Apollonian, in ever new births succeeding and mutually augmenting one another, controlled the Hellenic genius', and produced a flourishing culture in ancient Greece.

Yeats's attraction to this narrative can be explained, of course, by his own desire to produce a flourishing culture in modern Ireland, which might draw on elements of both folk and heroic poetry to generate a supreme form of artistic achievement. Like Nietzsche, the poet and playwright was intently focused on the question of what kind of culture modern men should endeavour to produce and what kind of values that culture should express. And like Nietzsche, he turned to the ancient past in order to find a potential response to the cultural and political decadence of the modern world, where an emphasis on rational and moral norms had separated men from the chaos and vitality of nature. The integration of Dionysian and Apollonian principles in modern tragic theatre promised to return the Irish to their relationship with these primordial forces, which had been suppressed by the decadent forces of modernity, of civilisation, of imperialism. At the same time, this new theatre promised another kind of transvaluation: to demonstrate that the cultural traditions of the 'half-barbarous' Irish were indicative of their strength, their well-being, the abundance of their own vitality: this was the genius of Greek culture, for Nietzsche; it could be the genius of Irish culture, claims Yeats. In *The Birth of Tragedy*, Nietzsche had identified the reemergence of such vitality in Wagner's musical dramas, which combined Dionysian and Apollonian elements into what the philosopher, at least initially, conceive of as an almost utopian form of cultural production capable of reviving the aesthetic energy of Attic tragedy. As Valdez-Moses points out, Yeats too had praised Wagner's 'The Ring' and 'Parsifal' not just because they provided examples of a national literature founded on ancient legends, 'but because of the influence both words and music are beginning to have upon the intellect of Germany and of Europe'.[104]

In two letters, written in the days following his lecture at Clifford's Inn, Yeats continues to explore Nietzsche's distinction between the Dionysian and Apollonian, moving from an attempt to explain the course of Irish cultural history to an effort to describe the trajectory of his own artistic development. If his earlier encounter with the philosopher's 'astringent joy' had prompted Yeats to think of his recent work as 'far more masculine', with 'more salt in it', now he was conceiving his recent writing as taking on a far more definitive shape, a far more robust structuring. He described this conversion to George Russell on 14 May 1903:

> The close of the last century was full of a strange desire to get out of form to get to some kind of disembodied beauty and now it seems to me the contrary impulse has come. I feel about me and in me an impulse to create form, to carry the realisation of beauty as far as possible. The Greeks said that the Dionysisic [*sic*] enthusiasm preceded the Apollonic and that the Dionysisic was sad and desirous, but that the Apollonic was joyful and self sufficient.[105]

This shift corresponds quite closely with Yeats's move from writing folk-inspired lyrics in the 1890s, with their Romantic yearning for other worlds, other states of existence, to his attempt to write plays – tragedies – based on heroic figures and bardic materials. But it is important to note that this was not an attempt to somehow replicate the established works of Irish tradition. Where previously he had sought after the dark energies of the natural world and a mystical sense of racial unity, he later turned toward more aesthetically refined and individuating arrangements that might accommodate these primal forces. The next day, Yeats elaborated on this distinction in a letter to John Quinn:

> I have always felt that the soul has two movements primarily: one to transcend forms, and the other to create forms. Nietsche [*sic*], to whom you have been the first to introduce me, calls these the Dionysic and the Apollonic, respectively. I think I have to some extent got weary of the wild God Dionysus, and am hoping that the Far-Darter will come in his place.[106]

Nietzsche had metaphorised the contrary elements of artistic subjectivity and, in doing so, provided Yeats with a means to articulate the evolution of his own aesthetic sensibility. Moreover, as is evident when the lecture and the letters are viewed together, the philosopher had given the poet and playwright a way to understand the significance of this personal transformation in relation to the course of Irish cultural history. Moving toward Apollonian form did not mean abandoning the primitive imagination of the folk, but shifting his emphasis to the heroic legends of the bards; it did not mean ignoring the chaos of natural forces, but giving them an aesthetic structure that might allow their improved contemplation. In this modernist mode of revival, his writing might better serve to reinvigorate the spirit of the Irish people (and to represent that spirit to audiences abroad) in the face of what he saw as the general malaise of the modern world.

American marginalia, Irish manifestoes

Nietzsche's philosophy continued to infiltrate Yeats's thoughts as he developed and refined his ideas about the Irish literary revival – especially the ethos of generosity linked to his understanding of Irish mythology, its heroes, and their status as exemplars for the citizens of modern Ireland – during his tour of America in late 1903 and early 1904. While he travelled the country delivering lectures such as 'The Intellectual Revival in Ireland', 'Heroic Literature in Ireland', and 'The Theatre and What It Might Be', he carried with him a copy of Thomas Common's anthology, *Nietzsche as Critic, Philosopher, Poet and Prophet* (1901), which had been provided to him by John Quinn in New York. The detailed marginalia that Yeats left in the anthology comprise a legible record of his engagement with Nietzsche and his autodidactic efforts at this crucial moment for Irish modernism. For instance, he marks a passage drawn from section 260 in the final chapter of *Beyond Good and Evil*, which Nietzsche titles 'What Is Noble?':

> The noble type of man regards *himself* as the determiner of worth, it is not necessary for him to be approved of, he passes the judgment: 'what is injurious to me is injurious in itself'; he recognises that it is he himself only that confers honour on things – he is a *creator of worth*. The type of man in question honours whatever qualities he recognises in himself: his morality is self-glorification. In the foreground there is the feeling of plenitude and power which seeks to overflow, the happiness of high tension, the consciousness of riches which would fain give and bestow; the noble man also helps the unfortunate, not (or scarcely) out of sympathy, but rather out of an impulse produced by the superabundance of power. The noble man honours the powerful one in himself, and also him who has self-command, who knows how to speak and keep silence, who joyfully exercises strictness and severity over himself, and reverences all that is strict and severe.[107]

The passage provides an early account of what Nietzsche means by 'master morality', which is composed of values that issue from the strength and self-confidence of the so-called 'noble type of man'. But this initial summary, which he would later expand upon at length in *A Genealogy of Morals*, also emphasises the kind of superfluity or overflowing fullness that Yeats had identified with the heroic life, as he planned the series of plays he would write during the first decade of the twentieth century. Crucially, this generosity does not stem from a sense of pity, indebtedness, or even kindness, which Nietzsche associates with slave morality, but from an excess of power – from the capacity *to give* itself – the same power with which the noble type bestows value on himself and all his actions. The noble type, that is, lives a life defined by Zarathustra's gift-giving virtue. Such a life is 'proud' and 'hard' precisely because it both glorifies itself and asserts control over itself, and yet it also participates in 'joyousness' because it relishes the exercise of the will to power over the self and the world.

In the margin, connecting these traits to the heroes of Irish mythology, Yeats inscribes, 'So Oscar's heart, but "hard" surely in the sense of scorning self-pity'. Identified as either the son or grandson of Finn Mac Cool (or Fionn Mac Cumhaill), Oscar (or Osgar) is known as the fiercest of the Fianna warriors, the best at spear-throwing and other feats of strength, though he was killed at the great battle of Gabhra as he slew the high king Cairbre Lifechair. In his preface to Gregory's *Gods and Fighting Men* (1904), an immense compendium of tales and fables, Yeats proposes that the stories 'of the Fianna, or of Cuchulain, or of some great hero' offer images of 'the fine life' for their readers and listeners: 'When Osgar complained, as he lay dying, of the keening of the women and the old fighting men, he too played his part; "No man ever knew any heart in me", he said, "but a heart of twisted horn, and it covered with iron; but the howling of the dogs beside me", he said, "and the keening of the old fighting men and the crying of the women one after another, those are the things that are vexing me"'.[108] The dying hero, with his enduring 'nobility', does not protest against his fate, but against the sorrow of those who are brought to tears by his demise; he has lived a life that honours his own 'feeling of plenitude and power' and he will not have that diminished by his death. As Laurence Lampert points out, the final chapter of *Beyond Good and Evil* provides a portrait of nobility that is meant to edify the reader as to how they might accomplish the great deeds in morals and politics set out in preceding chapters.[109] The heroes portrayed in *Gods and Fighting Men*, according to Yeats, demonstrate a mode of existence not governed by restrictive social expectations or moral norms, but 'pride and movement' pursued for 'the sake of joy', even their wars are fought for a delight in their warrior skills rather than anything that might be gained in victory. 'If we would create a great community' in contemporary Ireland, he reflects, then 'we must recreate the old foundations of life', the noble values of another age, as they were purveyed by the ancient storytellers, who could address the fools and the finest minds alike.[110] This is, in short, the Yeatsian project of revival.

Nietzsche too sees these lost virtues exemplified in ancient stories that, as we have just seen, were being revived in his time by Wagner's operas. The passage that Yeats marked in Common's anthology continues:

> 'Wotan has put a hard heart into my breast', says an old Scandinavian saga: it is thus rightly expressed out of the heart of a proud viking. Such a type of man is in fact proud of *not* being made for sympathy; the hero of the saga therefore adds, by way of warning: 'He who has not had a hard heart when young, will never have a hard heart'. The noble and the brave who think thus are furthest removed from the morality which sees precisely in sympathy, in acting for the good of others, or in *désintéressement*, the characteristic of morality; a belief in oneself, a fundamental hostility and irony with respect to 'selflessness', beyond distinctly to the higher morality, as do careless indifference and precaution in the presence of sympathy and the 'warm heart'.[111]

Nietzsche evokes the 'old Scandinavian saga' because it is demonstrative of values that have not been corrupted by modern ideals such as democracy, egalitarianism, and Christian pity. In 'A Note on National Drama', as we observed earlier, Yeats suggests that modern literature, including examples such as Ibsen's *Peer Gynt* and Wagner's *The Ring of the Nibelung*, had 'found new life in the Norse and German legends' (though he found even greater promise in 'the Irish legends, in popular tradition and in old

Gaelic literature');[112] contemporary writers had created characters who derived from the heroic figures of ancient myth and exemplified values that contrasted dramatically with those their own time. Wagner's Siegfried, for instance, was defined by his pride, his rashness, his reckless desire to defy everything that he encountered, at least until he came to know fear later in life. To be sure, beginning as early as 1898 with Shaw in *The Perfect Wagnerite*, commentators have long linked Siegfried, the scion of Wotan, with the image of the Nietzschean Superman, as an individual driven to stand up against external authority in an effort to realise his own values and to create himself in their image.[113] For Nietzsche, these figures from the past were available as models for the future, but not a future that would necessarily be regarded as progress, at least from the point of view of modern ideas about moral improvement and social equality. Instead, Nietzsche envisioned a future for Europe that would honour the best in its ancestors and claim their aristocratic legacy, including the kind of hard-hearted nobility that is the expression of the will to power in the highest achievements of a flourishing culture.

Yeats expresses increasing sympathy with the aristocratic morality of some earlier age that he finds articulated in Nietzsche, though he is concerned to preserve an element of gift-giving generosity as he sees it exemplified in Irish mythology. This is not to say that Yeats wants to amend or revise Nietzsche's ethics – 'by supplying', as Cullingford suggests, 'the generosity which Nietzsche so signally lacks' – but that he seeks to highlight or enhance an element of the philosophy that he finds understated.[114] What he provides, in other words, is a Yeatsian reading of Nietzschean philosophy, which suggests a central, even primary, place for generosity not just in ethics, but in politics. In doing so, he also clearly indicates one of the features that makes his contribution to modernism distinctive, that is, an early challenge to liberalism drawing on both master morality and his own sense of ancient heroism. On the very next page of *Nietzsche as Critic, Philosopher, Poet and Prophet*, the poet and playwright marks the following passage:

> The morality of the ruling class ... is more especially foreign and irritating to the taste of the present day, owing to the sternness of the principle that one has only obligations to one's equals, that one may act towards beings of a lower rank, and towards all that is foreign to one according to discretion, or 'as the heart desires', and in any case 'beyond Good and Evil'.[115]

The noble type is a member of an aristocratic class, which does not bow to the external authority of organised religion, normative ethics, or majority rule, but instead recognises only its own authority, derived from strength, health, and power. At one time these characteristics were directly aligned with the order of rank in a society, so that those of higher rank felt no need to attend to those of lower ranks. But in an age increasingly governed by democratic ideals, master morality seems out of place and anachronistic because it does not recognise the equality of all men and the values that Nietzsche associates with slave morality. The noble type, however, does not acknowledge the values of the slaves, especially the moral worth attributed to sympathy and subservience and the moral detriment of their own strength and vitality. They acknowledge only the validity of their own impulses – it is in this sense that they live beyond the categories of 'Good and Evil'.

Nietzsche recognises that the aim to recreate an aristocratic order will encounter resistance because the disruption of the settled order will seem illicit or barbaric; Yeats responds to these potential objections by again emphasising the generosity of the noble type: 'Yes', he inscribes in the margin, 'but the necessity of giving remains. When the old heroes praise one another they say "he never refused any man"'. In fact, Yeats is repeating verbatim a claim made in *Gods and Fighting Men* about Finn Mac Cool, who is said to be the best of men precisely due to his consistent generosity.[116] What 'Nitzsche [sic] means', Yeats goes on to clarify, is 'that the lower cannot create anything, cannot make obligations to the higher'. With these marginal notes, then, he supplements Nietzsche's aphoristic passage with his own ethical and political interpretation, as well as examples from his own literary preoccupations: he attempts to clarify that, for the noble type, generosity is to be considered a principal aim of the Revival. For Yeats, however, this generosity only reinforces the distinction between higher and lower ranks, between the artist and the mob, between the aristocratic and the common or vulgar, because it cannot be initiated or even properly reciprocated by the latter. He adds: 'This implies that victory achieves its end not by mere overcoming but because the joy of it creates friends – it is a new creation. Victories of mere brute force do not create'. Again, it is the heroes of Irish antiquity, with their pursuit of power *and* pleasure, who have provided the model for this ethos: as Yeats writes in his Preface, 'the very heroism of the Fianna is indeed but their pride and joy in one another, their good fellowship'.[117]

As he makes his way through the Common anthology, Yeats clearly remains concerned with the paradoxical nature of noble generosity, of the gift-giving virtue that is also a variety of selfishness, which emanates from the will to power rather than any attention to the will of others. In the remainder of the passage from *Beyond Good and Evil*, Nietzsche goes on to define slave morality as the ethos of those who are oppressed and weary and therefore condemn not just 'the virtues of the powerful' but 'the whole situation of man'. 'It is here that the kind helping hand, the warm heart, along with sympathy, patience, diligence, submissiveness and friendliness, attain to honour', because their qualities are useful in the presence of suffering and the burdens of existence.[118] On the next page, responding to the passage as a whole, Yeats writes in the margin: 'In the last analysis the "noble" man will serve or fail [fear?] the weak as much as the "good" man, but in the first case the "noble" man creates the *form* of the gift[,] in the second the weak' (original emphasis). For Yeats, that is, the distinction between master and slave morality can be summed up in the form of the gift, in the mode of generosity, associated with each. Although the 'good' man is sympathetic and friendly, the 'noble' man is equally capable of offering something to the weak. But the form of munificence exercised by the noble man does not seek to address the needs of the weak as they experience them: as a want of sympathy and friendship that might lighten the burdens of existence, as patience and diligence that might help to alleviate suffering. Instead, the proud and strong possess the aesthetic capacity to form, to mould, to give style to the excess or overflow of their own energies, their own existence.

Nietzsche insinuates in these passages that an aristocracy of noble types is really only possible if a people has accepted the value of aristocracy and organised itself according to a hierarchy of classes or categories topped by those who embody strength and heroism. Later in the anthology, recognising this very principle, Yeats notes that Nietzsche 'opposes organisation from resentment – denial to organisation from power – affirmation' as he responds to a passage taken from *A Genealogy of Morals*, which Common titles 'The Conflict of Master-Morality and Slave-Morality'. But the poet and playwright continues to inquire into the ethos of generosity to be found in the noble type and suggests that the philosopher's 'system seems to lack some reason why the self must give to the selfless or weak, or itself perish or suffer diminution – the self being the end'. Here Yeats appears again to be reading Nietzsche through the prism of Irish mythology and its pagan values, which necessitated giving as a means of affirming a heroic character or aristocratic status, rather than as fulfilment of Christian charity or some external obligation. If Finn or Osgar or their like would refuse hospitality in his home or assistance in the field, his reputation and his corresponding self-worth would be diminished. In this regard, moreover, Yeats's note seems to deny Nietzsche's sense that the value-creating and gift-giving capacity of master morality is not just an acceptance of the will to power, but also, somehow, a justification of it.

The passage in question explains the distinction between master morality and slave morality as the historical opposition between Rome and Judea, which saw Roman valuations regard Jewish culture as guilty 'of hatred of the entire human race' because it denigrated the aristocratic ideals of power and nobility. Although he decried antisemitism in contemporary Germany, Nietzsche was not averse to ascribing a central role to the Jewish people in the history of slave morality because they 'performed the miracle of inversion of values, by means of which life on earth received a new and dangerous charm for a couple of millenniums'. On the other hand, he describes the ancient Romans as the epitome of aristocratic bearing, because they looked down, with the pathos of distance, on the Jews as 'something like incarnated opposition to nature, a monstrosity, as it were, the very antipodes of themselves'. In this rendering, as Yeats points out, there is little sense of generosity, little sense of largesse, little sense even of noblesse oblige, on the part of the aristocratic peoples, who were in 'mortally hostile contradiction' with their slavish counterparts.[119] Nonetheless, the spiritual conflict between the two cultures remains in the background of modern moral distinctions, as aristocratic societies have given way to mass politics and democratic ideals.

Despite his reservations, Yeats would draw heavily on these terms and themes as he sought to articulate his vision for Irish culture in essays such as 'The Dramatic Movement' and 'First Principles', developed from his American lectures and published in *Samhain* prior to the opening of the Abbey Theatre in December 1904. These manifestos seek not only to describe the past activities of the National Theatre Society, but to detail the artistic ethos of the group – often over and against the Irish-Irelanders, Gaelic Leaguers, Catholic nationalists, and others who were competing to shape the national conscience – as the theatre moved forward in the hope of preparing a broader and more suitable audience for its work. 'The Dramatic Movement', for instance, warns against the hazards of ressentiment as a motivating force or organising principle, when the modern theatre is already in danger of drifting away 'from the living impulse of life': 'It is easy for us to hate England in this country, and we give that hatred something of nobility if we turn it now and again into hatred of the vulgarity of commercial syndicates, of all that commercial finish and pseudo-art she has done so much to cherish'.[120] Hatred of England, that is, must not be the slavish resentment of the master and his noble values, but rather the aristocratic disregard of its affinity for the modern, the vulgar, the commercial in its cultural values and artistic tastes, with the levelling tendencies that these forces produce. 'I would not be trying to form an Irish National Theatre', Yeats writes in 'First Principles', 'if I did not believe that there existed in Ireland, whether in the minds of a few people or of a great number I do not know, an energy of thought about life itself, a vivid sensitiveness as to the reality of things, powerful enough to overcome all those phantoms of the night'.[121] Even now, he can express gratitude for a 'ruling caste of free spirits' in Ireland, who have 'left the theatre in freedom', rather than the English censor, 'who forbids you to take a subject from the Bible, or from politics, or to picture public characters, or certain moral situations which are the foundation of some of the greatest plays in the world'.[122] Like the 'free souls' Yeats had praised to Gonne and the 'free spirits' whom Nietzsche addresses in the next section of the Common anthology, these leaders, at least in this rendering, possess a singular virtue: they have not succumbed to the constraints of slavish values, the vulgarity of popular tastes, or the prudery of moral conventions, unlike their counterparts in England.

As Yeats continued, even escalated, his advocacy for the separation of art and politics, literature and propaganda, in his writings on the theatre, he often coupled what amounted to the aesthetic and legislative functions of artistic production – and again, he found much of his source material for these ideas in Nietzsche's writings from Common's anthology. A few pages later, in a section titled 'The Natural System of Ranks and Castes' (derived from section 57 of *The Antichrist*), Nietzsche identifies the Manusmriti or *Law-book of Manu*, a Sanskrit text laying out the religious and legal duties of Hindus, as an example of a text that finally codifies and fixes the morality of a people after a long period of experience and experiment with values for living. Yeats marks the following sentence from the passage: 'At a certain point in the development of a nation, the book with the most penetrative insight pronounces that the experience according to which people are to live – *i.e.* according to which they *can* live – has at last been decided upon' (original emphasis).[123] According to Nietzsche, this is a crucial step in the history of a people because it brings an end to the process of experimentation by which values are tested, criticised, and selected; henceforth, these values no longer require conscious reflection and thus can become unconscious guides, integrated with instinct, which he claims is 'the prerequisite for every kind of superiority, for every kind of perfection in the art of living'. This passage has often been cited by those seeking a political philosophy in Nietzsche's writing because they identify in it a description of his ideal form of social and political organisation.[124] 'To draw up a law-book like that of Manu', he continues, 'means to permit a nation to get the upper hand, to become perfect, to be ambitious of the highest art of living'. Perhaps more than anything, as we witnessed in Chapter 1, Nietzsche advocates here for a politics that makes possible the emergence of 'the higher and the highest types', not so much the priestly caste protected by the laws of Manu as the great artists in life, the great innovators in morals, who have been suppressed by slave morality throughout history.[125]

At his most ambitious, Yeats envisioned the creation of a text that would somehow incorporate the great individual and his creative energy with the spirit of his people through a form of aesthetic striving. In the margin, he writes: 'A sacred book is a book written by a man whose self has been so exalted (not by denial but by an intensity like that of the vibrating vanishing string) that it becomes one with the self of the race'. This is, then, a model for his own work as an artist – the artist as legislator – who will promote the interest of the Irish people in a manner that transcends mere propaganda. As he writes in 'First Principles', 'this is because art, in its highest moments, is not deliberate creation, but the creation of intense feeling, of pure life'.[126] In this way, art asserts a life-affirming ethos that surpasses the codifications of laws or moral principles. But this is not to say that art has nothing to do with 'moral judgments'. Surely, he asserts, it has, 'and those judgments are those from which there is no appeal', as art clears away the old table of established standards in favour of new values founded on the aesthetic force of the creative personality, of the noble type. That the *Law-book of Manu* lays out a hierarchical vision of the social and political order, arranged according to 'natural' ranking of 'castes' and lead by an aristocracy of 'the fewest', 'the most intelligent men', is nonetheless crucial to Yeats: for only to this 'perfect caste' belongs the eminence 'to represent happiness, beauty, and goodness on the earth'. 'They rule', Nietzsche writes, 'not because they want to do so, but because they are rulers; they are not at liberty to hold the second place'.[127] 'Rulers, that is to say, the living, the wholly free, wholly self moving', Yeats clarifies in the margin as he links the code of Manu with the characteristics of those noble types who are free from the restrictions and ressentiment of slave morality. On the other hand, the lowest caste, which Nietzsche refers to as 'the mediocre', is associated with 'business, the unfree' by Yeats: 'they serve things, not life', he writes, as he links these ancient social distinctions with the crass materialistic and consumerist interests of the modern mob.

Whatever his concerns regarding those who 'serve things, not life', Yeats conjectures repeatedly during this period that Ireland is on the brink of revival, of 'awake[ning] into imaginative energy', to 'the seeming irresponsible creative power that is life itself', so that its artists can again 'create like the ancients', freed of the 'innumerable considerations of external probability and social utility'.[128] Unlike Nietzsche, he often connects this kind of creative energy to the belief in something 'immortal and imperishable' in the individual, but he declines to tie this faith to any doctrine or dogma: 'So long as that belief is not a formal thing, a man will create out of a joyful energy, seeking little for any external test of an impulse that may be sacred, and looking for no foundation outside life itself'.[129] More than anything, this means returning to the pagan 'faith' that is found in the 'old writers' and their bardic labours that 'keeps alive in the Gaelic traditions … a portion of the old imaginative life'. Yeats contrasts these native traditions with 'the rhetoric of newspapers' that 'mudd[ies] what had begun to seem a fountain of life with the feet of the mob', and threatens to sully 'the language of the Nation' and forfeit 'all that has made it worthy of revival, all that has made it a new energy of the mind'. But this is not a prescription for nativism or atavism. A writer is not less 'National', for Yeats, if he betrays the influence of foreign writers: indeed, if Ireland is on the verge of creating a literature of national importance its writers must open themselves to other national traditions and literary languages.[130] This kind of receptivity is necessary for any artist who would share her or 'his own intense nature' with an entire people – that is, any artist who would mould the collective conscience of a nation but not adhere to established models or succumb to communal pressures. In turn, his audience should have a kind of 'folk learning' that would connect them with the traditions of their people, even as they had enough highbrow culture and cosmopolitan tutelage to appreciate the value of foreign literatures. What is more, they should not expect patriotic propaganda or orthodox moral instruction from their writers. A national literature needs 'not to plead the National Cause, nor insist upon the Ten Commandments', but to persist in the 'praise of life'; it should not come to 'the defence of all that is codified for ready understanding ... but ... bring all the ways of men before that ancient tribunal of our sympathies'.[131]

Recasting Cuchulain and reconsidering the theatre

These concerns shed light on Yeats's continuing efforts to hone *On Baile's Strand* into a work suitable to his aims for a national literature: a work capable of sparking the imaginative energy of the Irish people, without resorting to popular sentiment or political oratory. While still on tour in the United States during January 1904, Yeats began revising the play for a proposed spring production in Dublin; a year later, after the opening productions at the Abbey Theatre, he returned to the play again, spending almost the entire year of 1905 reworking the manuscript. By 2 November, he could write that 'the first half of "Baile's Strand" is entirely new', as he had added a chorus of singing women, the oath of obedience for Cuchulain, and a more forceful and boastful presence for the hero.[132] Cuchulain begins by asserting his sense of duty to King Conchubar, though this dutifulness to political authority will not thwart his energy, his spirit: 'So much the better, for I have obeyed / In everything that touches peace and war. / But I will eat at whatsoever table / And sleep in whatsoever bed I fancy'.[133] As Yeats revised, this assertion of personal priority becomes more aggressive and assured: 'Why should I take it – why shou I be bound / Why should I not hunt & fish & ride / Where I ve [sic] a mind to – why not spread a sail / Or drop an oar into what tide I will / Why must I take this oath'.[134] Cuchulain will not, for now, bow to external restraints on his behaviour: he is, in other words, the exemplar of master morality, who 'regards *himself* as the determiner of worth, it is not necessary for him to be approved of, he passes the judgment ... In the foreground there is the feeling of plenitude and power which seeks to overflow, the happiness of high tension, the consciousness of riches which would fain give and bestow' (original emphasis).[135]

A national literature, according to Yeats, should provide a people with a 'scale of virtues', and, moreover, should teach them to 'value most highly those that approach the indefinable'. This aim will coalesce with the emergence of noble types in Irish society: 'Men will be born among us of whom it is possible to say, not "What a philanthropist", "What a patriot", "How practical a man", but, as we say of the men of the Renaissance, "What a nature", "How much abundant life"'. A national literature, that is, should stimulate an appreciation of these superior individuals: 'A feeling for the form of life, for the graciousness of life, for the dignity of life, for the moving limbs of life, for the nobleness of life, for all that cannot be written in codes, has always been greatest among the gifts of literature to mankind'.[136] In this regard, Cuchulain's acquiescence to Conchubar's oath is tragic precisely because it represents a capitulation to an authoritative code of conduct and a simultaneous defeat of the spirit, of his 'proud hard gift giving joyousness', as the knight pledges allegiance to the values and interests of the king – and, in the process, portends the Oath of Allegiance to the British Crown still required of Yeats's Irish contemporaries. Insofar as the great martial hero of antiquity is seen as an embodiment of Ireland itself, 'what is at stake here', as Doggett points out, 'is not simply Cuchulain's individual legacy but that of the Irish nation and by extension, the Celtic race'.[137]

The next few years, as Yeats continued his work as a dramatist, would severely test his ideas for a national theatre, for a national literature, and indeed his conception of the Irish nation itself. In October 1906, he was appointed one of the Directors of the Abbey Theatre, along with Gregory and Synge, and it was not long before controversy began to plague the operation, when riots broke out on the opening night of *The Playboy of the Western World* in January 1907. The story of the riots is too familiar to rehearse in any detail here, but suffice it to say that the play, with its portrayal of unscrupulous peasant men and women, had offended members of its audience on both moralistic and nationalistic grounds.[138] As Foster notes, cries of 'God save Ireland' alternated with 'Sinn Féin for ever'.[139] Writing in response to the riots, Yeats claimed for 'our writers the freedom to find in their own land every expression of good and evil necessary to their art, for Irish life contains, like all vigorous life, the seeds of all good and evil'.[140] The writer, that is, must not be bound to these moral categories in such a way that he is compelled to turn his eyes away from at least half of what Irish life contains. Instead, Yeats suggests, he must be granted, or grant himself, enough distance from the Irish people that he does not limit his depiction of them to the terms of slave morality. The riots at the Abbey Theatre represented, in his estimation, an assertion of this morality against the freedom of the artist and his assertion of an autonomous position in the field of cultural production. They represented, moreover, 'an increase of Irish disorder', because they challenged the hierarchical relationship between the aristocratic perspective of the writer and the slave values of 'the mob'. English artists may bend to the pressures of the priest and the censor, but Yeats declared that Irish artists 'did not learn in the houses that bred us a so suppliant knee' and thus implied that they should seek to impose their own standards on the production *and* consumption of national culture.[141]

From his perspective, the threat of disorder that Yeats now faced was due in no small part to the democratisation of the nationalist movement after the turn of the century, when its leaders passed their authority to the legions of young men who were forming cultural and political organisations during the period. At the time of the riots in Dublin, Yeats was lecturing to students in Aberdeen, Scotland, where he told his host, Sir Herbert J.C. Grierson, about his 'interest in Nietzsche as a counteractive to the spread of democratic vulgarity', before transitioning into a discussion 'of Sinn Féin (We Ourselves) and all he hoped from it for Ireland'.[142] But in the middle of the night, after Yeats's crowd-pleasing speech, Gregory's infamous telegram arrived at the Grierson home, notifying the poet and playwright of the riot, calling him back to the Abbey, and confirming his anxieties about the anarchic potential of the theatre-going public: 'Audience broke up in disorder at word shift' (Irish slang for an open-mouthed kiss). When he arrived back in Dublin for the subsequent performances of the play, Yeats commenced a vehement plea for artistic autonomy by denouncing the Sinn Féin 'Griffithites' and other upstart 'societies, clubs and leagues', which wielded their newly found influence, with 'tyranny and violence', against any supposed affront to their values.[143] He recognised, nonetheless, that he would have to struggle with these forces in order to impose his own vision of a legitimate national culture.

It was in the context of this perceived threat that Yeats turned to his next play on Cuchulain, *The Golden Helmet*, a play that has often been read as a satire on the mob mentality exhibited by the opponents of the Abbey Theatre. Finished in August 1907, the play projects an image of Cuchulain at his most noble and generous in contrast not just to his knightly counterparts, Laegerie and Conal, but to the general inhabitants of contemporary Dublin. *The Golden Helmet* opens with a scene demonstrating the basic pettiness of Laegerie and Conal, who resent what they imagine to be the 'victory and wealth and happiness flowing in on' Cuchulain during his sojourn in Scotland; they proceed to refuse hospitality to a traveller who approaches their abode, for they fail to recognise the figure as the returning hero himself.[144] In his absence, the two have endangered the land with their improvident behaviour, especially when faced with the Red Man, a spirit from the sea, to whom they owe the debt of one of their heads after entering into an ill-advised contest. In an expression of heroic generosity, of unfettered nobility, Cuchulain offers to pay the debt with his own head; his heroic actions, in sharp contrast to the behaviour of his intemperate friends and their haughty wives, promise to reestablish the honour of his people and the order to their society. When Yeats revised the play as *The Green Helmet* the following year, he retained the same basic scenario but translated the proud hard gift-giving joyousness of his hero into a compelling verse formulation, which the Red Man pronounces as he offers a prize to him at the conclusion of the play:

> And I choose the laughing lip
> That shall not turn from laughing whatever rise or fall,
> The heart that grows no bitterer although betrayed by all;
> The hand that loves to scatter; the life like a gambler's throw;
> And these things I make prosper, till a day come that I know,
> When heart and mind shall darken that the weak may end the strong,
> And the long-remembering harpers have matter for their song.[145]

With this, the Red Man identifies Cuchulain as the model of Irish nobility for all time to come. For he remains buoyant, despite all his trials and tribulations, and never becomes acrimonious, though his friends, his spouse, and his entire community have given him ample reason to be so. Instead, like Nietzsche's noble types, Yeats's hero is sustained by a sense of plenitude and power, which overflow in the form of bold actions and generous gifts. The Red Man, an embodiment of the force and vitality of nature, blesses these qualities and assures their continuance, at least until the day when the mendaciousness, the abasement, and the ressentiment of slave morality conquers noble values in modern Ireland.

Even as Yeats was recasting *The Golden Helmet* as *The Green Helmet*, he was becoming more and more dissatisfied with the national culture of his time and was taking up an increasingly aristocratic stance in relation both to Irish society and the Irish theatre. Synge's death in the spring of 1909 confirmed Yeats's alienation from an audience he found both resentful and philistine, a modern mass of men and women incapable of properly appreciating or perpetuating the ideals he sought to promote in his poetry and plays. During this period, with both Synge and Gregory suffering from ill health (and revisions to *The Golden Helmet* ongoing), Yeats became an even more imperious figure in the theatre: he presided over rehearsals with a firm hand and little regard for the feelings of his actors, stage crew, production designers, and other collaborators; he also composed a hectoring notice for 'playwrights who are sending plays to the Abbey', warning them to abstain from sending 'plays intended as popular entertainments' or designed 'to serve some obvious moral purpose'. Instead, he called for plays that 'contain[ed] some criticism of life founded on the experience or personal observation of the writer, or some vision of life, of Irish life by preference, important from its beauty or from some excellence of style'.[146] These were crucial matters of cultural distinction.

A few years earlier – when Yeats had insulted his sister, Elizabeth, in her role as principal of the Dun Emer Press – he was rebuked by his father for adopting what the elder Yeats considered to be a Nietzschean stance in his dealings: 'Is this the theory of the overman, if so, your demigodship is after all but a doctrinaire demigodship ... The men whom Nietzsche's theory fits are only great men of a sort, a sort of Yahoo great men'.[147] During this period, Russell had also upbraided him for assuming an autocratic approach to his work in the Abbey, to which Yeats responded in harshly Nietzschean tones that he desired 'the love of very few people, my equals or my superiors. The love of the rest would be a bond & an intrusion'.[148] The poet and playwright had confidently invested himself with the title of cultural nobility. Now, in 1909, he received a similar reproach from his longtime patroness, Annie Horniman, who accused him of doing business in a manner consistent with master morality as she prepared to withdraw sponsorship from the Abbey company:

> I know that you hold the Nietzschian [sic] doctrine that you have no duties towards those who have neither Genius, Beauty, Rank (race or family) nor Distinction, that there are 'Slaves' & that I am one of them & that no arrangement nor pact with me is of any importance ... If you can get people to take my place with whom you can feel on terms of Nietzschian equality the position would be much simpler ... It is very sad that it should have come to this between us (another bit of 'slave' sentiment;) but you have chosen your own course & I *accept* fully that you have a full right to it, in contradistinction to your contention that we poor 'slaves' should *bow* to everything said by a superman. (original emphasis)[149]

After a decade of contentious work in the theatre trade, Yeats's generosity of spirit had run out, at least in Horniman's view; despite his early assertion that 'the necessity of giving remains' for the noble type, he had grown more and more overbearing in his dealings with his many collaborators, not to mention his fickle audience. There would be no democracy of equals in the theatre. No doubt, as Foster suggests, Horniman's letter also adopts, though rather falteringly, a 'tone of imperious offensiveness', which befits this 'love-letter by other means', but together with the letters from Russell and his father, the missive corroborates Yeats's attempt to bring Nietzsche's philosophy to bear on his professional activities as a director of the theatre company.[150] Any attempt to soften the 'brutal implications' of his moral and political philosophy, which critics have located in Yeats's annotations to Common's volume, seems to have diminished; here, instead, there is more of the fierceness and arrogance that O'Brien warned against dismissing in both Nietzsche and Yeats.[151] The poet and playwright's professional stance placed him in tense conflict with other cultural workers, especially those women with whom he would collaborate, making the collective undertaking of a national theatre company nearly impossible. His position in the cultural field came at the cost of both abandoning the sense of generosity that is so central to the philosopher's ethical thinking and leaving behind the liberal cast of mind shared by his father and many of his colleagues.

Even as he became increasingly impatient with his work in the theatre, Yeats began to freely espouse the importance of 'Genius, Beauty, Rank' to his vision of Irish society, dismissing the value of democracy, equality, and sentimentality as belonging to a lower caste. In the journal entries published in 1909 as *Estrangement*, he went so far as to suggest that Ireland required 'a new statement of moral doctrine', which would espouse a 'lofty morality' in the interests of 'the most distinguished', even as it protected them from overthrow by a decadent 'classical morality', because it would also be accepted by 'the average man'.[152] He set himself up as a modern bard for the Irish people, but also the chosen artist of an elevated caste, a man of cultural 'Distinction' who might also speak to and for the masses and thereby transform the conscience of the Irish nation. At the same time, he began to align himself even more closely with the interests of the once-dominant Anglo-Irish Protestant Ascendancy in the hope of asserting his cultural power in the name of the values he associated with that class, whether or not the association was warranted by its history.

Nietzsche had provided him with a powerful articulation of pride and hardness that, while putting him at odds with his patroness and a large portion of his audience, nonetheless helped Yeats to develop a new vision for Irish national culture and the collective conscience of the Irish people. His contribution to Irish modernism during this period was not merely a repudiation of English cultural hegemony or revival of native cultural forms but a renovation of tradition to promote values that Yeats identified as a mark of nobility for his people, even as he made a claim to his own autonomy as a writer. And yet his disappointments in reaching an audience and imposing his sense of cultural and social distinction also reduced the generosity of his artistic spirit, as he grew ever more pessimistic about his theatrical project: 'The Abbey Theatre will fail to do its full work', he lamented in *Estrangement*, 'because there is no accepted authority to explain why the more difficult pleasure is the nobler pleasure'.[153] Yeats had tried to give his audience the gift of their own noble heritage, to provide them with a revived and enhanced image of themselves, but he had found them unwilling to accept his offering of aristocratic munificence. He was also becoming, like

Shaw, more interested in the new science of eugenics and more demoralised by what he called 'the new ill-breeding of Ireland, which may in a few years destroy all that has given Ireland a distinguished name in the world'.[154] In his estrangement, Yeats convinced himself of the 'analogy between the long-established life of the well-born and the artist's life', for he believed that both forms of existence aspired to something permanent, rather than the flotsam and jetsam of a modern world characterised by newspaper opinions and commercial interests. Both forms of life, moreover, 'despise the mob and suffer at its hands', finding happiness in distance and distinction, rather than participation or engagement.[155] Still, as we will see later in this study, Yeats maintained his ambition to forge a national conscience in the form of an aristocratic ethos, both proud and generous, both hard and joyous, suitable to the destiny of the Irish people, though his ambition would be inflected by new, and increasingly distressing, historical circumstances.

Notes

1. W.B. Yeats to Augusta Gregory, 26 December 1902, in John Kelly and Ronald Schuchard (eds), *The Collected Letters of W.B. Yeats, Vol. 3, 1901–1904* (Oxford: Clarendon, 1994), p. 284.
2. W.B. Yeats, 'William Blake and the Imagination', in Richard J. Finneran and George Bornstein (eds), *The Collected Works of W.B. Yeats, Vol. IV: Early Essays* (New York: Simon and Schuster, 2007), p. 85.
3. W.B. Yeats to Augusta Gregory, 26 December 1902, *Collected Letters*, p. 285.
4. W.B. Yeats, 'A Postscript', in Augusta Gregory (ed.), *Ideals in Ireland* (London: At the Unicorn, 1901), p. 105.
5. Marjorie Howes, *Yeats's Nations: Gender, Class, and Irishness* (Cambridge: Cambridge University Press, 1996), p. 66.
6. Qtd in W.B. Yeats, *The Collected Works of W.B. Yeats, Vol. II: The Plays*, David R. Clark and Rosalind E. Clark (eds) (New York: Scribner, 2001), p. 837.
7. W.B. Yeats, *The King's Threshold: Manuscript Materials*, Declan Kiely (ed.) (Ithaca: Cornell University Press, 2005), p. xxxvii.
8. Howes, *Yeats's Nations*, p. 83.
9. W.B. Yeats to John Quinn, 6 February 1903, *Collected Letters*, p. 313.
10. Over the course of his career, Yeats employs three different spellings of the mythic hero's name: Cuchulain, Cuchullain, and Cuchullin.
11. A sizeable critical literature has grown up around the impact of Nietzsche's writing on Yeats's career, beginning with the evidence from these letters in the early years of the twentieth century. The themes addressed by this literature cover the gamut of possible connections between the work of the philosopher and that of the poet and playwright: the concept of the hero, idea of the Superman, role of the artist, theory of personality, knowledge of the human psyche, notion of the mask, order of social rank, hostility to bourgeois materialism, aristocratic ideals

or morality, and conception of tragedy or tragic vision, to name just the most prominent topics. Many critics, beginning with Connor Cruise O'Brien in *The Suspecting Glance* (New York: Faber, 1972), have also attributed the more severe tone of Yeats's writing after the turn of the century to the influence of Nietzsche's philosophy, while others have traced this influence through his entire to career by comparing Yeats's theory of cyclical history and his conception of the connection between violence and culture, on the one hand, to Nietzsche's vision of eternal recurrence and his thesis on master morality, on the other. In *The Anxiety of Influence* (New York: Oxford University Press, 1973), Harold Bloom goes so far as to call Yeats 'Nietzsche's disciple' (p. 9). The critical literature has firmly established a connection between the two, but much of this criticism has been rather vague or speculative regarding the exact nature of the relationship, deploying terms and phrases such as 'major Nietzschean echoes', 'kinship', 'confluence', 'affinity', and even 'mildly Nietzschean themes'. Meanwhile, these critics have almost entirely overlooked the social and political forces that Yeats's art contended with as he read Nietzsche's philosophy. Francis Nesbitt Oppel's *Mask and Tragedy: Yeats and Nietzsche, 1902–1910* (Charlottesville: University of Virginia Press, 1987), for instance, does an admirable job of establishing Yeats's connection to Nietzsche: what he read, how he annotated it, and where direct signs of influence in his poems and plays are visible. But in its narrow insistence on Nietzsche's literary influence, the study often overstates its claims – largely ignoring not only other significant elements of the philosopher's thought, but also other historical matters bearing on the poet's work. See also Otto Bohlmann, *Yeats and Nietzsche: An Exploration of Major Echoes in the Writings of William Butler Yeats* (New York: Palgrave, 1982); Erich Heller, 'Yeats and Nietzsche: Reflections on Aestheticism and a Poet's Marginal Notes', in his *The Importance of Nietzsche: Ten Essays* (Chicago: Chicago University Press, 1988), pp. 127–40; Keith M. Mays, *Nietzsche and Modern Literature: Themes in Yeats, Rilke, Mann and Lawrence* (New York: Springer, 1990), pp. 16–44; Michael Valdez Moses, 'Nietzsche', in David Holdeman and Ben Levitas (eds), *W.B. Yeats in Context* (Cambridge: Cambridge University Press, 2010), pp. 266–75.

12 W.B. Yeats to Augusta Gregory, 14 January 1903, *Collected Letters*, p. 303.
13 While the many intertextual connections between Yeats and Nietzsche are undeniable, Denis Donoghue (*William Butler Yeats* (New York: Viking Press, 1971), pp. 53–57), Francis Nesbitt Oppel (*Mask and Tragedy*), Michael Valdez Moses ('The Rebirth of Tragedy: Yeats, Nietzsche, the Irish National Theatre, and the Anti-Modern Cult of Cuchulain', *Modernism/Modernity* 11:3 (September 2004), 561–79), and others have claimed that they were most insistent during the decade following Yeats's receipt of the three volumes from John Quinn. It may be that, as Roy Foster (*W.B. Yeats: A Life, I: The Apprentice Mage, 1865–1914* (Oxford: Oxford University Press, 1998), p. 272), Terence Brown (*The Life of W.B. Yeats* (New York: Wiley, 2001), p. 98), and others have argued, Yeats first encountered the writings or, at least, the name of Nietzsche through a series of articles by Havelock Ellis published in *Savoy* during the spring and summer of 1896. But there is no definitive evidence that the poet had developed

any interest in the German philosopher, much less read his work, until that fateful fall of 1902.

14 Quinn went on to offer '[a]nother reason' for his sending the copy of *Thus Spake Zarathustra*: 'I saw copy of it on [George] Moore's library table when I called at his house in company with your father the Saturday night before I went down to Galway. *If* he is writing a novel on the subject, he may be reading "Zarathustra" with the plan of the novel in his mind. This is only a supposition on my part. The two things may have no connection. Now that your play is finished you will not of course care to waste time on Nietzsche's *rhetoric*' (original emphasis). John Quinn to W.B. Yeats, 27 September 1902, in Richard J. Finneran (ed.), *Letters to W.B. Yeats* (London: Macmillan, 1977), p. 106.

15 Ibid., p. 106.

16 W.B. Yeats to John Quinn, 22 October 1902, *Collected Letters*, p. 239.

17 Qtd in Foster, *Yeats*, p. 269.

18 Qtd in Wim Van Mierlo, 'Introduction', in Wim Van Mierlo (ed.), Where There Is Nothing *and* The Unicorn from the Stars*: Manuscript Materials* (Ithaca: Cornell University Press, 2012), p. xxviii. Although Oppel acknowledges 'the extensive revisions appearing in 1903 were made after Yeats really read *Thus Spake Zarathustra*', she focuses only on the original 1902 version of the play, ignoring these revisions entirely in her analysis. The most she can say, then, is that 'it is easy to see how a look at Zarathustra might have fired Yeats, adding impetus to the creation of his already antisocial nonconforming hero' (Oppel, *Mask and Tragedy*, p. 49).

19 Van Mierlo, 'Introduction', p. xxix.

20 W.B. Yeats, *Where There Is Nothing* (London: A.H. Bullen, 1903), p. 92.

21 Friedrich Nietzsche, *Thus Spake Zarathustra: A Book for All and None*, Alexander Tille (trans.) (New York: Macmillan, 1896), p. 5.

22 Ibid., p. 3.

23 Ibid., p. 10.

24 Yeats, *Where There Is Nothing*, p. 106.

25 W.B. Yeats to John Quinn, 6 February 1903, *Collected Letters*, p. 312.

26 Yeats, *Where There Is Nothing*, p. 120.

27 Nietzsche, *Zarathustra*, p. 34.

28 Robert Gooding-Williams, *Zarathustra's Dionysian Modernism* (Palo Alto: Stanford University Press, 2001), p. 57.

29 Yeats, *Where There Is Nothing*, p. 98.

30 Foster, *Yeats*, p. 287.

31 Peter Sloterdijk, *Nietzsche Apostle*, Steven Corcoran (trans.) (Los Angeles: Semiotext(e), 2013), p. 57.

32 Gilles Deleuze, *Nietzsche and Philosophy*, Hugh Tomlinson (trans.) (New York: Columbia University Press, 2006), p. 85.

33 Richard White, 'Nietzsche on Generosity and the Gift-Giving Virtue', *British Journal of the History of Philosophy* 24:2 (2016), 348.

34 Sloterdijk, *Nietzsche*, p. 62.

35 W.B. Yeats, *The King's Threshold; and On Baile's Strand* (London: A.H. Bullen, 1904), p. 23.
36 Adrian Frazier notes that Nietzsche's influence on the play was even noticed by contemporary commentators, such as 'Chanel' in the *Leader* (31 October 1903), 'who regarded it as forgivable, because irrelevant to the plot' (*Behind the Scenes: Yeats, Horniman, and the Struggle for the Abbey Theatre* (Berkeley, University of California Press, 1990), p. 71).
37 Nietzsche, *Zarathustra*, p. 117.
38 Qtd in Frazier, *Behind the Scenes*, p. 68.
39 Yeats, *The King's Threshold; and On Baile's Strand*, p. 42.
40 Jane Francesca Elgee Wilde, *Ancient Legends, Mystic Charms, and Superstitions of Ireland* (Boston: Ticknor, 1888), p. 164.
41 Frazier, *Behind the Scenes*, p. 69.
42 Sloterdijk, *Nietzsche*, p. 48.
43 Ibid., p. 52.
44 W.B. Yeats to Augusta Gregory, 26 April 1903, *Collected Letters*, p. 348.
45 W.B. Yeats, 'A Canonical Book', in Colton Johnson (ed.), *The Collected Works of W.B. Yeats, Vol. X: Later Articles and Reviews* (New York: Scribner, 2010), p. 95.
46 Ibid., p. 96.
47 Ibid., p. 97.
48 Donald J. Childs, *Modernism and Eugenics: Woolf, Eliot, Yeats, and the Culture of Degeneration* (Cambridge: Cambridge University Press, 2001), p. 170.
49 Nietzsche, *Zarathustra*, p. 141.
50 See, for example, Elizabeth Cullingford, *Yeats, Ireland, Fascism* (New York: Springer, 1981), p. 49; Frazier, *Behind the Scenes*, pp. 66–67; Howes, *Yeats's Nations*, pp. 95–99.
51 Nietzsche, *Zarathustra*, p. 19.
52 See Joseph Hone, *W.B. Yeats: 1864–1939* (New York: Macmillan, 1962), p. 187; Suheil B. Bushrui, *Yeats's Verse-Plays: The Revisions 1900–1910* (New York: Clarendon, 1965), p. 115; and Oppel, *Mask and Tragedy*, p. 137.
53 Yeats, *The King's Threshold; and On Baile's Strand*, p. 66.
54 Bushrui, *Yeats's Verse-Plays*, p. 115.
55 Yeats, *The King's Threshold; and On Baile's Strand*, p. 55.
56 Nietzsche, *Zarathustra*, p. 8.
57 O'Brien, *The Suspecting Glance*, pp. 67–76.
58 Qtd in William Louis Strauss, *Joseph Chamberlain and the Theory of Imperialism* (American Council on Public Affairs, 1942), p. 79.
59 See Alan Graham, 'Sassenachs and Their Syphilization: The Irish Revival, Deanglicization, and Eugenics', in Kathryn Conrad (ed.), *Science, Technology, and Irish Modernism* (Syracuse: Syracuse University Press, 2019), pp. 203–14. See also Childs, *Modernism and Eugenics*, pp. 155, 189–93.
60 Friedrich Nietzsche, *A Genealogy of Morals*, William A. Haussmann (trans.) (New York: Macmillan, 1897), p. 38.
61 Ibid., p. 22.

62 Ibid., p. 23.
63 Ibid., p. 25.
64 Ibid., p. 26.
65 Friedrich Nietzsche, *The Case of Wagner, Nietzsche Contra Wagner, The Twilight of the Idols, The Antichrist*, Thomas Common (trans.) (London: Henry, 1896), p. 243.
66 W.B. Yeats, 'The Irish Literary Theatre, 1900', in Mary FitzGerald and Richard J. Finneran (eds), *The Collected Works of W.B. Yeats Volume VIII: The Irish Dramatic Movement, Volume VIII* (New York: Simon and Schuster, 2008), p. 162.
67 Ibid., p. 162.
68 Ibid., p. 161.
69 Ibid., p. 162.
70 Maude Gonne to W.B. Yeats, 7 May 1903, in Anna MacBride White and A. Norman Jeffares (eds), *The Gonne-Yeats Letters, 1893–1938* (Syracuse: Syracuse University Press, 1994), p. 169. Original emphasis.
71 Foster, *Yeats*, p. 287.
72 W.B. Yeats to Maude Gonne, late January 1903, in White and Jeffares (eds), *The Gonne-Yeats Letters*, p. 165. Original emphasis.
73 Foster, *Yeats*, p. 285.
74 Howes, *Yeats's Nations*, p. 103.
75 Nietzsche, *A Genealogy*, p. 20.
76 Maude Gonne to W.B. Yeats, 10 February 1903, in White and Jeffares (eds), *The Gonne-Yeats Letters*, p. 166.
77 W.B. Yeats, 'First Principles', in FitzGerald and Finneran (eds), *The Collected Works of W.B. Yeats Volume VIII: The Irish Dramatic Movement, Volume VIII*, p. 56.
78 A.C. Haddon and D.J. Cunningham, 'The Anthropometry Laboratory of Ireland', *Journal of the Anthropological Institute of Great Britain and Ireland* 21 (1892), 36.
79 Michael North, *The Political Aesthetic of Yeats, Eliot, Pound* (Cambridge: Cambridge University Press, 1991), p. 36.
80 Nietzsche, *A Genealogy*, p. 25.
81 North, *The Political Aesthetic*, p. 36.
82 See Gregory Castle, 'Introduction', in Gregory Castle and Patrick Bixby, *Standish O'Grady's Cuchulain: A Critical Edition* (Syracuse: Syracuse University Press, 2016), pp. 1–34.
83 Qtd in Hone, *W.B. Yeats*, p. 473.
84 Qtd in Claire Nally, *Envisioning Ireland: W.B. Yeats's Occult Nationalism* (New York: Peter Lang, 2010), p. 26.
85 Including: Oppel, *Mask and Tragedy*; Frazier, *Behind the Scenes*, p. 106; Norman Jeffares *W.B. Yeats: Man and Poet* (New York: Macmillan, 1996) pp. 152–53; Geraldine Higgins, *Heroic Revivals from Carlyle to Yeats* (New York: Palgrave, 2012), p. 108.
86 Higgins, *Heroic Revivals*, p. 109.

87 The recent publication of the manuscript materials of the play, painstakingly edited by Jared Curtis and Declan Kiely, makes it possible to do this work much more readily: W.B. Yeats, *On Baile's Strand: Manuscript Materials*, Jared Curtis and Declan Kiely (eds) (Ithaca: Cornell University Press, 2014).
88 Yeats, *On Baile's Strand*, p. 109.
89 Ibid., p. 119.
90 Ibid., p. 211.
91 Joseph Valente, *The Myth of Manliness in Irish National Culture, 1880–1922* (Urbana: University of Illinois Press, 2011), p. 175.
92 Yeats, *On Baile's Strand*, p. 207.
93 Nietzsche, *A Genealogy*, p. 20.
94 W.B. Yeats to Frank Fay, 20 January 1904, *Collected Letters*, p. 527.
95 Ibid., p. 527.
96 For an alternative reading of these dynamics, see Valdez Moses, 'The Rebirth of Tragedy', 561–79.
97 W.B. Yeats, *Poems, 1899–1905* (London: A.H. Bullen, 1906), p. 88.
98 Rob Doggett, *Deep-Rooted Things: Empire and Nation in the Poetry and Drama of William Butler Yeats* (South Bend: Notre Dame, 2006), p. 26.
99 Valdez Moses, 'The Rebirth of Tragedy', 561.
100 Ibid., 564.
101 Passages from the book, however, were translated and published in Thomas Common's 1901 anthology, *Nietzsche as Critic, Philosopher, Poet and Prophet*, which Yeats read and annotated during his American lecture tour in the winter of 1903–4. The episode demonstrates how Nietzsche's ideas circulated piecemeal in articles, in anthologies, and, perhaps most importantly, by word of mouth amongst writers and intellectuals across the British Isles and elsewhere during this period. But this does not mean that his writing was accessible everywhere. In an 8 October 1903 letter to the *Irish Times*, Yeats complains of the national library's policy of censorship: it has only just added books by Flaubert, and 'at this moment "The National Library" refuses to have any book written by Nietzsche, although it has a book upon his genius'. Qtd in W.B. Yeats, *Uncollected Prose*, John P. Frayne and Colton Johnson (eds) (New York: Macmillan, 1970), p. 5.
102 Arthur Symons, 'Nietzsche on Tragedy', *The Academy and Literature* LXIII (30 August 1902), 220.
103 H.W. Nevinson, 'Daily Chronicle. Office', *Daily Chronicle* (13 May 1903), 7.
104 W.B. Yeats, 'John Eglinton and Spiritual Art', in William Kirkpatrick Magee (ed.), *Literary Ideals in Ireland* (Dublin: T. Fisher Unwin, 1899), p. 31.
105 W.B. Yeats to George Russell, 14 May 1903, *Collected Letters*, p. 369.
106 W.B. Yeats to John Quinn, 15 May 1903, *Collected Letters*, p. 372.
107 Friedrich Nietzsche, *Nietzsche as Critic, Philosopher, Poet and Prophet*, Thomas Common (ed.) (London: Grant Richards, 1901), p. 110. Original emphasis.
108 W.B. Yeats, 'Preface', in Augusta Gregory, *Gods and Fighting Men* (London: John Murray, 1905), p. xxiii.

109 Laurence Lampert, *Nietzsche's Task: An Interpretation of* Beyond Good and Evil (New Haven: Yale University Press, 2001), p. 262.
110 Yeats, 'Preface', in Gregory, *Gods and Fighting Men*, p. xxiii.
111 Nietzsche, *Nietzsche as Critic*, p. 110. Original emphasis.
112 W.B. Yeats, 'A Note on National Drama', in Kirkpatrick Magee (ed.), *Literary Ideals in Ireland*, p. 18.
113 Bernard Shaw, *The Perfect Wagnerite: A Commentary on the Ring of the Niblungs* (London: Grant Richards, 1898), p. 48.
114 Cullingford, *Yeats, Ireland, Fascism*, p. 73.
115 Nietzsche, *Nietzsche as Critic*, p. 111. Original underlining.
116 Gregory, *Gods and Fighting Men*, p. 254.
117 Yeats, 'Preface', in Gregory, *Gods and Fighting Men*, p. xvii.
118 Nietzsche, *Nietzsche as Critic*, p. 112.
119 Ibid., p. 127.
120 W.B. Yeats, 'The Dramatic Movement', in FitzGerald and Finneran (eds), *The Collected Works of W.B. Yeats Volume VIII: The Irish Dramatic Movement, Volume VIII*, p. 44.
121 Yeats, 'First Principles', p. 56.
122 Yeats, 'The Dramatic Movement', p. 45.
123 Nietzsche, *Nietzsche as Critic*, p. 132.
124 Brian Leiter, 'Nietzsche's Moral and Political Philosophy', in Edward N. Zalta (ed.), *The Stanford Encyclopedia of Philosophy* (Winter 2015 Edition), https://plato.stanford.edu/archives/win2015/entries/nietzsche-moral-political/. Accessed 15 May 2021.
125 Nietzsche, *Nietzsche as Critic*, p. 134.
126 Yeats, 'First Principles', p. 56.
127 Nietzsche, *Nietzsche as Critic*, p. 134.
128 Yeats, 'First Principles', p. 58.
129 Ibid., p. 59.
130 Ibid., p. 64.
131 Ibid., pp. 65–66.
132 W.B. Yeats to A.H. Bullen, 2 November 1905, in *The Collected Letters of W.B. Yeats. Electronic Edition. Unpublished Letters (1905–1939)* (Charlottesville: InteLex Corporation, 2002), p. 237.
133 Yeats, *On Baile's Strand*, p. 281.
134 Ibid., p. 313.
135 Nietzsche, *Nietzsche as Critic*, p. 110.
136 Yeats, 'First Principles', p. 66.
137 Doggett, *Deep-Rooted Things*, p. 23.
138 For a nuanced view of the factors contributing to the riots, see David Cairns and Shaun Richard's landmark essay, 'Reading a Riot: The "Reading Formation" of Synge's Abbey Audience', *Literature and History* 13:2 (Fall 1987), 219–37.
139 Qtd in Foster, *Yeats*, p. 360.

140 W.B. Yeats, 'The Controversy over *The Playboy of the Western World*', in FitzGerald and Finneran (eds), *The Collected Works of W.B. Yeats Volume VIII: The Irish Dramatic Movement, Volume VIII*, p. 110.
141 Yeats, 'The Controversy', p. 111.
142 Grierson mistakenly remembers the visit to have occurred 'early in the year 1906', rather than 1907.
143 Yeats, 'The Controversy', p. 112.
144 W.B. Yeats, *'The Golden Helmet' and 'The Green Helmet': Manuscript Materials*, William P. Hogan (ed.) (Ithaca: Cornell University Press, 2009), p. 3.
145 Ibid., p. 137.
146 Qtd in George Cusack, *The Politics of Identity in Irish Drama: W.B. Yeats, Augusta Gregory and J.M Synge* (New York: Routledge, 2009), p. 15.
147 Qtd in John Kelly and Ronald Schuchard (eds), *The Collected Letters of W.B. Yeats, Volume IV, 1905–1907* (Oxford: Oxford University Press, 2005), p. 160.
148 WBY to Æ, 8 January 1906, in Kelly and Schuchard (eds), *The Collected Letters of W.B. Yeats, Volume IV, 1905–1907*, p. 290.
149 Qtd in Foster, *Yeats*, p. 406. Original emphasis.
150 Ibid., p. 407.
151 Connor Cruise O'Brien, 'Burke, Nietzsche and Yeats', in O'Brien, *The Suspecting Glance*, pp. 67–68.
152 W.B. Yeats, *Autobiographies: The Collected Works of W.B. Yeats, Volume 3*, William H. O'Donell and Douglas N. Archibald (eds) (New York: Scribner, 2015), p. 363.
153 Ibid., p. 362.
154 Ibid., p. 342.
155 Ibid., p. 350.

3

Joyce: 'James Overman'

On 13 July 1904, not long after he had commenced his first attempt to write a novel, a young James Joyce signed a brief note to George Roberts with the alias 'James Overman'. The self-applied label has been dismissed by many biographers and critics, including Richard Ellmann, as little more than an ironic attempt at self-enhancement – appended, as it is, to a comically hyperbolic letter card asking for the loan of a quid.[1] How else, after all, could we read this allusion to Nietzsche's most infamous creation? The reference, however, should not be so easily dismissed, if only to entertain the attitude behind Joyce's own suggestion in regard to another hero of his youth, so often associated with the philosopher: that a 'postcard written by Ibsen will be regarded as interesting and so will *A Doll's House*'.[2] Even if Joyce's note does not merit as much attention as *Ulysses*, *A Portrait of the Artist as a Young Man*, *Dubliners*, or *Stephen Hero*, it can help us to appreciate previously overlooked aspects of those texts, to shed some light on the complex relationship between Nietzsche and Joyce, and thus to understand better certain features of the novelist's modernist project, its ethical significance, and its affective investments. What could it mean for the young James Joyce – this shabby son of the new Catholic middle class in Ireland, colonial subject, provincial intellectual, cosmopolitan wannabe, unapologetic debtor, fledgling socialist, aspiring artist, great ironist – to call himself 'James Overman?' Addressing this question does not necessitate returning to an outmoded vision of Joyce as an isolated genius or international modernist, but observing anew the interplay between his Irish commitments, with their 'subaltern' or 'semicolonial' valences, and his flirtations with the avant-garde of European thought. To be sure, the multiple contexts and subject positions suggested in the question seem to promise not the isolation or foreclosure of meaning but the proliferation of interpretive possibilities. Moreover, the figure of the Overman or Übermensch possesses a stubborn, if evocative, indeterminacy of its own in Nietzsche's writing, which had so recently been translated into English and yet was so widely discussed and debated, casting the figure as a eugenicist daydream, evolutionary inevitability, heroic outcast, moral exemplar, atheistic monster, or masculinist archetype, to name just a few roles already assigned to him.

At the same time, there is virtually no closure to the ironic play of meaning in Joyce's oeuvre: the lifting and installing, the cutting and pasting into new contexts that he practised in his writing destabilise all hierarchical relations between the world and the word, with the use of allusions, quotations, echoes, and intertextual reactivations. There is in these techniques an element of mischief that pervades the texture of his writing, so that the reader must account for the simultaneous sanctioning and subversion of sources. And so his playful signature on a letter card can be read as an exemplary modernist gesture, confident, knowing, and slyly evasive. But a thick description of such utterances and their contexts is precisely what is needed to appreciate this early allusion, and other intertextual nods to Nietzsche's thought, from the greatest allusionist in modern literature. This approach, at the very least, can provide a starting point for understanding how Joyce's writing responds to a particular affective disposition, a complex set of feelings associated with Ireland's colonial status, which plagued both the artist and his people during the first decade of the twentieth century. Indeed, as we have witnessed, Nietzsche's Übermensch was already playing a significant role in shaping both the politics and the ethics of Irish modernism at this early moment in its history. But if Shaw had found in Nietzsche a vehicle for his socialist propaganda, if Yeats had sought in Nietzsche a means to rise above nationalist propaganda, Joyce had looked for something different in the philosopher, something more closely aligned with the concerns of individualism. The Übermensch postulated a means for breaking out of a history of personal and national *ressentiment*, those feelings of animosity that are a defensive reaction against the values of the powerful. Joyce's fictional alter ego, Stephen Dedalus, is fond of casting himself in the roles of various literary and mythological figures (the Count of Monte Cristo, Hamlet, and Jesus come immediately to mind) as a means to attain a satisfactory image of himself. As he set out on his career, Joyce similarly recognised himself in the image of the self-affirming individual, an image that promised a life beyond the social norms of bourgeois respectability, nationalist antipathy, and Catholic faith that had defined his youth. If the modernist artist in this conception comes to resemble that familiar heroic figure of literary history who somehow transcends the restrictions of his society and redeems its resentful values, the writer is nonetheless bound up in the same ecology of affects that generated those values and defined his national or racial conscience.

It may be rather unsurprising that Joyce entertained at least a passing interest in Nietzsche's thought during this period. After all, the budding novelist and the German philosopher shared a number of preoccupations:

not just the elevation of the exceptional individual, but the promises of the artistic vocation, the significance of classical culture, the shortcomings of Christianity and nationalism, the perspectival nature of human knowledge, and the emergence of certain affective orientations and their associated values. Ellmann suggests, moreover, that 'it was probably upon Nietzsche that Joyce drew when he expounded to his friends a neo-paganism that glorified selfishness, licentiousness, and pitilessness, and denounced gratitude and other "domestic virtues"'. But the celebrated biographer concludes that '[a]t heart Joyce can scarcely have been a Nietzschean anymore than he was a socialist; his interest was in the ordinary even more than in the extraordinary'.[3] This general assessment has been echoed in passing by numerous critics, sometimes with the desire to lump Nietzsche together with Ibsen and Hauptman as radical critics of modern society and bourgeois values, and often in an effort to lay the topic of Joyce and Nietzsche to rest by dismissing any allusion to the philosopher or his Übermensch as 'of a gratuitous and flippant nature'.[4] When critics have given more sustained attention to the relationship between the novelist and the philosopher, it has generally been to cite the 'affinities' in their perspectivist epistemologies or to read Joyce through Nietzschean themes such as the burden of history or the progress of the artist.[5] The focus of the present chapter is not so much affinity or influence as the possibility of tracing through Joyce's texts certain of Nietzsche's key ideas – including slave morality, bad conscience, the death of God and, of course, the emergence of the Übermensch – and of assessing the role that they played in the novelist's developing vision of the artistic vocation in relation to Irish society and its fraught colonial history.

To appreciate the significance of Joyce's epistolary gesture, then, it will be useful to outline the immediate context of the lettercard's composition. When Joyce wrote to Roberts, the young man was still suffering from bad conscience over the death of his mother and his inability to comfort her during her final illness, even as he was progressively adopting the spendthrift habits of his father, living as a debtor (that original form of bad conscience, according to Nietzsche) on what he could beg or borrow from others. His correspondence throughout the period – with Roberts, as well as Oliver St. John Gogarty and Constantine Curran – is made up of frequent and increasingly desperate requests for financial assistance. He signed these requests not only 'James Overman', but also 'Stephen Daedalus' or 'S.D.', indicating the proximity in his imagination between Nietzsche's Übermensch and the protagonist of his own recently commenced autobiographical novel. Padraic Colum, a friend of both Joyce and Roberts, later described the writer during this period as a 'borrower of small sums' and a 'shabbily dressed, penniless, lewd-spoken youth whose disreputability was striking because of the witticisms that rose out of it'.[6] There was, to be sure, something of the striking witticism, if not a bit of defensive irony, about his adopted pose as the self-overcoming Übermensch. There was also in Joyce's reference the flashing of some cultural capital, as the young man and aspiring artist offhandedly drops a reference to the most dangerous and disreputable figure in contemporary European letters. In writing to Roberts, who would become his nemesis as an editor at Maunsel and Sons some years later, he was appealing to a member of what Colum called a coterie of 'literary aspirants', who took tea and cakes at his mother's home to discuss Nietzsche, Ibsen, and Yeats, as they prepared themselves 'to take part in a revival of the Celtic spirit'.[7] Though he was not always welcome, Joyce had joined Roberts and Colum at meetings of the Irish National Theatre Society where the discussion ranged across the same topics discussed in the Colum home (it is worth noting that he had also visited with Yeats in London on 2 December 1902 and again later in the month, just as the poet was reading Nietzsche intently for the first time).

In the context of turn-of-the-century Ireland, Nietzsche supplied inspiration for an unconventional mode of *Bildung*, for overcoming not so much bourgeois morality or European decadence as the predicament of metrocolonial modernity and a specifically Irish variety of cultural malaise, including certain anxieties about manhood and masculinity in the context of British rule. His creation, the Übermensch, offered an inelegant young man like Joyce an alternative model of self-development, beyond gentility, respectability, and harmonious social integration; it offered the writer, what is more, an imported resource for envisioning his personal myth of the artist and his relation to his family, his friends, and his nation.

Two ways of understanding Nietzsche

Even as this attention to Nietzsche's writings exhibits a shared concern with the emergence or reemergence of a vibrant national culture, it also evinces the conflicts within and around the Revival movement – especially, as we saw in the Introduction, the debate at this time about the interrelations among international modernism, Irish Catholicism, and cultural nationalism. In his notorious broadside of 1904, 'The Holy Office', Joyce imagines himself 'Unfellowed, friendless and alone, / Indifferent as the herring bone, / Firm as the mountain ridges where / I flash my antlers on the air'.[8] The self-image provocatively combines Joyce's view of the fallen Home Rule leader Charles Stewart Parnell, as the defiant stag at bay, with what Ellmann would later identify as Zarathustra's mountaintop, above and beyond the provincial defenders of Irish art and culture. There, the young writer imagines that his strength has invoked the hatred of that 'motley crew' of the

Irish Literary Revival, including Yeats, Russell, Synge, and Gregory, as well as Colum, Roberts, Gogarty, and John Eglinton. The last of these figures was familiar to Joyce as a sub-librarian at the National Library, where the young man and his contemporaries would gather to deliver lectures and engage in debates as famously depicted in the 'Scylla and Charybdis' episode of *Ulysses*. Eglinton drew Joyce's ire in 1904 by rejecting the early autobiographical essay 'A Portrait of the Artist' for publication in his newly founded journal, *Dana*, where he would soon publish his own provocative article titled 'A Way of Understanding Nietzsche'. Sharing Joyce's sense of dissatisfaction with the parochial aspects of Irish cultural nationalism, the editors of *Dana* drew on their humanist rhetoric in a call for something like a belated Irish Enlightenment, which would help to create a generation, or at least a vocal minority, of free thinkers – a new literati who would refuse to submit to nationalistic fervour or religious authority, especially Catholic orthodoxy. In addition to contributions by the editors, the journal often published pieces by their friends such as George Moore and Russell, as well as articles with titles like 'On Reasonable Nationalism', 'Ireland in the New Century', 'The Policy of the Irish Party', and 'On the Possibility of a Thought Revival in Ireland', which challenged the reigning cultural and political dogmas of the day. Eglinton's essay on Nietzsche, as we also glimpsed in the Introduction, underwrites this project by asking Irish readers to consider the contributions of a radical European thinker. Yet Nietzsche is worth understanding, according to the essay, not simply for reasons of intellectual tourism or aloof cosmopolitanism, but precisely because the German philosopher speaks to native concerns, to the Irish mind and its dire want of 'independent thought'.

What is most striking about Eglinton's essay, particularly in relation to Joyce's writing, is that he frames his account of Nietzsche's work in terms of a national coming of age in Ireland, repeatedly employing tropes that suggest alternative modes of education and development. The piece opens by suggesting that, although Nietzsche may be described as 'a dangerous author', there is a natural safeguard against the corruption of his audience, the same 'as that which preserves the schoolboy from corruption by the more highly-coloured passages in the works of Horace and Ovid'.[9] Acknowledging that Nietzsche's philosophy 'stands or falls with the assertion that moral distinctions are … the creation of humanity itself', Eglinton explains the basic thesis of the 'First Essay' of *A Genealogy of Morals* by referring to the family, where parents impose slave morality on their children and it is a matter of expediency 'to whip little boys' out of the habit of lying.[10] Slave morality, he continues, 'points back to the creative power of "masters" who impose it' and is thus essentially reactive, rather than creative, and an impediment to 'virtue, in the old sense of manhood'.[11] Crucially, Nietzsche can teach

Eglinton's readers that, even when they give up or grow out of their servitude, they may still be prone to particular patterns of thought or habits of perception that keep them mired in a certain moral affect – ressentiment. Quoting from *Morgenröte* (*The Dawn of Day*), Eglinton stresses that 'we should change our *way of seeing* in order to arrive, perhaps very late, at changing our *way of feeling*' (original emphasis).[12] The Irish people, then, will be able to create new values for themselves only when they have learned to recognise their moral feelings as the aftereffect of the servitude that they have abandoned or are in the process of abandoning.

Eglinton goes on to suggest that the discussion of 'the morality of slaves and masters' leads inevitably to 'the doctrine of the Superman – that "far-off divine event" to which, according to Nietzsche, humanity moves'.[13] The Superman or Übermensch embodies the possibility of finally overcoming slavish values. It is here, however, that the critic parts company with the philosopher and a concept that, in a concession to Nordau and his influence, Eglinton finds 'undoubtedly a little crazy', because he believes that it represents a radical break from the humanist narrative of individual and collective development. Yet the idea of the Übermensch does provide Eglinton with an opportunity to address his abiding concern with the state of Irish culture, because the notion evokes in turn the fundamental idea of culture, as well as the social and the political conditions necessary for its flourishing. Considering the case of the great writer or artist, Eglinton claims contra Nietzsche that, while certain privileges are 'necessary for art', 'we must not therefore conclude that civilisation exists for the sake of the few'. To be sure, a year earlier in a review for the *United Irishman* titled 'The Philosophy of the Celtic Movement', Eglinton had chided Yeats for his increasingly aristocratic view of art along with his 'abandonment of the ordinary man, so to say, to his fate, and the contemptuous repudiation of all humanitarian ideals'. The critic concludes 'A Way of Understanding Nietzsche' in a manner that speaks both to the ambitions of Irish cultural nationalism in the early years of the century and to the modernist aspirations Stephen would articulate at the end of *A Portrait*: 'the efflorescence of art and culture is only a part of the life-history of a race' and '[b]ehind this efflorescence, and eventually displacing it, new ideas and new tendencies are germinating'.[14]

It is instructive to compare this perspective on Nietzsche to that of Thomas Kettle, a devout Catholic, a classmate of Joyce's, and another 'literary aspirant' in his coterie (albeit one with ambitions in politics, economics, and law, as well); for Kettle published two reviews of *Heralds of Revolt* by Father William Francis Barry in late 1904 and early 1905, which again help to make visible the structuring of the field of cultural production, its implicit rules and relations of force, during this key period for Irish modernism. Barry's book included chapters on topics such as Carlyle, the modern French novel, latter-day pagans, and Nietzsche, drawn from articles that the British Catholic priest had published in the *Dublin Review* and the *Quarterly Review* over a period of nearly twenty years. Kettle's reviews offer an account of 'Dr. Barry's point of view, which is, of course, in essentials *our* Catholic point of view, of the most crowded, shining, confused, intelligent, spacious and chaotic age of human experience' (original emphasis).[15] In stark contrast to Eglinton's call for independent thought, the reviewer shares in Barry's attempt to evaluate modern culture according to the beliefs, values, and sentiments that unite the members of the Catholic Church, especially in Ireland. Along with other Catholic university students, Kettle had protested the Irish Literary Theatre production of *The Countess Cathleen* in 1899 on the grounds that it had defamed the Irish Catholic peasantry, but he was no narrow-minded nationalist, having taken a sustained interest in both French and German culture early in his academic training. After graduating from University College Dublin with a Bachelor of Arts degree in Mental and Moral Science in 1902, he continued to gather with Joyce and their former classmates at the National Library and to attend other gatherings at UCD, where he sought to express the perspective of the new Catholic middle class in Ireland. But his receptiveness to a variety of international influences and his eagerness to engage with modern thought sometimes put him at odds with his fellow Catholic nationalists. In May 1904, he had attempted to publish a review of *Dana* in the *Freeman's Journal*, but it had been rejected by William Brayden on the grounds that the new journal was not worthy of serious attention; later in the year, he endeavoured to publish the review in the new UCD student publication, *St. Stephen's*, but was again denied, because the faculty supervisor, Rev. William Delany (who would later appear in *Stephen Hero* as the College President, Father Dillon), deemed that engaging 'in a deplorable controversy on the question of the existence of God, of elementary morality – and the like – [was] *utterly unsuited* to a magazine like this' (original emphasis).[16]

Kettle's reviews of *Heralds of Revolt* perform the Catholic 'duty' of interpreting 'the new thought' of Nietzsche and other 'great typical individuals' from the previous century 'in terms of our standards, of explaining the secret divergence from what presents itself to us as the supreme truth'. 'Catholicism and Modern Literature', originally a paper read at a National Library conference in December 1904 and later an essay published in *St. Stephen's* in January 1905, claims that this duty is the 'foundation of criticism', not just in England where his contemporaries are afforded more leisure for intellectual pursuits, but in Ireland, as well: 'For what we call the modernisation of Ireland has definitely begun'. This means that Catholics must try to understand the radical transformation of European thought in relation to God, man, and the world, and, indeed, 'to assimilate the most wholesome elements of contemporary culture'.[17] But here too is a vision of cultural flourishing. According to Kettle, at a moment when Catholicism across the Continent was coming to terms with artistic and theological modernism, Barry's book promised to 'inaugurate a creative florescence among richer Catholic minds' in Ireland, despite unaccommodating educational, economic, and political circumstances.[18] A month earlier, writing in the *New Ireland Review*, Kettle had identified Barry's chapter on Nietzsche as 'perhaps the best, and certainly the most "actual", chapter' in the study, because it deals directly with 'a great and original force' in the more general assault on Christianity over the course of the nineteenth century. In a journal known for its decidedly Catholic point of view, Kettle turns his attention to Nietzsche's 'Over-man' who 'imitating reality, rises above the distinction of good and evil, and lives as a pure artist, lives for ecstasy and rhythm'. In Nietzsche's philosophy, the pursuit of an uncorrupted aesthetic vocation creates 'an heroic glow', but according to Kettle, Barry's Catholic criticism strips this writing of its 'figured robes' to reveal the 'very madness of immorality'. Like Eglinton, Kettle diagnoses the idea of the Übermensch as the product of a kind of insanity, 'the absolute negation of social sense and spirit of pity and co-operation'. But despite this, he finds that Nietzsche's ideas have 'a tonic virtue', for they have an artistic and affective force, delivering 'the mind from that mawkish, merely sentimental pity which vainly effuses itself, utterly regarding the plain laws of life'. Nietzsche's illiberal and even misanthropic philosophy, with its unforgiving criticism of both modernity and Christianity, is thus partially redeemed by his exacting psychological insights. In the end, according to Kettle, his 'new thought' offers the collective conscience of the Irish an 'antidote against Puritanism and Pessimism', even as the Übermensch and his other key ideas deny any 'relish of salvation, social or philosophic'.[19] As we shall see in the next chapter, Kettle's subsequent commentaries on Nietzsche would play a crucial role in shaping the philosopher's reception in Ireland during the fraught years of world war and revolution.

Stephen Hero and the vocation of the artist

Making his first effort to write a novel in 1904 and 1905, Joyce began to respond to the provocation of this 'new thought', these trademark Nietzschean ideas, in his depiction of the emergence of a heroic artistic consciousness, as his protagonist seeks a type of secular salvation in the process of Daedalian self-fashioning and Nietzschean self-overcoming. Placed in the mouth of the eponymous protagonist of *Stephen Hero*, these allusions serve both to demonstrate what Seamus Deane calls Stephen's 'passion for thinking' and to estrange his developing interiority from the affective and ideological forces that have shaped his youth.[20] In Chapter 21 of the novel, which chronicles his early years at the university and his developing relationship with the devout Cranly, Stephen has begun to distance himself from religious authority, even as he remains reluctant to commit sacrilege. 'I am a product of Catholicism', he admits in conversation with his friend: 'I was sold to Rome before my birth. Now I have broken my slavery but I cannot in a moment destroy every feeling in my nature'.[21] Stephen's Bildung, his formation as an artist and a young man, will depend precisely on his ability to surmount this affective conditioning, this indoctrination into bad conscience and ressentiment fostered by Catholicism and its priests, and he announces here, for the first time, his refusal to 'submit to the Church'.[22] Like Nietzsche, Stephen suggests that Christian or 'slave' morality is characterised by debilitating feelings, which find solace in a form of imaginary revenge of the weak, needed in order to sustain a belief in their own 'good' in relation to the 'evil' of the strong. What Nietzsche calls 'self-overcoming' would require Stephen, the nascent 'Overman', to surmount slavish values and emotions through a process of brutal introspection and thus to open the way for a new set of values that proceed from strength to define the good according to his own noble valuation. The Overman, in this sense, is precisely one who has overcome himself. Übermensch is linked to *überwinden* (to overcome) in the sense of elevating man beyond the moralism of Christianity, the illusions of metaphysics, and the decadence of modernity, as well as the ressentiment and reactive values of the so-called herd. Catholicism is an obstacle to this process of personal development precisely insofar as it nurtures his ressentiment, which will therefore require, according to the ambitious young man, its removal from his thoughts and feelings, so far as that is possible.

Calling on Nietzschean terms again in Chapter 24, Stephen places his artistic ambitions in direct opposition to the sensibilities of his social class and his classmates at the university, who have entrusted their futures to the Catholic clergy and the promise of a world to come. In conversation again with Cranly, he proclaims that 'I will live a free and noble life', and further that '[m]y art will proceed from a free and noble source. It is too troublesome for me to adopt the manners of these slaves'.[23] The proclamation, like the ones that lead up to it, draws on terminology from *A Genealogy of Morals* to denote Stephen's aesthetic aspirations in terms of an ethical imperative developed out of a refined feeling or awareness that begins with the triumphant affirmation of the self and directs it attention to the affirmation of new values. With this proclamation, moreover, Stephen draws on the potential for self-affirmation that Nietzsche, more than anyone else, helped to initiate. The young man positions himself as one of what the philosopher calls 'the noble, the powerful, the higher-situated, the higher-minded', who regard 'themselves and their acting as of first rank, in contradistinction to everything low, low-minded, mean and vulgar'.[24] For Stephen, more than for Yeats, the emphasis here is ethical. Noble, in this sense, does not mean so much elevated in social rank as 'with lofty sentiment', or 'privileged in sentiment', where the *'pathos of distance'* from the herd affords the noble individual with 'the right of creating values' (original emphasis).[25] Again like Nietzsche, Stephen makes a strong differentiation between the active morality of strength and creativity, on the one hand, and the morality born out of weakness and conformity, on the other. The boys of the college bear 'the stamp of Jesuit training', which for all its scholarly seriousness cultivates a passive respect for the 'spiritual authorities of Catholicism and patriotism, and the temporal authorities of the hierarchy and the government', while muting 'the call to a larger and nobler life'.[26] The Jesuit fathers, who are expected to train 'the youth of Ireland for the higher walks of life', have instilled in them an admiration of 'Gladstone, physical science and the tragedies of Shakespeare' and a belief in 'the adjustment of Catholic teaching to everyday needs, in the Church diplomatic'.[27] Stephen, too, bears the stamp of this Jesuit training, which has provided him with crucial intellectual resources. But he is practising, or attempting to practise, an alternative form of self-cultivation as he declares his independence from clerical teachings and the 'manners of these slaves', while announcing the right to express himself on his own terms. The form of Nietzschean Bildung that Stephen pursues will not depend on respect for spiritual and temporal authorities, but on the cultivation of what is rare, noble, or 'aristocratic' in the exemplary individual, who is capable of generating his own values, his own ideals.

This Nietzschean ethos can already be glimpsed in Stephen's aesthetic theory as laid out in his essay 'Art & Life', which the young man reads to the students and faculty gathered for a meeting of the university debating society earlier in the novel. His theory of art is described as 'applied Aquinas', but the narrator lets us know that 'he set it forth plainly with a naïf air of discovering novelties', indicating both that he has taken Thomist philosophy beyond its original scope and that, in doing so, the enthusiastic undergraduate has unknowingly wandered into established domains of aesthetic theory.[28] In November 1904, not long after he settled in Trieste, Joyce himself had drawn on his rather sketchy schoolboy knowledge of Aquinas's *Summa Theologiae* (likely derived from the *Manuals of Catholic Philosophy* used at UCD) to write out a series of reflections on the nature of beauty in a notebook later housed in the National Library.[29] What is perhaps most striking about the integration of these materials into *Stephen Hero* is the degree of self-consciousness exhibited by the budding novelist who, acknowledging that Aquinas does not offer a theory of beauty per se, has Father Butt confess 'that it was a new sensation for him to hear Thomas Aquinas noted as an authority on esthetic philosophy'.[30] Thus, while we might agree with Colum's early claim that Stephen 'is unable to analyse his ideas or shape his life except in terms of the philosophy that the Catholic Church has evolved or adopted', we can also see what William York Tindall, Francis Fergusson, and others soon asserted of Joyce: that he made liberal and self-conscious use of these materials for very different ends than their original author.[31] In this case, his radical reinterpretation – we might even say, transvaluation – of Thomist principles leads Stephen into territory increasingly associated with Nietzsche and the avant-garde of European letters. For instance, he claims rather hyperbolically that

> In fine the truth is not that the artist requires a document of licence from householders entitling him to proceed in this or that fashion but that every age must look for its sanction to its poets and philosophers. The poet is the intense centre of the life of his age to which he stands in a relation than which none can be more vital. He alone is capable of absorbing in himself the life that surrounds him and of flinging it abroad again amid planetary music. When the poetic phenomenon is signalled in the heavens, exclaimed this heaven-ascending essayist, it is time for the critics to verify their calculations in accordance with it. It is time for them to acknowledge that here the imagination has contemplated intensely the truth of the being of the visible world and that beauty, the splendour of truth, has been born. The age, though it bury itself fathoms deep in formulas and machinery, has need of these realities which alone give and sustain life and it must await from those chosen centres of vivification the force to live, the security for life which can come to it only from them. Thus the spirit of man makes a continual affirmation.[32]

One would scour the works of Aquinas in vain for any analogous sentiments. But Nietzsche frequently proclaims that the affirmation of life is effectively an aesthetic undertaking by which the individual creatively and artistically comes to see existence as beautiful. Like Nietzsche in *Twilight of the Idols*, Stephen protests against the '*moralizing* tendency in art' (original emphasis), but again like Nietzsche, he does not argue in favour of *l'art pour l'art* – art with no other end than itself.[33] Instead, they both suggest that art should contribute to and participate in the overflowing of energy, which in turn strengthens or weakens certain valuations. This becomes the very precondition of art as what Nietzsche calls 'the great stimulus to life', so that artistic creation cannot be understood as purposeless or aimless, even if it also has the capacity to make manifest 'much that is ugly, harsh, and questionable in life'.[34] In *The Joyful Wisdom*, he professes the desire 'more and more to perceive the necessary characters in things as the beautiful: – I shall thus be one of those who beautify things. Amor fati: let that henceforth be my love! I do not want to wage war with this ugly ... And all in all, to sum up: I wish to be at any time hereafter only a yea-sayer!'.[35] This revaluation, as an assertion of the will to power, akin to what Stephen calls 'the force to live', works through the artist to take the life that surrounds him – the good, the bad, the ugly – and transform it into the beautiful. In this sense, the aesthetic and the ethical merge.

It may be no surprise that, after a *pro forma* vote of thanks to the essayist, the audience soon launches into a 'general attack' on his 'strangely unpopular manifesto', which concludes that the 'the moral welfare of the Irish people was menaced by such theories'.[36] The language of cultural conflict surrounds Stephen's aesthetic theorising. Even before its first public appearance, when Madden 'vaguely wonder[s] what state of mind could produce such irreverence', Stephen presents the manuscript to his friend as 'the first of my explosives'[37] in a manner that would become synonymous with Nietzsche, who understood himself as 'a philosopher – a terrible explosive in the presence of which everything is in danger', and who would famously claim that 'I am not a man, I am dynamite'.[38] What Stephen shares, or aspires to share, with Nietzsche is a commitment to symbolic transgression that, when joined to radical aestheticism and political scepticism, produces a direct opposition to the late-colonial petit-bourgeois moralism of his peers and professors in the college. This means that the work of art and its creator necessarily enter into conflict with both the 'oaths to his patria' that call for the loyalty of his peers and the very standards that Kettle attributes to Irish Catholic society and identifies as the foundation of criticism.[39] In 'Catholicism and Modern Literature', under the heading of 'Art for Art's sake', Kettle regrets the absence of 'pure artists' in Ireland, because he recognises that 'adherents of established things, like ourselves', have consistently advocated for the moral value of art and failed to appreciate its capacity 'to break up old moulds, and bring us back to the vital and throbbing stuff of sensation and feeling'.[40] As noted above, Eglinton had made similar appeals for an art that was 'the outcome of a strong interest in life itself',[41] and during this period Yeats had increasingly called for an art that was 'the creation of intense feeling, of pure life'.[42] But a young man in the debating society, Magee, deems the implications of the theory articulated by Stephen, despite their ostensible source in Thomist thought, as 'conceived in a spirit ... hostile to the spirit of religion itself', not least because it was the Church that 'had sustained and fostered the artistic temperament'.

As the criticisms mount, it becomes clear that they derive not only from a sense of religious devotion, but also a cultural nationalism aided, rather incongruously, by the dismissive theories of artistic decadence derived from Max Nordau and his followers. Magee goes on to say that he does not 'know much about Ibsen as Mr Daedalus did – nor did he want to know anything about him – but he knew that one of his plays was about the sanitary condition of a bathing-place'.[43] To be sure, this is precisely the kind of partial and partisan knowledge of Ibsen to be drawn from the chapter treating his work in *Degeneration*, which dedicates a number of pages to his *An Enemy of Society* only to reduce it to a play about 'bathing in contaminated water'.[44] As detailed in the Introduction, Nordau links Ibsen and Nietzsche as the poet and philosopher of 'ego-mania', the mental affliction of those degenerates who demonstrate an inappropriate preoccupation with interiority, and often exhibit a perversion of the instincts that leads to anti-social behaviour. Magee's invocation of Ibsen prompts another audience member to pronounce Stephen's essay 'a jingle of meaningless words, a clever presentation of vicious principles in the guise of artistic theories, a reproduction of the decadent literary opinions of exhausted European capitals'.[45] These are the very terms that Nordau uses to denounce the egomaniacal scribblings of Ibsen, to whom are attributed an 'empty jingle of words devoid of all import' and 'meaningless phrases', and Nietzsche, to whom are ascribed a 'jingle and clatter of words' and 'wholly incomprehensible, meaningless sounds'.[46] But, more than this, demonstrating a pervasive anxiety about racial and national collapse, the audience heaps scorn on any affiliation with metropolitan fin-de-siècle culture, which Nordau saw not as the acme of civilisation but as a breeding ground for nervous maladies associated with modern artistic schools: 'The peasant population, and a part of the working classes and the *bourgeoisie*, are sound. I assert only the decay of the rich inhabitants of the great cities and the leading classes'.[47] For his 'professed cosmopolitism', Stephen is condemned as a 'renegade from the Nationalist ranks', whose 'insidious theory that art can be separated from morality' had offended the general acceptance of 'moral art, art that elevated, above all, national art'.

The battle lines in this skirmish over literary ideals have been clearly drawn. 'The climax of aggressiveness was reached', we are told,

> when Hughes stood up. He declared in ringing Northern accents that the moral welfare of the Irish people was «menaced by such theories.» They wanted no foreign filth. Mr Daedalus might read what authors he liked, of course, but the Irish people had their own glorious literature where they could always find fresh ideals to spur them on to new patriotic endeavours.[48]

Stephen, for his part, holds that 'it cannot be urged too strongly on the public mind that the tradition of art is with the artists and that even if they do not make it their invariable practice to outrage these limits of decency the public mind has no right to conclude therefrom that they do not arrogate for themselves an entire liberty to do so if they choose'.[49] To accomplish this task, he must reject the morality of the Catholic Church and the 'oaths of his patria',[50] the value of altruism, and even happiness, all in order to produce what Nietzsche calls a more 'severe self-love'.[51] It would be too easy to dismiss this as mere posturing on the part of a young artist in a restrictive social environment – that is, to see these details as contributing all too directly to the romantic modernist cliché of the artist as a heroic outsider. What is less evident, but more important, is the way that Stephen draws on the modernist culture capital of writers like Ibsen and Nietzsche, so that he might, however desperately, elevate himself to a leading position in a society of outsiders, who draw on native and foreign resources alike in their efforts to assert distinction for their side in a cultural civil war.

In the midst of this struggle, Stephen is subject to the entreaties of the Catholic authorities, who send 'an embassy of nimble pleaders' to state their case – though it appears from the way they are implicated in Stephen's reflections that these pleaders are, in fact, internalised ones who have infiltrated his conscience and now 'address every side of his nature in turn'. With this shift towards interiority, and away from the more conventional dialogical form that dominates the earlier chapters of the novel, the scene may be read as dramatising the difficult process of self-overcoming that is taking place inside the young man, even as he is hailed to take his place within a certain ideological formation. Recognising the social and cultural forces that impinge on Stephen's 'individual liberty', the ambassadors of the Church also acknowledge his 'modern' reluctance to make pledges and his need to see 'himself [as] the greatest sceptic concerning the perfervid enthusiasms of the patriots'.[52] The members of the priestly caste, as educators and spiritual guides, are largely responsible for breeding such enthusiasms among the Irish people, who (so Stephen seems to believe) have come to resent the very traits with which he associates himself – nobility, intellect, creativity. But as the entreaties continue, they become more and more cynical, until they even suggest sympathy with various Nietzschean positions: they caution against 'convictions' in light of the changeability of the human mind and later endorse Stephen's belief in the 'eminence of the aristocratic class and in the order of a society which secures that eminence'.[53] The ambassadors, moreover, cynically appeal to Stephen's sense of superiority in a way that recalls Nietzsche's descriptions of aristocratic or master morality: 'Do you imagine that manners will become less ignoble, intellectual and artistic endeavour less conditioned, if the ignorant, enthusiastic, spiritual slovens whom we have subjected subject us?'[54] With these queries, Stephen's interlocutors claim sympathy with his sense of superiority, which positions his 'nobility' over and against the manners and mores of the so-called slaves, with their religious and patriotic enthusiasms.

This cynical will to power becomes definitive of the Church's role in Ireland. In Stephen's thoughts, at least, the ambassadors of the Church are willing to acknowledge his fondness for proclaiming that 'the Absolute is dead' – and even to entertain the notion themselves – though they refuse to accept the consequence of the proclamation.[55] Although Stephen's denial of the Absolute may have roots in the relativism of Walter Pater, Anatole France, and others (the 'ambassadors' recognise that it is 'a mark of the modern spirit to be shy in the presence of all absolute statements'), his formulation is cleary right out of Nietzsche, with its prophetic, quasi-religious phrasing.[56] Again, his claim is hyperbolic, even arrogant, inviting us to recognise its modernist cachet as a form of cultural dissent, but in the same moment revealing the overweening arrogance, however defensive, of the young man. Borrowing on the shock value of the notorious assertion that 'God is dead', first made in *The Joyful Wisdom* and then repeated in *Thus Spake Zarathustra*, Stephen's claim denies the existence of some metaphysical source of authority that might offer universal foundations for religious, ethical, or moral codes. As the ambassadors of the Church repeat his claim back to him, Stephen becomes (at least in his own mind) a quotable cultural dissident like his infamous German predecessor, and, even in this slightly tempered form, his pithy obituary forms an eminently modern and modernist challenge to the status of all values that claim ontological privilege or the validation of an ultimate order. The modernising emissaries of the Church seem untroubled by all this, however, as they offer the young man a position in their 'patrician order', from which he can continue 'to exercise his contemptuous faculties' against belief even as he enjoys the rewards attained by the very doctrines he challenges.[57] The priests in Stephen's mind appear to have slid from cynicism to nihilism in *both* senses of the latter term that Walter Kaufmann identified in Nietzsche's thought: 'in asserting the existence of God and thus robbing *this* world of its ultimate significance, and also in denying God and thus robbing *everything* of meaning and value' (original emphasis).[58] In the end, the ambassadors of the Church compel Stephen to recognise that 'in temper and in mind [he is] still Catholic', that 'Catholicism is in [his] blood', and, with another query, that his desire to overcome this in himself is misguided: 'can you be fatuous enough to think that simply by being wrong-headed you can recreate entirely your mind and temper or can clear your blood of what you may call the Catholic infection?' They counsel not a personal revolution that might forge his conscience anew but instead 'a course of moderation', which can only seem like a slow defeat for a young man of Stephen's enthusiasms.[59]

This allusion to Nietzsche's philosophy provides an important point of reference for understanding Stephen's conception of his role as an artist in Irish society, a role that casts him as an inventor of personal and communal values. It provides, moreover, a significant context for appreciating Joyce's use of the moniker James Overman, for at the close of the first book of *Thus Spake Zarathustra*, the prophet proclaims: '*Dead are all Gods: now we will that beyond-man* [Übermensch] *live*' (original emphasis).[60] After the demise of the divine or the Absolute, man is open to an ethical transformation and a renovated culture to fill the void left behind: as Eglinton puts it, in a manner designed to provoke his Catholic readers, those who have repudiated God 'will be called upon, in a world bankrupt in ideals, to create new moral values and new Gods'.[61] The alternative is nihilism. The ambassadors in Stephen's mind, having accepted that they may well be wrong regarding their belief in the Absolute, ask if anything remains then for the young man 'but an intellectual disdain'. This question serves as a rejection of Nietzschean critique and an invitation to comradeship with them. In joining their order, the emissaries of the Church suggest that Stephen will protect himself from the 'revolutionary notions' – the critical, dissenting, even heretical thoughts – that might derail his career as an artist in their conception.[62] As Gregory Castle points out, the Jesuits are inviting him into the safety of an established institution, which would assure him something like the telos of traditional Bildung, and his story something like the narrative trajectory of the conventional Bildungsroman; but they also threaten to 'short-circuit the Bildung process, shunting him off the pathway leading to the fulfilment of his artistic aspirations'.[63] Stephen believes that the responsibility for taking the place of God, for establishing new ideals or standards, falls to the artist: that exemplary individual who becomes the only source and guarantor of what is to be valued, to be sought after, to be recognised as beautiful and true. The Nietzschean idea thus becomes a mark of cultural dissidence. The Nietzsche of the young Joyce, in other words, shares much with the Nietzsche of Kaufmann, who recuperated the philosopher's image from the taint of National Socialism by transforming him into the prophet of an alienated artistic heroism. In the context of turn-of-the-century Ireland, where the Catholic Church, the British Empire, and the Irish nationalist movement all exert their powerful influence, Nietzsche and his Übermensch offer a model of individual dissent, of individual freedom, that Stephen (and Joyce) fails to find in these ideological formations.

'A Painful Case', *A Portrait*, and *A Genealogy*

That the terms in Stephen's thoughts derive, in no small part, from Joyce's reading of Nietzsche's philosophy is substantiated by evidence in his *Dubliners* story, 'A Painful Case', written at the same time as these late chapters of *Stephen Hero*. Throughout the summer of 1905, the young writer worked alternately on the story and the novel, completing Chapters 24 and 25 of *Stephen Hero* by the end of June and likely beginning composition of 'A Painful Case' the same month, completing the second draft of the story by 15 August. The dates of composition are significant here because in the first draft of the story Joyce places two volumes of Nietzsche's writing on his protagonist's bookshelf: *The Gay Science*[64] and *Thus Spake Zarathustra*, the texts in which the philosopher announces the demise of God and rise of the Übermensch. There is no doubt that James Duffy shares certain characteristics and predilections with Stephen and with Joyce himself, especially their affection for German culture, including not just the philosophy of Nietzsche, but the drama of Gerhardt Hauptman.

This affection for avant-garde Continental culture is emblematic of their artistic and intellectual aspirations, as well as their sense of being outsiders to Dublin society, each cultivating an anti-social demeanour in relation to the 'rabble' of the city. Given these details, critics have often associated Duffy with the figure of the Übermensch, as an aloof, freethinking, self-sufficient individual, who offers an image of self-criticism on Joyce's part in the wake of his own flirtations with Nietzsche's philosophy (flirtations that, according to this line of thinking, had already ceased). But we should also sense the irony here: Tom Steele and Simon Joyce both note that, like Duffy, many '*petit-bourgeois* intellectuals denied the opportunity of constructing themselves like gentlemen', instead 'sought expression in its opposite, the superman'.[65] Or, as Sloterdijk puts it, 'Nietzsche's free spirit brand ran a greater risk of being imitated by a success-hungry movement of losers'.[66] To be sure, after severing ties with his only real human relation, Mrs Sinico, Duffy develops an attraction to the newly fashionable brand of Nietzschean individualism, which speaks to the lofty sense of self enjoyed by one who has 'neither companions nor friends, church nor creed'.[67] But, his desire for cultural distinction, which Duffy attempts to satisfy through a lonely autodidacticism, conflicts with his life of Irish petit-bourgeois penury, made evident in the drab surroundings of his room and the nearly comic deficiency of his bookcase. The apparent heterogeneity of his tastes – 'a complete Wordsworth stood at one end of the lowest shelf and a copy of the Maynooth Catechism, sewn into the cloth cover of a notebook, stood at one end of the top shelf' – the ostensible muddle of genres and ranks, the seeming arbitrariness of his acquisitions, all speak to his tenuous hold on cultural capital.[68]

The problem with Duffy, in this sense, is precisely that he is not 'Nietzschean' enough and that the character, some two decades older than his creator, represents a cautionary tale for Joyce or Stephen should either not follow the path of self-overcoming. Duffy is the undesirable outcome of the cultural malaise or 'paralysis' that afflicts Joyce and his contemporaries, who suffered from a form of material and intellectual deprivation that threatened their capacity for self-development. Rather than a bohemian, an anarchist, or a revolutionary, Duffy is a meek middle-aged, middle-class man: he entertains socialist ideas but abandons them at the first sign of difficulty; he thinks of robbing the bank where he works but realises the correct circumstances will never arise; he fancies himself in the mode of an artist and man of culture, but he stolidly retains his clerkship; finally, when Mrs Sinico presents him with the possibility of an unconventional – that is, adulterous – relationship, he retreats back into his previous isolation and idleness. Unlike Stephen, who seeks to rise above the conditions of deprivation that define his youth in Dublin, Duffy remains mired in his all-too-Irish state of self-delusion as 'a suburban would-be Nietzschean'.[69] In another instance of irony, as the volumes of Nietzsche sit neatly arranged on his bookshelves, Duffy dines moderately every evening at George's Street and 'reads the evening paper for dessert', internalising the conventional values of late Victorian Dublin.[70] Later, as he reads the details of Mrs Sinico's death in the newspaper, 'the threadbare phrases, the inane expressions of sympathy, the cautious words of a reporter won over to conceal the details of a commonplace vulgar death attack his stomach' and he feels 'degraded'.[71] Duffy may at least feign to share Nietzsche's famous antipathy towards 'newspaper ethics', but book ownership only works towards the accumulation of cultural distinction if one can prove that one has read the books. Indeed, the satire works on the assumption that many of his books remain unread. Despite his pretensions to moral, or more accurately, amoral superiority, Duffy is finally unable to overcome the social norms that restrain his thought and behaviour. James Duffy is, in short, a failed 'James Overman'.

Joyce's subsequent novel, *A Portrait of the Artist as a Young Man*, may be read as the story of how Stephen finally arrives at his vision of an alternative future. In chronicling Stephen's early life, which is largely absent from what survives of *Stephen Hero*, *A Portrait* presents us with an individual still prey to slave morality, ressentiment, and bad conscience, as it loosely recapitulates the broader narrative of decadence laid out so influentially by Nietzsche's *A Genealogy of Morals*. Like many of his counterparts in the history of the novel, Joyce's protagonist grows up in the context of the moral authority and religious pedagogy of the Church, though he experiences the torments of sin and confession even more intensely than most. The imagery of the famous hell-fire sermon in Chapter 2 vividly imparts the lesson that damned souls will experience an intense 'pain of conscience': 'Just as in dead bodies worms are engendered by putrefaction so in the souls of the lost there arises a perpetual remorse from the putrefaction of sin, the sting of conscience, the worm, as Pope Innocent the Third calls it, of the triple sting'.[72] Here, transforming ressentiment into self-righteousness, the Catholic priest ministers to his sick herd and in the process cultivates a sense of self-hatred or bad conscience, all as a means to transvalue the meanings of power and vitality. Stephen's stern teacher, Father Arnall, then describes at length and in horrifying detail 'the triple sting' of conscience suffered by these miserable wretches, to whom God imparts His own knowledge of sin, so that they may understand how their actions appear in his eyes. Soon after hearing the protracted sermon, Stephen manifests what might be called a textbook example of bad conscience, endured by an individual who has transgressed religious authority and who, out of fear as much as anything else, has promised to amend his ways. The young man, that is, has become conscious of a debt to be repaid to his progenitor, who 'called [his] soul into existence out of nothing', loves him 'as only a God can love', and will receive him with open arms even though he has 'sinned against Him'.[73] Stephen feels the pangs of bad conscience all the more acutely because he has so recently and so often succumbed to the 'wasting fires of lust', which have led him, 'like some baffled prowling beast' through gloomy backstreets of Dublin and into the arms of a series of prostitutes. Prior to his experience of the sermon, at the end of Chapter 2, Stephen had revelled in his burgeoning sexuality precisely as a form of social and theological transgression: 'he wanted to sin with another of his kind, to force another being to sin with him and to exult with her in sin'.[74] In the midst of these transgressions, the young man comes to see that 'his soul lusted after its own destruction' and 'a certain pride, a certain awe' at the perceived gravity of his offence holds him back from prayer and devotion.[75]

But, with his interminable sermon, Father Arnall takes this raw material and compels Stephen to reinterpret his inchoate feeling of guilt – what Nietzsche calls the 'animal "bad conscience"' – as 'sin' in the direst sense and, in doing so, accomplishes precisely what the philosopher identifies as the aim of the ascetic priest, 'this real artist in feelings of guilt': turning cruelty inward to 'the make the chords of the human soul resound with every kind of lacerating and ecstatic music'.[76] As the sermon comes to an end, Stephen prays 'with his heart':

– my God! –
– my God! –
– I am heartily sorry –
– I am heartily sorry –
– for having offended Thee –
– for having offended Thee –
– and I detest my sins –
– and I detest my sins –[77]

And so on. Later, returning to his room alone that evening, he continues the process of self-laceration:

> Could it be that he, Stephen Dedalus, had done those things? His conscience sighed in answer. Yes, he had done them, secretly, filthily, time after time and, hardened in sinful impenitence, he had dared to wear the mask of holiness before the tabernacle itself while his soul within was a living mass of corruption.[78]

It is only when Stephen resolves to confess, to 'abas[e] himself in the awe of God' that the 'ache of conscience' he has suffered begins to subside and he is able to distance himself from that 'bestial part of the body able to understand bestiality and desire bestiality'.[79]

Stephen's story, at this point, has become the clichéd tale of a repentant sinner, but in following this plotline, the young man also adheres closely to the details of Nietzsche's genealogical account of guilt, bad conscience, asceticism, and ressentiment. By reinterpreting his emotional experience – his suffering from self – with the aid of the ascetic priest, the young man moves further and further in the direction of bad conscience as he ruminates incessantly on his past deeds. In Chapter 4 of the novel, responding to his intensified 'ache of conscience', Stephen adopts the ascetic ideal much as described in the 'Third Essay' of *A Genealogy of Morals*:[80] 'here', according to Nietzsche, 'physiological thriving itself – especially, its expression, beauty and joy, is viewed with dark and jealous eye; whereas a satisfaction is felt and *sought* in all abortive, degenerate growth, in pain, in mishap, in ugliness, in voluntary detraction, in self-mortification, in self-castigation, in self-sacrificing' (original emphasis).[81] Dedicating each day of the week to a strict form of devotion, and each part of the day to his new duties, Stephen enters into a regime of penitence that includes the mortification of each of his five senses 'with the most assiduous ingenuity of inventiveness' that in seeking out 'bad odours', sitting in the 'most uncomfortable positions', and suffering 'patiently every itch and pain'.[82] 'His course of intricate piety and self-restraint',[83] emphasising prayer and fasting, vividly exemplifies the naysaying ethic of what Nietzsche calls 'the self-racking sinner' by which spiritual values are elevated above sensual pleasures and worldly ambitions.[84] But it also gives Stephen, ever the object of irony, the sense that he is paying back his debt and even accruing a kind of spiritual capital: 'he seemed to feel his soul in devotion pressing like fingers the keyboard of a great cash register and to see the amount of his purchase start forth immediately in heaven'.[85]

His course of devotion and redemption thus follows precisely the trajectory that Nietzsche traces in his *A Genealogy*:

> And truly, by means of this system of processes, former depression, heaviness and weariness were completely *conquered*; life once more became *very*

> interesting. Waking, forever waking, overwatched, glowing, charred, pining and yet not tired – thus looked the man, the 'sinner', who now had become initiated in *these* mysteries.[86]

No better summary could be articulated of Stephen's journey through asceticism toward redemption, as abortive and ironic as it is. As he carries on, he thrills at the knowledge that at any moment he might surrender to the 'voice of the flesh', and in the power that he wields over the fate of his eternal soul, which is preserved from destruction only 'by a sudden act of will or sudden ejaculation'.[87] When his devotion attracts the attention of the director of Belvedere College, who summons Stephen to his office and asks the young man whether he has considered the priestly calling, it is precisely the power of the position that the clergyman emphasises:

> No king or emperor on this earth has the power of the priest of God. No angel or archangel in heaven, no saint, not even the Blessed Virgin herself has the power of a priest of God: the power of the keys, the power to bind and to loose from sin, the power of exorcism, the power to cast out from the creatures of God the evil spirits that have power over them, the power, the authority, to make the great God of Heaven come down upon the altar and take the form of bread and wine. What an awful power, Stephen![88]

And it is precisely the power of the priesthood that attracts Stephen, for it confirms the sense of power that he has already experienced in his private reflections: 'A flame began to flutter again on Stephen's cheek as he heard in this proud address an echo of his own proud musings. How often had he seen himself as a priest wielding calmly and humbly the awful power of which angels and saints stood in reverence!'[89] It is in this sense that Nietzsche identifies the ascetic life as 'a self-contraction': 'Here a most extraordinary resentment prevails, – the resentment of an insatiate instinct and will to power, which would fain lord it – not merely over something in life but over life itself, over the deepest, strongest, and most fundamental conditions of life'.[90] The ascetic priest must be 'sick' like those whom he presides over but he must also be strong, so that he can more completely master himself and his will to power, in order to secure his position over them as a 'an opposition, a support, a constraint, a taskmaster, a tyrant, a god for them'.[91]

Compelled by some vague instinct, Stephen will presently reject the offer of life defined by 'social or religious orders' in favour of a university career and its promise of a worldlier form of knowledge, though the rejection leaves him mired in his dreary everyday existence in metrocolonial Dublin.[92] Even after his grand artistic epiphany at the end of Chapter 4, which hails him to a life beyond 'dull gross voice of the world of duties and despair', his vision of ecstatic affirmation of life – 'Yes! Yes! Yes! He would create proudly out of the freedom and power of his soul, as the great artificer whose name he bore, a living thing, new and soaring and beautiful, impalpable, imperishable' – founders on the dismal reality of his surroundings.[93] The novel highlights the mundane details of his morning routine, which persist long after he has abandoned his enthusiastic asceticism: he eats his sparse and unappetising breakfast, his mother straightens the battered alarm clock and then cleans him behind the ears, while somewhere in the street outside, a maniac screeches. All this threatens to 'humble the pride of his youth', because it offers material reminders of the family's inferior social position and his own lowly position in the material world, without the assurances of power and prestige afforded by the priesthood.[94] While a university education might offer the promise of future social and cultural distinction, even a place in the local Catholic aristocracy, the depression and weariness of his current existence have translated into apathy for his studies. As he walks across the city to the university, however, he draws on an alternative curriculum – his increasingly rich store of literary knowledge, which he accumulates from both authorised and unauthorised sources – to transform the dreary scenes around him by meditating on the 'silverveined prose of Newman ... the dark humour of Guido Calvacanti ... the spirit of Ibsen', later turning his mind to 'the spectral words of Aristotle and Aquinas' and 'the dainty songs of the Elizabethans'.[95]

In this sense, his foreign cultural resources provide a desired detachment from his immediate surroundings. As he makes his way through Dublin, Stephen constructs an internal realm of culture against everything that is low, common, or vulgar and, in the process, he aspires to a new kind of social attainment through a process of self-transformation. His developing aesthetic disposition requires what Bourdieu calls 'an objective and subjective distance from the world, with its material constraints and temporal urgencies', so that his longing for artistic autonomy and cultural capital develops in direct opposition to the declining financial capital of his family.[96] But success will be difficult for a metrocolonial petit-bourgeois young man of diminishing means and declining social position, especially when the physical environment he traverses repeatedly draws him back to his personal and communal entanglements:

> The grey block of Trinity on his left, set heavily in the city's ignorance like a dull stone set in a cumbrous ring, pulled his mind downward; and while he was striving this way and that to free his feet from the fetters of the reformed conscience he came upon the droll statue of the national poet of Ireland.[97]

Together, the imposing edifice of Trinity College Dublin and the rather awkward monument to Thomas Moore (1779–1852) serve as humiliating reminders of young man's social positioning, as well as the provincial quality of Dublin's cultural life. The city's Protestant university opened its doors primarily to members of the Anglo-Irish ruling class, but despite its relative prestige and royal charter it does little, in Stephen's mind, to elevate the city's status on the world stage or to illuminate the minds of the local inhabitants – not least, because it discourages the likes of him from access to its social and cultural capital. The statue of the poet, on the other hand, merely serves to undermine the stature of Moore's stridently Catholic voice and the standing of his embattled native culture, since the monument is not only what a contemporary commentator in *The Irish Builder* called a 'hideous caricature of the national bard' by a London-based sculptor, but one with a rather embarrassing history of accidental decapitation and faulty repair (not to mention the fact, noted in *Ulysses*, that the monument shares a traffic island with the public toilets) that further inclined its 'servile head', so that 'it seemed humbly conscious of its indignity'.

The passage also reintroduces the question of conscience into the narrative. Stephen attempts to dance free of the 'fetters of the reformed conscience' that holds sway over the Protestant institution, only to find his movement impeded by a monument to that arbiter of communal conscience, 'the national poet of Ireland'.[98] But these lines also make clear that it is not so easy for the young man and his contemporaries to escape the feeling of ressentiment that both the university and statue threaten to engender in members of their class and religious affiliations (and even more so in those who do not share Stephen's urban background and cosmopolitan ambitions). Joyce repeatedly suggests that the collective conscience of the Irish has been shaped by the chastened economic and political circumstances of turn-of-the-century Ireland, where the possibilities of wealth and prestige, power and influence, are largely denied to a generation of young men; and by the ideological response to these circumstances formulated by both the Irish Catholic Church and the Irish nationalist movement, especially in its cultural nationalist mode. The mildly absurd image of the national bard, 'in the borrowed cloak of a Milesian' (referring to those early settlers of Irish myth), makes Stephen think of 'his friend Davin, the peasant student', whose 'rude Firbolg mind' (referring to other early settlers from Irish myth) had fascinated him with its quaint and courteous disposition, but also repulsed him with its 'bluntness of feeling' and worship of 'the sorrowful legend of Ireland'.[99] The narrator describes the impact of this influence on Davin's 'rude imagination', which stands towards 'the broken lights of Irish myth ... in the same attitude as towards the Roman catholic religion, the attitude of a dull witted loyal serf'. These forces, the combined weight of national and religious traditions, have rendered the Irish people slavish insofar as faith in them has made them weak, incapacitated, degenerate; these forces, in other words, have rendered them slavish in the very manner that Nietzsche associates with slave morality to the extent that their values have been determined not by their own strength, but in reaction to the strength of others: 'whatsoever of thought or feeling came to [Davin] from England or by way of English culture his mind stood armed against'.[100] Davin's ressentiment has become productive of values, reaffirming the distinction between the ruler and the ruled by reversing the hierarchy with reference to native myths, native history, and native beliefs, but simultaneously reinforcing the very cultural oppositions levied by imperial power.

For Nietzsche, the slave defines himself in relation to the master, saying 'No to something "exterior", "different", "not-self"':[101] this necessary glance outward instead of inward upon oneself is definitive of ressentiment, that defensive reaction against the values of the powerful. No doubt Joyce himself was both a keen sufferer from and diagnostician of ressentiment, recognising that communal values are essentially dependent on collective affects, which provide a people with its fundamental mode of judgement or evaluation. The sociological significance of ressentiment derives from its creative power, which eventually leads to the transvaluation of national or communal values in a manner that vilifies the values of the society originally conceived as superior. Ressentiment at the level of national consciousness thus typically results in the privileging of indigenous traditions over and against their foreign counterparts, associated with the 'original' national principle. Rather controversially, Edward Said has identified this dynamic in the 'tremendous ressentiment of nativism'[102] found in anti-colonial cultural movements ranging from Senghor's negritude to Yeats's mysticism, which are 'limited by an essentially "negative" and defensive apprehension of their own society and, relatedly, of "civilised" European modernity'.[103]

What links these various versions of nationalism is precisely their effort to harness the national imaginary for the regulation of affect, deploying rhetorical practices to direct the intensities of feeling that gather around particular communal allegiances and socio-political conflicts. Addressing this subject in his 1907 lecture, 'Ireland: Island of Saints and Sages', Joyce leads off with the claim that 'nations, like individuals, have their egos', and goes on to suggest that it is easy enough to 'understand why the Irish citizen is reactionary and Catholic, or why, when he curses, he mixes the names of Cromwell and the Satanic pope', given the brutal history of conquest in Ireland.[104] In this sense, ressentiment is the extension of bad conscience to the entirety of a culture, so that it becomes productive of an entire metaphysics of good and evil on an international scale. The diagnosis is eminently Nietzschean insofar as it uses psychological terms to describe a sociological collective, which has succumbed to a sense of defensiveness and acrimony in the face of the values of a powerful antagonist, identified as evil by virtue of that very power. But Joyce ends the lecture by decrying this ressentiment, so often expressed in the heightened affect of nationalist speechmaking, because he does not 'see the use in bitter invectives against England, the despoiler', and of the attendant claims for an unacknowledged cultural superiority, which trap Ireland in a self-defeating vision of its own victimhood.[105] It bears noting here that, responding to a number of earlier studies, Andrew Gibson claims in *Joyce's Revenge* (2005) that ressentiment 'is surely a key theme for Joyce criticism' because the writer had such a deep understanding of and, indeed, identification with the phenomenon.[106] But if Joyce 'repeatedly demonstrates that those of his characters who are caught in *ressentiment* are also still in thrall, subordinate to power in the very intensity of their reaction to it ... he also had deep misgivings about it and worked to overcome it or leave it behind'.[107]

Race, affect, and value in *A Portrait*

Stephen's Bildung, his development as an artist and young man, in this environment is necessarily a struggle with ressentiment in the effort to affirm a self that is contingent neither on the recognition of the powerful nor the devaluation of the noble. If *A Portrait* is a loose recapitulation of *A Genealogy*, it is also the story – however unsuccessful or infelicitous – of how one might extricate oneself from this ethical impasse, of how the artist might emerge from his society to create an art that proceeds 'from a free and noble source', rather than from 'the manners of slaves'. When Stephen abandons the possibility of becoming a priest for the vocation of an artist, his aesthetic formulations initially constitute something of an overreaction to his circumstances and, even more fervently than in 'Art & Life', he theorises a static art divorced from moral concerns. To separate himself from the slaves would be to abandon their morality, their sense of good and evil, for a mode of aesthetic perception that has no truck with such categories. But the traumatic experience of Irish history makes the severance difficult, if not impossible, since that experience is always influencing the development of the young man and depleting the will to innovate in his art. His eventual revolt thus can be read as an act of Nietzschean heroism, as he seeks to overcome the very forces that have shaped his conscience: as he famously tells Davin in Chapter 5, 'when the soul of a man is born in this country there are nets flung at it to hold it back from flight. You talk to me of nationality, language, religion. I shall try to fly by those nets'.[108] Stephen's 'non servium' is precisely a refusal to acquiesce to slavish values. To overcome himself and achieve true distinction it will be necessary to combat the conventions that have come to define him as a metrocolonial subject and to begin redefining his opinions of what is noble and good, to begin creating independently a new table of values. Yet the young man will not find it so easy to fly off to artistic independence when nationality, language, and religion are as closely woven as they are in Irish history and in his own mind. His declaration announces a modernist revolt that seeks out the creation of new values, both personal and communal, for the artist-hero and his readers, even as it rejects the social accommodation that is the telos of traditional Bildung and the conventional Bildungsroman. To create new values would require him to overcome the self-estrangement he has been subjected to by the forces of Irish history. His revolt requires, above all, surmounting of the negative affects – the bad conscience and ressentiment – that have defined the lives of Stephen and many of his fellow countrymen, so that they might regard themselves as measures of value in their own right – confident, judicious, and fully independent.

In declaring his prophetic ambition to forge 'the uncreated conscience of [his] race' at the end of the novel, Stephen recognises his own bad conscience for what it is and, in this recognition, opens up the possibility of creating new, nobler values through his art. Recent scholarship has given considerable attention to the term 'race' in Stephen's declaration, and while that term remains important here, I want to add emphasis to the connection between conscience and affect, value and emotion, in these well-known lines. To be sure, these relationships are highlighted in the lines that immediately precede Stephen's declaration: 'Welcome O life! I go to encounter for the millionth time the reality of experience'.[109] In this final epiphany, this ecstatic moment of feeling, Stephen has adopted the life-affirming stance that, according to Nietzsche, privileges strength, health, and power over the life-denying morality of the so-called slaves, associated with weakness, pathos, and ressentiment. Moreover, this is a stance based on direct contact with the material world, of 'the earth beneath him, the earth that had borne him', rather than a retreat from lived experience into otherworldliness, spirituality, or metaphysics.[110] What Stephen seeks in this moment of heightened affect is something radically new, which breaks from the manners and mores of the national community and the pervasive feeling of ressentiment – and he declares this to be his central artistic aim.

Robert Gooding-Williams has identified a similar aim in Zarathustra and his desire to produce 'novelty-engendering interruptions of received practices and traditions': in other words, Nietzsche's protagonist 'is a *modernist* who, articulating his vision of the overman, aspires to create new, non-Christian-Platonic values that will transform European humanity' (original emphasis).[111] Joyce's protagonist is equally a modernist who aspires to create new post-ressentiment (and postcolonial) values that will renovate the Irish future by, to paraphrase both Frantz Fanon and Edward Said, moving racial conscience beyond national consciousness. This aspiration, of course, also represents the possibility of Stephen overcoming his own antipathy, his own ressentiment, toward the 'slaves' or 'herd', as his effort at self-overcoming merges with the interests of his 'race'. When the young man first begins to formulate this project, as he embarks on his long stroll with Cranly in Chapter 5, he wonders about the Irish 'patrician' class: 'How could he hit their conscience or how cast his shadow over the imaginations of their daughters ... that they might breed a less ignoble race than their own'?[112] Earlier in the novel, Stephen is dismissive of the idea 'that every physical quality admired by men in women is in direct connexion with the manifold functions of women for the propagation of the species', because he believes that 'it leads to eugenics rather than to esthetic'.[113] But, as his artistic ambitions expand to an almost comical extent for an unpublished writer (and take on an increasingly Nietzschean thrust in the process), the young man now seems to harness the aesthetic in service of the eugenic, as he speculates on the power of his artistic vision to transform his fellow Irishmen – 'a race', as the philosopher would have it, of 'men of resentment [ressentiment]' into a 'noble race', or at least, as Stephen muses, 'a less ignoble race'.[114] This might be accomplished by 'hitting' the conscience of the aristocratic classes directly with the impact of his art or more gently wooing their daughters into some clandestine activity with his writing, so that they might 'breed' a new generation of superior individuals, of Overmen – a project, as observed in earlier chapters of this study, closely associated with Nietzsche's philosophy at the turn of the century. These eugenicist implications complicate the nationalist connotations that, as Vincent Cheng and Pericles Lewis have both pointed out, began to inflect the term 'race' during this period; and they also throw into question the possibility of forging an as-yet uncreated conscience for a collective understood to be already determined by a complex mixture of cultural, historical, and biological factors.[115]

The usage of the term in English translations of Nietzsche's work exemplifies and even compounds the complexities that surrounded the concept of 'race' at the end of the nineteenth century. In its racialised etymological and anthropological speculation, *A Genealogy* associates 'noble' in the sense of 'with lofty sentiment' or 'privileged in sentiment' with the lighter complexions of the 'conquering race', including the 'Celts' who were 'throughout a blond race' and asserts that Gaelic, as well as the Iranian, Slavic, Greek, and Latin languages, define such nobles against those with 'the dark-complexioned, especially the black-haired man'.[116] Nietzsche is often prone to write of race in this manner, which links the moral and physiological traits of a class within a given society to form a distinct ethnic set or genetic stock, such as when he describes 'noble races' that are set off from 'a race of ... men of resentment'.[117] But, at other times, he writes of race as a more variegated category that may contain internal disparities of moral and physiological disposition, such as when he suggests that 'the ascetic priest ... does not belong, exclusively, to any one race; he flourishes anywhere; grows out of all classes'.[118] At still other times, he suggests racial and national unities that override any intramural diversity. Although the 'ethnographical maps of Germany' that Nietzsche refers to demonstrate a variety of ethnic origins that align with certain 'intellectual and social instincts', he also writes of Germans as a 'nation of thinkers' who have conquered 'their fundamental mob-instincts and their brutal bluntness' thanks to a common tradition of brutal punishment that endowed them with a particular capacity for memory and, with it, a capacity for reasonableness and reflection.[119] It is, Nietzsche argues elsewhere in *A Genealogy*, the race of men of resentment that, with its ability to remember, to stay silent, to remain patient, 'will at last, of necessity, be more *prudent* than any noble race' (original emphasis).[120] Although he does not use the term in a single, clearly defined manner, each usage does suggest a broadly Lamarckian sense that race was a matter not just of inherited physiological characteristics, but also of the values and customs acquired by successive generations. While Shaw, in his comments on race, was inclined to deny the existence of a specifically Irish or English race and to concern himself instead with the breeding of the human race 'to heights now deemed superhuman',[121] Yeats had imagined the emergence of 'the great race that is to come' from the ethnic stock of the Irish people, who had already become 'a harder, a more masterful race than the comfortable English of our time'.[122] Both responses combine aesthetic and ethical concerns insofar as the writers saw their artistic work as a means of bringing about these racial transformations, just as both responses, albeit from opposing perspectives, offer ways of combatting the disparaging and even dehumanising claims made about the Irish in the ethnographic discourses issuing from England at the time. What is most significant for Joyce is precisely the possibility, however implausible, of literature making anew the conscience, the values or moral characteristics, of the Irish people, whether this means 'the patricians of Ireland', many of whom presumably trace their heritage back to England, or the peasants of the country with their 'rude Firbolg mind[s]'.[123]

The success of Stephen's artistic project depends ultimately on the question of 'conscience' and indeed *A Portrait* often refers to the issue over the course of its five chapters; but while critics have frequently noted the importance of the term, they have not accounted for it in relation to Nietzsche's moral philosophy. The Catholic priests who reign over Stephen's youth oblige the young man and his peers 'to examine the state of [their] conscience' and to acknowledge their debt to 'God's holy will';[124] and, in the aftermath of his various sexual encounters, he feels that 'the preacher's knife had probed deeply into his disclosed conscience', so that he can sense 'that his soul was festering with sin'.[125] Father Arnall deploys a full arsenal of rhetorical weapons – more than thirty pages of frightful images, fervent commands, strident exclamation, pressing rhetorical questions – to inflict Stephen and the gathered students with 'the pain of conscience', 'the ache of conscience', 'the sting of conscience', and, most vividly, 'the worm of conscience', which inflicts the 'most cruel sting'.[126] Stephen has thus become one of those 'modern men' who, according to Nietzsche, 'are heirs to the vivisection of the conscience and self-torment of thousands of years in which we have had our longest practice', as men have learned to regard their 'natural bents' in a way that binds them to 'bad conscience'.[127] But 'it was only in the hands of the priest, this real artist in feelings of guilt', that these feelings 'took form – and Oh, what form! "Sin" – for this name is the priestly reinterpretation of the animal "bad conscience" (of cruelty turned inward) – was the greatest event so far in the history of the sick soul. It is the most dangerous and fatal artist-feat of religious interpretation'.[128]

Conscience, in the Catholic tradition, may be conceived as a form of self-knowledge, rooted in an awareness of the moral principles adopted by an individual and forming the motivation to act according to those principles. It is in this sense that Father Arnall implores his listeners to examine 'the state of [their] conscience'; but Joyce makes it clear that, in the lessons Stephen receives, conscience is always addressed in terms of '*bad* conscience', burdened by the negative feelings of fear and guilt. All the religious teachings of his youth, distilled into the prolific rhetoric of the hell-fire sermon, serve to burn this message into his memory and to demand his compliance: 'You will promise God now that by his His holy grace you will never offend Him any more by that wicked sin. You will make that solemn promise to God, will you not? ... Promise God now that you will give up that sin that wretched wretched sin'.[129] The 'reformed conscience' of the Protestant Church, which he seeks to escape as he makes his way past Trinity College, offers him no better alternative because in rejecting the 'terrorization of conscience' by the Catholic Church it nonetheless made the question of conscience, of bad conscience, even more central to the concerns of Christianity.[130] In *Beyond Good and Evil*, Nietzsche claims that 'the preacher was the only one in Germany who knew the weight of a syllable or a word, in what manner a sentence strikes, springs, rushes, flows, and comes to a close'.[131] It is thus the preacher alone who 'had a conscience in his ears, often enough a bad conscience', and it is Luther, the nation's 'greatest preacher', who has produced 'the masterpiece of German prose' with his translation of the Bible – that is, at least until Nietzsche transformed that prose in *Thus Spake Zarathustra*.[132]

In *A Genealogy*, Nietzsche sets out to define 'the concept "conscience"' at 'its final, almost strange phase of development', which has been reached after its 'long history and transmutation of forms'.[133] This history is synonymous with the history of 'man' as an animal reared to make promises, to take on responsibility and thereby to render himself 'uniform, equal among equal beings, regular and consequently reckonable'.[134] This undertaking, which has unfolded over the protracted saga of the species, has been carried out by what Nietzsche calls 'the morality of custom' that, despite the combined forces of tyranny and absurdity, has managed to produce 'the social strait-jacket', making man both predictable in his actions and accountable for their consequences. But for Nietzsche the story of human society and its morality of custom is all preamble to the emergence of 'the *sovereign individual*', who is at last delivered from these external restraints, which were, in the final analysis, only a means to produce this new kind of man: 'autonomous, supermoral (for "autonomous" and "moral" are mutually preclusive terms), in short, the man of private, independent and long will who *may promise* – and in him a proud consciousness vibrating in all his fibres, of *that which* finally has been attained and realised in his person, a true consciousness of power and freedom, a feeling of human perfection in general' (original emphasis).[135] This kind of consciousness can be glimpsed in the moment of Stephen's artistic epiphany: 'Yes! Yes! Yes! He would create proudly out of the freedom and power of his soul'.[136] For Nietzsche, 'to be able to pledge for one's self and to be, consequently, also able to *say yes* to one's self' is the long-awaited outcome of the history of conscience, which has only been reached after a long and bitter struggle with the morality of custom (original emphasis).[137] Only when one is freed from this morality can he be said to possess an 'infrangible will' and to acquire his own '*standard of valuation*', so that he may judge according to that standard whether others are to be honoured and despised (original emphasis).[138] And only when one is freed in this way can he be said to truly promise, which he does so only cautiously, after much deliberation, because he feels that he is strong enough to honour his pledge 'even against misfortune, ay, even against fate'.[139] It is in this sense that Stephen, combining his aesthetic and ethical impulses, commits to discovering 'the mode of life or of art whereby [his] spirit could express itself in unfettered freedom'[140] and doing so, as he confides in Cranly, at the risk of great hardship: 'I do not fear to be alone or to be spurned for another or to leave whatever I have to leave. And I am not afraid to make a mistake, even a great mistake'.[141] It is only when, according to Nietzsche, 'the consciousness of this rare freedom, of this power over self and fate, has penetrated into the inmost depth of his personality and become instinct, dominating instinct' that the sovereign man has surmounted the long history of the 'morality of custom'. 'By what name will he call it, dominating instinct …? … This sovereign man', Nietzsche tells us, 'will call it his *conscience*' (original emphasis).[142]

In this context, we can better appreciate Stephen's infamous artistic pledge to 'forge the uncreated conscience of his race'.[143] With his influential account in *A Genealogy*, Nietzsche helped to renovate the moral significance of 'conscience' by the beginning of the twentieth century; drawing on these associations, the conscience that Stephen seeks to articulate out of nothing would be one somehow freed from the stifling traditions, restrictive institutions, and chastening history that have cultivated bad conscience and ressentiment in the Irish. According to its well-established pattern, *A Portrait* culminates on an affirmative note, with Stephen pronouncing his ambition to create new values, a new collective conscience, through an act of artistic will. It is this sense of conviction – and its association with the Übermensch or overman – that is presented to the young man in an abandoned final scene from a late draft of *A Portrait* (presumably from 1912 or 1913, though later revised and incorporated into the opening chapter of *Ulysses* when he began writing it in 1914) when Doherty implores him with an incipient irony, 'Dedalus, we must retire to the tower, you and I. Our lives are precious. I'll try to touch the aunt. We are the super-artists. Dedalus and Doherty have left Ireland for the Omphalos'.[144] Yet, like *Thus Spake Zarathustra*, Joyce's youthful masterpiece (in the final version published in 1916, without the prospective tower episode) leaves open the question of whether or not the creation of new values is indeed possible. Will Stephen Dedalus, the namesake of that 'fabulous artificer', forge a modern art for Ireland and help to deliver it from a history of bad conscience and ressentiment? Can he accomplish this task without merely reacting against the structures of authority imposed by imperial power or becoming mired in his own bitter resentment of 'nationality, language, religion'? Can he perform this radical break from his cultural or racial past, whether through flight or withdrawal, in order to create as yet uncreated values? Will the young man find a way to become a singular, independent, autonomous artist and somehow speak for the vast collective of his 'race' at the same time? Or will he, despite his best efforts, stumble upon what Gooding-Williams identifies as 'a possibility inherent in modernism: namely, that of failing, despite one's efforts, to make an innovative break with a received cultural practice or tradition'?[145] In this sense, the 'uncreated conscience' is a consummate modernist trope, perpetually open to the future, to the innovative, to the new in anticipation of a mode of feeling and valuation that, ironically, may never come into existence, that may remain only a potentiality or, at best, an ongoing and uncertain process of becoming. The wager that Stephen must enter into – to leave behind the familiar comforts of home, including the consoling illusions of 'nationality, language, religion' – at the risk of making a great mistake is one that represents only the distant possibility of adequate compensation through what Sloterdijk calls the 'as yet unproven mobilization of creative counter-energies'.[146] The often-remarked distance between Joyce and Stephen, between the novelist and his creation, can be read not only as the gap between the mature artist and the young man, but as a scepticism about the result of this wager that, dampening all prophetic ecstasy, throws all possibility of forging new values into question.

Ulysses, Zarathustra, and cultural revolution

This scepticism and uncertainty carry over to the first chapter of *Ulysses*, where a number of Nietzschean references appear and confirm the significance of Nietzsche's project for Joyce's fiction. At the opening of the novel, we find Stephen – 'the hawklike man' now 'Lapwing. Icarus.' – returned to Ireland and now ensconced in the Martello Tower with his enthusiasm for forging the 'uncreated conscience' of his race severely diminished. Playing at the role of a Jesuit father, as we witnessed at the opening of this study, Buck Mulligan scolds Stephen for his callous behaviour towards his dying mother: 'I'm hyperborean as much as you. But to think of your mother begging you with her last breath to kneel down and pray for her. And you refused'.[147] Calling on Nietzsche's evocation of the Hyperboreans in the opening pages of *The Antichrist*, Mulligan takes on the ironic role of a Nietzschean priest who identifies himself and his charge with those mythical peoples who live in far off northern climes, looking upon the moral codes of modern men with a cold eye (this, even as he wants to preserve the value of a son's love for his mother). Nietzsche, in his own sly manner, appeals to his readers to identify with him and to share in this perspective – 'Let us look one another in the face. We are Hyperboreans – we know well enough how much out of the way we live' – even though he had no grounds to suppose that he might have followers wanting to view the world around them from such an icy remove.[148] The real-life Buck Mulligan, Oliver St John Gogarty, wrote a series of letters from the tower during this period demonstrating his easy familiarity with Nietzsche, whom he linked with both classical sources and a strident 'satire against mediocrity'.[149] Mulligan's reference to the Hyperboreans in *Ulysses* is similarly an invitation to distinction, to participate in a form of elevated inquiry that carries the inquirer away from the comforts of a familiar community and from the accommodations of established values: 'We have discovered happiness', Nietzsche writes, 'we know the way, we have found the exit from entire millenniums of labyrinth'.[150] This would be a particularly strong appeal for Stephen, who has attempted to fly past the Dedalian maze of 'nationality, language, religion', for it offers identification with a mythos that was for Nietzsche, as Sloterdijk puts it, 'a way of describing his sojourn in the cold as a gay and voluntary exile'.[151] But

Mulligan's entreaty – with its casual, even clumsy evocation of Nietzsche's philosophy – cheapens the value of this appeal so that it only serves to diminish the significance of Stephen's exile from Ireland and to undermine his efforts to assert a sovereign selfhood. The young man remains haunted by his past, his home, and his family, returning to the habitual brooding he displayed in *A Portrait* as a sufferer of bad conscience, now rendered as 'agenbite of inwit' (usually translated as 'remorse of conscience').[152] Stephen mournfully recalls not only the bedside scene with his dying mother, but also his conversation in the previous novel with Cranly, who had pointed out that his mind continued to be 'supersaturated with the religion' he claims to disbelieve.[153]

What Stephen imagines in its place is a rather degraded alternative, which mixes a blithe disdain for the modern institution of the Church with strains of ancient aristocratic values and assertions of Irish nationalist sentiment. The Greek literary tradition contains texts that identify the Hyperboreans, living far to the north, with the Celts, so that reference to the mythic peoples takes on a more complicated set of associations: not just with the sense of a detached perspective and exilic consciousness, but also with something much closer to home – that is, the actual peoples regarded as ancient inhabitants of Ireland, who migrated there at some point during the Iron Age. Mulligan, regretting the bitterness of his friend, soon takes Stephen's arm and implores him: 'God, Kinch, if you can I could only work together we might do something for the island. Hellenise it'. Stephen's elliptical string of thoughts in response to this appeal – 'to ourselves ... new paganism ... omphalos'[154] – locates the Martello tower at the centre of a prospective cultural revolution that would lead a 'priest-ridden Godforsaken race' into a new future defined by classical values. Critics have long recognised the opening of this peculiar pledge as a variation on 'ourselves' or 'we ourselves' (or commonly, but inaccurately, 'ourselves alone'), the English translations of *Sinn Féin*, which had become a rallying call for Irish nationalists and part of the slogan for the Gaelic League beginning in the 1890s, as the organisation asserted the sovereignty of the Irish people and promoted the revival of the Irish language. Seemingly at odds with this, 'new paganism' was another slogan that was pronounced with increasing insistence in the 1890s to hail a nascent epoch defined by a return to pre-Christian modes of spirituality and morality, neatly exemplified in Nietzsche's call to other modern 'Hyperboreans'. Reference to the 'omphalos' aligns with this interest in Hellenic culture, for the term means 'navel' or 'navel of the earth' in Ancient Greek and recalls the Omphalos of Delphi, a monument said to be placed by Zeus at the centre of the earth where the Oracle of Delphi was to reside. Hans Walter Gabler has suggested that Doherty's invitation to Stephen in the abandoned first draft of the chapter 'would seem to imply an intention of figuring the concept of exile which concludes *A Portrait* into a retreat to the tower, where the young aesthetes, seeking unfettered freedom in an abandonment of Nietzschean élitism, isolate themselves from society; or to preface Stephen's departure into an exile alone in the world by the attempt and failure of a retirement to the *omphalos*, the navel of friendship and art'.[155] But the evocation of the 'omphalos' in *Ulysses* suggests a position that is at once peripheral, providing the necessary aesthetic distance from which to articulate an alternative vision of Irish culture, and central, placing Ireland and, more specifically, the tower at the crux of a cultural revolution that will remake the values of the modern world.

The evocation of the omphalos also places Stephen and Mulligan in the roles of modern-day oracles, updated versions of those ancient priests who had the prophetic capacity to see into the future and utter confident predictions. Richard Begam has claimed that 'for Stephen both the nationalism represented by the phrase "sinn féin" and the aestheticism represented by the phrase "new paganism" are the deadends of the Nineties, examples of *omphalos* or navel-gazing'.[156] But I would suggest that, as the action of the novel takes place on 16 June 1904, both slogans still held some promise, however dubious, for a more assertive future. In 1905, Arthur Griffith adopted the name 'Sinn Féin' for the new political party he created in the effort 'to establish in Ireland's capital a national legislature endowed with the moral authority of the Irish nation' and, indeed, as Matthew Bevis notes, Gogarty spoke alongside Griffith at the first National Council convention of the party in November of that year.[157] We have also seen that they had troubled Yeats during the period of the *Playboy* riots in 1907. Joyce knew well by 1914, as he drafted the Telemachus episode, that the party had struggled politically, but that it had also merged its membership with the Irish Volunteers in the desire 'to secure and maintain the rights and liberties common to the whole people of Ireland'.

The promise of the new paganism, with its assault on bourgeois Christian values, might have been thought to perish with the death of Oscar Wilde, who, as Joyce had written, 'deceived himself that he was the bearer of good news of neo-paganism to an enslaved people. His own distinctive qualities, the qualities, perhaps, of his race – keenness, generosity, and a sexless intellect – he placed at the service of a theory of beauty, which, according to him, was to bring back the Golden Age' (and which had been dismissed by the likes of Nordau and Stutfield for demonstrating the 'true inwardness of modern aesthetic Helenism').[158] But in his 1904 essay on Nietzsche, Eglinton had also linked the philosopher's denunciation of Christianity and its slave morality to a period 'when Europe was filled with renunciants and ascetics', and 'paganism was still able to unfold before the eyes of men the most shining examples, not indeed of holiness, but of manhood (virtue)'.[159]

This conflict continued on into the present. To be sure, in the early years of the twentieth century, Nietzsche's name became closely associated with a pagan ideal that valued the affirmation of embodied existence and affiliation with the natural world over the otherworldly and anti-natural beliefs of Christianity, which were seen to corrupt and weaken the aristocratic basis of life. In *A Genealogy*, the philosopher had remarked the 'Greeks for the longest time used their gods just for keeping "bad conscience" at a safe distance, in order to enable them to remain happy in their freedom of the soul; *i.e.*, reversely from the practice of Christianity in the application of its God!'[160] This strain of the new paganism was to reassert the natural, the healthy, and the virile in order to imagine higher creatures capable of living in a manner free of bad conscience and liberated from ascetic impulses. This ethos can be glimpsed in what Michael Valdes Moses calls 'Yeats's investment in the Nietzschean recuperation of aristocratic pagan values' in his Cuchulain plays, which in harkening back to the Iron Age hero presented the Irish people with an image of native masculinity. In addition to playing a role in a 'specifically anti-Christian project', this updated paganism also provided a means both to avoid the sectarian conflicts that had plagued Irish nationalism and to combat the colonial discourses that had labelled the Irish as feminine, slavish, and incapable of self-rule. Mulligan, with his robust health and masculine swagger, becomes an embodied signifier of these competing and coalescing possibilities for the future of Irish culture, which can only be said to produce a highly ambivalent response from Stephen.

Mulligan's heretical mass, delivered in the guise of a Nietzschean priest, is a parodic riposte to those priests in *Stephen Hero* and *A Portrait* who worked to cultivate ressentiment and bad conscience even as they courted cynicism and nihilism. His deceptively complex mode of speech, which travesties the elevated rhetoric of both Zarathustra and the Jesuit fathers, draws on the authority, the cultural capital, of their modes of speech even as his wry mockery (along with Joyce's comic rendering of his character) undercuts this authority – and fashions his address to Stephen into a loaded invitation to join his neo-pagan Nietzschean cult. As his oration nears an end, Mulligan begins to disrobe and ready himself for a plunge into the sea, only to break off his banter in mock alarm and frantically grope under his flapping shirt: 'My twelfth rib is gone, he cried. I'm the *Uebermensch*. Toothless Kinch and I, the supermen'.[161] The playful reference to a missing rib links Mulligan to Adam in the Judeo-Christian creation myth, even as the equally playful reference to Nietzsche suggests a new creation myth of the Übermensch, who has arisen precisely to overcome the image of man cultivated by the Judeo-Christian tradition. The good news of the Übermensch, who promises to rise above or beyond man, is a radical compensation for the bad news of the fall of man and an omen of the creative potentialities of the will to power.

Like Mulligan's earlier allusion to the Hyperboreans, moreover, this cry of the Superman works to interpolate Stephen into a Nietzschean vision of sovereign selfhood, even as this double-edged invitation undercuts the young man's potency by addressing him as 'Toothless Kinch', the dull knife that cannot fulfil the purpose for which it was created. That Stephen indeed suffers from dental neglect ('My teeth are very bad ... Ought I go to a dentist, I wonder, with what money? That one. Toothless Kinch, the superman. Why is that, I wonder, or does it mean something perhaps?', he later reflects in 'Proteus') suggests the comic pathos of this invitation to a young man who has fallen a long way from his lofty aspirations.[162]

Taken seriously, the invitation demands that its addressee abandon all traditional forms of illusion and live beyond all forms of social accommodation. Citing Nietzsche, Mulligan calls Stephen to run afoul of the repressive ideologies that predominate in Ireland – Catholicism, Imperialism, nationalism – and to embrace an individualism predicated on access to enough cultural capital to produce a subject opposed to its 'societal preconditions'.[163] But the form of the invitation also cheapens these aspirations for aesthetic achievement and artistic autonomy, precisely because it blithely announces the Übermensch as the brand name of an individualist trend that had only grown in force by the turn of the twentieth century. The names in Mulligan's address, 'Uebermensch ... Toothless Kinch', work to interpolate Stephen as a subject, a would-be artist as a young man and a member of the metrocolonial petit bourgeoisie – a concrete individual who aspires to the status of an autonomous and authoritative subject, but who cannot afford proper care of his physical person, of his teeth. In this sense, Mulligan is yet another of the 'nimble pleaders' who appeals to Stephen's defiant sense of self. On his lips, the trope of the Übermensch risks becoming merely another ideologeme that contains an increasingly hegemonic attitude towards gender, class, race, and nation, though an altogether more insidious one because it stands in for a set of values that Stephen already identifies as his own, as the necessary way to live as an artist in relation to Irish society.

Mulligan's citation of Nietzsche's philosophy, lifting a few key words and phrases out of their original context, provides him with the opportunity to garner a certain kind of cultural capital, but only through the subversion of earlier discursive forms. Stephen turns away from the mocking priest and walks away from the tower, but not before repaying his debt to Mulligan for a pint by tossing two pennies on the soft heap of his dressing gown. The gesture is a corrupted version of the offertory, that closing ritual of the Catholic Mass when alms are collected from the congregation for benefit of the poor; in response, as we saw in the Introduction, Mulligan concludes his parodic sermon by playfully transvaluing Proverbs 19:17 – 'He who stealeth from the poor lendeth to the Lord' (in place of 'He that hath pity upon the poor lendeth unto the Lord') – and then pronouncing 'Thus Spake Zarathustra'.[164] In doing so, he again rather cruelly draws attention to Stephen's destitute condition and, at least for the purposes of his joke, advocates for Nietzschean selfishness, impiety, and pitilessness, in opposition to Christian pity. But, more broadly, his pronouncement participates in the denigration of biblical or sermonic speech, which can no longer guarantee the speaker a profit because the condition of transmission for messages of this type has transformed. To utter such speech earnestly would only be to reveal oneself as someone 'who had not yet properly learned the procedures of modernity to be able to take up the word to advantage'.[165] Geoffrey Hartman suggests that, despite his elevated aims, Nietzsche could only parody and not appropriate the high seriousness of such language in *Thus Spake Zarathustra*, because 'its weight and resonance make a fool of whatever modern writer dares impersonate it'.[166] For Sloterdijk, the book that Nietzsche referred to as 'the fifth "gospel"' also represents 'an odd renewal of eulogistic energies' because in it 'an alternative linguistic current first opens onto a proposition designed to transmit via speech an evangel propped upon on a "dis-evangel"'.[167] It is a book that, with utmost seriousness (and mirthful laughter), sets out to destroy all the illusions that had maligned life in the name of otherworldly values and thus a book that offered itself as a work of incomparable worth. It is, moreover, a book that turns on declarations, not arguments or justifications. Mulligan's pronouncement neatly exemplifies such 'an evangel propped upon a "dis-evangel"', but in doing so it also questions the potency of this renewal, for his comic attempt to spread the 'fifth gospel', to initiate a new eulogistic chain, threatens to render him ridiculous. In his mouth, Nietzsche's refrain appears to have lost much of its weight or seriousness, calling attention both to its waning force, with each reiteration, in *Thus Spake Zarathustra* and to the difficulty of pronouncing new values in late colonial Ireland. If the aim of the citation – indeed, the aim of the entire mock mass – is his self-enhancement, Mulligan also seems to have misjudged the costs that he would incur and the diminishing narcissistic returns he would enjoy. This is punctuated by the comic baptismal rite that concludes his liturgy, as 'his plump body plunge[s]' into the sea at the base of the tower.[168]

The return of the Overman and the ethics of Irish modernism

Despite these evocations of Nietzsche's philosophy, Stephen seems entirely nonplussed by Mulligan's heretical rite and can be seen mutely walking away up the path away from the tower at its conclusion, thereby refusing initiation into his Zarathustrian cult. So what has become of Stephen's heroic modernist project and its Nietzschean inspiration in the opening pages of *Ulysses*? What, we might also ask, has become of Joyce's interest in Nietzschean thought during the decade stretching from 1904, when he signed the lettercard to Roberts, to 1914, when he began drafting the early chapters of his great novel? The 'Overman' was to be a radically new type of human being, one capable of overcoming bad conscience, ressentiment, and the nihilistic drift of Western culture by confidently generating a new set of values that affirmed life in a changing and chaotic modern world. Mulligan's speech hails Stephen to take his place as an individual or, better, individualist in this mould: to be a consumer of the brand of individualism with which Nietzsche had become so closely associated (and, thus, to recognise himself as a subject capable of such overcoming). In 1904, Eglinton had recognised 'the doctrine of the Superman – that "far-off divine event" to which, according to Nietzsche, humanity moves' – as the natural next step past a 'consideration of the "morality of slaves and masters"'; but he had also recognised the doctrine as 'undoubtedly a little crazy' due not so much to its radical rejection of Christianity as to its elevation of 'the Cæsars and Napoleons, those idols of the average man', who nonetheless exist as the expense of all men.[169] This is, no doubt, a rather vulgar reading of the Übermensch. But it is exemplary of the way that, shortly after Nietzsche's death, 'a wave of demands began turning Zarathustra into a fashionable prophet and the "will to power" into a password for social climbers'.[170]

As the dissemination of Nietzsche's ideas posthumously transformed the field of cultural production, his most prominent creations risked being relegated to the status of something déclassé or worse. Before the turn of the century, Brandes had already recognised that the philosopher was 'now more or less understood, now misunderstood, now involuntarily caricatured'. Soon, Shaw and Yeats had each taken up his philosophy for their artistic enterprises, though they were quickly accompanied by all manner of other readers across Europe who found value in Nietzsche for their various efforts at attaining distinction. 'A Painful Case', as Simon Joyce points out, had demonstrated the association between Nietzschean ideas and those like James Duffy seeking to elevate themselves 'through the means of culture'.[171] And Jean-Michel Rabaté, recognising the role that 'fashionable Nietzscheism' had played for Joyce in 'a deliberate dramatization of his farewell to Dublin', has suggested that in *Ulysses* the writer was working 'satirically, taking Nietzsche as a straw man useful to expose the limitation of an earlier egotistic posturing' that had been dominant in his earlier writing.[172] To be sure, Mulligan's strategies of citation secure neither Stephen's discipleship nor his own participation in the supreme advantages promised by Nietzsche's claim, much less the attribution of excellence to his own person. His strategies fail not least because they draw on a few distorted fragments of Nietzsche's philosophy to appeal to an audience of one, who is simultaneously denigrated as impotent and impoverished.

This is not to say that the role of Nietzsche's philosophy in Joyce's writing should be dismissed ultimately as that of a 'straw man' or 'stage prop'. Rather, we should read Stephen's return to Ireland, the return of his bad conscience, and Mulligan's playing at Zarathustrian prophecy together as signs of Joyce's acknowledgement that the project of creating new values is necessarily a vexed one, especially in the context of Irish history. As noted earlier, it is often suggested that a central concern of the so-called Telemachus chapter is the state of Irish culture and the contest over its future between not just Dedalus and Mulligan, but also the Englishman Haines. In this contest, Joyce appears to be conducting a thought experiment of sorts, examining the challenges faced by the creator of new values and the significance of Nietzschean concepts for Irish culture. When Mulligan holds out his broken mirror to Stephen, so that he may examine his visage, that of the 'dreadful bard', the young man famously remarks, playing on an aphorism from Wilde: 'It is a symbol of Irish art. The cracked lookingglass of a servant'.[173] Despite his best efforts, Stephen has not been able to create an art that proceeds from a 'free and noble source' and has instead come to 'adopt the manners of these slaves', who have failed to represent themselves as a sovereign and self-confident people through the means and mores left to them by history. Rather than aspiring to the status of an Übermensch, capable of forging his own morality in a feat of artistic will or aesthetic achievement, Stephen concedes to being 'the servant of two', or rather three, 'masters': the Imperial British state, the Holy Roman Empire, and the Irish nation itself.[174] His ressentiment is manifest – he remains enslaved. He is in no position to take up the Nietzschean 'mandate for art, and for the entire dimension of history': to affirm true nobility, one that has not been known by the Irish or anyone else, a nobility based on a world-affirming, creative attitude towards life.[175] No doubt, as Zarathustra himself recognises, the Übermensch cannot be invoked through discipleship, since he must learn to help himself, independent of God, Christian doctrine, and the will of others. Unlike the young Joyce who had proclaimed himself 'James Overman' in 1904, Stephen denies identification with Nietzsche's image of the self-overcoming individual; the denial may be seen, nonetheless, as a sign of Stephen's enslavement insofar as he has failed to overcome himself, to somehow transcend what his youth in Ireland has made of him, to finally, that is, 'kill the priest and the king' that reside in his mind, as he suggests much later in the novel.[176] 'Telemachus' instead seems to suggest a species of historical fatalism: Stephen, like Duffy and many of Joyce's other Dubliners, cannot forge a flourishing modern culture in Ireland, precisely because his efforts to produce new values depends on historical conditions and ideological forces that make such a project all but impossible. His return to earth in *Ulysses* raises the question of whether overcoming these historical conditions can be a matter of individual striving and personal transformation or whether overcoming these conditions must involve a collective effort to contend with the economic and political forces that perpetuate them.

Mulligan's Nietzschean hailing, and its call for Stephen's allegiance, nonetheless offer an important point of departure for understanding the project of cultural transformation undertaken by Joyce's art and the ethics of modernism negotiated within the pages of his masterpiece. Stephen's project takes place in relation to a variety of external authorities and pursues the desire to create oneself as a subject, without relying on the recognition of those authorities. This means that the possibility of forging a postcolonial conscience is, in the sense that Nietzsche's thought suggests, the possibility of overcoming ressentiment and conquering slave morality. There is a doubling and dissembling potentiality in this to the degree that Stephen, as an artist, seeks to be different from those who are different and entertains the impossible dream of being the same as the masters that have defined Irish history – an impossibility that haunts the process of his Bildung and his bold proclamation to make anew the conscience of the Irish. There is further dissembling in this to the degree that Stephen's rejection of this calling is, in an important sense, the necessary precursor to asserting an autonomous subjectivity like that suggested in Nietzsche's Übermensch. These are contradictions that are not finally resolved in *Ulysses*. Nietzsche's philosophy – his rhetoric, tropes, trademark ideas – with its assertive quality eventually elicits resistance from Joyce's writing, but these terms nonetheless infiltrate his fiction, evoke a memory, and provide an incitement from his earlier writings that he cannot let fade entirely. Joyce's novel allows him to personify this 'modernist will to cultural change', which represents the possibility – if not the necessity or even probability – of escaping the received cultural conditions that threaten the will to innovate and of opening up the future as a void into which new forms, new content, and new values might issue. It also allows him, in the story of his younger alter ego, to attain the pathos of distance necessary to diagnose the negative affects and historical contingencies that plague any such project. This distance is not indicative of aesthetic alienation, then, but of an ethically engaged modernism that depends on both formal experimentation and scepticism about the solidity of all ethical and moral pronouncements. Nietzsche's thought thus offers not just an 'antidote to Puritanism and Pessimism', but an impetus for thinking through the aesthetic, affective, and ethical issues arising for Joyce and the Irish people in the early years of the twentieth century.

Joyce's fiction takes up the provocation to create the 'uncreated conscience' of the Irish, one that would not be yoked to the consequences of imperial authority, religious hegemony, and communal animosity; one that, instead, would issue from a position of nobility in order to open up a richer potential. The citation of Nietzsche's work does not simply seek to draw on the distinction of a particular philosopher who had become synonymous with individualism, but instead it demonstrates how those who seek to spread his words risk descending to the low, common, or vulgar, if not simply ridiculous. As we will see in the next chapter, even as Joyce was writing the 'Telemachus' episode in 1914, selective references to Nietzsche were being employed for vulgar propagandistic ends by those who sought to further their resentful nationalist and militaristic agendas in the early months of the First World War, despite the surplus of anti-nationalist and anti-militaristic sentiments in his writing. But in its opening chapters, *Ulysses* poses the question of whether it is possible, for the future of Ireland, for the future of humanity, to overcome both personal and national ressentiment as the most powerful and pervasive historical forces. Rather than concentrating his attention on a solitary 'James Overman', the heroic creator of values who emerges in *A Portrait*, Joyce decentres this hyperbolic ego (and developmental historicism) at the focus of his Bildungsroman in favour of a more expansive ethical perspective, centred on the everyday or mass man in Leopold Bloom, who is far less concerned with the quest for sovereign individualism. Joyce does not generate a prescriptive ethics that claims for itself any kind of moral obligation, acknowledging instead uncertainty and futurity in the mode of cultural and cognitive pluralism beyond all attempts at unification or codification. His should not be understood as a moral or national art, then, but as an ethical and political one, which despite its seeming aloofness is all the better positioned to create images, voice perspectives, and provoke feelings that might transmute the collective conscience of the Irish people and the broader community of its readers.

Notes

1 James Joyce to George Roberts, 13 July 1904, in Stuart Gilbert (ed.), *The Letters of James Joyce* (New York: Viking, 1957), p. 56.
2 Qtd in Mary Colum and Padraic Colum, *Our Friend James Joyce* (Gloucester: Peter Smith, 1968), p. 33.
3 Richard Ellmann, *James Joyce* (Oxford: Oxford University Press, 1983), p. 142.
4 David S. Thatcher, *Nietzsche in England, 1890–1914: The Growth of a Reputation* (Toronto: University of Toronto Press, 1970), p. 135. See also Christopher Butler, 'Joyce, Modernism, and Post-Modernism', in Derek Attridge (ed.), *The Cambridge Companion to James Joyce* (Cambridge:

Cambridge University Press, 1990), pp. 259–82; Klaus Reichert, 'The European Background of Joyce's Writing', in Attridge (ed.), *The Cambridge Companion to James Joyce*, pp. 55–82; Jacques Aubert, *The Aesthetics of James Joyce* (Baltimore: Johns Hopkins University Press), pp. 24–26; Jean-Michel Rabaté, *Joyce and the Politics of Egoism* (Cambridge: Cambridge University Press, 2001), pp. 19–22; Brett Foster, 'Biography of James Joyce', in Harold Bloom (ed.), *James Joyce* (New York: Chelsea House, 2003), p. 21.

5 Joseph Valente ('Beyond Truth and Freedom: The New Faith of Joyce and Nietzsche', *James Joyce Quarterly*, 25:1 (Fall 1987), 87–103), for instance, acknowledges that 'in Nietzsche's superman [Joyce] found an empowering myth for his struggle against the mind-forged manacles of Irish society', but suggests that as Joyce's interest matured, he 'came to regard the Übermensch in light of the hermeneutical apocalypse Nietzsche heralds' (pp. 87–88). It is here, in the increasingly syncretic vision of the mature Joyce, that Valente locates Nietzsche's importance for the novelist, who appropriated elements of his thought to formulate a sceptical epistemology of 'aesthetic incertitude'. More recently, in the first book-length study to address the connection between Joyce and Nietzsche, Sam Slote (*Joyce's Nietzschean Ethics* (New York: Palgrave, 2013)) has elaborated on the affinities between Joyce's 'multifarious art of style' and Nietzsche's theories of artistic innovation and perspectival knowledge in order to demonstrate not just their shared concerns regarding aesthetics and epistemology, but also the ethics of style or individuation operative in their writing. Nietzsche is relevant to Joyce, then, not because he provided the writer with raw materials for his art or with theories of artistic practice, but because the recognition of certain parallels between their projects can teach the reader something about the 'ramifications' of Joycean style or styles (p. 2).

6 Colum and Colum, *Our Friend*, pp. 21–22.
7 Ibid., p. 59.
8 Qtd in Theodore Spencer, 'Introduction', in James Joyce, *Stephen Hero* (London: Jonathan Cape, 1944), p. 27.
9 John Eglinton, 'A Way of Understanding Nietzsche', *Dana: An Irish Magazine of Independent Thought* 1:6 (1904), 182, 184.
10 Ibid., 185.
11 Ibid., 185, 187.
12 Ibid., 186–87.
13 Ibid., 187.
14 Ibid., 188.
15 T.M. Kettle, 'Catholicism and Modern Literature', *St. Stephen's* (January 1905), 131.
16 Qtd in J.B. Lyons, *The Enigma of Tom Kettle: Irish Patriot, Poet, British Soldier, 1880–1916* (Dublin: Glendale, 1983), p. 57.
17 Kettle, 'Catholicism', 132.
18 Ibid., 133.
19 T.M. Kettle, 'Dr. William Barry's Report on Modern Literature', *The New Ireland Review* 22:4 (December 1904), 250.

20 Seamus Deane, *Celtic Revivals: Essays in Modern Irish Literature, 1880–1980* (Winston-Salem: Wake Forest University Press, 1985), p. 75.
21 Joyce, *Stephen Hero*, p. 123.
22 Ibid., p. 123.
23 Ibid., p. 164.
24 Friedrich Nietzsche, *A Genealogy of Morals*, William A. Haussmann (trans.) (London: Macmillan, 1897), pp. 19–20.
25 Ibid., pp. 23, 20.
26 Joyce, *Stephen Hero*, p. 154.
27 Ibid., p. 153.
28 Ibid., p. 64.
29 See Fran O'Rourke, 'Philosophy', in John McCourt (ed.), *James Joyce in Context* (Cambridge: Cambridge University Press, 2009), pp. 320–30.
30 Joyce, *Stephen Hero*, p. 90.
31 Padraic Colum, 'James Joyce', *Pearson's Magazine* 39:1 (May 1918), 40.
32 Joyce, *Stephen Hero*, p. 68.
33 Friedrich Nietzsche, *The Case of Wagner; Nietzsche Contra Wagner; The Twilight of the Idols; The Antichrist*, Thomas Common (trans.) (London: H. Henry, 1896), p. 182.
34 Ibid., p. 186.
35 Friedrich Nietzsche, *The Joyful Wisdom*, Thomas Common (trans.) (New York: Macmillan, 1910), p. 213.
36 Joyce, *Stephen Hero*, p. 89.
37 Joyce, *Stephen Hero*, p. 68.
38 Friedrich Nietzsche, *Ecce Homo and Poems*, Oscar Levy (trans.) (New York: Macmillan, 1911), pp. 81, 131.
39 Joyce, *Stephen Hero*, p. 64.
40 Kettle, 'Catholicism', 131.
41 Eglinton, 'Understanding Nietzsche', 188.
42 W.B. Yeats, 'The Dramatic Movement', in Mary FitzGerald and Richard J. Finneran (eds), *The Collected Works of W.B. Yeats, Volume VIII: The Irish Dramatic Movement* (New York: Scribner, 2008), p. 60.
43 Joyce, *Stephen Hero*, p. 89.
44 Max Nordau, *Degeneration* (New York: Appleton, 1895), p. 353.
45 Joyce, *Stephen Hero*, p. 89.
46 Nordau, *Degeneration*, pp. 388, 395, 415, 463.
47 Ibid., p. 2.
48 Joyce, *Stephen Hero*, p. 89. Editorial marks used by the editors of *Stephen Hero* to indicate phrases Joyce had slashed with a crayon.
49 Ibid., p. 67.
50 Ibid., p. 64.
51 Nietzsche, *Ecce Homo*, p. 140.
52 Joyce, *Stephen Hero*, p. 204.
53 Ibid., p. 205.
54 Ibid., pp. 205–6.

55 Ibid., p. 206.
56 Ibid., p. 205.
57 Ibid., p. 206.
58 Walter Kaufmann, *Nietzsche: Philosopher, Psychologist, Antichrist*, 4th ed. (Princeton: Princeton University Press, 1974), p. 101.
59 Joyce, *Stephen Hero*, p. 206.
60 Friedrich Nietzsche, *Thus Spake Zarathustra: A Book for All and None*, Alexander Tille (trans.) (New York: Macmillan, 1896), p. 109.
61 Eglinton, 'Understanding Nietzsche', 182.
62 Joyce, *Stephen Hero*, p. 206.
63 Gregory Castle, *Reading the Modernist Bildungsroman* (Gainesville: University Press of Florida, 2015), p. 177.
64 An anachronism. Joyce was likely familiar with both *Die Fröhliche Wissenschaft* (1882) and its Italian translation as *La Gaia Scienza* (1905), but Nietzsche's book was not published in English until 1910, and then as *The Joyful Wisdom*, translated by Thomas Common and published in London by T.N. Foulis.
65 Qtd in Simon Joyce, *Modernism and Naturalism in British and Irish Fiction, 1880–1930* (Cambridge: Cambridge University Press, 2015), p. 186.
66 Peter Sloterdijk, *Nietzsche Apostle* (Los Angeles: Semiotext(e), 2013), p. 77.
67 James Joyce, 'A Painful Case', in James Joyce, *Dubliners* (London: Grant Richards, 1914), p. 132.
68 Ibid., p. 130.
69 Joyce, *Modernism and Naturalism*, p. 111.
70 Joyce, 'A Painful Case', p. 137.
71 Ibid., p. 140.
72 James Joyce, *A Portrait of the Artist as a Young Man* (London: Egoist, 1916), p. 147.
73 Ibid., p. 155.
74 Ibid., p. 112.
75 Ibid., p. 117.
76 Nietzsche, *A Genealogy*, p. 196.
77 Joyce, *A Portrait*, p. 155.
78 Ibid., p. 158.
79 Ibid., pp. 160–61.
80 Ibid., p. 160.
81 Nietzsche, *A Genealogy*, p. 161.
82 Joyce, *A Portrait*, pp. 174–75.
83 Ibid., p. 175.
84 Nietzsche, *A Genealogy*, p. 197.
85 Joyce, *A Portrait*, p. 171.
86 Nietzsche, *A Genealogy*, p. 197. Original emphasis.
87 Joyce, *A Portrait*, p. 177.
88 Ibid., p. 183.
89 Ibid., p. 183.
90 Nietzsche, *A Genealogy*, p. 161.

91 Ibid., p. 173.
92 Joyce, *A Portrait*, p. 188.
93 Ibid., p. 197.
94 Ibid., p. 203.
95 Ibid., p. 257.
96 Pierre Bourdieu, *Distinction: A Social Critique of the Judgement of Taste* (New York: Routledge, 2013), p. 377.
97 Joyce, *A Portrait*, p. 188.
98 Ibid., p. 209.
99 Ibid., pp. 209–10.
100 Ibid., p. 210.
101 Nietzsche, *A Genealogy*, p. 35.
102 Edward Said, 'Yeats and Decolonization', in Terry Eagleton, Fredric Jameson, and Edward Said (eds), *Nationalism, Colonialism, and Literature* (Minneapolis: University of Minnesota Press, 1990), p. 82.
103 Leela Gandhi, *Postcolonial Theory: A Critical Introduction* (New York: Columbia University Press, 1998), p. 109.
104 James Joyce, 'Ireland: Island of Saints and Sages', in Kevin Barry (ed.), *Occasional, Critical, and Political Writing* (Oxford: Oxford University Press, 2000), pp. 108, 120–21.
105 Ibid., p. 125.
106 Andrew Gibson, *Joyce's Revenge: History, Politics, and Aesthetics in Ulysses* (Oxford: Oxford University Press, 2005), p. 17. Enda Duffy characterises *A Portrait* as taking on 'the general air of *ressentiment*', carrying over into the opening chapters of *Ulysses*, where the Bildung-narrative indulges the 'bitter pleasures of personal ressentiment' within the still feted air of 'the most hackneyed nationalism' (*The Subaltern Ulysses* (Cambridge: Harvard University Press, 1994), pp. 13, 27, 31). Seamus Deane has suggested that Joyce's critique of the Irish tendency towards both paralysis and fantasy 'arose out of colonial conditions, involving derivativeness, economic backwardness, internalised submissiveness to established external authority, a *ressentiment* directed towards oneself and one's own culture' ('Dead Ends: Joyce's Finest Moments', in Derek Attridge and Marjorie Howes (eds), *Semicolonial Joyce* (Cambridge: Cambridge University Press, 2000), p. 33).
107 Gibson, *Joyce's Revenge*, pp. 17–18.
108 Joyce, *A Portrait*, p. 238.
109 Ibid., p. 299.
110 Ibid., p. 200.
111 Robert Gooding-Williams, *Zarathustra's Dionysian Modernism* (Palo Alto: Stanford University Press, 2001), pp. 3, 5.
112 Joyce, *A Portrait*, p. 280.
113 Ibid., p. 244.
114 Nietzsche, *A Genealogy*, p. 38.
115 See Vincent J. Cheng, *Joyce, Race, and Empire* (Cambridge: Cambridge University Press, 1995), pp. 15–76; Pericles Lewis, *Modernism, Nationalism, and the Novel* (Cambridge: Cambridge University Press, 2000), pp. 1–51.

116 Nietzsche, *A Genealogy*, pp. 23–25.
117 Ibid., pp. 41, 38.
118 Ibid., p. 161.
119 Ibid., pp. 26, 70.
120 Ibid., p. 38.
121 Bernard Shaw, *Man and Superman: A Comedy and a Philosophy* (New York: Brentano's, 1905), p. 125.
122 W.B. Yeats, *The Collected Works in Verse and Prose of William Butler Yeats: The Hour-Glass, Cathleen ni Houlihan, The Golden Helmet, The Irish Dramatic Movement* (Stratford-upon-Avon: Shakespeare Head Press, 1908), p. 151.
123 Joyce, *A Portrait*, pp. 280, 210.
124 Ibid., p. 124.
125 Ibid., p. 131.
126 Ibid., pp. 147–48, 160.
127 Nietzsche, *A Genealogy*, p. 123.
128 Ibid., p. 196.
129 Joyce, *A Portrait*, p. 167.
130 Ibid., p. 209.
131 Friedrich Nietzsche, *Beyond Good and Evil*, Helen Zimmern (trans.) (Edinburgh: T.N. Foulis, 1909), p. 182.
132 Ibid., p. 204.
133 Nietzsche, *A Genealogy*, p. 67.
134 Ibid., p. 65.
135 Ibid., p. 66.
136 Joyce, *A Portrait*, p. 197.
137 Nietzsche, *A Genealogy*, p. 68.
138 Ibid., p. 66.
139 Ibid., p. 67.
140 Joyce, *A Portrait*, p. 290.
141 Ibid., p. 292.
142 Nietzsche, *A Genealogy*, p. 67.
143 Joyce, *A Portrait*, p. 299.
144 James Joyce, *The Workshop of Daedalus*, Robert Scholes and Richard M. Cain (eds) (Evanston: Northwestern University Press, 1965), p. 108.
145 Gooding-Williams, *Zarathustra's Dionysian Modernism*, p. 4.
146 Sloterdijk, *Nietzsche*, p. 41.
147 James Joyce, *Ulysses* (London: Egoist, 1922), p. 5.
148 Nietzsche, *Antichrist*, p. 241.
149 Oliver St. John Gogarty, *Many Lines to Thee: Letters to G.K.A. Bell from the Martello Tower at Sandycove, Rutland Square, and Trinity College, Dublin, 1904–1907*, James Francis Carens (ed.) (Dublin: Dolmen, 1972), p. 69.
150 Nietzsche, *Antichrist*, p. 241.
151 Sloterdijk, *Nietzsche*, p. 40.
152 Joyce, *Ulysses*, p. 17.
153 Joyce, *A Portrait*, p. 283.

154 Joyce, *Ulysses*, p. 7.
155 Hans Walter Gabler, 'Joyce's Text in Progress', in Attridge (ed.), *The Cambridge Companion to James Joyce*, p. 221.
156 Richard Begam, 'Joyce's Trojan Horse', in Michael Valdez Moses (ed.), *Modernism and Colonialism: British and Irish Literature, 1899–1939* (Durham: Duke University Press, 2007), p. 193.
157 Matthew Bevis, *The Art of Eloquence: Byron, Dickens, Tennyson, Joyce* (Oxford: Oxford University Press, 2010), p. 235.
158 Qtd in Seamus Deane, 'Joyce the Irishman', in Attridge (ed.), *The Cambridge Companion to James Joyce*, p. 35.
159 Eglinton, 'Understanding Nietzsche', 187.
160 Nietzsche, *A Genealogy*, pp. 120–21.
161 Joyce, *Ulysses*, p. 22.
162 Ibid., p. 50.
163 Sloterdijk, *Nietzsche*, p. 66.
164 Joyce, *Ulysses*, p. 22.
165 Sloterdijk, *Nietzsche*, p. 28.
166 Geoffrey H. Hartman, *Criticism in the Wilderness: The Study of Literature Today* (New Haven: Yale University Press, 2007), p. 134.
167 Sloterdijk, *Nietzsche*, p. 39.
168 Joyce, *Ulysses*, p. 23.
169 Eglinton, 'Understanding Nietzsche', 187.
170 Sloterdijk, *Nietzsche*, p. 38.
171 Joyce, *Modernism and Naturalism*, p. 171.
172 Jean-Michel Rabaté, *The Pathos of Distance* (London: Bloomsbury, 2016), p. 52.
173 Joyce, *Ulysses*, p. 16.
174 Ibid., p. 20.
175 Sloterdijk, *Nietzsche*, p. 58.
176 Joyce, *Ulysses*, p. 481.

4

War: 'The duel between Nietzsche and civilisation'

Thomas Kettle's introduction to the English translation of Daniel Halévy's *The Life of Friedrich Nietzsche* begins by declaring that already, in 1911, 'the duel between Nietzsche and civilisation is long since over; and that high poet and calamitous philosopher is now to be judged as he appears in the serene atmosphere of history'. A few years later, after the Irish parliamentarian and economics professor had turned gunrunner and war correspondent, Kettle would have cause to retract his claim (indeed, as we shall see, he also played a significant role in resuming the duel), but in his introductory commentary he could write with confidence that 'the crowd, the common herd, the multitude', which the philosopher famously railed against, 'has dismissed Nietzsche's ideas in order to praise his images ... The immoralist who sought to shatter all the Tables of all the Laws, and to achieve a Transvaluation of all Values, ends by filling a page in *Die Ernte* and other Anthologies for the Young'.[1] If Nordau had first taken up arms against Nietzsche in the name of protecting civilisation from the philosopher's egomaniacal assault on established values, transcribed into a tumultuous prose that was indicative of his 'bellowing insanity', Kettle seems to settle the conflict some two decades later by relegating Nietzsche's oeuvre to the domain of *mere* style.[2] Of course, by dismissing his writing as exemplary poetry for juvenile readers, Kettle also endeavours to diminish any threat that it might continue to represent: to defuse the philosophical dynamite of his prose, which had assailed, at least for a brief time, the status of the Christian faith as the dominant moral system in Western culture. To be sure, in *Thus Spake Zarathustra* and many of his other works, Nietzsche had deployed his aphoristic style to attack Christianity as a decadent faith, guilty of exalting otherworldly values while disparaging instinct, vitality, creativity, and embodied existence. But Kettle, with the presumed force of mass opinion behind him, is pleased to consign 'the gospel of this ambiguous prophet' to the category of rhetorical bluster, albeit some of the finest prose in the German language:[3] 'malice' like that of Nietzsche, he avers, 'always writes briefly and well'. Yet, according to Kettle's introduction, even the most unrefined reader could readily disarm the philosopher's most disturbing teachings by simply reading them as literature ('that gnomic and aphoristic tongue which sneers, preaches, prophesies, chants, intoxicates and dances' through his writing) and then, like Buck Mulligan, sarcastically repeating the refrain 'Thus Spake Zarathustra'.[4] No doubt there is something of a rear-guard action in Kettle's refusal to take Nietzsche's philosophy seriously, as his commentary reasserts the authority of a Christian civilisation (and a Catholic nation) too pious, too moral, and too rational to be imperilled by these exclamations any longer.

Nonetheless, Kettle's brief commentary occupies a noteworthy, though almost entirely forgotten, place in the history of Nietzsche's reception. More incisively than earlier criticism, his introduction advances the argument that insofar as Nietzsche can be said to have 'a doctrine', he makes his assertions in the name of literature, harnessing the imaginative intensity of art to advance his vision:[5] 'the life of his soul', Kettle claims, 'was an incessant creative surge of images, metaphors, symbolisms, mythologies'.[6] What Nietzsche offers, more than anything, is 'a new mode of speech'. With this claim, Kettle predicts the position of critics such as Sarah Kofman, Jacques Derrida, and Alexander Nehemas, involved in rehabilitating the philosopher in the 1970s and 1980s as the so-called 'New Nietzsche', by focusing attention squarely on the aesthetic and rhetorical dimensions of his work.[7] But while these commentators generally acknowledge a productive tension between the categories of literature and philosophy generated by Nietzsche's style, Kettle's introduction contributes to another strain of criticism that sought to exclude his writing from serious consideration (and thereby delegitimise his brand of cultural production) by suggesting that he was not really a philosopher at all so much as a would-be prophet or mystic whose nonsense was only 'redeemed by the lyricism of his language'.[8] Worse, for Kettle as for Nordau, these stylistic flourishes have only served to dress up a series of ideas that Nietzsche and too many of his readers failed to recognise as essentially derivative, so that his rhetorical innovations could be relegated to the conventional terms of Western thought: 'after all, there were sceptics, optimists, tyrants and poets before Zarathustra'.[9] But, worse still, 'the evangel of Zarathustra dissolves into mere sound and fury', because in the rush of his language Nietzsche loses sight of 'reasonable particularity' and falls into poetic assertions without internal consistency or external reference, dazzling paradoxes without sufficient justification or sensible resolution.[10] What Kettle refuses to countenance is the possibility that Nietzsche's polysemous 'images, metaphors, symbolisms, mythologies' might be perceived as necessary, even integral, to his thought, rather than as distractions from some more fundamental doctrine or truth. The 'New Nietzsche' would be recognised for the way that his mobile rhetoric worked to disrupt the dogmatic assertion of certain rational positions or unconditional values precisely by drawing attention to the way that language imprisons us in its conceptual categories. In this sense, his 'new mode of speech' could be seen to not only break free from established systems of thought and belief, but also to aspire to the creation of new myths, the assertion of new perspectives, beyond 'the reactive tradition of theology, metaphysics, and morality'.[11] This was perhaps the biggest danger, then: not the heretical force of some doctrine regarding the death of God, the will to power, or aristocratic values, but the formulation of a rhetoric that could not be understood according to some privileged referent or fixed basis outside the movement of the text itself.

Nietzsche's 'gospel' is, in this sense, *necessarily* 'ambiguous'. His images and metaphors issue in a relentless profusion that resists any attempts on the part of his readers to systematise them precisely because they remain active and mobile. But part of what troubles Kettle – and, indeed, many later commentators – is what he identifies as a series of (largely unintended) 'practical consequences' that have arisen when Nietzsche's readers have attempted to impose various forms of intelligibility on his words as they are inserted into new social contexts or related to new political circumstances:

> Zarathustra is, by a natural kinship, a prophet of the Anarchists, but he hated Anarchism; by a strange transformation, the genius of a certain school of Socialists, but he despised Socialism. German officials in Poland may find in him a veritable Oppressors' Handbook; he danced through the streets at the victory over France, but he derided the German State and Empire as a new idol. He contemned women, but praised indissoluble marriage. He preached pleasure, but celebrated chastity in a noble hymn. He was all for authority and inequality, 'a Joseph de Maistre', says Fouillée, 'who believes in the hangman without believing in the Pope'; but when he looked at a criminal on trial he acquitted everybody except only the judge. He denounced Bismarck and the Kaiser for being too democratic; he regarded Science, too, as disastrously democratic, because it subjected all phenomena, great and small, to the same uniform laws. Will was his god, but he saw the world under the aspect of a Mahometan determinism, and submitted himself to a resignation, an adoption of the hostile ways of existence, an *amor fati* which a Stoic might think extravagant.

For Kettle, then, this is not philosophy or even literature so much as a rather potent – for being so poetically captivating, so rhetorically enticing – form of propaganda, which was available to competing and sometimes contradictory social and political agendas. In the early 1890s, as we observed in the Introduction, Nordau could already denounce Nietzsche's writing, with its 'crazy shower of whirling words' full of 'mazy digressions or useless phrases', as confusing his readers to such an extent that it had become a rallying cry for all manner of 'degenerates', be they anarchists, feminists, or socialists.[12] Not long before Kettle wrote his introduction, Wolfgang Becker expressed similar bewilderment in *The Nietzsche Cult* (1908), which marvelled at the broad range of intellectuals and artists attracted to the philosopher's writings, though he also suggested that these readers failed to appreciate the more brutal aspects of his thought.[13] During intervening years, particularly after the success of Elisabeth Förster-Nietzsche's biography of her brother, there was increasing attention paid to his life as a key to understanding his philosophy. Halévy's biography, which was heavily indebted to the earlier book, sought to retrace the outlines of Nietzsche's philosophy, which had been intentionally distorted by his sister's biography in ways that eventually led to its nationalist and later fascist appropriation. But according to Kettle, in doing so, *The Life of Friedrich Nietzsche* had only succeeded in demonstrating the incongruity between the man and his work: 'It exhibits him as better than his gospel, a hundred times better than most of those disturbers of civilisation who call themselves his disciples'.[14]

Good Europeans and an Irish Nietzsche

The publication of the biography and, especially, Kettle's introduction, was greeted with considerable enthusiasm by the Irish popular press – indeed, *The Freeman's Journal* hailed the volume as 'An Irish Study of Nietzsche', despite its French author, due to the involvement of Kettle and Joseph Maunsel Hone, the Irish publisher, critic, and biographer, who translated the book.[15] For the *Irish Times*, the fact that Nietzsche was 'already known in Ireland', his name having circulated in intellectual circles on the peripheries of the Continent for some time, was proof that he had secured a 'European reputation'.[16] In any case, Halévy's biography did have the distinction of being the first full-length account of Nietzsche's life to appear in English, preceding the translation of the first volume of Förster-Nietzsche's biography by a year. George Moore, a friend of Halévy's since the 1880s and later the subject of a biography by Hone, helped to facilitate the translation. The novelist had praised highly the original French version, *La Vie de Frédéric Nietzsche* (1909), which he recommended to his younger brother as a model for his own attempt to write a biography of their father, the politician George Henry Moore.[17] The anonymous reviewer in the *Irish Times* expresses admiration for Halévy's ability to shed light on Nietzsche's 'solitary combats of thought, with their hidden sufferings, their invisible dangers', which led the 'mild-mannered and modest hypochondriac' to 'think of himself as something of a soldier' as he engaged in his intellectual quarrels.[18] But for both Irish reviewers, the book's 'immediate attraction' was its introduction, even if they were also quick to note that 'Mr. Kettle is not Nietzschean'. He is praised, nonetheless, for his contribution to 'making us "good Europeans"' due to his role in explaining the Nietzschean vogue, if rather belatedly, to the broader reading public in Ireland.[19]

Intriguingly, at this moment in Irish cultural history, the formulation – 'making us "good Europeans"' – negotiates the relationship between the national and perhaps nationalist 'us' and the broader international assemblage. In doing so, the phrase abandons the United Kingdom as an international collective, while it suggests the need to 'make' the Irish into better Europeans, as if that element of their identity still needs to be both invented and enforced. To be sure, as Nietzsche uses the phrase in *Beyond Good and Evil*, 'good Europeans' refers to those cosmopolitan 'free spirits', whether German or Irish or otherwise, who have not succumbed to crude forms of nationalist sentiment or the internecine politics of collective ressentiment. The reviewers, however, are always interested in positioning Nietzsche's thought in relation to Irish culture, even if they are also careful to note, repeating Kettle's position, that there are many 'disturbers of civilisation' who have misappropriated the philosopher's ideas since his death in 1900.

As indicated in the last chapter, Kettle had approached criticism as a Catholic 'duty', which he took up in his early essays and reviews to interpret 'the new thought' emerging from Europe 'in terms of our standard, of explaining the secret divergence from what presents itself to us as the supreme truth'. It was not that Kettle sought theological or doctrinal ends for literature and philosophy so much as a means to accommodate Irish culture to what he viewed as 'all but a matter of faith': 'that the most "modern" writers reject or fail to receive [traditional Christianity] in a completely undogmatic sense'. This attitude helps explains Kettle's interest in Nietzsche's philosophy, which was exemplary not just of this rejection but more broadly of 'the most crowded, shining, confused, intelligent, spacious and chaotic age of human experience'.[20] At the same time, Kettle identified a key role for the Catholic Church in brokering any cultural accommodations in Ireland, since in his estimation the institution was in a position to teach the people the enlivening power of art and to benefit from their heightened relationship with the beautiful, above and beyond the degradations of everyday life. It is for this reason, as the anonymous reviewer in *The Freeman's Journal* notes, 'Mr. Kettle, while he gives unstinted praise to Nietzsche the artist, scarcely conceals his contempt for the philosopher'. Certainly, according to the reviewer, Kettle's introduction undertakes 'an easy task' in pointing out the 'fallacies' of Nietzsche's philosophy and exposing the inconsistencies in his ideas, which 'must' force his followers 'to choose between two antithetical aspects of their master's thought'. Again, style is the culprit insofar as Nietzsche's mobile rhetoric, swarming with images, metaphors, and aphorisms, can be blamed for confusing his thought and confounding or, worse, corrupting his readers. But, as the reviewer claims, Kettle's analysis of these stylistic idiosyncrasies is itself 'disfigured by a verbal jungle ..., the tendency to which is one of the snares of Kettle's temperament', even if, in the end, he 'has a style worth preserving from blemish – eloquent, arresting, individual, full of colour'. The review concludes by claiming that despite, or indeed because of, these peculiarities, 'the book is worth study by any Irishman who desires to share the title, held in highest honour by Mr. Kettle as by Nietzsche of "good European"'.[21]

Kettle, who had been a fellow pupil of Joyce at both Clongowes Wood and UCD, went on to a career that spanned law, politics, and higher education, as well as poetry and journalism, including writing articles for a number of periodicals in both Dublin and London. While still a student at UCD, as his nationalist views were developing and strengthening, he not only wrote essays and reviews featuring Nietzsche, but he also demonstrated his broader intellectual interests by studying language and literature in Germany. After graduation, Kettle entered the Honourable Society of King's End to read law in 1903 and was called to the bar in 1905; he went on to practice law in Dublin and serve briefly as editor of *The Nationist* (which touted itself as an organ of 'complete independence', but displayed clear sympathies for the Parliamentary Party), before he was elected as MP for East Tyrone in 1906. Two years later, he was appointed as the first Professor of National Economics at UCD and, although he was reelected to Parliament in 1910, he soon resigned his seat in order to dedicate his energies more fully to his academic duties. Despite this, Kettle remained devoted to the political views of John Redmond, the Irish Parliamentary Party leader, who believed in a moderate, constitutional path toward Home Rule in Ireland. In the preface of *The Day's Burden* (1910), a collection of his essays published as he began his academic career, Kettle describes his political agenda for Ireland as 'equal parts Home Rule and the Ten Commandments', but he also announces his commitment to the notion that 'in order to become deeply Irish we must become European'.[22] Comprised of essays on topics ranging from 'The Philosophy of Politics' to 'Otto Effertz: Gentleman Socialist' and 'A Frenchman's Ireland', the volume addresses a range of intertwined concerns that he calls simply 'problems'. In this introduction, Kettle anticipates the objection that might follow from his audience: 'glancing at the foreign names which recur in these pages ... what has all this to do with Ireland'. His response is characteristic of his broadly cosmopolitan, if also devoutly Catholic, attitude: 'There is no ecstasy and no agony of the modern soul remote from her experience'.[23] The international outlook expressed in *The Day's Burden* nonetheless earned him more than a little suspicion from some of his nationalist readers: reviewing the book in the *Catholic Book Bulletin*, Father T.H. Fitzgerald asked pointedly, 'Is it not possible to go too far with the European cult?'[24]

If the interest of singular writers such as Shaw, Yeats, and Joyce never amounted to a 'Nietzsche cult' in Ireland, especially given their frequent and sustained absences from their native country, the philosopher and his ideas did come to occupy a more prominent position in public discourse in the years after the publication of *The Life of Friedrich Nietzsche*. No doubt this increased attention also owed something to the long-overdue translation of the remainder of Nietzsche's oeuvre into English, including titles such as *Human, All-Too-Human* (1909), *The Joyful Wisdom* (1910), and *Ecce Homo* (1911), as well as the publication of book-length studies such as J.M. Kennedy's hagiographic (and Shavian) *The Quintessence of Nietzsche* (1909), all of which were reviewed in the *Irish Times*. As we have already seen (and as Nietzsche himself had indeed foreseen), the philosopher's name was evoked in the service of a variety of causes, which drew on a variety of competing interpretations and contradictory associations. For instance, in his Preface to a new edition of John Mitchel's *Jail Journal* (1913), Arthur Griffith described the author of the day-by-day account of five years in a British penal colony as 'a sane Nietzsche', because Mitchel 'laughed at theories of human perfectability and equality, and despised the altruism which sees in the criminal a brother to be coaxed, not a rogue to be lashed'.[25] In his work as a writer, journalist, newspaper editor, and founding president of Sinn Féin, Griffith had often looked to the example of Mitchel, who had advanced his illiberal brand of nationalist rhetoric as one of the chief members of the Young Ireland movement in the 1840s, alongside the likes of Thomas Davis, Michael Doheny, John Blake Dillon, and Charles Gavin Duffy. In 1848, Mitchel had resigned from his position with *The Nation*, the newspaper closely associated with the movement, because as he witnessed the ravages of the Famine he came to believe in the need for 'a more vigorous policy' of resistance against the British Government than the moderate course of action advocated by his colleagues. He founded *The United Irishman* in an effort to rally public opinion behind a program of 'passive resistance reinforced at strategic points by aggressive action',[26] including the acquisition of arms by 'every free man, and every man who desired to become free' that they might defend 'the moral and material wealth' of Ireland.[27] But, in Griffith's estimation, an enervated and effeminate Ireland was incapable of taking up such a cause: 'In a land so lost to reason, the voice of sanity was deemed mad. Ireland failed Mitchel because it failed in manhood'.[28] The strident tone of *The United Irishman* would later become the model for Griffith's newspaper of the same name, founded in 1899, but Mitchel's advocacy of 'spontaneous revolution' also resulted in his arrest, conviction, and sentencing to fourteen years of penal servitude under the Treason Felony Act of 1848.

In his Preface to *Jail Journal*, Griffith seeks to assert the continuing relevance of his predecessor's example of 'intellectual courage in following out unshrinkingly a thought, an opinion, a conviction to its logical conclusion, however terrible the conclusion might be'; but he also attempts to recuperate Mitchel's reputation from the terrible conclusion he had reached after escaping to America and taking up the cause of the Confederacy: that the people of the United States should be 'proud and fond of [slavery] as a national institution, and advocate its extension by re-opening the [slave] trade'.[29] Defiantly, Griffith evokes Nietzsche as a counterpoint to 'the flabby doctrine that has gained some vogue in Ireland – mortally afraid of being esteemed behind "The Age", or limping in the rear of "Progressive Thought" – that an Irish Nationalist must by very virtue of being a Nationalist subscribe to and swallow all the Isms of Sentimentalism, has presumed to apologise for Mitchel – even sometimes to chide his memory'. Rather than excuse or occlude his hero's foulest opinions, Griffith uses the name of Nietzsche to emphasise Mitchel's resistance to 'tyranny' masquerading as 'Enlightenment, Benevolence, Philanthropy, and Progress': like the German philosopher, the Irish nationalist was an untimely figure insofar as 'his blasphemies' shocked the 'ruling gods of his time' – 'Cant and Humbug' – which, Griffith claims in 1913, 'are not dead gods yet'. 'The right of the Irish to political independence', he concludes, 'never was, is not, and never can be dependent upon the admission of equal rights in all other peoples'.[30]

Even as Griffith was summoning Nietzsche for a radical, masculinist, anti-liberal vision of Irish nationalism, others were turning to the philosopher as they advocated for the extension of the franchise to women and a more inclusive view of the advanced nationalist movement. On 25 February 1913, at a weekly meeting of the Irish Women's Suffrage League (IWSL), a frequent contributor to these discussions named Violet Jameson delivered a lecture titled 'Nietzsche and Women', which was published a few weeks later in the feminist newspaper associated with the organisation, *The Irish Citizen*. The organisation had been founded in 1908 by Kettle's sister-in-law, Hanna Sheehy-Skeffington, and his brother-in-law, Francis Sheehy-Skeffington, along with Margaret Cousins and her husband James Cousins, who a few years later went on to found and edit the associated newspaper. In early 1913, the IWSL was in the middle of an extended debate regarding the role of militancy in the suffrage movement. Margaret Cousins and several other members of the organisation had recently been arrested for smashing windows at Dublin Castle in protest of the Third Home Rule Bill (later known as the Government of Ireland Act), which had omitted the issue of suffrage entirely – and they were still imprisoned and on hunger strike at Tullamore Jail when the meeting took place in late February. After some remarks from the IWSL Secretary 'on the present hysterics of the Press regarding militancy', Jameson commenced her speech by acknowledging Nietzsche as the 'greatest modern German philosopher, one of the greatest thinkers that ever lived, and one of the most perfect artists' and a 'man [who] has done more to advance thought, to awaken it, to create order out of chaos, than any other thinker of the nineteenth century'. She went on to concede that, despite his status as 'the greatest apostle of progress the world has ever seen', Nietzsche's ideas regarding 'women and the woman's movement' would seem to represent a troubling 'weak spot in his greatness'.[31] But Jameson's intention (not unlike George Egerton's two decades earlier) was to present her audience with 'a very different Nietzsche – the real Nietzsche, as it seems to me – the inspired prophet, the artist, the creator of that marvellous poem, "Thus Spake Zarathustra"', who could be regarded as the messenger of 'the real truth about woman': 'the real tragedy of what occurs when woman has been imbued with false ideals, and lower moral standards' by a society that does not recognise the capacities of her sex. His 'theory of the Superman', moreover, demonstrates that men and women alike, but only with the help of each other, 'can attain these stupendously high ideals'.[32]

A few months later in May 1913, Jameson would address the IWSL again, this time under the title of 'Patriotism: True and False', to argue in response to the likes of Griffith that advanced nationalists had betrayed their own cause insofar as they had excluded women from their ranks. She contended further that forceful activism was the natural outcome of women's continued subjugation and disenfranchisement in Ireland and that, considering their own efforts to gain political freedom, 'Irishmen ... should blush with shame if they dare to make militancy an excuse for the betrayal of Irishwomen's interests'.[33]

Soon, as he surveyed recent political developments in Europe, Kettle would invoke the name of Nietzsche in relation to a much broader militant trend that was spreading across the Continent with alarming swiftness. In an article titled 'Is Peace Possible?', published in the *Daily News* on 13 June 1913, he questioned the 'mixture of moral evil and economic waste' that was leading to increased military spending, as jingoistic voices in both Great Britain and Germany called for accelerated production of heavy guns, warships, and warplanes. The article goes on to review four new publications on the peace movement and recent Hague conferences, but it also acknowledges that 'there is that apologia for war which roots in the very depth of what is somewhat too largely called human nature'. For all its wickedness, he suggests, war is undeniably a romantic enterprise as attested by 'critics of the Nietzschean school [who] fear the softness of peace, for they see that men have need of hardness'. In response, Kettle argues that those calling for peace must advocate for 'a new ideal of "toughness"' which could counter the 'thrills' that have led 'the instinctive imagination of mankind' to surround war with 'every glory of sound and colour'.[34] Only in this way can a solution be found to the perennial problem of war at a moment when an international arms race threatened bloodshed on a scale never before seen in human history.

Already in Ireland there was considerable debate in the popular press about where the nation might position itself should peace prove impossible: would Irish leaders – John Redmond, in particular – be satisfied with the terms offered by England or would they receive a greater benefit from siding with Germany? Could the war be the opportunity for Ireland to secure its freedom at last? When the Irish Volunteers were formed at a provisional meeting in November 1913, Kettle and his brother, Larry, were among the thirty initial members, who shared the desire to protect Irish Home Rule interests against the Ulster Volunteer Force sworn to oppose them. During the ensuing months, Kettle became an increasingly important figure in the Irish Volunteers, collaborating on a draft of their constitution in April 1914 and helping to formulate their mission – to protect 'the common liberties' of the Irish people. By July, the Irish Volunteers Executive felt the need to arm the group with modern rifles to fulfil this mission and Kettle was sent to procure the guns in Belgium, due primarily to his knowledge of European culture and his facility with the French language. He was still to be found there in early August when Germans troops invaded the country and effectively touched off the First World War, with Great Britain entering the fray shortly thereafter. Occupying a front-row seat for the so-called 'Rape of Belgium', Kettle immediately offered his services to the *Daily News* as a war correspondent, writing a series of articles in the following weeks that place the blame for German militarism squarely at the feet of none other than Friedrich Nietzsche. Kettle was convinced that the sovereignty of another small nation like Ireland must be protected from foreign aggression, but he also believed that something larger was at stake: the fate of Christian civilisation itself. Presenting the terms of the war in this way, Kettle helped to initiate a prominent strain of propaganda that would take hold in newspapers, magazines, pamphlets, and books across the Allied powers in the weeks and months that followed.

The 'big blonde brute' versus Christendom

Kettle commenced his case against Nietzsche in an article that framed the conflict in the starkest language, as 'Europe against the Barbarians'. The title evokes a binarism that had become commonplace by the early decades of the twentieth century and, in doing so, it also reiterates a faith in the idea of Europe, not so much as a diverse collective of national cultures, but as the ordained sanctum of Christian civilisation. The 'issue of war', according to Kettle, thus overwhelmed the mind like 'a vision of terror from the Apocalypse' – an idea that would gain additional currency in the early days of the fighting, as commentators across the Allied powers sought to impress the significance of recent events on newspaper audiences desperate for information and understanding. According to Kettle, the authentic 'Teuton touch', which threatened the Latinate and Catholic strain of European culture he held dear, had pushed aside 'all plain, pedestrian Christian standards' at the moment when the German army had violated the Belgium frontier. His heightened rhetoric attributes the blame for this violation to the 'big blonde brute' which

> stepped from the pages of Nietzsche out on to the plains about Liege. Brought suddenly to think of it one realises the corruption of moral standards for which Germany has in our time been responsible. Since Schopenhauer died nothing has come from her in the region of philosophy except that gospel of domination. And now we suddenly understand that the Immoralists meant what they said. We were reading, not as we thought a string of drawing room paradoxes, but the advanced proof sheets of a veritable Bullies' Bible.[35]

The image of the 'blond beast' ('*blonde Bestie*'), one of Nietzsche's most provocative metaphors, is here coopted and corrupted as the 'big blonde brute' to emphasise a connection with the Aryan myth of racial superiority developed by French aristocrat Arthur de Gobineau in the mid-nineteenth century. Nietzsche does argue that what we call civilisation, under the pervasive influence of Christianity, has consistently thwarted human instincts in the name of the 'moralities of taming', which have only succeeded in 'sickening' and 'domesticating' 'the finest specimens of the "blond beast"' by seducing them 'into the monastery'.[36] But here Kettle's rhetoric, drawing on Nordau's example, stresses the ruthless quality of Nietzsche's figure because it serves well the image of Teutonic barbarism that he seeks to construct, affirming the distinction between the Christian civilisation of Europe and the aggressive militarism of German culture. Translated from the book to the battlefield, then, the image of the 'big blonde brute' speaks to the ideological force that Kettle's reporting attributes to Nietzsche's thought, even as it attests to a fundamental shift from the realm of metaphor and theory to that of propaganda and praxis.

There is, the article suggests, a lesson in exegesis to be had here. The 'good news' of the gospel, with its indisputable message about personal salvation and the kingdom of God, has been challenged by an alternative faith, which may deal in irony and indirection, but which ultimately provides a fearsome doctrine. Nietzsche's philosophy is reduced to the status of 'a gospel of domination … a veritable Bullies' Bible', so that the present conflict becomes a holy war, a battle against enemies who are not just a threat to a nation or a coalition, but to Christian civilisation itself. What his writing manages to do in this way is to make a rhetorical assault on Christian values, a rhetorical assault that has been translated into a literal attack on the Belgian nation and its people. His warrior rhetoric at last pushed the 'monstrous contradiction in terms – an armed peace' that had defined international relations in Europe into armed conflict, as all other interests – financial, political, or humanitarian – had surrendered to a bellicose passion. Of course, this assumes a kind of semantic closure: the dazzling paradoxes of Nietzsche's writing should no longer be entertained as rhetorical strategies calling for interpretive efforts that might resolve or possibly further elaborate their apparent contradictions. Instead, they had been fixed in the form of an immoral doctrine. Thus Kettle's article attributes a direct racial and national significance to Nietzsche's metaphor of the 'blond beast', even though the philosopher associated the image with, among other things, the strength of a lion, the ideal of a Greek hero, the founders of the state, and the early settlers of Italy. In a manner that would be repeated over and over in the following months, Nietzsche's dynamic rhetoric was immobilised and turned against him, even as his assertions regarding the mobile and metaphorical quality of his language, of all language, were studiously ignored. Ironically, as we know, the philosopher had referred to *Thus Spake Zarathustra* as a 'fifth Gospel' and a 'new "holy book"', but it was a text that proclaimed its status precisely through the parodic subversion of earlier forms of evangelical discourse. According to Kettle, after the outbreak of war, Nietzsche should no longer be read for the images and metaphors, the parodies and paradoxes, that coursed through his writings but for the articles of a counter-faith, a dis-evangel, that aligned him with 'the General Berhardis who have been teaching Germany to desire war, to provoke it, to regard it as a creative and not a destructive act'.[37]

This is the clear verdict of Kettle's commentary: Germany, under Nietzsche's corrupting influence, has commenced a direct assault on Christian civilisation. The ostensible evidence against the philosopher includes his assertion that 'Nothing is true, everything is permitted', which the war correspondent quotes from *A Genealogy of Morals*, though he appends 'to the strong' to the phrase. Again, Kettle adds something to the source material in order to underscore his interpretation, but, in this case, it should also be noted that Nietzsche himself was quoting another source, for which he did not take full responsibility. Instead, he ascribes it to the Order of Assassins encountered by Christian crusaders, though this attribution is also contested: commentators from Albert Camus to Arthur Danto have identified the phrase as coming from Dostoevsky's *Brothers Karamazov*, but only the second half, 'everything is permitted', can be found in the novel. Nietzsche and subsequent adopters of the phrase, such as William Burroughs, source the slogan to Near Eastern thought, specifically Hassan-i Sabbāh, the twelfth-century cult leader of Isma'ilism. In any case, Nietzsche opposes this daring assertion to the values of Western civilisation: 'Has a European, a Christian free spirit ever, become involved in this sentence and its labyrinthine consequences?' he asks.[38] The function of the proposition in *A Genealogy* is particularly to challenge the ascetic ideal and its epistemological significance which, for Nietzsche, has come to dominate modern men – even the 'pallid atheists, antichristians, immoralists, nihilists; these sceptics, ephetics, spiritually *hectics* of the spirit' (original emphasis) who continue to believe in absolute truth, and to value it as an enduring ideal. But for Kettle, it has become a dangerous slogan put into action by the German war effort: 'at the end of the process a monster, gorged with blood and with the torn limbs of civilisation, is to lie sprawled over all Central Europe, while some new metaphysician from Berlin booms heavily into his self-intoxicated brain some new fable of preordination'.[39] This terrifying vision of Imperial Germany as the embodiment of a philosophy of brutality and conquest plays on themes that would become prominent motifs in the holy war rhetoric of Allied propaganda throughout the extended conflict: the monstrosity, immorality, and bloodthirstiness of the enemy, which threatened to bring about a kind of apocalypse, wiping Christian civilisation off the map of the European Continent in favour of a horrifying Teutonic culture.

Just a few days after Kettle published his first article on the war, that vision seemed already to have become a reality, as he observed the burned-out hulk of the Malines Cathedral in northern Belgium. 'My mind said to me', he wrote in the *Daily News*, '"This is how Nietzsche, from his grave, spate, as he wished to spit, upon Nazareth"'.[40] Acknowledging his point of view as 'an Irish Catholic', Kettle describes his response upon walking into 'the Grand Place' and seeing the destruction wrought by German guns, a response that does not register the material cost of the bombardment so much as the spiritual injury.[41] He continues: 'A picture came of that sinister Quixote, who made cruelty his sacrament, and who was yet so humanly dear in some of his moods, standing behind a great Krupp howitzer and shouting, "Charlottenburg *contra* Christ. I back Charlottenburg!"'[42] Together, these images, metaphors, and other tropes form a compelling piece of propaganda. Nietzsche, long dead at the time of writing, has been revived by the German war effort, which is viewed as a defilement of all Christendom, rendered metonymically in the form of Nazareth. If Kettle's article, even in the midst of this demonising rhetoric, preserves a space for Nietzsche's humanity, it nonetheless depicts the eccentric figure as worldly and 'sinister' enough to operate a Krupp howitzer (or 'Big Bertha'), the latest and most horrific example of modern military technology. In this guise, the philosopher becomes a radical Teutonic chauvinist, who bellows patriotic slogans that pit Germany (also rendered metonymically in the form of the affluent Berlin borough of Charlottenburg) against the Saviour himself. The complexities of the war's origins, still fiercely debated by historians today, are neatly reduced to a personified dualism – Nietzsche versus Christ. By structuring Kettle's rhetoric, the dualism effectively complements the other details of this early example of atrocity propaganda as it catalogues the destruction rained down on the cathedral.

In both articles, Kettle links the events in Belgium to concerns in Ireland, asserting the general European importance of the recent invasion and the broad cosmopolitan concerns of the Home Rule movement, while reaffirming the boundary between civilisation and barbarity, which he believed now united Ireland and its allies against a common German enemy. 'Europe', he claims pointedly, is 'tortured to the pattern of a new devilry'. Then, addressing the readers of the *Daily News* across Great Britain and Ireland, he identifies the only appropriate response to the situation: 'you say to yourself, as you hear all the world saying: *C'est incroyable*! It is not to be believed. It is a nightmare! And then the conviction shapes itself clearly, settles upon and masters your mind, that this German assault on civilisation has got to be repelled and utterly shattered once and for all'. With a slip into French, Kettle indicates his sympathies and advocates the same response from his audience, who must acknowledge their status as 'good Europeans' and band together against this threat to their shared civilisation: 'There can be no more isolation', from 'the comity of Europe'. Kettle reminds his readers, both English and Irish, that Redmond had previously offered 'friendship' (i.e. an alliance) in return for 'justice' (i.e. Home Rule), though 'never in such dramatic circumstances' as those taking shape in August 1914. 'It is assumed', then, that Great Britain 'has reconciled Ireland' and it is affirmed by the war correspondent that 'a reconciled Ireland is ready to march side by side with her into any desperate trial'. For England to do otherwise would be tantamount to the 'Prussian program' against civilisation and like the brutal invasion of Belgium, 'it is incredible', according to Kettle.[43]

One of the many ironies of Kettle's activity as a war correspondent is that his Nietzschean thesis became an important early component of British propaganda – in what would become the most powerful propaganda machine that the world had ever witnessed. As we have observed in Chapter 1, Britain saw the rise of its own Nietzsche cult at the end of the nineteenth century, with the publication of his works in English and the emergence of several avowedly Nietzschean journals, such as *The Eagle and the Serpent* (1898–1902) and *Notes for Good Europeans* (1903–9), edited by Thomas Common, and *The New Age* (1907–22), edited by another important Nietzschean exponent, Alfred Orage, with financial help from George Bernard Shaw. But, in the years leading up to the war, a number of British journalists and intellectuals had also expressed scepticism and even dismay at the Nietzschean vogue that had made its way into English culture. As early as 1907, in a review of Orage's *Friedrich Nietzsche: the Dionysian Spirit of the Age*, Shaw was bemoaning this defensive reaction:

> All that can be said here is that if half the energy that has been wantonly devoted to persuading England that ... Nietzsche was the unscrupulous apologist of every selfish bully in Europe, had been employed in keeping English culture reasonably up to date, our generation would have gained at least thirty years in comparative enlightenment ... The journalists have read in one another's paragraphs a certain sentence about 'the big blonde beast'; and from this misunderstood sample they construct an imaginary Nietzsche of impossible mental and moral inferiority to themselves.[44]

With the outbreak of the war, British commentators moved quickly from scepticism and dismay to denunciation, following Kettle's lead in characterising Nietzsche as the villainous inspiration for German militarism. For instance, just a month before the war commenced, when Thomas Hardy had been invited to honour the seventieth anniversary of the philosopher's birth, the British novelist and poet had written that 'it is a question whether Nietzsche's philosophy is sufficiently coherent to be of great ultimate value, and whether those views of his which seem so novel and striking appear thus only because they have been rejected for so many centuries as inadmissible under human rule'.[45] But by 7 October 1914, as he lamented the German bombardment of the Reims Cathedral in a letter to the *Manchester Guardian*, his assessment had harshened: 'Should it turn out to be a predetermined destruction ... it will strongly suggest what a disastrous blight upon the glory and nobility of that great nation has been wrought by Nietzsche, with his followers Treitschke, Bernhardi, etc'. What Hardy finds most perplexing in this state of affairs is that 'the profound thinkers in Germany, and to some extent, elsewhere, can have been so dazzled by the writer's bombastic poetry – for it is a sort of prose-poetry – as to be blinded to the fallacy of his arguments – if they can be called arguments which are off-hand assumptions'.[46]

As the British propaganda campaign against Germany unfolded it transformed Nietzsche's most provocative tropes – including the Übermensch and 'the blonde beast' – into caricatures of jingoism and brutality. In this way, the campaign succeeded in harnessing the media ecology of 1914, with the newspaper as the principal means of information dispersal, to demonise the philosopher as the progenitor of mass violence, while deflecting blame from the interests of the propagandists, who idealised their own motives for entering the war. Recent historical accounts suggest that rather than being the *outcome* of mass jingoism and anti-German antagonism, the war was in fact the *cause* of 'massively increased anti-Germanism and popular patriotism':[47] the *Daily News*, along with the *Manchester Guardian*, had run a strong anti-war campaign right up to 4 August, but the outbreak of war precipitated a change in tone in many outlets of the British press. This touched off a discursive eruption that was organised in part by the War Propaganda Bureau, which enlisted major authors and intellectuals such as William Archer, Arthur Conan Doyle, Arnold Bennett, Ford Maddox Ford, Rudyard Kipling, H.G. Wells, and Hardy himself. Nicholas Martin has detailed the way that the figure of Nietzsche (that is, as both a trope and a historical personage) was put to use by the propaganda effort to explain to the British reading public the supposed bloodlust of their enemy. Archer, for instance, wrote a pamphlet called *Fighting a Philosophy*; Wells expounded on the evils of Nietzscheanism; even Holbrook Jackson, a prominent journalist and avowed Nietzschean, used his editorial post at *T.P'.s Weekly* to opine on the German philosopher's foul influence. Kettle himself would go on to pen additional attacks on Nietzsche for a new iteration of the publication, *T.P'.s Journal of Great Deeds of the War*. The effects of this loosely orchestrated campaign, as Martin notes, were twofold: first, to lower Nietzsche to the status of a 'melodrama villain'; second, to raise his profile from that of a relatively little-known philosopher to that of a 'household name'. But in the process, 'the British Nietzsche of 1914' came to bear 'only a passing resemblance to the ironic and incisive, elliptical and elusive Nietzsche who emerges from his texts ... What emerged instead was a swaggering Prussian brute'.[48]

Response to 'frightful doctrines' in Ireland

In early September 1914, shortly after Kettle published his article on the destruction of the Malines Cathedral, his collaborator on *The Life of Friedrich Nietzsche*, Joseph Hone, published a rebuttal of sorts: a letter to the editors of the *Irish Times* titled simply 'Nietzsche and the War'. The immediate stimulus for the letter was a front-page article from the 2 September issue of the newspaper, which had followed Kettle's lead in 'attributing the origins of the present war to the "frightful doctrines" of Frederick [*sic*] Nietzsche'. Hone begins his response by questioning whether those doctrines 'are so frightful as they can be made to appear from a few popular quotations taken out of context from Nietzsche's later works'. After criticising recent newspaper propaganda for conveniently misconstruing Nietzsche's words in a manner that served its own partisan objectives, Hone attempts to absolve the philosopher from blame for those words by claiming that they were 'written at a time when [he] was on the verge of madness'. Nietzsche may have been his own worst enemy in this regard, not just because his metaphorical and aphoristic claims lend themselves to appropriation for a range of political ends, but because they retain the taint of his own biography – his words can be twisted, but all the more easily because they were twisted in the first instance. This nonetheless throws into doubt the notion that his claims could be taken as 'doctrines' in any proper sense, and Hone is careful to use the inverted commas when he reiterates the term in the subsequent sentence. He is also careful to point out that these 'doctrines', however errant or elusive, 'were never accepted in Germany, where [Nietzsche] was regarded, both in his life and after his death, as an enemy of the State, a poet of anarchy'. Nonetheless, the Irish commentator must acknowledge that Nietzsche was responsible for claims such as 'a good war justifies any cause', and even that 'this aphorism is popular in Prussian militarist circles', though this is again an opportunistic appropriation of his thought, no better and no worse than that performed by anti-German propagandists. But rather than explore the metaphorical implications of such statements, Hone pursues the course of biographical criticism in order to seek the authentic centre of the philosopher's position on violence and warfare. Asking his readers to recall that, in the Franco-Prussian War, Nietzsche served as an ambulance driver, the Irish commentator quotes from the philosopher's reflections on the experience: 'war ... obliges men to seek an ideal order, an order of beauty and duty, the ends of a life which are too cruel'. Perhaps guilty of the same kind of selectiveness that he faults in others, Hone finds in these words clear evidence that, contrary to popular opinion, 'Nietzsche was at bottom the most tender of men'.[49]

In the weeks that followed, as Ireland's commitment to the war effort became an increasingly urgent matter, Nietzsche's philosophy and Germany's threat to Christian civilisation were evoked repeatedly in the popular press. On 5 September 1914, for instance, the *Leitrim Observer* published an anonymous article titled 'Nietzsche on War', which comprised its own riposte to Hone's letter two days earlier in the *Irish Times*. Acknowledging, with no small irony, that Nietzsche might be described as gentle and mild, the article leads off with the strident claim that 'Germany has produced many philosophies of violence, but chief among them' was that of the 'will-to-power' and 'the superman'. Blame for the current conflict is attributed less to the spirit of these notions than to their susceptibility to misprision: 'it is very easy to twist his will-to-power idea into false doctrine, and in every country in Europe and America weaklings have guzzled his brave words until they have half imagined themselves supermen'. Nietzsche's rhetoric, relying on bold claims as much as 'philosophical argumentation', on provocative metaphors as much as precise concepts, is seen as more dangerous than any agenda or intention that may reside behind its various utterances, which are often taken 'to heart without waiting to probe too deeply into their meaning'.[50] Unfortunately, according to the article's anonymous author, this is particularly the case regarding his claims about war. Nietzsche's latter-day apologists, from Walter Kaufmann to Robert Solomon and Kathleen Higgins, have been at pains to demonstrate that, although his choice of the term has prompted much misunderstanding, when Nietzsche refers to 'war' the word is, almost invariably, 'used metaphorically':[51] 'the term was associated with a struggle for knowledge as the outcome of Socratic dialogue' or 'his own struggle within himself, with health, with his Christian bourgeois upbringing, with his own feelings of meekness, pity and ressentiment'.[52] The author of 'Nietzsche on War' is willing to concede that the philosopher 'was not pro-Prussian' and that he had little respect for 'hereditary symbols of power'; but the commentator nonetheless finds 'little doubt of his violent predilections', as they review a number of the philosopher's provocative claims, lifted from their original context and inserted into the circumstances of the present conflict. Yet, for all the professed certainty regarding Nietzsche's 'violent predilections', this assessment of his work is profoundly ambivalent, full of terms and phrases such as 'apparently', 'sort of', and 'may have'. That is, in an effort to account for the metaphorical and fragmentary qualities of Nietzsche's writing, the article undermines any propagandistic claims it seeks to advance because it fails to make the categorical assertions on which that mode of speech often relies.

That is the case except for where Nietzsche comments not on war, but on England; here, at least in the eyes of this anonymous commentator, his position appears to be unequivocal, even if the current implications of his position remain uncertain. The 'fire-eating Prussians' who have taken his comments on war far too literally have 'imbibed Nietzsche's contempt for England with even greater relish'. This contempt was to become a key element of the emerging debate in Ireland precisely because it severs allegiances that are made of other grounds: if the vast majority of Irish readers could agree that an advocacy of war – and an attack on Christian civilisation – were regrettable components of Nietzsche's thought, his attitude towards England was another matter. 'One of Nietzsche's main principles', the article tells us, 'is that the desire of happiness is a sign of weakness, so when he writes, "Man does not desire happiness, only the English man does that", we can imagine his scorn'. To be sure, as we have already seen, the German philosopher harshly criticises the English temperament as something base, particularly the utilitarian philosophy that had dominated nineteenth-century English thought with its call for 'the greatest happiness of the greatest number'. Nietzsche identified this brand of philosophy as not just a failure of the imagination, but a threat to the future of Europe and the West, which would continue to decline as long as they remained wedded to this strain of ethical and political thought. As the author tells us, Nietzsche 'hated English democratic institutions and advised Germany against imitating them, and he was convinced that Britain's world-Empire was detrimental to the fulfilment of Europe's destiny in which Germany, in his view, was to play the part of broker and middleman'. With this grand vision, the anonymous author at last seems to address the real stakes of the current conflict, but the article ends here without further commentary. Are the readers of the *Leitrim Observer* to resist Nietzsche's antipathy for 'English democratic institutions' and 'Britain's world-Empire', which must be saved through the spilling of blood, including Irish blood, on the battlefields of Europe?[53] Or might they be tempted to throw in their lot with Nietzsche and Germany, at least an idea of Germany, as proponents of a different vision of European destiny, including the rise of a sovereign Irish republic?

On the very day that 'Nietzsche on War' was published, 5 September 1914, the Supreme Council of the Irish Republican Brotherhood, pursuing their aim to establish an 'independent democratic republic' in Ireland, held a meeting at the Gaelic League headquarters on Rutland (later Parnell) Square. There, the gathered leaders of the oath-bound organisation agreed that the outbreak of the European conflict represented the opportunity for an armed insurrection in Ireland – and, in so doing, they touched off a momentous series of events. Several days later, a larger meeting was called to include other advanced nationalist leaders, including Patrick Pearse, James Connolly, and Joseph Plunkett, as well as representatives from Sinn Féin and the Irish Volunteers, who resolved to take action before the war had ended. Indeed, those advocating for physical force nationalism had revived the title of an 1845 article by John Mitchel as their slogan: 'England's Difficulty Is Ireland's Opportunity'. On 18 September 1914, the British Parliament did finally pass the Government of Ireland Act, granting the Irish an interim form of Home Rule, only to immediately suspend its implementation until the end of the war. Nonetheless, the legal achievement of self-government was important for Redmond who, just two days later, urged the Irish Volunteers to join the British war effort in his infamous speech at Woodenbridge, County Wicklow. In that oration, as Keith Jeffrey observes, Redmond 'drew on grand causes and Big Words', and in that way, I would add, advanced the same rhetoric that Kettle had deployed in his newspaper reports from Belgium:[54] 'The interests of Ireland – of the whole of Ireland – are at stake in the war. This war is undertaken in defence of the highest principles of religion and morality and right'. On this basis, Redmond announced a twofold duty to the gathered volunteers: 'Go on drilling and make yourself efficient for the Work, and then account yourselves as men, not only for Ireland itself, but wherever the fighting line extends, in defence of right, of freedom, and religion in this war'.[55]

The impact of this rhetoric was not entirely what Redmond had desired. Instead of galvanising support for the war among the volunteer forces, the speech enraged the anti-English contingent of the Irish Volunteers, leading to a split that divided the group into the minority Irish Volunteers led by Eoin MacNeill and the National Volunteers loyal to Redmond. Meanwhile, Sir Roger Casement, the former British diplomat turned ardent Irish republican, was making plans to travel to Berlin so that he could negotiate an alliance with the Kaiser and raise arms for a coming rebellion. Soon, in an anonymously published pamphlet, Casement would directly counter the pervasive rhetoric framing the British war effort as a fight for civilisation: 'once the chief factor governing the conflict is perceived, namely, the British claim to own the seas and to dominate the commercial intercourse of the world, then the cause of Germany became the cause of European civilisation at large'.[56] Jeffrey further observes that with this rhetoric and its 'Big Words' – especially that increasingly resonant term, 'civilisation' – Casement marshalled a 'mirror image of those of John Redmond, Thomas Kettle, and others in support of the Allied War effort'.[57] But such rebuttals could not alter the fact that Redmond had made an official declaration of allegiance to the British crown and its military forces, calling for the assent of not just the Volunteer forces, but the Irish people, who were now committed, at least nominally, to the Allied cause.

With Ireland at last implicated in the conflict, Catholic and Protestant religious leaders began to weigh in on the matter in a propaganda campaign that pitted pro-recruiting Redmondites against advanced nationalist groups such as Sinn Féin, which strongly opposed Irish participation in the British war effort. Following Kettle's lead, the pro-recruiting commentators, who were in the majority, often employed the figure of Nietzsche as an emblem of German brutality, in a conflict that was fought not for short-sighted political or economic ends, but for the fate of Christian civilisation itself. German culture, with Nietzsche as its figurehead, was cast as wholly anti-Christian, even demonic, while the Allied war effort was portrayed as pursuing God's will in a conflict between good and evil. To be sure, the portrayal replicated a set of images now prominent in propaganda across the Allied powers (and mirrored in German propaganda), but in Ireland it took on an added urgency given the nation's tenuous relationship with Great Britain. For instance, a 28 September article in the Redmondite *Freeman's Journal* titled 'Nietzsche's Teachings Put into Practice: Irish Priest's Accusation', summarises the claims of Rev William Delany: 'How much of German vandalism in the war is to be attributed to the teachings of some of the modern anti-Christian writers of the country is a matter of which the authors of the burning of Louvain and Malines, and of the destruction of the Cathedral of Rheims can best be cognizant'. A prominent Jesuit priest and educationalist, Father Delany had served as President of University College Dublin during Kettle's time as a student and had also overseen the publication of *St. Stephen's* when Kettle's writing had appeared in the periodical. In *The Freeman's Journal*, Delany answers his own query by proclaiming that 'some of the most striking abominations of Nietzsche's so-called "philosophy"' have 'practically been adopted by a large number of Germans, not only in the lower but of the military class and it helps to explain the barbarity of their actions in war'. The next section of the article, headed 'Counsel of Barbarism', reasserts the binary opposition that divided Ireland from its enemies: 'Nietzsche ... not only approves of expressly of such barbarity, but counsels it in order to get rid of the greatest of all curses – Christianity'. Germany has been thoroughly corrupted, Delany argues, because it has allowed the teaching of Nietzsche's 'doctrines' in its universities and approved the action of military leaders, including the Kaiser himself, who attacks 'all that is Christian or that honours Christian virtue'. The causal relationship between these doctrines and the present conflict is clear for Delany, who concludes by asking if it is any wonder, 'with such teachings by a University Professor, and adopted by a large number of educated Germans, ... that Louvain was destroyed or the Cathedral at Rheims? Is it not the lesson which was expressly inculcated by the miserable man who died in a lunatic asylum?'[58] With this last *ad hominem* swipe, then, Delany seeks to confirm the barbarity of the German cause, while affirming the civilised, rational, and fundamentally righteous character of the Allied war effort that unites Ireland and England.

Over the next two months Nietzsche's name and his 'doctrines' were invoked in newspapers across Ireland – from the *Irish Times* to the *Catholic Bulletin*, *Irish Independent*, *Westmeath Examiner*, *Southern Star*, and *Freeman's Journal* – as bywords for barbarism, Kaiserism, and German militarism. On 13 October, for instance, the *Irish Times* reported on an address given by the Methodist Reverend R. Lee Cole, titled 'Kaiserism vs. Christianity', which 'dealt with the influence of Nietzsche's philosophy on German ideals. By the Nietzsche doctrine he meant Kaiserism'.[59] The calculation had become obvious: Nietzsche's 'incessant surge of images, metaphors, symbolisms, mythologies' had been reduced to a militaristic doctrine, deployed to instruct the German people in the ways of war and prepare them to exert their will on Christendom. On 30 October, the *Irish Times* published an article reporting on the fiftieth Synod for the Diocese of Meath, which was headed by the provocative subtitle 'Poisonous Doctrines of Nietzsche'. Addressing the Synod, the Reverend Dr John Bennett Keane, Bishop of Meath, attested that

> a few years since, knowing the popularity in Germany of the philosopher Nietzsche, whose name had recently become so familiar, he ... procured whatever of his writings he found accessible, and, being impressed by the dangerous anti-Christian tendencies of the doctrines of which Nietzsche was the prophet, he called the attention of the Synod to the pernicious effect upon the world their acceptance by a country of such light and leading as Germany might exercise.

The war was seen as a 'striking exemplification' of just this effect. The philosopher was best viewed as the prophet and pedagogue of German militarism, and together the teacher and his pupils were to be recognised as the enemies of all Christendom.

Just how 'anti-Christian' Nietzsche's teachings were could be illustrated readily by a single resounding example – his infamous dismissal of 'The Sermon on the Mount'. According to Reverend Keane, the philosopher offers a kind of counter-sermon for the express purpose of moral, or rather immoral, instruction, delivered by a member of an anti-Christian priesthood, who represents a direct threat to the Irish people and the Allied nations. The true lesson of all this is clear to the clergyman: the Germans, incapable of putting Jesus's teachings – 'the lofty precepts expanded in that wonderful sermon' – into practice, have adopted Nietzsche's alternative faith as a national call to arms, exemplifying the corruption of both their culture and their cause.[60]

The Davis centenary and continued debate

The contradictory effects of this propaganda campaign were demonstrated rather dramatically by events surrounding a centenary celebration for the nationalist poet and newspaper publisher Thomas Davis on 20 November 1914. Davis, the principal organiser and poet of the Young Ireland movement, had promoted cooperation between Protestants and Catholics, arguing that nationality was not a matter of blood or sect, but of commitment to the Irish nation. Dedicating his short life to the cause of Irish nationalism, he founded the *Nation* newspaper in 1842 (which would publish contributions by John Mitchel until 1848) and wrote a number of nationalistic ballads for its pages. In the twentieth century, he became a hero to many nationalist leaders who were eager to promote not just national independence but a unique and vibrant national identity. The centenary celebration of his life and legacy, organised by the Trinity College Gaelic Society, was originally planned to take place on the campus of the university; however, the Vice

Provost, Professor J.P. Mahaffy, posted a letter to the organisers forbidding the event on his campus after he learned that 'a man called Pearse' would be on the rostrum.⁶¹ By November 1914, Patrick Pearse had become famous, or rather infamous, for his anti-recruiting activities across Ireland. The student leaders of the Gaelic Society responded in writing that the meeting was being organised to honour the memory of Davis and that 'the matter of the present European war' would not be introduced.⁶² Even after the entire correspondence was published in the Dublin papers on 14 November, the Vice Provost would not relent. To go forward with the event, while including a member of the advanced nationalist movement, an organisation called the Students' National Literary Society had to step in and secure an alternative venue – the Antient Concert Rooms in Dublin, the site of the inaugural production of the Irish Literary Theatre, *The Countess Cathleen*, fifteen years earlier. The young president of the Society, Denis Gwynn, immediately contacted W.B. Yeats with an invitation to speak in honour of Davis at the meeting; he also extended an invitation to Thomas Kettle, who had recently returned to Ireland from Belgium – but only after volunteering for service in the Royal Dublin Fusiliers, an infantry regiment of the British army. Given his rhetorical talents, but also his poor health, he was assigned to the duties of a recruiting officer and had spent the previous weeks travelling throughout Ireland in the effort to secure additional volunteers for the British war effort. These duties were in line with his commitment to the Redmondite position and his belief in the cause of small nations, but they made Kettle a rather controversial figure.

The Davis centenary celebration, which was described in detail the next day by Dublin papers and later by the poet Austin Clarke in his memoir, *A Penny in the Clouds*, finally took place on 21 November in a 'long dusty hall downstairs' at the Antient Concert Rooms. As Gwynn gave his opening address, explaining how the event came to be held in the hall, Yeats and Pearse were seated near him on the platform, though a seat next to them, intended for Kettle, remained empty. Gwynn then introduced Yeats, who had just begun to speak when heavy footsteps were heard resounding through the hall, as Lieutenant Kettle, dressed in his British officer's uniform, entered from the back. 'It was obvious', Clarke reports, 'that he had his fill of Irish whiskey in order that he might defy more confidently the small group of Sinn Féiners'.⁶³ After this disruption, Yeats began his speech by addressing the decision by Professor Mahaffy to exclude Pearse from the rostrum at Trinity, a decision that 'had puzzled him (Mr. Yeats), because there was a maxim which they all accepted – that they should never refuse to listen to a scholar on his own subject, even though they greatly objected to his politics. (Applause)'.⁶⁴ 'I am not', Yeats continued, 'more vehemently opposed to the Unionism of Professor Mahaffy than I am to the pro-Germanism [of Pearse], but we are here to talk about literature and about history'.[65] Before addressing the topics himself, however, Yeats confessed that 'I have friends fighting in Flanders, I had one in the trenches in Antwerp, and I have a very dear friend [Maud Gonne] nursing the wounded in a French hospital. How can I help feeling as they feel and desiring a German defeat?'[66] Then, turning to his ostensible theme, the poet delivered a long oration that compared Davis's love of Ireland to Mitchel's hatred of England and claimed that such animosity soon turned back on one's own countrymen. Davis's life and work, according to Yeats, provided an antidote to such antipathy and ressentiment.

When Yeats had finished, the chairman called on Kettle to propose a vote of thanks to Yeats – and as Kettle walked to the platform 'he was greeted with hisses and some applause, and there were cries of "Turn him out"'. Defiant, Kettle addressed the crowd and, after acknowledging the controversy created by Mahaffy and the timely comments made by Yeats, 'perhaps, their greatest master', he asserted to the increasingly unruly crowd that 'it was not proper to exploit the memory of Davis for the furtherance of any [political] opinions'. 'He hoped that Mr. Pearse and all his other enemies would have the opportunity of stating everything they knew, whether through the medium of hissing or some more articulate medium (Applause.)' This exhibition of barbed wit earned Kettle applause and, to his credit, Pearse seconded the motion. Gwynn, in putting forward the motion, took the opportunity to assert that 'Davis would not have been the great man he was if he had not been educated in Trinity College. Ireland never needed Davis more than to-day. (Applause)'. The *Irish Times* reported the next day that 'Mr. Yeats, in reply, quoted from Nietzsche, whom he described as the great German idealist and philosopher. (Applause.) He had done that on purpose, for he would never hear Nietzsche applauded again by a Dublin audience, and he wished to hear him applauded once. (Laughter)'.[67]

What are we to make of this rather astonishing turn of events, concluded by an equally astonishing turn of phrase? Clarke reports that Yeats's remark was a 'simple device', made with the sole intention of bringing 'in irreverently the name of Nietzsche, for the German poet and philosopher of the Superman was regarded with horror in all of our pro-British press during the First Great War'. The propaganda campaign had only 'annoyed' Clarke who had been reading with 'guilty delight' a number of Nietzsche's works and had developed a particular fascination with his 'theory of Dionysian and Apollonian moods'. Certainly, the sense of 'horror' with which Nietzsche was regarded could be attributed in no small part to Kettle's work as a war correspondent; clearly, Yeats's comments were aimed as much at Kettle and his efforts as at the sentiments of the crowd gathered in the Antient Concert Rooms. Nonetheless, as Clarke notes, the morning after the centenary celebration newspaper placards appeared across Dublin 'with the startling announcement: Dublin audiences cheer Nietzsche'.[68] Yeats had struck a chord with the anti-British, anti-recruiting members of his audience who had come to know Nietzsche, through newspaper reporting across Ireland, as an enemy of their enemy more than as a prophet of barbarism or an evangelist of the Antichrist.

This does not necessarily harmonise with Yeats's comments about his own impartiality earlier in the evening. Flippant as it may have been, his allusion to Nietzsche represents a more general protest against the appropriation of the philosopher for propagandistic or political ends (or, at least, propagandistic and political ends that Yeats did not endorse). 'In Ireland above all nations', he had claimed in the opening lines of his lecture, 'where we have so many bitter divisions, it is necessary to keep always unbroken the truce of the Muses'.[69] If his allusion to Nietzsche was meant, in part, to goad Kettle and the pro-recruiting movement, it was also an attempt to depoliticise Nietzsche's philosophy in a manner akin to Hone's earlier defence. It was, moreover, a rather mischievous ploy, as he took the occasion to celebrate this 'dangerous' Continental thinker for an audience primed by circumstances to play along with the ruse. In other words, his reference to Nietzsche was less an attack on pro-recruiting or pro-British sentiments in Ireland than on the appropriation of philosophy and literature for propagandistic purposes. Ironically, as Marjorie Howe points out, Yeats had long complained that Davis's poetry was symptomatic of the colonial situation in Ireland, which silenced national traditions and thus guaranteed that 'much Irish art would serve nationalist propaganda rather than the vision of an individual artist'. This complaint in turn 'enabled him to negotiate between his disdain for Davis's verse and his interest in and sympathy for the nationalist feelings it aroused'.[70] By the time he delivered his speech in the Antient Concert Rooms, Yeats's attitude towards Davis's poetry had softened to a degree, but he still recalled the sense that his 'generation could not do its work unless [it] overcame the habit of making every Irish book, or poem, shoulder some political idea'.[71] As indicated in Chapter 2, this was a rather vexed issue, especially when it comes to Yeats. For in this and many other instances, the poet and playwright himself courted propaganda (even in his claims to the contrary) insofar as his assertions attempt to undermine the efforts at public persuasion made by others – as he engaged in a form of address that might be called, oxymoronically, anti-propaganda propaganda.

The use of Nietzsche in the holy war rhetoric of pro-British and pro-recruitment propaganda would reach an apex just two days later, on 23 November, with an article headed 'What We Are Fighting against / Humanity against Savagery / Moral and Religious Issues at Stake', printed in the Redmondite *Freeman's Journal* and reprinted in papers across Ireland in the following week. In the piece, Rev Stanislaus Curran advances an increasingly prominent claim, designed in part to deflect lingering animosities regarding British interference in Ireland: 'The real purpose of Germany is to establish a world-wide empire, to crush and subdue the whole of Europe under the iron heel of brute force'. Unlike the 'soft power' exerted by Great Britain in Ireland, then, the German war effort sought to 'enforce the reign of Might against Right and to set back the register of human progress to the wretched conditions that obtained 14 centuries ago'. It is, in short, a direct threat to Christian civilisation. The Catholic priest likens the threat to 'nothing less than another Reformation: instead of Faith alone, we shall now have Culture alone, the raving Nietzsche succeeds to apostleship of the raving Luther, Militarism is the new evangel, blood and iron driving the driving and convincing power, and the restoration of all things shall be fulfilled, not in Christ, but in the Superman'. Again, Nietzsche is cast as a frenzied madman and his philosophy as a kind of barbaric religion; the 'Prussian militarism' that he inspires in his 'multitudinous disciples' has nothing to do with heroism or chivalry, but with the negation of these virtues. Nietzschean transvaluation here takes the form of 'Might over Right, that the weak must ever go to the wall, that the world is not for the best but the strongest, and that blood and iron are the real civilise[r]s of humanity'. All this is confirmed for Father Curran by 'the proud boast of [Gerhart] Hauptman[n], that every German soldier goes to battle with a copy of Nietzsche in his pocket', carrying the gospel of this fiend with him rather than the New Testament. In this way, from beyond the grave, Nietzsche 'has created a diabolically anti-Christian atmosphere in which the armies of the Kaiser live and move'. The stakes of the present conflict may thus be summed up by a striking, but increasingly familiar, set of binary oppositions: 'it is a war of Humanity against Savagery, of Liberty against Tyranny, of Right against Might, of Christ against Anti-Christ'.[72]

This kind of rhetoric continued to appear in Irish publications over the next six months and more – and in many of the same publications Halévy's biography of Nietzsche was also advertised, highlighting Kettle's introduction and inviting the Irish reading public again and again to contend with the life and work of this dangerous thinker. Meanwhile, Kettle could be found on the recruiting trail, making his case for the alliance with Britain and the threat to Ireland and Christian civilisation produced by the German war effort. At a recruiting meeting at the Young Men's Society Hall in late January 1915, he was joined on stage by Sir Nugent Everard – a prominent member of one of the oldest Anglo-Irish families in Dublin, as well as High Sheriff and Lord Lieutenant for Meath – who followed a now customary line of argument: 'The German nation as a whole had been demoralised by the anti-Christian teachings of Nietzsche and the modern school of German philosophy. Such teaching explained much of the brutality of the German Army in the eyes of the civilised world'. When Kettle took the rostrum to a warm reception, he chastised those in Ireland who had, until very recently, remained detached from the war, believing it had nothing to do with Ireland: 'their business was to wait until the sky of European civilisation fell, and they were to bother in the meantime only about recipes for cooking the larks they were to catch. (Laughter)'. Kettle's tone speaks not just to his frustration with the attitude of many of his fellow countrymen, but to his own attitude toward European civilisation, which he saw as the principal victim of the Great War. His frustration was only increased, he continued, by men who occasionally wrote:

> little articles in little papers setting forth that if Davis, Stephens, Emmet, or Wolfe Tone – (applause) – were alive they would also be engaged in keeping themselves warm at comfortable fires and praising the barbarism of Berlin, or, in the alternative, they would be in Berlin itself like that wild man from the Congo, Sir Roger Casement – (laughter) – offering to sell for a scrap of paper written in German – the only language in which apparently you could not keep treaties – (laughter) – the pledged honour of Ireland.

This was clearly an attack on the propaganda efforts of advanced nationalists: 'The masters of adjectives, who in order to gratify a sham hatred for an England that no longer exists, had raised a paean to Prussia and accepted its whole gospel of murder, arson, and outrage'. In opposition to this militant gospel, Kettle's claim was that the majority of the Irish people, 'above all the men of Ireland who in the old days fought England and English policy in this country were heart and soul with the Allies in their battle for justice, and for the foundations of civilisation'. The grand causes, then, were also the causes of Ireland. When the advanced nationalists appealed to their countrymen in the name of nationalist heroes like Davis to side with German interests (and what Kettle would soon call 'the Gospel of the Devil'), he could only assert that such an appeal belied 'the gospel of Irish nationality'. Ireland stood to compromise both its honour and its own political interests if it were to allow the values of 'Prussianism' to triumph within its borders.[73]

It should be noted that during this fractious period – the final months of 1914 and early months of 1915 – there were a number of Irish intellectuals and clergymen prompted to take a closer look at Nietzsche's philosophy and to offer a more nuanced view of what they found there, one that disrupted the strict binaries and univocal statements of Kettle and his pro-recruiting allies. In December 1914, A.J. Rahilly, 'controversialist' and lecturer in the Department of Mathematics and Mathematical Physics at University College Cork, published an article in *Studies* (formerly *The New Ireland Review*) titled 'The Gospel of the Superman', reiterating a key phrase from

Kettle's 1911 introduction to *The Life of Friedrich Nietzsche*. Rahilly's essay shares Kettle's view that the war was not just a battle between nations but between ideals – moreover, that understanding the views of Nietzsche was in some way essential to understanding 'the larger problem of German policy and culture', which, in his view, had strayed a considerable distance from those of other European nations.[74] The article emphasises, however, that to critique, or even to condemn, German thought was not to praise or legitimise English ideals, since England had entered into the war to safeguard its own interests and Ireland had good reason to be sceptical about English attitudes towards small nations. For Rahilly, Nietzsche was not an aberration, but an embodiment of the 'Zeitgeist', which had transformed 'the biological speculations of Darwin' into an ethics that, in emphasising strife and struggle between men, was directly counter to 'the Spirit of Christianity'. Confirming some of the most strident claims made by Kettle, Rahilly asserts that 'Nietzsche deliberately set himself to found a sect of "Antichristians", to establish a religion of irreligion. He even wrote a Gospel of his own, his "Thus Spake Zarathustra"'.[75] But 'Nietzsche', he continues, 'was not altogether wrong when he described contemporary Christianity as a "soft moralism" and he was certainly right in combating the enervating pessimism of Schopenhauer' (whom Kettle continued to hold in high regard, even in his reporting on the Rape of Belgium). With Nietzsche, Rahilly shares the perspective that 'exquisite squeamishness, the overcivilised humanitarianism, the anaemic aestheticism of the present age are signs of decadence'.[76] He thus denies that 'as some would have it ... Nietzscheanism was "the cause of the war"', although in the final analysis Rahilly does see the philosopher's ethics as developing, by some peculiar feat, into a foreign policy that denies the agreement of 'the civilised world' on 'the humane principle of equity without appeal to brute force'.

As we have already witnessed, this kind of condemnation was by no means universal, not even among the clergy. Rev P. O'Keefe, Professor of Scholastic Philosophy at Queen's University Belfast, opens an article in *The Irish Ecclesiastical Record* by suggesting that 'to the discerning mind the charm of Nietzsche, amid all his wilfulness and error, springs first from a hard, relentless logic, and then from a certain keenness of insight'; notwithstanding his constant provocation of Christian sensibilities, 'his theory of morals contains in a sense a valuable stimulus for thought'.[77] For Nietzsche is no 'orthodox evolutionist, like Herbert Spencer', whose thought merely overlays evolutionary theory onto Christian morals – indeed, suggests O'Keefe, 'Nietzsche establishes once for all their essential disparity'. In this case, the priest is ready to agree with the philosopher, if only on other grounds. But O'Keefe, much like Hone before him, is most concerned to demonstrate the 'essential disparity' between Nietzsche's thought and 'the

German soul', in which the philosopher found merely a 'boorish indifference to taste'.[78] What his philosophy primarily offers, according to this reading, is a theory of cultural distinction, which asserts its own opposition between vitality and vulgarity, and O'Keefe's article goes on to emphasise Nietzsche's critique of the German culture, especially his condemnation of the pride taken in Teutonic civilisation after the Franco-Prussian war: 'Is it merely barbarism fortified to the best of its ability, but lacking the freshness and savage force of original barbarism'. According to O'Keefe, Nietzsche attributes this cultural and intellectual decline to the foundation of the Empire and a general 'moribund estrangement' generated by the rise of nationalism across Europe. Although, as the article points out, the philosopher had a 'high opinion of French culture', which he saw as a font of 'European noblesse – of sentiment, taste, manners', he aspired to the cosmopolitan title of the 'Good European', who has overcome 'the atavistic attacks of patriotism and soil attachment' – and, moreover, he dreamed of the formation of a united Europe.[79] This would require 'a new culture, a new education, radically opposed to the Philistinism at present in vogue', a culture that would value personal attainments and give rise to great men: individualism, not Germanism or militarism, was at the heart of Nietzsche's 'moral system'. If he valued war, it was not for the expansion of the German Empire, but for the role that it could play in the emergence of a superior type of human being. 'That such is the object of any form of modern militarism', O'Keefe acknowledges, 'is not at all likely, and that the so-called lust for empire should have been fostered by Nietzsche's glorification of war seems too ironical even for history'.[80] In any case, the priest concludes, 'in his own country Nietzsche's influence was slight'.[81]

The Ways of War and the 'Gospel of the Devil'

During this period and the months that followed, Kettle continued to perform his recruiting duties across Ireland, giving nearly 200 speeches, as well as writing articles, pamphlets, and parts of *Battle Songs for the Irish Brigades*, which repeatedly stressed the threat to European civilisation posed by German militarism. In the midst of these efforts, he also made numerous attempts to have himself sent to the Front, though he was turned down each time due to his poor health, made no better by his worsening alcoholism. After the Easter Rising, his resolve to recruit men to fight for Britain was severely strained: responding to the execution of the rebels, he memorably commented that these men 'will go down to history as heroes and martyrs, and I will go down – if I go down at all – as a bloody British officer'.[82] Finally, in the summer of 1916, he received his commission and left for France on Bastille Day. During his time at the Front,

Kettle continued to write in defence of his position; tragically, he was never to see the Allied war effort or the Home Rule movement come to fruition, for he was killed in action at the Battle of the Somme on 9 August 1916. His remains were never recovered.

In the summer of 1917, Kettle's widow, Mary, published a collection of his writings under the title *The Ways of War*, a book that forms his last, most complete, statement on the stakes of the Great War and the motives for Ireland's participation – and again Nietzsche's name features prominently. In a chapter titled 'Gospel of the Devil', which had originally appeared in *T.P'.s Journal of Great Deeds of the War*, Kettle develops his argument against Nietzsche in a far more detailed manner than he had in his previous pieces as a war correspondent for the *Daily News*. He claims, as so many others now had, that what the Allies face is nothing less than a doctrine of the Antichrist: the revelation of a belief system directly counter to that of Christian civilisation. But Nietzsche's 'defenders' have misread his gospel and sought to prove that 'the calamitous prophet of Hohenzollernism', who foretold the militaristic ideology of Prussian Kings and German emperors, actually 'meant this fine thing, and that, and did not mean blood and domination'. His apologists in England have thus 'allowed themselves to be tarred with the Nietzschean brush. They made a cult of him, a boom, a pinnacle of superior vision'. It seems that the central issue of the war, then, is to eradicate Nietzsche's influence, which has helped give rise to 'Hohenzollernism' or 'Prussianism' not just in Germany, but across Europe, so that Christian civilisation has been threatened with extinction. For Kettle, this is a matter of exegesis. He argues that the current 'vogue of the Supermaniacs' (for this, Shaw and his colleagues, including Thomas Common and Alfred Orage, doubtless share some of the blame) has taken hold of a weakness in 'the English mind', which is characterised by a 'curious lack of seriousness in dealing with ideas'. This weakness is evinced in receptivity to other, mostly German, thinkers and theologians, such as Adolf von Harnack and Rudolf Christoph Euckens, who 'attempt to deny all authenticity to the "scraps of paper" on which Christian belief if founded'.[83] At the same time, the English have been guilty of reading 'the Gospel of the Devil' rhetorically, tropologically, playfully, rather than literally, plainly, or, as Kettle has it, seriously: 'When your Prussian says: "Fill me a bath of blood!" he means blood. When your English critic reads this, he says, too often: "What a vivid image!"'[84] Nietzsche, with his dazzling style, is the chief offender: a maniacal poet who has managed to convince his countrymen and their enemies alike of the cause of Prussianism, with his vivid images, his captivating metaphors, his dexterous turns of phrase, which, Kettle now claims, have far more power to sway the opinions of his readers than direct statements or logical propositions.

For Kettle, the cause of civilisation depends on a kind of sober reading that will allow for no deception or corruption, precisely because it provides utter certainty: 'Of the "deep damnation" which lies at the heart of Nietzschean philosophy no doubt is admissible'. Such an approach to interpretation, then, requires the reader to penetrate to the fixed centre of this corrosive doctrine without being misled by the multiple perspectives and shifting assertions of its distinctive rhetoric: 'it is idle to say that [Nietzsche] contradicted himself at twenty turns'. Too often Nietzsche's German readers, like his English readers, have read his mobile rhetoric only in terms of their own political interests: 'Of all his writings Germany took and absorbed just as much as fitted in with her mood of domination and Empire'. That is to say, these readers have read selectively, latching on to only those words and phrases, images and ideas, that suited a nefarious ideological purpose they had already laid out for themselves. Paradoxically, his prose thus provides a 'lucid brutality' all its own. 'Not since Lucifer', Kettle tells us, 'was so much light put to such dark ends ... The devil was always a good stylist, and it is not inappropriate that when his gospel is at its worst, his prose should probably be at its best'. Nietzsche, in this sense, wrote both brilliantly and deliberately, calling on the full resources of language in order to prepare the minds of readers to receive the most dangerous messages about power and superiority that he intended to deliver. His worst readers have refined this faith the same way that good Christians have done with their own, through close contact with the scripture; but where the Allied troops can be found reviewing a copy of the New Testament, 'if you open the knapsack of a German soldier', Kettle tells us, reiterating Gerhart Hauptmann's claim, 'you will probably find in it a copy of *Thus Spake Zarathustra*'.[85] Kettle suggests, rather charitably, 'that those whom he led off the plain paths of life into his foul and blood-bathed jungles, were taken captive, not by his message, but by his music'.[86] The poetry of Nietzsche's writing, then, is precisely what renders it such a corrosive force. Latter-day commentators have hailed Nietzsche's style as integral to his general effort to challenge 'the rational, objective, and unconditional authority of certain values or positions';[87] others have suggested that his use of metaphorical and aphorism 'wants to be understood only by those who are commonly related by a common set of refined perspectives',[88] and Derrida takes this a step further in his *Spurs* (1978) by arguing that Nietzsche's fragments defy wholeness and interpretation altogether. Still others, such as Arthur Danto, have doubted the possibility of 'deflecting readers from taking his interpretations and injunctions literally and urging them to attend instead to the poetry of his expression', precisely because 'his vivid images and incendiary language' possess the power to rouse susceptible individuals to senseless acts of violence.[89] For

Kettle, this brilliant style is all part of a dangerous subterfuge, beneath which lurks the malevolent core of 'the Gospel of the Devil'.

The principal tenet of this gospel – 'his creed – or rather vision' – is clear enough for Kettle and his manner of reading, even though Nietzsche 'was the mystagogue of Prussianism, who chanted but never explained':[90] 'the whole task of life is to impose your power on others *an andern Macht auslassen*. With what aim? To evolve the Superman'. Again, he claims 'it is idle to remind us that Nietzsche touched life at other points, and that in his flaming incoherence you will find contradictions of this vision'.[91] Kettle, instead, tries to provide Nietzsche with a kind of coherence by selecting passages that speak to his diabolical vision of the morality of war, the shame of empathy, the ills of democracy, the degeneration of the masses, and the elevation of his own ego. No matter what he may have thought of the style of such passages in the past, Kettle now believes that this 'very coherent doctrine' should not be 'explain[ed] away' as 'poetry', in the manner that his contemporaries and many latter-day commentators have attempted to do, precisely because it speaks to the experience of war.[92] Whatever their contradictions, whatever their incoherence, then, the passages are all based on the same 'centre of corruption, the Will-to-Power'. But what most disturbs Kettle's sensibilities, of course, is Nietzsche's assault on 'that special mode of worship called Christianity, upon which all justice, love, pity, and help of our neighbours, is, in the tradition of Europe, immovably based'.[93] There is a real threat in this verbal attack insofar as English, Irish, American, and German readers have been willing to contemplate the 'metaphysics of bullying' while they have largely ignored the French intellect and its more refined sensitivities.[94] This recognition forces Kettle to reevaluate the claim he had made at the beginning of his introduction to Halévy's biography: 'The duel between Nietzsche and Civilisation is over'. 'I was wrong', he concludes, 'it is not over. But between Prussianism and Civilisation it is that this epical war is joined; there is not room on earth for the two'.[95] And so Kettle ends his final statement on Nietzsche by reiterating the fundamental binary opposition that structures his entire propagandistic argument and by insinuating that despite their differences Ireland and England must stand together in the fight for Christian civilisation.

The fate of civilisation and 'The Second Coming'

Of course, the war took a great toll on this civilisation and resulted in a fundamental rethinking of the very idea of 'civilisation' itself. If the nineteenth century had been preoccupied with the notion of progress in technological, biological, and many other senses, the generation that came of age in the war years was just as consumed by worries about the collapse of social and cultural structures altogether. The First World War led thinkers as varied as Arthur Spengler and H.G. Wells to speculate on the fate of Western civilisation, while others, like Leonard Woolf, denounced the 'delusions of the civilised' that had justified fighting in Europe, colonisation in Africa and Asia, and the maintenance of social hierarchies at home in England.[96] W.H. Auden claimed that 'The Age of Anxiety' had commenced in August 1914, when a 'breakdown of the faith in the existence of God, in the goodness of man, and in the possibility of progress' was announced across Europe.[97] This sentiment is captured nowhere better than in the closing paragraph of George Duhamel's landmark account of the war, *Civilisation, 1914–1917*, which the French physician and army surgeon published in 1918:

> The world seemed to me confused, incoherent and unhappy; and in my opinion it really is so. Believe me, Monsieur, when I speak with pity of civilisation I know what I'm talking about; and it's not the wireless telegraph that can make me change my views. It's all the sadder, because there's nothing one can do about it: you can't climb back up a slope like that down which the world is going to roll from now on.

Whether this crisis was seen as beginning with the war or as the culmination of a long decline, it was a generalised concern that scholars and pundits have now commented on for over a century. Perhaps more than any other work of literature, Yeats's 'The Second Coming' has been cited as capturing the sense of crisis and anxiety about the fate of Christian civilisation generated by the war. If the poet had been notoriously silent about the Great War during the course of the conflict, this poem seems to brutally concentrate this anxious mood – and it has found its place not just in the canon of Irish modernism and in innumerable anthologies of modern literature, but in textbooks, courses, and commentaries on modern European history, for that very reason. Critics have long speculated about the link between Yeats's cyclical vision of history and Nietzsche's notion of the Eternal Recurrence, going so far as to suggest that Zarathustra millenarianism could in fact have been the forerunner of the basic time consciousness of both *A Vision* and 'The Second Coming'.[98] But, with the wartime debate over Nietzsche in view, it is also possible to see a series of more direct and telling links between the iconic poem and his philosophy, as well as the propagandistic deployment of the idea of 'civilisation' during the war.

What Yeats had refused to write was a poem that endorsed the Allied war effort or otherwise played a propagandistic role in addressing the conflict. To be sure, his attitude towards the war was more complex than many scholars have acknowledged: if he was initially sympathetic to the Allied war effort, which involved a number of his friends and loved ones, he came to see the British contribution as an imperial misadventure and he increasingly distanced himself from the conflict as it dragged on. But this is not to say that he was entirely mute on the matter. Although he famously declared, in his short verse 'On Being Asked for a War Poem', 'I think it better that at times like these / we poets keep our mouths shut', he did write nearly a dozen poems that address the war with varying degrees of directness.[99] He was deeply affected by the violence of the war, as well as of the Easter Rising and the Russian Revolution, each of which has been linked with the vision of intensity and chaos found in 'The Second Coming'. He was also, in his aloof way, interested in what Nietzsche might be able to teach him about the significance of the war and of struggle or strife in general. On 5 August 1914, one day after Germany invaded Belgium and Britain declared war, he wrote to Lennox Robinson, wondering 'how the war will affect the minds of what audience it leaves to us. Neitsze [sic] was fond of foretelling wars for the possession of the earth that were to restore the tragic mind, & banish the mass mind which he hated'.[100] Late in the war, as he moved farther from the realities of the moment and deeper into his esoteric period, he would place the philosopher in the twelfth or 'heroic' phase of his 'Phases of the Moon' (addressed at length in the next chapter), where Nietzsche follows on the bellicose Achilles and Hector. In both instances, as in 'The Second Coming', Yeats seems less concerned with the costs of the war than with the potential of what it might bring, what values might emerge, and what might arise after the fall of Christian civilisation.

'The Second Coming', as has long been recognised, hinges on the notion that a phase of civilisation is winding down, opening the way for a new era of unknown but fearful possibilities. To be sure, as Yeats wrote the poem in the weeks immediately after the armistice, political events seemed to bear out these prospects, not just in the European conflict, but in the gathering storm of political and military upheaval in Ireland after the Easter Rising. 'The Second Coming' sets poetry and prophecy against propaganda, and in doing so works to unsettle the dearly held vision of civilisation that had been affirmed again and again by Allied commentators. Drafts of the poem, written during the final weeks of the war, indicate that the threat of chaos in the opening stanza was inspired by the destruction of political stability and aristocratic hierarchy in recent conflicts across Europe and Russia. But rather than responding directly to these conflicts, Yeats offers a grand historical and artistic vision, first announced in the image of the falcon and the falconer. The metaphor, drawn from an age defined by aristocratic and Christian values, both exemplifies a loss of authoritative control and evokes an esoteric historical system of alternating gyres, which leads to an image of generalised fears and common costs: 'The blood dimmed tide is loosed, and everywhere / The ceremony of innocence is drowned'.[101] The use of the present tense suggests a diagnosis of the current state of affairs, and yet the language and imagery, just like the title, evoke the Book of Revelation along with its deeper history and broader significance. Whereas the biblical book had foretold the ultimate triumph of good over evil at the end of the current age, the poem begins to loosen the familiar Christian topoi from their established implications and to open the way for a transvaluation of their entrenched ideals.

Like the priests and propagandists of the war years, Yeats draws on the familiar lexicon of Christian belief, but not so much to provoke paralysing fears or promote political agendas as to render its meaning and the future it promises radically uncertain, if insistently foreboding. The concluding lines of the stanza seem to pass judgement on those promising individuals in the recent conflict who either lacked sufficient conviction to act or who drove the violence on with their 'passionate intensity'. But the lines can also be read to define 'the best' as precisely those who lack all conviction – to kill and die for God, country, or civilisation – while the worst are those who have the most zeal for such deeds and ideals; the lines thus challenge precisely the affects generated by wartime propaganda, affects that had driven millions to slaughter and be slaughtered during the long years of the war. In the face of the recent conflict and the heated rhetoric that surrounded it, Yeats mobilises the forces of myth and metaphor to reimagine the stakes of the war and offer an alternative vision of their significance. The poem, in this way, exhibits a strange mix of confidence and uncertainty: confidence in the power of poetic vision, reiterated in the opening lines of the second stanza – 'Surely some revelation is at hand; / Surely the Second Coming is at hand' – but uncertainty at what that vision might reveal about the future to come. It is precisely these possibilities – and their attendant ambiguity – that prevent the poem from becoming didactic in the mode of propaganda or propagandistic verse, but 'The Second Coming' is nonetheless a riposte to the feverish sloganeering and emotional appeals of wartime rhetoric. This is not simply to oppose poetry to propaganda, but to see modernist verse as working in relation to – with and against – a mode of writing that had come to dominate the mass media and public debate during the war years.

This is nowhere more evident than in Yeats's adoption and adaptation of certain key images from Nietzsche's writing. The 'vast image out of Spiritus Mundi' that 'troubles [the] sight' of the visionary poet can also be seen as a set of images drawn almost directly from Chapter 3 of Book I of *Thus Spake Zarathustra*, 'Of the Three Metamorphoses'. There, Nietzsche deploys a series of bestial metaphors to depict the spiritual stages of becoming an Übermensch: 'in the loneliest desert however cometh the second metamorphosis: there the spirit becometh a lion. Freedom it will take as its prey and be lord in its own desert'.[102] Like Yeats's 'somewhere in sands of the desert / A shape with lion body and the head of a man', Nietzsche's images borrow from Biblical sources only to transform them into a picture of the Antichrist. From a common storehouse of images, which finds examples in both *Thus Spake Zarathustra* and the Bible, Yeats articulates a vision that assaults the claims made in defence of Christian civilisation throughout the war. According to this vision, there is neither a possibility of thwarting the blond beast in the desert nor a promise of Christ returning in his grandeur and founding a New Kingdom on earth. The image of the beast, that is, announces a brutal end to the 2,000-year historical cycle defined by Christianity. But like Nietzsche's mobile rhetoric, Yeats's visionary poetics belies any stable relationship between such images and a particular ethical or political position. In *Thus Spake Zarathustra*, the lion is largely defined by his revolt against the reign of Christian morality, and the beast of prey seeks to supplant or transvalue that morality and assert a new form of authority. In the Bible, it should be recalled, Satan is symbolised as a lion – who is stealthy, savage, pitiless – but so is Christ, because he exhibits a kind of majestic power, which will enable him to rule over his kingdom in the coming times. To be sure, in Yeats's vision there are afterimages of not just Nietzsche's rhetoric and the Bible's symbolism, but also Sophocles' drama, Shelley's poetry, and many other sources, which suggest other interpretative possibilities, but no final end to the interpretive process.

Ample critical attention has been given to the complex functioning of images and symbols, emblems and metaphors, in Yeats's poetry and especially to how these forms of signification served his evolving artistic agenda, as he moved from romantic earnestness and nationalist sentiments to esoteric detachment and authoritarian inclinations. Yet this criticism has not addressed these issues at any length in connection with Yeats's career-long negotiation of the relationship between poetry and propaganda: his continual struggles to free literature from a narrow political purpose and his simultaneous efforts to shape the conscience of his readers. Nor has existing criticism addressed these issues in connection with Nietzsche's rhetoric, which raises a number of pressing questions regarding the relationship between literature and propaganda, poetry and philosophy, metaphor and concept, especially in view of the way his rhetoric was deployed during the First World War.

It is thus worth pursuing further interpretation of Yeats's image as Nietzsche's blond beast in the guise of the lion. This fearsome creature supplants Nietzsche's first metamorphosis, the camel, which is associated with subservience to or passive acceptance of Christian morality, and the blond beast thus hastens the way to a world without doctrine, without dogma, without authoritative values: 'now it must find illusion and arbitrariness even in the holiest'.[103] In the schema laid out in *Thus Spake Zarathustra*, the lion contests for victory with 'the great dragon', which is another a Biblical metaphor for Satan, but which is equally representative of Christ and Christianity for Nietzsche: 'values a thousand years old are shining on these scales'. As in Yeats's poem, the lion's will is to supersede the moral principles that have dominated the previous epoch: '"Thou shalt" is the name of the great dragon', who has coerced humanity throughout the Christian era; 'But the lion's spirit saith: "I will"', as he asserts his own strength against the authority of tradition.[104] Yeats's Sphinx-like figure promises a new era, not least because it possesses the strength, aggression, and wildness of the lion body together with the intelligence of the human head. But, this is nonetheless a monstrous creature, who embodies a violent assault on Christian civilisation. In drawing on this figure for his prophetic vision, Yeats both acknowledges its frightful qualities and suggests an emergent or imminent transvaluation: they become not just signs of the Antichrist or the portents of the Apocalypse, but the promise of a new future, the purging of a past that will no longer impede transformation and transvaluation.

In the process, the blond beast is also transvalued: no longer the omen of a dark age or a threatening force that must be conquered, he is the bringer of his own good tidings. The gaze of Yeats's beast, 'blank and pitiless as the sun', evokes Zarathustra's repeated exhortations that his followers must overcome their debilitating proclivity for Christian pity; the gaze also conjures Nietzsche's frequent references to the sun or to daybreak, which brings clarity to the consideration of values and reveals their constructedness, contingency, and interestedness by bringing all this out into the light. The dawn also brings the power of a natural force to expose the machinations and petty fabrications of Christian civilisation. The birds that circle the beast, their shadows cast down by the sun, recall Zarathustra's eagle, which soars high in the sky, flirting with the sun in a show of 'strength and cruel nobility'. This is not to say that Nietzsche's images substitute a metaphor for a fixed concept or thing, but that together the elements of his bestiary suggest the 'pitiless'-ness of the 'The Second Coming', which will sweep away all inherited values and stifling traditions.

To borrow the phrase that Kettle had applied to Nietzsche, this 'incessant creative surge of images, metaphors, symbolisms, mythologies' is entirely apposite to the uncertain future projected by the poem. According to Zarathustra, to 'create new values – that even the lion is not able to do: but to create for itself freedom for new creating, that the lion's power is enough'. The capacity for new beginnings, for creating new values, belongs to youth and, therefore, with the third metamorphosis, the 'preying lion' must 'become a child also'.[105] Reflecting on the spontaneous joy of the creative process, Yeats had written in his diary of 1909 that 'Nietzsche had it doubtless at the moment when he imagined the 'Superman' as a child';[106]

for Zarathustra, 'the child is innocence and oblivion, a new starting, a play, a wheel rolling by itself, a prime motor, a holy asserting'.[107] This assertion, eminently Nietzschean in explaining a metaphor with a series of metaphors, suggests that the third and final metamorphosis results in a being freed from any reactionary relationship with what has come before. In the concluding lines of Yeats's poem, a similar metamorphosis is described in rather more ominous terms: the visionary poet now comes to the realisation that after 'twenty centuries of stony sleep', during the Christian era, something entirely new is imminent. The somnambulism of the past, which meant passively accepting a set of values guaranteed by some external authority, has been disrupted by a rocking cradle, containing a new being, a new creature, whose hour has 'come round at last'. The 'rough beast', slouching towards Bethlehem (in another corruption of the Biblical source), makes his way to be born; 'the lion', Zarathustra declares, becomes 'at last a child'.[108] Ending with its famous question mark, which queries the nature of this beast and the infant that will soon emerge, the poem indicates equivocation and open-endedness. We might sense here some intimations of Yeats's drift toward authoritarian sympathies, and the barely articulate desire for the birth of some severe form of political control. To be sure, Nietzsche's imagery would soon be taken up into such a cause. But the qualities of this new being, and the values that he or she might produce, remain indeterminate: like Nietzsche's child, Yeats's monstrous progeny represents the potentiality of new values, of a new era, but it prescribes nothing explicit, no new belief systems or political institutions. There may not be much comfort in this. But, with these provocative images, the poem suggests a species of hope, a prophetic optimism – that is, paradoxically, consonant with both the Christian typos of the Second Coming and the Nietzschean metaphor of the childlike Superman – that a postwar Europe and a postcolonial Ireland might emerge in some radically new form from the chaos and strife of epochal transition.

Notes

1. T.M. Kettle, 'Introduction', in Daniel Halévy, *The Life of Friedrich Nietzsche*, J.M. Hone (trans.) (London: Adelphi, 1911), p. 7.
2. Max Nordau, *Degeneration* (New York: D. Appleton, 1895), p. 417.
3. Kettle, 'Introduction', p. 12.
4. Ibid., p. 8.
5. Ibid., p. 13.
6. Ibid., p. 8.
7. See David B. Allison, 'Introduction', in David B. Allison (ed.), *The New Nietzsche: Contemporary Styles of Interpretation* (Cambridge: MIT University

Press, 1985), pp. xi–xxxvi; Sarah Kofman, *Nietzsche and Metaphor*, Duncan Large (trans.) (London: Athlone, 1993) (original French, 1972); Jacques Derrida, *Spurs: Nietzsche's Styles*, Barbara Harlow (trans.) (Chicago: Chicago University Press, 1979); Alexander Nehemas, *Nietzsche: Life as Literature* (Cambridge: Harvard University Press, 1985).
8 Arthur C. Danto, *Nietzsche and Philosophy* (New York: Columbia University Press, 2005), p. xvi.
9 Kettle, 'Introduction', p. 13.
10 Ibid., p. 15.
11 Allison, 'Introduction', p. xii.
12 Nordau, *Degeneration*, p. 417.
13 See Steven E. Ascheim, *The Nietzsche Legacy in Germany: 1890–1990* (Berkeley: University of California Press, 1992), p. 40.
14 Kettle, 'Introduction', p. 18.
15 'An Irish Study of Nietzsche', *The Freeman's Journal* (4 February 1911), 5.
16 'Nietzsche', *The Irish Times* (3 March 1911), 10.
17 George Moore to Maurice Moore, 16 April 1912, in Helmut E. Gerber (ed.), *George Moore on Parnassus: Letters (1900–1933)* (Newark: University of Delaware Press, 1988), p. 218.
18 'Nietzsche', 10.
19 'An Irish Study of Nietzsche', 5.
20 T.M. Kettle, 'Catholicism and Modern Literature', *St. Stephen's* (January 1905), 131.
21 'An Irish Study of Nietzsche', 5.
22 T.M. Kettle, *The Day's Burden: Studies, Literary and Political* (London: T. Fisher Unwin, 1910), p. ix.
23 Ibid., p. viii.
24 T.H. Fitzgerald, 'Is It Not Enough to Be Anglicised?', *The Catholic Bulletin and Book Review* 1 (1911), 85.
25 Arthur Griffith, 'Preface', in John Mitchel, *Jail Journal* (Dublin: M.H. Gill, 1913), p. xiv.
26 Ibid., p. ix.
27 Qtd in P.A. Sillard, *The Life of John Mitchel* (Dublin: J. Duffy, 1908), pp. 87–88.
28 Griffith, 'Preface', p. ix.
29 Qtd in William Dillon, *Life of John Mitchel, Vol. II* (London: Kegan, 1988), p. 106.
30 Griffith, 'Preface', p. xiv.
31 Violet Jameson, 'Nietzsche and Woman', *The Irish Citizen* (8 March 1913), 331.
32 Violet Jameson, 'Nietzsche and Women: Part II', *The Irish Citizen* (15 March 1913), 339. The lecture was followed by a response from Maud Joynt, a Celtic studies scholar and German literature teacher, who stressed Nietzsche's 'view on the dependence of man on women', but went on deprecate the 'recent militant developments' in the suffrage movement, thus touching off 'an animated

discussion' among the leaders of the organisation (*The Irish Citizen* (28 June 1913), 5).

33 Violet Jameson, 'Patriotism: True and False', *The Irish Citizen* (28 June 1913), 5.
34 T.M. Kettle, 'Is Peace Possible?,' *Daily News* (13 June 1913), 3.
35 Thomas Kettle, 'Europe against the Barbarians', *Daily News and Leader* (10 August 1914), 4.
36 Friedrich Nietzsche, *The Case of Wagner*, Thomas Common (trans.) (London: H. Henry, 1896), pp. 148–49.
37 Kettle, 'Europe against the Barbarians', 4.
38 Friedrich Nietzsche, *A Genealogy of Morals*, William A. Haussmann (trans.) (New York: Macmillan, 1897), p. 210.
39 Kettle, 'Europe against the Barbarians', 4.
40 T.M. Kettle, 'Under the Heel of the Hun', in Mary S. Kettle (ed.), *The Ways of War* (New York: Scribner, 1917), p. 127.
41 Ibid., p. 126.
42 Ibid., p. 127.
43 Kettle, 'Europe against the Barbarians', 4.
44 George Bernard Shaw, 'Our Book-Shelf', *Fabian News* 17 (April 1907), 37.
45 Qtd in Patrick Bridgwater, *Nietzsche in Anglosaxony* (Leicester: Leicester University Press, 1972), p. 143.
46 Thomas Hardy, 'On the War,' in Thomas Hardy, *Life and Art* (London: Greenberg, 1925), pp. 137–38.
47 Adrian Gregory, *The Last Great War* (Cambridge: Cambridge University Press, 2008), p. 39.
48 Nicholas Martin, '"Fighting a Philosophy": The Figure of Nietzsche in British Propaganda of the First World War', *Modern Language Review* 98:2 (1 April 2003), 378.
49 Joseph Hone, 'Nietzsche and the War', *Irish Times* (3 September 1914), 7.
50 'Nietzsche on War', *Leitrim Observer* (5 September 1914), 7.
51 Walter Kaufmann, *Nietzsche: Philosopher, Psychologist, Antichrist* (Princeton: Princeton University Press, 1974), p. 386.
52 Robert Solomon and Kathleen Higgins, *What Nietzsche Really Said* (New York: Schocken, 2000), p. 41.
53 'Nietzsche on War', 7.
54 Keith Jeffery, *Ireland and the Great War* (Cambridge: Cambridge University Press, 2000), p. 13.
55 Qtd in Stephen Gwynn, *John Edmond's Last Years* (Dublin: Arnold, 1919), p. 155.
56 Qtd in Jeffery, *Ireland and the Great War*, p. 48.
57 Ibid., p. 47.
58 'Nietzsche's Teachings Put into Practice', *Freeman's Journal* (28 September 1914), 7.
59 'Kaiserism vs. Christianity', *Irish Times* (13 October 1914), 6.
60 'Poison Doctrines of Nietzsche', *Irish Times* (30 October 1914), 8.

61 Denis Gwynn, 'Foreword', in W.B. Yeats, *Tribute to Thomas Davis* (Cork: Cork University Press, 1965), p. 5.
62 Ibid., p. 8.
63 Austin Clark, 'From *The Yeats We Knew*', in Gregory A. Schirmer (ed.), *Reviews and Essays of Austin Clarke* (Gerrards Cross: Colin Smythe, 1995), p. 23.
64 'Thomas Davis Centenary', *Irish Times* (21 November 1914), 10.
65 Yeats, *Tribute to Thomas Davis*, p. 12.
66 'Thomas Davis Centenary', 10.
67 Ibid., 10.
68 Clark, 'From *The Yeats We Knew*', p. 24.
69 Yeats, *Tribute to Thomas Davis*, p. 12.
70 Marjorie Howes, 'Yeats and the Postcolonial', in Marjorie Howes (ed.), *Cambridge Companion to W.B. Yeats* (Cambridge: Cambridge University Press, 2006), p. 218.
71 Yeats, *Tribute to Thomas Davis*, p. 18.
72 'What We Are Fighting Against', *Freeman's Journal* (23 November 1914), 4.
73 'Ireland and the War', *Irish Times* (18 January 1915), 6.
74 A.J. Rahilly, 'The Gospel of the Superman', *Studies* (December 1914), 381.
75 Ibid., 387.
76 Ibid., 394.
77 Rev P. O'Keeffe, 'Some Aspects of Friedrich Nietzsche', *The Irish Ecclesiastical Record* (April 1915), 363.
78 Ibid., 364.
79 Ibid., 366.
80 Ibid., 369.
81 Ibid., 372.
82 Qtd in John Benignus Lyons, *The Enigma of Tom Kettle: Irish Patriot, Essayist, Poet, British Soldier, 1880–1916* (Dublin: Glendale, 1983), p. 293.
83 T.M. Kettle, 'The Gospel of the Devil', in Kettle (ed.), *Ways of War*, p. 220.
84 Ibid., p. 221.
85 Ibid., p. 221.
86 Ibid., p. 222.
87 Nehamas, *Life as Literature*, p. 4.
88 Kofman, *Nietzsche and Metaphor*, p. 114.
89 Arthur Danto, *Nietzsche as Philosopher* (New York: Columbia University Press, 1995), p. xvi.
90 Kettle, 'The Gospel of the Devil', p. 222.
91 Ibid., p. 223.
92 Ibid., p. 225.
93 Ibid., p. 226.
94 Ibid., p. 228.
95 Ibid., p. 229.
96 See Brian W. Shaffer, *The Blinding Torch: Modern British Fiction and the Discourse of Civilisation* (Amherst: University of Massachusetts Press, 1993), p. 28.

97 Jewel Spears Brooker, '"The Second Coming" and "The Waste Land": Capstones of the Western Civilisation Course', *College Literature* 13:3 (Fall 1986), 242.
98 See John R. Harrison, 'What Rough Beast? Yeats, Nietzsche, and Historical Rhetoric in "The Second Coming"', *Papers on Language and Literature* 31:4 (Fall 1995), 362–88.
99 W.B. Yeats, 'On Being Asked for a War Poem', in W.B. Yeats, *The Wild Swans at Coole* (New York: Macmillan, 1909), p. 68.
100 W.B. Yeats to Lennox Robinson, 5 August 1914, in John Kelly and Ronald Schuchard (eds), *The Collected Letters of W.B. Yeats: Unpublished Letters (1905–1939), Electronic Edition* (Charlottesville: Intelex, 2002), p. 249.
101 W.B. Yeats, 'The Second Coming', in Richard J. Finneran (ed.), *Collected Poems of W.B. Yeats* (New York: Simon and Schuster, 2008), p. 187.
102 Friedrich Nietzsche, *Thus Spake Zarathustra*, Alexander Tille (trans.) (New York: Macmillan, 1896), p. 26.
103 Ibid., p. 27.
104 Ibid., p. 26.
105 Ibid., p. 27.
106 W.B. Yeats, *The Collected Works of W.B. Yeats Vol. III: Autobiography*, William H. O'Donnell and Douglas N. Archibald (eds) (New York: Simon and Schuster, 2010), p. 351.
107 Nietzsche, *Zarathustra*, p. 27.
108 Ibid., p. 25.

5

Postwar: 'The Forerunner'

On 8 December 1922, as the first President of the Executive Council of the Irish Free State, W.T. Cosgrave, was bringing debate in the Dáil Éireann to a close, the leader of the opposition and head of the Labour Party, Thomas Johnson, interrupted to end the proceedings on his own terms: 'I have never made any protestations of my religion', he claimed, 'but this is a question of Christianity or Nietzscheism'. The occasion for Johnson's assertion – and for the debate that had occupied the entire parliamentary session – was the execution that morning of four anti-Treaty Republican leaders in reprisal for the assassination of the pro-Treaty Sinn Féin Teachta Dála (Member of Parliament) Sean Hales and attempted assassination of Deputy Speaker Pádraic Ó Máille the previous day. The actions represented a disturbing escalation of violence in the recently founded Irish Free State, which was struggling to establish law and order in the early days of its existence. The Civil War that followed the contentious ratification of the Anglo-Irish Treaty a year earlier had now reached a fever pitch as former allies in the fight for Irish freedom slaughtered each other in brutal ambushes and summary executions. Earlier in the Dáil debate, Sean Milroy, a Sinn Féin TD and veteran of the Easter Rising, had sought to justify the executions by arguing that the assassinations and the anarchy they represented had gripped the 'the Irish nation ... by the throat' and 'challenged the right of this nation to say what its decisions will be and what its future will be'. Noting that only two days had elapsed since the formal proclamation of the Irish Free State, Johnson protested bitterly that 'almost the first act is utterly to destroy in the public mind the association of the Government with the idea of law. I am almost forced to say you have killed the new State at its birth'.[1] His Labour Party had declared neutrality in the dispute over the Anglo-Irish Treaty and again when the hostilities led to Civil War, but now he condemned the brutal measures taken by the state to put down the activities of the anti-Treaty Irregulars. Drawing on the opposition made familiar by Thomas Kettle and the propagandists of the Great War, his concluding remark addresses the issues at stake for the national conscience: would the coming years be characterised by civilisation or barbarism, the assumed spiritual force and gentle values of the gospels or the supposed brutality and depravity of Nietzschean doctrine? It was a question that, in a number of variations, would play a role in defining the future of both Europe and Ireland.

Nietzsche himself had foreseen that the twentieth century would be a time of escalating warfare between ideological forces that were emerging in this own time and that would eventually represent an existential threat to civilisation. He had also predicted that Western culture would have to wait until the twenty-first century to finally come to terms with the crisis of nihilism, which had long been part of its history. The propagandists of the Great War had helped to cement the association between Nietzsche and nihilism by claiming over and over again that his philosophy provided inspiration for murder and mayhem on an immense scale by preaching an absolute indifference to human life: 'nothing is true', they had him say, 'everything is permitted to the strong'. But more attentive readers of Nietzsche knew that his writings provide an exhaustive diagnosis of nihilism as a chronic 'disease of the will' that had entered a new phase when 'the Death of God' opened the way for a whole array of secular faiths.[2] According to Nietzsche, his contemporaries sought cures in anarchism, socialism, communism, nationalism, and other mass movements that were only so many means to avoid recognising the full consequences of the disease. The catastrophic events of the war years had further shaken the secular faith in social and scientific progress, along with the Christian faith in a benevolent God, and impelled a stark encounter with the nihilistic implications of European modernity. But Nietzsche could be looked to not just as a scapegoat or diagnostician, but also as what he called a 'physician of culture'. His philosophy, that is, refuses to accept the present conditions that define a culture and instead, through imaginative leaps and visionary intuitions, seeks to transcend prevailing historical processes and realise new possibilities (even a new politics) for life. The Übermensch is just such a 'mythos of the future'.[3] Nietzsche had urged his contemporaries, and the generations to come, to meet the peril of nihilism head-on by overcoming the legacy of Western culture and becoming the creators of new life-affirming values, even as he suggested that the ascendancy of nihilism remained incomplete and that its complete overcoming would have to wait for a future epoch. It is in this regard that Nietzsche attributes to art an ethical capacity, so that whatever new values come into being do so as a result of artistic will, no longer restrained by what had been considered 'given' or 'transcendent' or 'redemptive'.

It is little wonder, given the tumultuous intensity of the war years and the urgent questions they raised about the fate of both Ireland and Europe, that writers such as Yeats, Shaw, and even Joyce turned their attention toward prophetic modes of discourse: increasingly, they composed in ways that passed judgement on the current state of Irish culture and Western civilisation more broadly, intimated a range of reasons for their judgement, and, most importantly, offered a revelation of events to come. Writing during this period of historical tumult – beginning during the First World War and continuing through the Anglo-Irish War and the Irish Civil War – Yeats sought in *A Vision* (1925) to offer a systematic, if highly idiosyncratic, account of the patterns of human history that might also reveal something about how those patterns would project into the future. In other words, like another admirer of Nietzsche, Arthur Spengler, he set out to write a new kind of totalising history that not only announced the doom of Western civilisation, but could also predict world-historical events to come.[4] Meanwhile, in his preface to *Back to Methuselah* (1921), Shaw wondered 'whether the human animal, as he exists at present, is capable of solving the social problems raised by his own aggregation, or, as he calls it, his civilisation'.[5] The five-part play that follows attempts to translate the tenets of his vitalist Lamarckian philosophy of Creative Evolution into the legends of a new religion that rewrite the story of the Garden of Eden, comment directly on the political failings of the present, and project a posthuman future some 30,000 years hence. Like Yeats, then, he took on the role of modernist as heroic seer (not to mention artistic celebrity) capable of transvaluing the values of his own time. Insofar as their prophecies owe something to Nietzsche they worked towards a wilful demolition of existing moral and ethical standards in order to open the way for new ideals that might transcend the rising tide of nihilism in the postwar years. At the same time, like many of their contemporaries after the war, Yeats and Shaw also became increasingly enamoured with the biopolitical potential of eugenics to overcome the counter-selective effects of the recent war and to breed the human race into fitter or more effective political animals. Joyce, for his part, demonstrates considerable scepticism about such eugenicist efforts and the utopian dreams they cultivated, but he is nonetheless preoccupied with human breeding and the question of futurity in the later chapters of *Ulysses* (1922). Among the many competing discourses that addressed these issues in Ireland and beyond, Nietzschean philosophy is again a crucial point of reference, precisely because it remains open to multiple interpretations, multiple potentialities for the future of humanity, or rather a future beyond humanity, when at least certain individuals will live according to new codes, new values, and new ideals.

Yeats's *A Vision* and Nietzsche's personality

With its peculiar admixture of mythology, cosmology, eccentric historiography, and pervasive esotericism, *A Vision* manages to speak to this era of chaos and destruction while distancing itself from any direct commentary on contemporary events. Sounding an apocalyptic note, the book instead translates these events into signs of the culmination of a doomed era, 'the purging away of our civilisation by our hatred', which will give birth to a new era defined by antithetical values.[6] Yeats's mouthpiece, Michael Robartes, sums up this transition in the following terms: 'after an age of necessity, truth, goodness, mechanism, science, democracy, abstraction, peace, comes an age of freedom, fiction, evil, kindred, art, aristocracy, particularly, war'.[7] The abstraction of Yeats's system, which famously maps these historical attributes and many more besides onto a series of intersecting cones or tinctures, is made more concrete through the assignation of certain historical individuals to the 'Phases of the Moon' that help to structure his schema – and in this way, Nietzsche's persona, along with a number of his key ideas, continued to occupy an important place in Yeats's imagination. Throughout the long, strange process of composition – a kind of revelation conducted in a dialogue between the poet, who asked the questions, and his new wife, George, who provided the answers in a state of hypnotic trance – personal archetypes were collected, analysed, and attached these lunar phases. As early as 1 January 1918, Yeats was asking questions regarding exemplars and features, when George told him that Nietzsche should be placed in Phase Twelve, which would include the year that had just begun, and Zarathustra in Phase Eighteen, which is the phase that George herself would occupy. Significantly, Phase Twelve would later become 'the phase of the hero', also occupied by Yeats's perennial protagonist Cuchulain. But when initially queried about the placement of Nietzsche, George responded: 'Wisdom of thought is an unlasting thing it never creates a philosophy of time only one of space it is generally a propaganda a will to change forms of existing thought a metaphysician is a nihilist not a Creator'.[8] Despite the obliqueness of her comment, and its rather esoteric, even abstruse, logic, George appears to be responding rather directly to the uses made of Nietzsche and his name during the war years, when his reputation had been swept up into the Allied propaganda machine: like so many of her contemporaries, George attributes to the philosopher the very nihilism of which he had been such a strident critic. In her estimation, his thought could clear the ethical or ideological field, synchronically, but it could not project new values into this void and thus could not carry civilisation forward into a new era, diachronically.

Still the question remained for Yeats as to why Nietzsche and these other figures should be placed where they were in his developing system. In May 1918, as he continued to sort out the relation between phases and exemplars, 'he asked if there were anti-deformities at 12 to make primary allurements impossible' and he went on to suggest that 'various forms of intellectual ugliness' might be the answer, citing the 'violence' of both Nietzsche and

Ezra Pound as illustrations.⁹ When Yeats published 'Phases of the Moon' the following year in a reprint of *Wilde Swans at Coole*, Nietzsche had officially taken his place alongside Achilles and Hector in the 'hero's crescent' of Phase Twelve. Later to appear as the introduction to the 'Great Wheel' section of *A Vision*, the poem is a philosophical dialogue between Michael Robartes and John Aherne, which provides a comprehensive exposition of the twenty-eight-phase lunar cycle that governs the book's intertwined schema of history and personality. As the moon grows full, man becomes increasingly self-conscious, whipped by the 'cat-o'-nine-tails of the mind', even as his body has become well-formed. It is here that Nietzsche and his peers can be found:

> Eleven pass, and then
> Athene takes Achilles by the hair,
> Hector is in the dust, Nietzsche is born,
> Because the hero's crescent is the twelfth.

As the physical heroism of Achilles and Hector moves toward its end, the moral and intellectual courage of Nietzsche emerges, so that the violent impulse is turned inward on the conscience, with the kind of stringent self-love that leads to the possibility of self-overcoming. The succeeding stage, the thirteenth phase of the moon, 'sets the soul at war / In its own being', until 'under the frenzy of the fourteenth moon, / The soul begins to tremble into stillness' and finally to succumb to death in 'the labyrinth of itself'.¹⁰ The poem thus turns Nietzsche into a sign or metonym for this inward-turning gesture, but also, as we will see, the kind of exemplar on which the future of humanity must depend.

Yeats would go on to elaborate on these rather cryptic claims in 'The Great Wheel' section of *A Vision*, where he introduces Phase Twelve with the following schematic heading:

Will – The Forerunner.
Mask (from Phase 26). *True* – Self-exaggeration. *False* – Self-abandonment.
Creative Mind (from Phase 18). *True* – Subjective Philosophy.
False – War between two forms of Expression.
Body of Fate (from Phase 4) – Enforced intellectual action.
Example: Nietzsche.¹¹

Here we find something like Yeats's final judgement on Nietzsche's life and work; indeed, this section from the 1925 version of the text appears virtually unaltered in the 1937 version of the text, which is otherwise thoroughly revised. The philosopher, with his egomaniacal bluster, offers the advance copies of a volatile doctrine, based not on some absolute ground or external authority, but rather on the force of his own personality. His name is transformed into an event, a destiny, which initiates a break from the history of previous mentalities and precipitates a new wave of individualism that will spread relentlessly through the modern world. Christ too had been referred to as 'the forerunner': for instance, in the final lines of Hebrews 6 where he enters ahead of his followers into the holy place as their representative and champion. But Nietzsche, of course, is the representative and champion of an alternative faith.

The passage that follows under this heading can be read as a Yeatsian explication of the Nietzschean faith, especially as articulated in the 'fifth "gospel"' of *Thus Spake Zarathustra*, as well as an assessment of the psychology of the philosopher – all of which are integrated with occult systems and esoteric terminologies to create a singular Yeatsian-Nietzschean discourse in this section of *A Vision*. Returning to his interest in the theme of generosity, Yeats begins the text proper with the claim that 'The man of this phase is out of phase, is always in reaction, is driven from one self-conscious pose to another, is full of hesitation; or he is true to phase, a cup that remembers but its own fullness';[12] the claim reiterates, even as it reevaluates, Part I of Zarathustra's prologue: 'Bless the cup which is about to overflow so that the water golden-flowing out of it may carry everywhere the reflection of thy rapture. Lo! this cup is about to empty itself again, and Zarathustra will once more become a man'.[13] After ten years in the mountains, communing with the natural world, Nietzsche's prophet has stored up a superabundance of wisdom and has now decided to return to the company of men. Ready to empty himself of this wisdom, he brings to them the gift of his visionary teachings – of the Übermensch, of the transvaluation of all values, of the Eternal Recurrence – and in the process he begins to embrace his own humanity again. For Yeats, when true to his station, the man of Phase Twelve – whether Nietzsche, his creation, Zarathustra, or some other hero – is poised at this moment of ecstatic awareness of his own plenitude, his own wholeness and self-sufficiency, without need of the affirmation of other men who cannot be counted on to understand or appreciate his gifts; but this same hero, as Yeats suggests, is always in danger of falling out of phase and into a debilitating self-consciousness, which generates various postures and pretences in a strained performance for the benefit of others. Indeed, it might be said that this is precisely what Zarathustra risks as he leaves his mountaintop home and returns to the world of men, who are not ready to receive the message he brings with him.

Yeats proceeds to offer a detailed account of the psychology to be expected of the courageous individual belonging to this phase, who for all his heroism is now less a man of action than a man of ideas. Such a hero turns away from the slings and arrows of the world and instead directs his animosity towards himself; but in doing so he also defines himself according to his developing conscience, his moral and intellectual becoming rather than his physical action in the world of men. One must possess a kind of heroism of the soul in order to generate the self-hatred necessary to move beyond the limitations that define the current self: this is the necessary precondition of future human possibilities, of the overcoming of man and coming of the Übermensch. In the prologue of *Thus Spake Zarathustra*, as Stanley Rosen points out, 'the great contempt' designates 'the proper attitude of human beings toward their own existence, in contrast with that of the superman'.[14] For Yeats, the man of Phase Twelve possesses the 'immense energy' necessary for such as task, 'because the *Four Faculties* are equidistant. The *oppositions* (*Will* and *Mask*, *Creative Mind* and *Body of Fate*) are balanced by the *discords*, and these, being equidistant between *identity* and *opposition*, are at their utmost intensity' (original emphasis). Together, the faculties have fallen into an arrangement that produces the greatest possible intellectual and emotional force in Phase Twelve: the Will, the as-yet undirected inclination or propensity of the ego, is poised in tension with the shaping and conducting function of the Mask (much discussed in the existing scholarship on Yeats and Nietzsche),[15] with its capacity to create a sense of coherence or unification of the self; the Creative Mind, the faculty of perception and interpretation that works to make sense of the phenomena it encounters and is balanced in opposition to its object; and the Body of Fate, the outward context of brute reality that affects a particular individual. This arrangement of tensions means that 'the nature is conscious of the most extreme degree of *deception*, and is wrought to a frenzy of desire for truth', which, as we have observed in Nietzsche's philosophy, is turned inward through probing self-inspection to root out the frauds imposed by convention and conformity.[16]

Yeats associates the 'frenzy of desire for truth' and its heightened intellectual and emotional energies, with the project of value creation or what he calls 'the greatest possible belief in all values created by personality'.[17] This is, in an important sense, the central preoccupation of *Thus Spake Zarathustra* and much of Nietzsche's philosophy: the creative impulse to destroy or overcome the inherited values of the Platonic-Christian tradition, which descend from some eternal elsewhere, and to replace them with new values derived from yea-saying, life-affirming impulses. It hinges on what Gooding-Williams calls 'a fundamental opposition between a traditional philosophy that seeks ontological truth and a philosophy of the future involving the creation of new values'.[18] Nietzsche's masterpiece is, in this regard, a response to what the German philosopher saw as the creeping nihilism of European culture. Yeats's book tells us (again deploying a

Nietzschean vocabulary) that this is 'therefore before all else the phase of the hero, of the man who overcomes himself, and so no longer needs, like Phase 10, the submission of others, or like Phase 11 conviction of others to prove his victory'.[19] Healthy individuals in Phase Twelve, moreover, embrace 'the Body of Fate' because they recognise that their past has made them who they are today, but this embrace of their past and present by the 'Creative Mind' also orients them towards a future destiny that they will shape for themselves out of everything that has come before. But 'pursued by a series of accidents', the man of Phase Twelve is in danger of falling into a series of 'temporary ambitions' in the social and political world that bind him to 'some small protesting sect', despite his inclinations towards interiority and individualism. Once drawn into the world of historical contingencies in this way, the man of Phase Twelve passes his life in a reactionary agitation, taking up 'some commonplace pose' in defence of the cause of the moment or 'a dogmatism which means nothing, apart from the circumstances that created it'[20] – a phrase that suggests the 'passionate intensity' of competing nationalisms that had so recently thrown both Ireland and Europe into violent turmoil.

There is another possibility, however. The man of Phase Twelve, moving away from these collective entanglements and towards greater and greater individuation, may respond to the Body of Fate with 'a noble extravagance, an overflowing fountain of personal life', and thereby detach himself from 'all that is topical and temporary' and focus his mind on the Zarathustrian creation or recreation of the self. The 'True Mask' of Phase Twelve is derived from 'the terrible Phase 26', which has exhausted all 'the old abstraction, whether of morality or of belief',[21] leaving man to an entirely solitary existence in part due to his 'physical deformity' – for this reason, Yeats calls this phase that of 'the Hunchback'.[22] In doing so, he associates the 'True Mask' of Phase Twelve with not only emotional detachment and the end of abstraction of Phase Twenty-Six, but also with the Hunchback of *Thus Spake Zarathustra*, who urges the prophet, having come out of his solitude, to speak not just to the folk but to 'us cripples' in 'Of Salvation'. The provocation leads Zarathustra to reflect on his vocation: 'A prophet, a willing one, a creator, a veritable future, and a bridge unto the future – and alas! besides, as it were, a cripple at that bridge'.[23] He then launches into a series of lessons for his disciples on the limitations of the will, its relation to the movement of time and the spirit of revenge, and lastly its entanglement with the question of salvation. As he comes to an end, the Hunchback is there to question the authenticity of his teachings: '"But why doth Zarathustra speak unto to us in different wise from that in which he speaketh unto to his disciples?" … But why doth Zarathustra speak in different wise unto his disciples from that – in which he speaketh unto himself!'[24] The Hunchback, who Yeats tells us 'is his own Body of Fate', has the last word here because he is the embodiment of *amor fati*, who must love his own fate and call Zarathustra to love the fate of men, which has rendered them but fragments and limbs.[25] 'In the future Zarathustra envisages', Gooding-Williams claims, 'individuals will re-create themselves by compelling their passions (the fragments of their bodies) to function in concert with each other'; but, at the same time Zarathustra, worries that the kind of redemption 'involved in willing backwards ... and thus in preserving his belief that man can be overcome, must compromise the very connection to man that creating new values and overcoming man presupposes'.[26]

'Dove or Swan' and Nietzschean prophecy

These Nietzschean perspectives, as rearticulated in Phase Twelve of *A Vision*, go on to play a critical role in the grand mythico-historical schema formulated in the book as a whole. By the time that Yeats came to draft 'Dove or Swan', which provides his most direct and sustained treatment of history in the volume (and which was one of the few sections that did not 'fill [him] with shame' as he revised *A Vision* over the next decade and more), he had recalculated – in his suggestive and impressionistic, rather than rigorous or empirical way – the relationship between the phases and their historical epics, so that his present day was to be found in Gyre Ten at Phase Twenty-Two of the Christian era and at the very cusp of Gyre Eleven, which would open in 1927 and coincide with Phases Twenty-Three, Twenty-Four, and Twenty-Five of the Moon or the opening of its last quarter. Nietzsche properly belongs to Gyre Ten, with those few men of the previous century – including William Blake and, perhaps surprisingly, Coventry Patmore – who have emphatically endeavoured through the 'Creative Mind' to express 'the new emotion' that could counter the long, slow collapse of Western civilisation.[27] Since the end of the war, Yeats had eagerly anticipated the reconstruction of Europe through totalitarian rule, and he had come to admire the achievements of Mussolini in Italy, as an antidote to democratic decadence. Writing 'Dove and Swan' while travelling in Italy, Yeats pushed the coming of an antithetical era off into a more distant future than the immediacy of 'The Second Coming' suggests: a more distant future that will only arrive after a long period of gradual and multiform counter-movement against the current religious and political dispensation.[28] Although Yeats increasingly shied away from prophecy as he wrote and rewrote *A Vision*, he dedicates the concluding pages of 'Dove or Swan' (the last section of the 1925 volume to be written) to his vision of this future. Like Nietzsche, he predicts a deepening decadence brought on 'by perpetual moral improvement', as the present epoch winds to its end; and, like Nietzsche, he associates this decadence with the decline of the Greco-Roman world, though the near future holds a worse fate for it will be democratic and sapped of all vitality.[29]

But, as we know from 'The Second Coming', Yeats sees on the horizon a new era defined by values antithetical to those of the primary Christian era – an era, moreover, that will be welcomed by a select group of individuals who have already embraced its antithetical values. The new era will not call into being a community based on traditional Christian values, the 'virtues of delight', mercy, pity, peace, and love that Blake associates with 'the human form divine'; it will not render man in the image of a living God nor model him on the all deities that 'reside in the human breast' insofar as they are associated with these ideal human qualities. But, as the poet waxes prophetic here, this is also not – or not yet, as Yeats's choice of conjunction may suggest – the epoch of 'Nietzsche's superman', who overcomes the Christian virtues instilled in man and creates his own values in the absence of God. That future remains still more distant. Rather than envisioning the emergence of ethically superior individuals, Yeats foresees the rise of physically and intellectually advanced collectives, evolving naturally out of the decadent multitudes of men. If Yeats's racial imaginings owe something to Nietzsche's close association with ideas about the future of the human race, as his philosophy was repeatedly linked with Darwinian evolutionary theory and the associated field of eugenics, this vision is also indebted to his genealogical narrative of Western morality. 'Dove or Swan', like *A Genealogy of Morals*, rests on a basic duality between Greek and Christian culture: Yeats's mythico-historical narrative begins with Zeus's 'annunciation' made in the form of a swan and then takes up the story of the ensuing Christian era, with the annunciation made to Mary by the Holy Spirit in the form of a dove. He goes on to envision 'new races ... seeking domination, a world resembling but for its immensity that of the Greek tribes' and a reassertion of archaic values associated not with 'the brood of the Sistine Chapel', and their 'virtues of delight', but with the 'brood of Leda, War and Love', as they were manifest long ago in the pre-Christian era.[30]

Nietzsche too distinguished clearly between Christian and Greek moral thought, and often pointed toward the superiority of the master or noble morality that grounded the latter, because it embraced the passions of war and love, rather than flagellating itself with bad conscience and ressentiment. The tribes of Greek antiquity had learned to attribute their suffering to external forces and to assign responsibility for their passions, as well as their fate, to their gods in a way replicated by Yeats in 'Leda and the Swan'. In doing so, they had resisted the temptation to assume guilt for their nature or to moralise their actions, and they had thereby succeeded in avoiding the debilitating effects of bad conscious and instead embraced the unrestricted exercise of the will to power, the affirmation characteristic of noble morality. Yeats also shares Nietzsche's sense that a return to this ethos would require a bodily or physiological transformation into something like the ancient Greeks, a healthy and resilient race that could replace the 'the dull, sluggish races' of modern Europe: 'Above all', the poet tells us in a Nietzschean vocabulary, 'I imagine everywhere the opposites, no mere alternation between nothing and something like the Christian brute and ascetic, but true opposites, each living the other's death, dying the other's life'.[31] Nietzsche had seen 'the *great* danger threatening mankind' (original emphasis) and 'the doom of Europe' in the drift towards nihilism, which was not the inverse of Christian thought but rather the natural outgrowth of that tradition and a clear sign of 'the degeneration of life'.[32] The ascetic ideal was a response to a 'physiologically aborted and depressed' condition – the condition, according to Nietzsche, of 'the *majority* of mortals' (original emphasis) – by thinking themselves '"too good" for this world'.[33] With the advent of the new era, however, Yeats sees the emergence of a new collective, which forms a 'true opposite' to these Christian exemplars because it has been cured of 'the final disease', this turn towards 'nothing', and has instead adopted a noble morality that arises from a triumphant 'yea-saying' to life.[34]

As in 'The Second Coming', Yeats sees the emergence of this new dispensation not as an interruption of the Christian era, but as its culmination, an enunciation that has been prepared by the two millennia that preceded it. He sees, moreover, a 'falling into two of the human mind', with the increasing separation between the 'cultivated classes' and the slavish masses, who remain mired in the ethos of the Christian era. With the increasing separation of these groups as the eleventh gyre commences in 1927, there will arise a form of philosophy that Yeats has already associated with Nietzsche, who has paved the way as a thinker who 'almost belongs' to that gyre. Some 200 years hence, in the twelfth gyre, Yeats sees this philosophy becoming 'religious and ethical', as genealogical critique moves towards the positive articulation of these new values that challenge and replace the primacy of Christian morality. The Nietzschean qualities of this new 'religious and ethical' dispensation soon become manifest: 'It will be concrete in expression, establish itself by immediate experience, seek no general agreement, make little of God or any exterior unity, and it will call that good which a man can contemplate himself as doing always and no other man doing at all'.[35] Perhaps there could be no better summation of the philosophical project undertaken by Nietzsche. He shunned abstractions and metaphysics in favour of poetic images and genealogical inquiry; he wrote for those with the ears to hear him, and his Zarathustra sought only those disciples ready for his message; in neither case was the intention to indoctrinate an audience, but to spur independent thought; and in neither case did the philosopher and prophet seek the outside authority of God or any other metaphysical presence or principle of unity as a guarantor of meaning. More important, as we have seen throughout this study, Nietzsche identified not just the possibility, but the history, of a morality based on the self-affirmation of 'the noble, the powerful, the high-situated, the high-minded' who regard 'themselves and their acting as of first rank, in contradistinction to everything low, low-minded, mean and vulgar'.[36] In the new era to come, according to Yeats, 'men will no longer separate the idea of God from that of human genius, human productivity in all its forms'.[37] God will not be evoked to shore up human political institutions or explain the teleological movement of history or even undergird and render infallible the human capacity for reason. Rather, human genius will be given the task of reinventing humanity, transvaluing all values, and remaking human life.

It is in this necessarily speculative mode that Yeats begins to suggest not just a new religious and ethical orientation but the political orientation that will attend it: in the era to come, the democratic will to mutuality will give way to the heroic politics that he had already begun to glimpse in the early 1920s. For the poet, the well-born of the future – the enemies of the ascetic ideal to whom Nietzsche alludes only obliquely in *A Genealogy of Morals* – will not be wedded to one branch of knowledge or one source of wealth; and, more important, they will pursue learning and riches, explore new styles of knowing and new forms of living with a libidinous lust for life. This ethos becomes a politics because those who best 'express' this lust for life will be rewarded with influence and authority. Crucially, they will be rewarded thus not due to what they might accomplish with their influence and authority, whether social benefits or political transformations, but due to their embodiment of this new libidinous force. Echoing 'The Second Coming', Yeats emphasises that this new political orientation will not 'interrupt the intellectual stream' that flows from the primary Christian era into the antithetical Nietzschean era to come, but emerging out of it and extending from it, the new epoch 'may grow a fanaticism and a terror' that oppresses the ignorant and perhaps also the innocent who do not share in this new ethical and religious orientation. In this sense, then, the new era is a reverse image of the Christian era that had in its turn 'oppressed the wise' who did not share in the slave morality of the masses or herd. And yet, in its affirmation of life in its totality, the religious and ethical dispensation in Gyre Twelve also suggests (at least the possibility of) a fundamental integrity, a truce between the temporal self and the immortal soul, between a temporal fate and an eternal destiny. For, Yeats concludes, the time will come when 'the two halves of man', the ignorant and the wise, the slavish and the masterful, the life-denying and the life-affirming, can be reconciled as the 'Sun in Moon, Moon in Sun', and so escape out of 'the Wheel'[38] of history into a final and complete 'Unity of Being'.

Back to Methuselah and Creative Evolution

Given the devasting impact of the First World War on European society and the concurrent events in Ireland, it is not surprising that during the same period Yeats was grappling with these epochal issues, his estranged countryman, Shaw, was wrestling with many of the same concerns: the fate of Western civilisation, the future of humanity, and the desire for a new politics. Nor is it surprising that, given their shared interest in the philosopher, both writers had reference to Nietzsche as they formulated their responses to these concerns. Like his dramatic avatar in *Man and Superman*, John Tanner, Shaw continued to believe in the need for the Superman and that 'the need for the Superman is, in its most imperative aspect, a political one', though now, after the cataclysm of the war, his political vision took on a grand millennial scope far surpassing anything imagined by the technocratic Tanner in his 'Revolutionist's Handbook'.[39] Shaw returned to his role as an eccentric political philosopher – but, by the time he began drafting *Back to Methuselah* about six months before the conclusion of the war, he had given up his faith in Fabian gradualism and parliamentary politics entirely and instead took up a kind of cosmic evolutionary gradualism. He joined Yeats in casting his attention back to the beginnings of Christian civilisation in order to provide a genealogy of sorts that might explain the terminus at which Western culture had arrived; Shaw too looked into the future in the effort to understand the trajectory of contemporary history by extrapolating from the present by reviewing the implications of the previous epoch; and he too drew on a wide range of generic conventions and discursive modes in the production of a novel aesthetic form, which in his case contributes to the genres of both science fiction and utopian literature. His five-part play, subtitled *A Metabiological Pentateuch*, commences in 4004 BCE with 'In the Beginning' and ends in the distant future, 30,000 years after his own era, that is 31,920 CE, with 'As Far as Thought Can Reach'. In between these temporal poles, Shaw seeks to articulate a new mythology for his religion of Creative Evolution, which would greatly elaborate and extend the scope of the Life Force philosophy he had first addressed in *Man and Superman*.

The preface of his massive dramatic work sets out to examine the underlying causes of the war, diagnose the condition of European society after its conclusion, and, more generally, address a question that 'had grown steadily in [his] mind during [his] forty years' public work as a Socialist', namely: whether the human species at it had evolved was indeed capable of overcoming the social and political ills generated by what it calls 'civilisation'.[40] Of course, the war had made this question all the more pressing, and an affirmative answer all the more doubtful. Shaw attributes 'the betrayal of Western Civilisation' to the rise of 'Neo-Darwinian' political thought in the years leading up to the conflict, as partisan opportunism had corrupted parliaments across Europe and created internecine conflicts between nations. In response to this state of affairs, Shaw translates evolutionary theory into international relations and suggests that 'if the Western Powers had selected their allies in the Lamarckian manner intelligently, purposefully, and vitally, *ad majorem Dei gloriam*, as what Nietzsche called good Europeans, there would have been a League of Nations and no war'.[41] Leaving aside Shaw's strange analogical misprision, equating the dynamics of biological evolution with those of modern statesmanship, we can nonetheless note the significance of his evocation of Nietzsche's famous phrase, which the philosopher deploys in a section of *Beyond Good and Evil* titled 'People and Countries' to describe those exceptional individuals who rise above chauvinism and narrowminded nationalism. Although 'good Europeans' may occasionally relapse into national sentiment, these individuals – he cites nineteenth-century examples such as Napoleon, Goethe, Beethoven, Stendhal, Heine, Schopenhauer, and even Wagner – do not long remain mired in this condition, unlike the 'duller spirits' and 'sluggish, hesitating races' that cannot 'surmount such atavistic attacks of patriotism and soil-attachment'.[42] Looking around him at the end of the nineteenth century, Nietzsche sees his fellow Europeans becoming increasingly detached from the climatic and hereditary circumstances that had separated the various tribes, peoples, or races of the Continent so that 'an essentially *super-national* and nomadic species of man' (original emphasis) with increased powers of adaptation is emerging everywhere.[43]

A connection between the Übermensch and the good European begins to emerge. Although the 'process of the *evolving European*' (original emphasis) has repeatedly been slowed or even derailed by the resurgence of national sentiment, and although the same civilising and democratising forces that generated the possibility of a super-national species also contribute to a 'levelling and mediocrising of man', Nietzsche contends that these forces may 'give rise to exceptional men of the most dangerous and attractive qualities': 'the strong man will necessarily, in individual and exceptional cases, become stronger and richer than he has perhaps ever been before – owing to the unprejudicedness of his schooling, owing to the immense variety of practice, art, and disguise'.[44] Prescient as ever, the philosopher foresees both the spread of democracy and the rise of tyrants across the European Continent. In the early 1920s, Shaw despaired of the 'purely circumstantial opportunist selection'[45] in the realm of international relations that had led to such horrible consequences in the recent past, and his Pentateuch makes it clear that monarchs and statesmen who allowed the war to happen may have been doing their best to guide their respective societies through vexed historical circumstances, but 'succeeded in all-but-wrecking the civilisation of Europe'.[46] Shaw is again at pains to deny the influence of Nietzsche on his work, by reminding his audience that the German philosopher was hardly 'the first man to whom it occurred that morality and legality and urbanity lead nowhere', but it is just as clear that the playwright owes much to Nietzsche as he formulates a response to the cataclysm of the war.[47] Like Nietzsche, he prophesies the emergence of a higher type of European, a higher type of man, a politically adequate animal capable both of transcending nationalist sentiment or petty chauvinism and of governing the increasingly complex societies of the future. The difference for Shaw is that this new man would develop the wisdom during the course of his greatly extended lifespan and thus overcome the trifling competitiveness that had led to so much conflict and bloodshed. For man in his present state, according to the playwright, does not live long enough to acquire the training and experience necessary to 'organise socialism', which is tantamount to 'organise civilised life'.

Back to Methuselah attempts to repackage the Life Force philosophy articulated in *Man and Superman* two decades earlier as the new faith of Creative Evolution, which Shaw claims is 'the genuinely scientific religion for which all wise men are now anxiously looking', with an anxiety generated by the sense that evolution should proceed according to some underlying moral imperative, if not a divinely ordained plan.[48] For to Shaw, whose 'new gospel' again draws heavily on the work of Samuel Butler, 'self-control' is the 'highest moral claim' of 'Evolutionary Selection', a fact that the Darwinians have overlooked *even though* it was an implication of their theoretical framework as much as of the neo-Lamarckian perspective, with its assertion of the existence of some metaphysical force behind organic creativity. This is a mistake, according to Shaw, that the 'Vitalist philosophers' have avoided: 'Nietzsche, for example, thinking out the great central truth of the Will to Power ... had no difficulty in concluding that the final objective of Will was power over self, and that seekers after power over others and material possessions were a false scent'.[49] Shaw makes his own mistake in continuing to attribute a purely teleological motive to the will to power, which Nietzsche conceived of as irrational and unconscious, but this teleology is a central article of faith for Creative Evolution, just as it was essential to the Life Force doctrine: as the former cleric, Franklyn Barnabus, says in the third play of the Pentateuch, 'the force behind evolution, call it what you will, is determined to solve the problem of civilisation; and if it cannot do it through us, it will produce some more capable agents'.[50] This is the renewed promise of the Shavian Superman. If the statesmen of contemporary Europe were incapable of governing the Continent during the recent conflict due to their lack of experience and intellect, the statesmen of the future could be expected to develop longer lifespans in order to acquire more experience – and develop more advanced cognitive abilities in order to better process that experience.

Shaw was motivated to produce his massive Pentateuch because he believed that Creative Evolution could not 'become a popular religion until it has its legends, its parable, its miracles'.[51] In this sense, like the other books discussed in this chapter, *Back to Methuselah* participates in the modernist obsession with mythic and prophetic modes that owes far more to Nietzsche's *Thus Spake Zarathustra* than it did to, say, J.G. Frazer's *The Golden Bough* or Jessie Weston's *From Ritual to Romance*. For Shaw, with his more direct social and political motives, the recourse to legends was driven by a desire to reach an audience of common men, as well as the 'professional politician and administrator', who is not adept in the interpretation of unfiltered philosophy or prophecy.[52] The role of the 'artist-prophet' (a step beyond the 'artist-philosopher' of *Man and Superman*), as Shaw came to conceive it, was to serve the cause of progress by effectively translating the implications of neo-Lamarckian evolutionary theory into 'the new Vitalist art'.[53] Like Yeats, Shaw sees a prescient exemplar in Michelangelo, who 'could paint the Superman three hundred years before Nietzsche wrote *Also Sprach Zarathustra* and Strauss set it to music'.[54] *Back to Methuselah* is thus framed as a 'second legend of Creative Evolution', after *Man and Superman*, as well as a radical revision of the Christian mythos of the perfectibility of mankind that reaches into a posthuman future.[55] It is fitting, then, that the Pentateuch opens in the Garden of Eden, where we find Adam and Eve discovering the possibilities of procreation, death, and eventually murder. After Cain slaughters his brother, he proclaims: 'There is something higher than man. There is hero and superman'; to which Eve answers, 'Superman! You are no superman: you are Anti-Man ... When you die, men will say, "He was a great warrior; but it would have been better for the world if he had never been born"'.[56] With this Shavian genealogy of morals, the stage is set for dramatising the legend of Creative Evolution and exploring the qualities of the Superman towards which it leads.

The next two parts of the Pentateuch, 'The Gospel of the Brothers Barnabas' and 'The Thing Happens', begin to envision the political significance of such a figure. The first, set immediately after the First World War, is a satirical drawing-room comedy very much in the mode of *Man and Superman*, both plays populated by various social types, propelled by courtship intrigues, and scripted in the form of ideological debates, often focused on the foibles of bourgeois manners. But, in the aftermath of the war, these debates take on an added intensity: Franklyn tells a statesman that his task is 'beyond human capacity', because he must control 'our huge armaments, our terrible engines of destruction', which should not be 'entrusted to an infinitely experienced and benevolent God, much less to mortal men whose whole life does not last a hundred years'.[57] His brother Conrad, a professor of biology, adds that 'some authorities hold that the human race is a failure, and that a new form of life, better adapted to high civilisation, will supersede us as we have superseded the ape and the elephant'. This does just not mean 'the superman', as the statesman presumes, but 'some being quite different than us', according to Conrad.[58] Wedding science and religion to politics, the brothers announce their program – 'only that the term of human life shall be extended to three hundred years' – as the only possibility for mankind to acquire the experience and know-how necessary to govern highly complex societies.[59] As its title suggests, 'The Thing Happens' demonstrates the initial outcomes of this program and the radical transformation of geopolitics that has ensued. The year is 2170 and the unimpressive politicians of 'The Gospel of the Brothers Barnabas' have now become the ostensible rulers of the British Isles; but the real business of governing the English is mostly left to outsiders from Africa and China, who have attained the wisdom and expertise needed to successfully lead what is left of the British Empire. This scenario provides Shaw with ample opportunity to mock the political shortcomings of the English and their claim to being a 'great race', when even those who have lived for more than two centuries remain unable to effectively govern their own people.[60] At the same time, it also offers him the occasion to consider the characteristics of a political Superman in the figure of Confucius, who not only sees through the foolish pretensions of the English but counters them with the wisdom of some future philosopher king, dedicated to creating the conditions under which 'the Government' can 'think'.[61]

Yet, as Shaw extends his vision into the distant future of human evolution, the image he sees is an increasingly ambivalent one. The fourth part of the Pentateuch, 'The Tragedy of an Elderly Gentlemen', is set on 'a fine summer day in the year 3000 A.D.', on 'the south shore of Galway Bay in Ireland', where a party of 'shortlivers' has come to consult with the 'longlived people' who now inhabit the island: here is the prophesied race that has the ability to manage its political affairs with infinitely greater efficiency.[62] By the time the play is set, war has all but eradicated the 'pseudo-Christian civilisation' of the previous epoch, and the leaders of the British Empire, who have travelled from Baghdad to Galway Bay, hope to learn from this race of Supermen and women in order to preserve what remains of their domain.[63] Writing during a period of violent conflict in Ireland, Shaw mocks the Irish inclination for ardent nationalism by having his characters explain that, because the English finally left them to themselves there in Ireland, the Irish people have long since emigrated to other parts of the British Empire 'where there was still a Nationalist question'. The elderly gentleman of the title, however, has come to the island on a pilgrimage to see the place where the members of this diaspora had attempted an ill-fated return; he is cynical enough to claim that, after the Irish left Ireland, they 'lost all their political faculties by disuse except that of nationalist agitation' and 'owed their position as the most interesting race on earth solely to their sufferings'.[64] On the other hand, the new inhabitants of the island, the so-called 'longlived people', have become something like the 'good Europeans' Shaw imagines in his preface: not only have they conceded all claims to nationality, they have also given up all national sentiment as childish and misguided. On the other hand, along with patriotic feeling, they have also parted with passion and poetry. Having developed the most refined political faculties, they have simultaneously developed into what must be the least interesting race on earth, so dry, so bloodless, and so hyperrational that they have also lost the capacity to laugh, cry, and even understand figurative speech. These are creatures, then, who have evolved far beyond anything Nietzsche had envisioned, for whatever physiological process created them as 'an essentially *super-national*' (original emphasis) species, immune from 'atavistic attacks of patriotism and soil-attachment', has also drained them of the spirit of what the philosopher calls the 'more profound and large-minded men', the 'masters of new modes of speech' in his century, the Napoleons, Goethes, and Beethovens.[65]

The question is whether Shaw sees this forfeiture as a hazard or a necessity. He offers an answer of sorts by bringing Napoleon himself (or at least the 'Emperor of Turania', masquerading under that name) on stage in Act II to meet with 'the Oracle', a long-liver who might advise him on how '[he] is to satisfy [his] genius for fighting until [he] die[s]'.[66] The scandalous query derives from a supreme confidence that he is 'a man gifted with a certain specific talent in a degree altogether extraordinary' – that is, a talent for 'the shedding of oceans of blood, the death of millions of men'.[67] To be sure, what Shaw is offering in the person of Napoleon is a parodic response to the vulgarised version of the Superman that had gained increasing currency during the war years. As noted in Chapter 1, Shaw had already defended Nietzsche (and himself) in the preface of *Major Barbara* (1907) from what the playwright deemed to be an unwarranted reputation in England: 'it is assumed, on the strength of the single word Superman (Übermensch) borrowed by me from Nietzsche, that I look for the salvation of society to the despotism of a single Napoleonic Superman, in spite of my careful demonstration of the folly of that outworn infatuation'.[68] Fifteen years later – on the other side of the most destructive armed conflict in European history, as well as the concerted propaganda campaign implicating Nietzsche – Shaw takes up this defence again in *Back to Methuselah* in order to clarify his vision of human futurity, which pits the superhuman wisdom and rationality of the long-livers against the all-too-human pettiness and hostility of Napoleon and his bellicose breed. Certainly, despite his frequent praise of Napoleon, Nietzsche had admired not so much his talents as a general or even as a statesman, but his ability to create a personal morality and to give style to his character. More than this, the 'mysterious labour' of his soul represented a broader tendency to anticipate 'the Europe of the Future' insofar as it transcended the nationalism of the herd with a 'love of the ego ... much more powerful than the love of old, used-up, hackneyed "fatherland"'.[69] Against the 'will to levelling' that, according to Nietzsche, was epitomised in the decadent impulses behind the French Revolution, Napoleon sounded the 'rapturous counter-cry of the privilege of the fewest' as they appeared 'the incarnate problem of the noble ideal as such'. It is precisely this problem that Shaw takes up by calling him to the stage, though Nietzsche had already summed up the issue with his characteristic pith in *A Genealogy of Morals*: 'Napoleon, this synthesis of monster and *beyondman*' (original emphasis).[70]

'As Far as Thought Can Reach' and Shavian posthumanism

In the end, the Shavian Superman is something very different from anything Nietzsche had envisioned, although the playwright and the philosopher do share a sense that in the centuries to come the function of politics will inevitably be bound up in a redefinition of the human species.[71] The final part of the Pentateuch, 'As Far as Thought Can Reach', brings the trajectory of Creative Evolution to a telos appropriate to the playwright's political, ethical, and, it could be said, broadly religious orientation, if only through an implicit dialogue with Nietzschean images, concepts, and values. Indeed, the drama helps to clarify Shaw's objections to Nietzsche's vision of a higher humanity, objections that he had made since first addressing the philosopher's ideas in his reviews and prefaces at end of the previous century. 'As Far as Thought Can Reach' is set in something like a second Garden of Eden – 'a sunlit glade' on a 'summer afternoon in the year 31,920 A.D.' – when the short-livers are nothing more than a distant memory and the long-livers, after a brief childhood as 'youths', spend centuries in detached contemplation as 'ancients'.[72] Although the values announced by the 'ancients' of the play align with those to which Shaw returned repeatedly throughout his career (and increasingly in the last decades of his life), their articulation by these 'mild' and 'bland' messengers threatens to lapse into a kind of parody.

As the drama opens, a dance of youths is underway in a meadow, but an ancient, deep in thought, soon wanders into their midst and explains that he has long since given up dancing, singing, and mating, as mere childish pastimes. Nothing could be further from Nietzsche's life-affirming ethical vision: images of dancing appear throughout his oeuvre and can be found in some of his most often repeated aphorisms, frequently as an affirmation of Dionysian energies in the face of Christian enmity towards bodily existence. Conversely, as Zarathustra claims, it is the failure of the so-called 'higher men' to dance – 'to dance beyond yourselves' – that indicates their implication in the decadent values of the modern European culture and their inability to reach the status of Übermenschen.[73] After the demise of God, these artists and statemen have pursued new forms of meaning, but they have been thwarted in their efforts precisely insofar as they continue to abide by the ascetic ideal and allow their bodies to remain exhausted and passionless.

Denigration of the body and all it involves – its pleasures and passions, as well as its weaknesses and limitations – is central to Shaw's vision of superhumanity in this final part of *Back to Methuselah*. The denizens of 31,920, who are born fully grown from giant eggs, have lost all interest in romantic love, in caressing and cavorting, by the age of four; they have begun to see this all as 'silly', as they turn their attention to higher – that is to say, for Shaw, more intellectual – pursuits. Rather drolly, the play quickly dispatches all the romantic intrigues that had characterised Shaw's earlier comedies, including *Man and Superman*, by having a suitor, Strephon, pursue 'the Maiden' who soon after her birth has already begun to withdraw from the life of the physical passions for a solitary life of the mind. Rejecting his advances, the Maiden explains that she prefers 'thinking, thinking, thinking; grasping the world; taking it to pieces; building it up again; devising methods; planning experiments to test the methods'.[74] Again, the response to Nietzsche's vision of the Übermensch is a stark contradiction. For the philosopher, overcoming oneself does not mean an overreliance on the intellect, but rather the shaping of one's impulses or drives according to the demands of one's better instincts. While condemning Darwin for the oversight ('that was English!', he exclaims), Nietzsche even attributes greater intellect to the weak than to the strong, because the weak require 'foresight, patience, craft, dissimulation, grand self-control, and all modifications of *mimicry*' as a means to survival (original emphasis).[75] In his 'ancients', on the other hand, Shaw elevates intellectual powers to the status of an evolutionary telos, which requires little or no bodily experience, while allowing for a profound understanding of the structural features of reality. Nietzsche repeatedly affirms that mental activity is inextricably intertwined with physical activity: for instance, in *Twilight of the Idols*, he scolds German philosophers for forgetting 'that thinking requires to be learned as dancing requires to be learned, as a mode of dancing'.[76] Shaw, on the other hand, envisions the process of evolution as moving towards the eradication of the body altogether: 'the day will come', an oracular she-ancient foretells, 'when there will be no people, only thought'.[77] Freed from their mortal coils, the superhumans to come will exist as a vortex of energy capable of roaming unhindered among the stars and contemplating endlessly the mysteries of the universe.

Perhaps, given the rather dour tone and unyielding beliefs of his ancients, it should be expected that Shaw's scientific religion of Creative Evolution has some rather disturbing social and political implications, even if it was Nietzsche's philosophy that was coopted by fascist regimes in Italy and Germany in the succeeding decades. No doubt these implications go some distance in explaining Shaw's own support of these regimes, with their utopian claims, in the 1920s and 1930s. His vision of Creative Evolution, reaching into a far distant future, prophesies an end to the Anthropocene era and the beginning of a kingdom to come, of something posthuman – of something, as his title suggests, almost unthinkable. In a sense, he has radically extended Fabian gradualism over an evolutionary time-scale of 30,000 years; but, in another sense, he has abandoned all faith in socialist agitation to project a utopia beyond the end of history, where there is no need for laws, governments, even civilisation as he knew it. Instead, a radical biopower is vested in the sublime intelligence of the ancients, who possess an unchecked authority over life and death for each new generation: when a 'child' emerges from her egg, an ancient examines her critically, feeling her head like a phrenologist, gripping her muscles and shaking her limbs, looking over her teeth and her eyes, before pronouncing, 'She will do. She may live'.[78]

Shaw became increasingly vocal in the 1920s and 1930s about a program of negative eugenics that would eliminate unproductive, intractable, or in some way unfit individuals from society: 'extermination', as he put it in his preface to *On the Rocks* (1933), 'must be put on a scientific basis if it is ever to be carried out humanely and apologetically as well as thoroughly'.[79] Such a program, whatever its scientific claims, was ultimately in service of the religion of the Life Force, which through such practices would expedite the evolutionary process towards a telos like that depicted so vividly, so frighteningly, in 'As Far as Thought Can Reach'. In doing so, Shaw's play had nonetheless edged towards a thanatopolitics, a politics of death. At the end of the play, he stages a return of those characters who initiated his legend in 'In the Beginning', with each speaking in turn: Cain feels unneeded because the strong have slain each other and the weak live forever, but Eve is pleased since the fighters have perished and the 'clever ones have inherited the earth' (the value of cleverness for Shaw persists).[80] The last word is reserved for Lilith, the original emissary of the Life Force who created Adam and Eve long ago: observing that their descendants have accepted the burden of eternal life and given up the yoke of bodily existence, she wonders if this is enough or if she should start the project of creation all over again. One is tempted to conclude, in turn, that Shaw's vision is deeply misanthropic, projecting a form of posthuman existence that transcends all that he found displeasing in human life, especially the baggage of embodiment: pain, disease, decay, physical violence, corporeal disability, but also sexual expression, carnal pleasure, aestheticised enjoyment, all of it. In this sense, *Back to Methuselah* radically transvalues the Nietzschean Übermensch. Moreover, if we adopt Daniel Conway's notion of *the political* in relation to Nietzsche's thought – namely, '*what ought humankind to become?*' (original emphasis) – then it is clear that the philosopher and the playwright have very different ideas about how to answer 'the founding question of politics'.[81] The philosopher had postulated superior individuals capable of moving beyond the accrued history of resentment, bad conscience, and moral decadence that had come to define *Homo sapiens* as 'man' in modern Europe, precisely by enlisting the best impulses and accepting the worst limitations of his animal existence. The playwright, in the face of modern European history, refuses to affirm human existence in all of its shortcomings and restraints, but instead envisions an escape into an eternal and ethereal utopia, by any means necessary.

'Oxen of the Sun' and Irish futurity

A different species of futurity is to be found in Joyce's writing, albeit a futurity bound up in the same concerns about breeding, eugenics, and the chaotic state of both Ireland and Europe in the years immediately following the First World War. Again, Nietzsche's philosophy plays an important role in the consideration of these issues, especially in episode fourteen of *Ulysses*, the so-called 'Oxen of the Sun' chapter; and, again, the effects of the recent conflict on the Continent, along with the increasing nationalist agitation and political violence in Ireland, form crucial contexts for appreciating the urgency of these concerns. Having sent a draft of the chapter to Ezra Pound in October 1919, Joyce began writing the earliest surviving version of 'Oxen of the Sun' in February 1920 and worked on it in ten separate copybooks during the next two months, before publishing part of the chapter in the September–December 1920 issue of *The Little Review*. In other words, the chapter was written as the Irish War of Independence raged in the distance, with Joyce beginning composition at the same time the British were outlawing the Irish Dáil and finishing his drafts not long after Westminster passed the 'Better Government of Ireland Bill' – a period that saw raids, ambushes, and assassinations on both sides and near-constant tumult throughout the island. Enda Duffy has suggested that the intensification of anti-colonial and nationalist conflicts in Ireland during the composition of *Ulysses*, beginning with the Easter Rising and continuing through the War of Independence, had given the author little optimism for the future of the nation-state as a form of social, political, and geographical community. Moreover, the recent war on the Continent, which the self-exiled writer circumnavigated according to the famous itinerary delineated at the end of the novel – 'Trieste – Zurich – Paris' – could have done little to bolster any utopian hopes for the current modes of socio-political organisation or the prevailing forms of psycho-social cultivation, for that matter. It was nonetheless clear that, as Joyce wrote 'Oxen of the Sun', a new era was being born both in Ireland and Europe after the First World War, a new era that he, like Yeats and Shaw, envisioned with the aid of Nietzsche, as well as the discourses surrounding birthing and breeding that contributed to his great modernist opus.

The episode is best known for its integration of a series of prose styles, which come to signify the long gestation of the English language, with a series of discourses that bear on the development of the human embryo. In the century since it was written, much has been made in Joyce criticism of the relationship between the style and the content of the chapter. It is only relatively recently, however, that scholars have given sustained attention to the assorted discourses on maternity, fertility, birth control, and the nation that circulate through the various imitations of literary style making up the chapter. Both Richard Brown and Mary Lowe-Evans have demonstrated how the chapter deploys arguments from Catholic theologians and nationalist concerns about declining birthrates, on the one hand, and proponents of birth control such as Fabian socialists and members of the Malthusian League, on the other.[82] It is worth noting here that, not long before beginning work on 'The Oxen of the Sun', Joyce had also read the preface to Shaw's *Getting Married*, which argues that while there could be no viable alternatives to marriage, the future of the institution requires the reform of divorce laws in order to ensure the well-being of both the adults involved and their children.

In an important contribution to our understanding of these issues in *Ulysses*, Duffy emphasises the nationalist stake in birthrates in the aftermath of the First World War, when the relationship between population growth and the maintenance and development of a 'healthy' nation took on the utmost importance.[83] By 1919, as Duffy points out, Ireland was one of a small number of European countries where birthrates were increasing, though it was also, rather ironically, one of the few European countries where the population had fallen over the previous century – due primarily to the Famine and its consequences. Responding to earlier critics, however,

Duffy shows how 'once the tenor of a given setting is considered, what appears at first to be narrative in support for what Ellmann called "the fecundity of the natural order" can turn out to be a parodic mimicry of a rhetorical line that the overall narrative seems loath to accept'.[84] To be sure, the multiplying parodies that make up the chapter generate numerous lines of argument and a range of shifting perspectives, as Joyce not only attempts to disrupt nationalist discourses that called for population growth or promoted the symbolic power of motherhood, but also undertakes to redefine 'traditional paternalist narratives of male worth' that 'were coming under intense pressure' during this period.[85]

What is missing from all these analyses is any sustained attention to the role that Nietzschean allusions play in the Joycean excursion into various verbal styles and the ideologies they transmit. Early in the chapter, as a group of young men drink and prattle in a backroom of the National Maternity Hospital, a medical student named Dixon turns the conversation to why Stephen has abandoned his earlier interest in a religious vocation, and another young man follows up with rumours of how Stephen had strayed into sexual adventures that had corrupted at least one young woman. In the style of Sir Thomas Malory, Stephen responds with an anecdote about the playwrights John Fletcher and Francis Beaumont who, at least according to him, had not only collaborated on the bawdy romance, *The Maid's Tragedy*, but had also shared a single lover. The increasingly drunken repartee reaches a blasphemous climax of sorts, when Stephen punctuates his story with a mock Biblical verse:

> Greater love than this, he said, no man hath that a man lay down his wife for his friend. Go thou and do likewise. Thus, or words to that effect, said Zarathustra, sometime regius professor of French letters to the university of Oxtail nor breathed there ever that man to whom mankind was more beholden. Bring a stranger within thy tower it will go hard but thou wilt have the secondbest bed. Orate, fratres, pro memetipso. And all the people shall say, Amen.[86]

The passage lifts a line out of the Gospels – John 15:13, to be exact – gives it a vulgar twist, and then attributes it to Nietzsche's prophetic alter ego, who is also given a kind of vulgar twist with his new title, profession, and institutional affiliation. Duffy reminds us that 'Stephen's priestly parodies ... are merely imitations of Buck Mulligan, one of which opens *Ulysses*: what he presents then is a parody of a parody'.[87] To this, I would add that Mulligan himself is not just parodying a priest in 'Telemachus', but – most notably in his travesty of Proverbs 19:7, which he follows with 'Thus Spake Zarathustra' – he is parodying Nietzsche's messianic protagonist – who in turn, it should also be added, is parodying the heightened rhetoric of Biblical verse on virtually every page of *Thus Spake Zarathustra*. What Stephen offers here is thus more accurately described as a parody of a parody of a parody. One effect of this mimicry and mockery is to again taint the priesthood with a scandalous Nietzschean association: what better way for Stephen to respond to the chiding of his peers about his departure from the Church? Another effect, however, is to further destabilise the authority of the Nietzschean refrain and to throw additional doubt on the project of forging new values in late colonial Ireland. That Zarathustra is here identified as a 'sometime regius professor of French letters to the university of Oxtail' suggests a further slight insofar as it attributes to him an academic appointment (in a foreign literature, no less) to a chair founded by a British sovereign and filled by a royal appointment – a nomination, moreover, to a derisively renamed Oxford University, that bastion of English learning.[88] In short, Zarathustra has been reduced summarily to the status of a mild academic, albeit one with an apparent penchant for bawdy Biblical parody.

No doubt there is still much more to this: as is the case throughout the novel, these playful allusions carry with them various associations, and these multiplying parodies come with multiplying rhetorical effects. The biblical verse that Stephen parodies – 'Greater love hath no man than this, that a man lay down his life for his friends' – amounts to a new commandment, which Jesus delivers to his apostles as he washes their feet and thus demonstrates the need for them to serve humbly. This is a pivotal and particularly moving moment in the Gospels because Christ, foreseeing his own death, has just told his disciples that 'where I am going, you cannot come' and now explains what will bind them together in his absence – namely, their self-sacrificing love for one another. The travesty of the verse in *Ulysses* – 'Greater love than this, he said, no man hath that a man lay down his wife for his friend' – may undo the powerful communal sentiment present in the original, but it also postulates another kind of bond: one that undermines both the institution of marriage and the Catholic imperative for reproductive sexuality.[89] Christine Froula argues, for instance, that there is a homoerotic charge to the sexual triangle of Fletcher, Beaumont, and their lover, a charge that transfers to the triangle of Mulligan, Haines, and Stephen as the mock-Christian proposal is linked to their living arrangements in the Martello tower and the cult of new paganism that might be founded there. Perhaps Zarathustra – the modern messiah as Antichrist, who prattles on to his disciples – is the perfect messenger for such a message. Perhaps even more so is 'the regius professor of French letters at the University of Oxtail', if we consider that 'French letters' was common slang for condoms or that, despite its derivation from a castrated animal, oxtail has long been linked with aphrodisiac effects.

In addition to his amusing association with royal authority and academic refinement, then, Zarathustra is also linked to an enhanced, if nonreproductive, sexuality – and its private, carnal pleasures, rather than familial or communal concerns. The hyperbole that follows his academic title – 'nor breathed there ever that man to whom mankind was more beholden' – echoes the grandiose tone of *Thus Spake Zarathustra*, while it both asserts and undercuts a central lesson of that text: that mankind owes deep gratitude to the secular prophet because he has taught them what the Christian priests cannot. He has taught them, that is, the Übermensch, who should be loved (rather than their neighbour) precisely because he surpasses humanity in its current state. All this is again linked back to the earlier exchanges between Stephen and Mulligan regarding the future of Irish culture by reference to 'thy tower', where 'the stranger' – that is, the Englishman, Haines – has usurped the place of Stephen and left only the 'secondbest bed' to Mulligan, according to a phrase that invokes Shakespeare's rather ungenerous bequest to his wife, Ann. Moving to an end, Stephen – now fully, if ironically, inhabiting the Mulliganean role of Nietzschean priest – pronounces '*Orate, fratres, pro memetipso*' ('Brothers, pray for me myself') in imitation of the celebrant at the end of the Liturgy of the Eucharist, who calls on the assembly to request that their sacrifice might be acceptable to God. Then, bringing his brief mock mass to a close, Stephen intones: 'And all the people shall say, Amen'.[90]

This mockery is shortly challenged by yet more mockery. When Mulligan arrives on the scene at the maternity hospital, he comes bearing a freshly printed visiting card that presents him as 'Mr Malachi Mulligan, Fertiliser and Incubator, Lambay Island' and he soon announces his desire 'to devote himself to the noblest task for which our bodily organism has been framed'. Citing concerns about the 'sterility' of Ireland, he explains (in the style of Joseph Addison and Richard Steele's essays) his plan to:

> purchase in fee simple for ever the freehold of Lambay island from its holder, lord Talbot de Malahide, a Tory gentleman of note much in favour with our ascendancy party. He proposed to set up there a national fertilising farm to be named *Omphalos* with an obelisk hewn and erected after the fashion of Egypt and to offer his dutiful yeoman services for the fecundation of any female of what grade of life soever who should there direct to him with the desire of fulfilling the functions of her natural.

Evidently abandoning his earlier scheme to set up a neo-pagan cult in the tower, the ribald young man now mirthfully suggests relocating the 'omphalos' (now with a phallic Egyptian obelisk) to an island off the coast of Dublin, where he will personally offer stud services to the women of Ireland. His plan amounts to an erotic reverie for masculinist nationalism, as Mulligan plots to take full and irrevocable ownership of land belonging to a once-powerful Anglo-Irish Protestant family, so that he can begin his eugenicist effort to repopulate the country with little Mulligans. In this way, his scheme also counters Stephen's mockery of Zarathustra as a randy but nonreproductive academic by hyperbolically reasserting one of the 'traditional paternalist narratives of male worth' that Duffy identifies. Yet, coming from Mulligan's mouth, the narrative also highlights the perverse patriarchal expectations involved in such nationalist and eugenicist fantasies, which simply presume female sexual consent rather than giving the matter any serious consideration. Nothing could be farther from George Egerton's feminist transvaluation of Nietzsche's thought in 'The Regeneration of Two', discussed at the beginning of this study: the founding of a utopian community, where unwed mothers and their children, once ostracised from society, can create a new social order based on their own needs and values.

There is something quite serious, then, to be found in all this joking, for these passages from 'Oxen of the Sun' bear on the vision of Ireland offered by the chapter as a whole, which is profoundly concerned with discourses of breeding and paternity – and what they might say about the future of Ireland, as foreshadowed both by the birth of a child and by the conversation of the young men in the hospital. When, after a difficult labour, the long-awaited baby Purefoy is finally born in the maternity ward down the hall, the gathered youths break into a raucous celebration of paternity: 'By heaven, Theodore Purefoy, thou hast done a doughty deed and no botch! Thou art, I vow, the remarkablest progenitor barring none in this chaffering allincluding most farraginous chronicle'.[91] The prose now emphasises what Geoffrey Hartman calls 'the impure or extravagant element in the diction' of Thomas Carlyle to the point of achieving a carnivalesque quality that verges on unintelligibility.[92] Although he is absent from the scene, the new father is incited to continue his reproductive efforts like a ferocious animal: 'Cleave to her! Serve! Toil on, labour like a very bandog and let scholarment and all Malthusiasts go hang. Thou art all their daddies, Theodore. Art drooping under thy load, bemoiled with butcher's bills at home and ingots (not thine!) in the countinghouse? Head up! For every newbegotten thou shalt gather thy homer of ripe wheat'.[93] And, in this vulgar way, Purefoy is urged on in the face of those who would suggest that Ireland is not capable of sustaining, much less increasing, its population. In his highly influential *An Essay on the Principle of Population* (1798), Thomas Malthus argues that, while population growth in any society would occur in a geometric progression, the food supply would increase only in an arithmetic progression. According to this calculus, the size of a population will continue to increase only until it is checked and returned to a sustainable level by what came to be known as a Malthusian catastrophe: war, disease, or starvation. During the course of the nineteenth century, politicians and political economists in England came to hold the vulgar Malthusian view that Ireland suffered from poverty – and from the devastating effects of the Famine – due to a surplus of Irishmen. Malthus had contended that the only way to avoid such catastrophes was to be found in 'preventive checks', including curbing marriage between impoverished or otherwise defective individuals and imposing 'moral restraint' on sexual activity.[94] Latter-day Malthusians came to advocate birth control through the use of contraceptives at the same time that the eugenics movement was gaining momentum in Great Britain and elsewhere.

The scattered allusions to Nietzsche contained in the chapter are thus integrated into a discursive environment that contains all manner of other conceptual formulas bearing on the same concerns; the prose style of Carlyle, moreover, seems to be a particularly apt model for the passages in question since it recalls through form, if not through content, his perspective on these same issues: travelling across Ireland in the latter stages of the Famine, accompanied by the nationalist Charles Gavan Duffy, the Victorian sage had noted with disgust the 'pauperism in geometrical progression' that had created 'brutal … human swineries' across the island.[95] Andrew Gibson argues that, while Joyce's chapter rejects the Malthusian analysis of the Irish situation, it nonetheless connects with that tradition by placing the population issue in the Irish political context; more important, according to this argument, the chapter also 'massively supplements or radically extends the tradition, most of all precisely in its playfulness'. For Gibson, this playfulness inserts 'a new and assertive buoyancy' into a novel way of thinking about Ireland that had only just begun to emerge at the turn of the twentieth century:[96] that is, that an increase in the population might move Ireland further away from the trauma of the Famine and closer toward 'modern independence and modern political and cultural health'.[97] In this sense, the concatenation of voices that make up the chapter, including Nietzschean parodies as well as all the bawdy talk of sex and reproduction, does contribute to something like a utopian view of the future of Ireland.

Just as the allusion to Zarathustra had troubled his discursive authority, the parody of Carlyle both undermines the 'oracular gravitas' that characterises so much of his work and contributes to a perspective at odds with his own (though a perspective that eventually fragments into a kaleidoscopic melee of allusions, expressions, and bits of popular wisdom):[98] 'Copulation without population! No, say I! Herod's slaughter of the innocents were the truer name. Vegetables, forsooth, and sterile cohabitation! Give her beefsteaks, red, raw, bleeding! She is a hoary pandemonium of ills, enlarged glands, mumps, quinsy, bunions, hayfever, bedsores, ringworm, floating kidney, Derbyshire neck, warts, bilious attacks, gallstones, cold feet, varicose vein'.[99] Shouted in the streets of Dublin, this jocular refutation of the birth control movement calls on Biblical precedent, Victorian dietary recommendations, and a gruesome litany of diagnoses, drawn from the studies of the medical students. Together, they suggest not so much a faith in the utopian potentiality of the Irish race as shallow sloganeering and dubious advice further undercut by lingering, if playfully discounted, fears regarding decadence and degeneration.

Zarathustra and mother's milk for Ireland

It is in this frenzied discursive milieu that the conversation among the young men incorporates another Nietzschean allusion: 'How saith Zarathustra? *Deine Kuh Trübsal melkest Du. Nun trinkst Du die süsse Milch des Euters*'.[100] The lines, from Section 5 of *Thus Spake Zarathustra*, 'Of Delights and Passions', appear in Alexander Tille's 1896 translation as 'thou didst milk the cow of sorrow – now though drinkest the sweet milk of its udder',[101] and harken back to a mention of Ireland as 'a land flowing with milk and money' earlier in the chapter, though here the threat of 'bitter milk'[102] has become the promise of 'sweet milk'. John Burt Foster argues that 'the strained, bombastic qualities of Zarathustra's style become apparent when it is placed among the parodies of English prose in the "Oxen of the Sun"'.[103] This is, in fact, the only place in *Ulysses* where the words attributed (or nearly attributed) to Zarathustra actually belong to Nietzsche's text,[104] rather than to Mulligan's or Stephen's biblical parodies, though this third attribution compounds the parodic effect of pronouncing Nietzsche's refrain by diminishing its authority yet again with this playful repetition (even more playful, if we note that the actual quotation from *Thus Spake Zarathustra* is the one that receives only doubtful attribution: 'How Saith ... ?'). But one more time we should note that what is strictly speaking a quotation also serves as a parody of a parody (and, possibly, of a further parody, if we attribute the quotation in *Ulysses* to Stephen rather than Mulligan), for the mocking 'saith' both emphasises Nietzsche's parodic use of the biblical idiom in the German original and evokes the language of the King James Bible. At the very least, the prophetic has been rendered mock-prophetic. Hartman suggests that Nietzsche, like Carlyle, could only parody and not appropriate the high seriousness of such language because 'its weight and resonance make a fool of whatever modern writer dares impersonate it'. In this passage of 'Oxen of the Sun', which 'interlards Carlyle and Nietzsche', Joyce might be praised for calling the 'bluff' of both writers, but to simply praise the text for taking down these heightened styles is to overlook the complex ideological work that these lines do in relation to the other discourses comprising the passage.[105] To begin with, it might be noted that, as the language of the chapter progressively fragments and degenerates, the quotation from Nietzsche mixes with not just biblical references, but medical terminology, Dublin slang, and other popular discourses in the mouths of these young men, suggesting that his philosophy has entered into a common idiom bandied about during a pub crawl.

Yet the quotation, even in this remarkable new setting, carries vestiges of its original articulation in the pages of *Thus Spake Zarathustra*, where Nietzsche advocates for a transvaluation of the human passions: as Zarathustra, addressing his followers, says in the lines immediately preceding the quotation, 'out of thy poisons thou brewedest a balsam for thee'.[106] With this curious pharmakon, he encourages his listeners to acknowledge the value of what comes from the passions by abandoning the valuations that have condemned them as sins or vices and instead adopting, or creating, a new set of valuations that celebrates the same passions as life-affirming. In other words, Zarathustra incites his followers to abandon the Christian ethos that makes a virtue of abstinence by turning the will to power against the passions, including sexual passion, in order to suppress or eradicate them. For all the facetiousness that accompanies it, this is nonetheless a crucial idea for the chapter. Zarathustra offers a perspective counter not just to the so-called Christian virtues but to the Malthusians who would impose 'moral restraints' on sexual activity in the name of political economy or population control. More than this, however, he urges his listeners (and, in this new context, the audience to be found in the public spaces of Dublin) to affect a personal transvaluation of the bodily passions – and, if we follow Zarathustra, to move towards the status of Übermenschen, by overcoming the forms of selfhood enforced by the values of Christian tradition or imposed by the privations of Irish history.

This obscure German phrase, 'holler[ed] down the street', thus becomes a kind of ebullient, if facetious, rallying call for individual autonomy: for all those within earshot to reorder their passions, to give them style, to create, moreover, a self that relishes in the passions that it incorporates.[107] In this sense, the drunken exclamation also offers an exemplification of Stephen's heretical suggestion earlier in the novel that God is 'A shout in the street', made in response to headmaster Deasy's claim that, 'All history moves towards one great goal, the manifestation of God'.[108] Here, the sacred is not some otherworldly destination to be reached only in some distant future, but rather something already present in the contingencies of the material world – in the rollicking passions of these young men as they make their way through the dirty alleys and avenues of Edwardian Dublin. The exuberant language that follows the quotation emphatically reinforces this message, even as it comically mixes in all manner of other references in a muddled celebration of milk, fatherhood, and drinking:

See! It displodes for thee in abundance. Drink, man, an udderful! Mother's milk, Purefoy, the milk of human kin, milk too of those burgeoning stars overhead, rutilant in thin rainvapour, punch milk, such as those rioters will quaff in their guzzlingden, milk of madness, the honeymilk of Canaan's land. Thy cow's dug was tough, what? Ay, but her milk is hot and sweet and fattening. No dollop this but thick rich bonnyclaber. To her, old patriarch! Pap! *Per deam Partulam et Pertundam nunc est bibendum!*[109]

The excessiveness of the language compounds the excessiveness of the decree, but it does so by offering some comic relief from the high seriousness of Nietzsche's language – or, perhaps more accurately, by vividly demonstrating both the comic and serious potentials of his language. Allusions to *Macbeth*, Exodus, and Roman deities combine with boisterous Dublin dialect to affirm life in a celebration of milk as a tangible, gratifying, and nurturing substance, which, of course, is also closely associated with the maternal body. The abundance of the maternal body, as opposed to the privations and betrayals of Irish history, promises a kind of utopian potentiality in 'the honeymilk of Canaan's land'; the colloquial paraphrase of Zarathustra's injunction – 'Thy cow's dug was tough, what? But her milk is hot and sweet and fattening' – suggests a further transformation of historical difficulties into new Irish prosperity, emphasised in the Anglicised Gaelic term, 'bonnyclabber'. This verbal merriment comes to a comic climax in the Latin acclaimation of Partula and Pertunda, the Roman goddesses who presided over birth and the loss of virginity, and who suggest how far all this has strayed from Christian puritanism, as they bind the celebration of milk and maternity to that of alcohol and sexuality. Having feted the powers of milk the young men move on to their own Dionysian thirst for something more potent.

Of course, Joyce's mobile rhetoric does not allow any utopian vision to persist for long: the group of youths, these representatives of a national community of the future, carry on with their bawdy banter and their language continues to degenerate. When Mulligan, in a final Nietzschean allusion, jestingly proposes a toast to Stephen – 'Mead of our fathers for the *Uebermensch*' – he evokes the potential of his gifted peer, who might come to embody what the progenitors of past generations had dreamed or hoped for the Irish (or even what Yeats had imagined of those dreams in his plays and poetry).[110] No doubt this is pale prophecy. The passing suggestion, following on all this talk of birth and breeding, is that Ireland may indeed have seen the emergence of a truly exceptional individual, capable of overcoming the aesthetic, ethical, and affective limitations of his fellow men, or at least his compatriots: it is Stephen who has evaded their enslavement to the Imperial British state, the Holy Roman Empire, and the Irish nation itself, at least for a moment. Yet, in this comic context, the allusion to the Übermensch also works to demythologise this mythos of the future, to undercut the heroic individualism that it promises. The toast cheerfully points out the failures of the returned exile, who continues to find himself alienated from his community precisely insofar as he rejects the forces of imperialism, Catholicism, and nationalism that have shaped its history. Repeated here, the salute to the Übermensch, however ironic, also recalls Stephen's earlier dismissal of Mulligan's Nietzschean invitation in the 'Telemachus' episode, which hails him to join the pagan cult of the tower and take up the project of cultural transformation. The young man rejects the call, at least in part, because it pays no heed to his personal and national past, to the struggles of those who suffered and died in the Famine or those, like his mother, who were likewise victims of Irish history. For all his efforts at cultural distinction, Stephen has not yet attained, or cannot attain, the kind of nobility that would allow him to make promises to himself or to engage in a generosity towards the future. In the closing pages of the 'Oxen of the Sun', moreover, the toast takes its place among innumerable other calls – Revivalist imaginings, Shakespearean parodies, Irish nationalist anthems, Latin musings, Dublin slang, and so on – that compete for the attention and allegiance of the young man. Taken together, they suggest a vast and eclectic array of possibilities for the Ireland to come, even as their sheer incoherence presages a chaos of misunderstanding and contention far more than some lasting harmony of communal affiliation and fellow feeling.

Irish modernism, Irish classics

In a pithy summation of the long and varied history of Nietzsche's reception, Peter Sloterdijk suggests 'that never has an author so insisted on distinction and yet attracted such vulgarity'.[111] This is the case, in large part, because Nietzsche's writing persistently eludes definitive interpretation, and instead offers itself up, in a form of boundless generosity, to all manner of appropriation as it circulates through new national cultures, media environments, institutional settings, and political circumstances. This is also the case, however, because his philosophy sets out on a radical program of illusion-destruction, which has few parallels in the history of Western thought, even as it engages in a concomitant project of illusion-creation, generating new myths, new metaphors, new values by which to live. His Zarathustra thus prophesies the rise of nihilism in the aftermath of the death of God, but also insists on filling this moral vacuum with the cultivation of new meanings, however open or uncertain, in the form of the Übermensch. Through the intervention of his early disciples, detractors, and interpreters, Nietzsche quickly became associated with a range of modern myths, including the grand mythico-historical schema of *A Vision* and the new religion of Creative Evolution in *Back to Methuselah*, as well as fascist myths addressed to the renewal of civilisation and humanity through the collectivity of the state. Nietzsche and his creation, Zarathustra, also find their way into the mythic method of *Ulysses*, if only as means of questioning the promises of individualism as embodied in the Übermensch and the possibilities for overcoming the historical force of *ressentiment*. What is unquestionable is that, as elusive as this writing may seem, in each case these fragments of Nietzschean vocabulary, these glimpses of Nietzschean images continued to well up in the writing of these Irish modernists as they sought to create their own visions of the postwar world. His philosophy had heralded the final collapse of a shared mythos that had provided Western civilisation with a sturdy bulwark against the tumultuous forces of history, but it had also helped to usher in a new myth-making project that was based on the unrestrained freedom of artistic creation.

No doubt there is also the potential for something deeply troubling in this. The fascist appropriation of Nietzsche in the 1930s created a totalitarian cult of war and violence to fill the spiritual vacuum that the philosopher had foreseen as the outcome of a general drift towards nihilism in Western civilisation. Selective reading and strategic redaction allowed the propagandists of National Socialism to transform the pluralism of his writing into a form of vengeance politics, though they could not retain his corrosive criticism of antisemitism, German chauvinism, modern militarism, and so many other signs of decadence. In his T.S. Eliot Memorial Lectures at the University of Kent, delivered in November 1969 (and later published as *The Suspecting Glance* in 1972), Conor Cruise O'Brien nonetheless lamented the 'malign influence' that Nietzsche had exercised over Yeats and contested Richard Ellman's suggestion that the poet had 'discarded the brutal implications of Nietzsche's ethics'.[112] 'In fact', O'Brien claims, rather than leave behind these implications, 'fierceness, violence, arrogance and war were to become more attractive to Yeats towards the end of his life', when, as evinced by his hectoring eugenicist tract, *On the Boiler* (1938), he had been reading Nietzsche again with great relish. To be sure, Shaw also drifted further into these turbulent waters during the 1930s, as evinced in the preface to *On the Rocks*, where he followed up his recent praise of the British fascist leader, Oswald Mosley, by accepting the apparent necessity of dictatorships and pondering the desirability of negative eugenics in the form of mass exterminations, much like those being prepared in Germany.

The degree to which any of this can be blamed on Nietzsche is highly contestable. O'Brien, like Thomas Kettle long before him, deems the philosopher guilty by association with those who had adopted some of his most notorious aphorisms for their nefarious ideological and militaristic purposes – and, again like Kettle, he denounces those who, especially in England, would overlook this 'ferocious' Nietzsche in favour of the 'gentle' Nietzsche, recognised as a dazzling writer, incisive critic, or penetrating psychologist. 'When Nietzsche praises, as he so often does, war and cruelty', O'Brien echoes Kettle, more than fifty years later, 'we are told we must understand him as calling for spiritual struggle and a stern mastery over the self'.[113] Lecturing in the aftermath of the Third Reich and its appropriation of Nietzsche (and just months after his own election to the Dáil Éireann as a member of the opposition Labour Party), he attributes to the philosopher a coherent ethical system, which elicits – or, at least, seems to elicit – from him a kind of absolute certainty about its dire social and political implications. As he concludes his reflections on Yeats and Nietzsche, O'Brien looks forward at the world to come from the vantage of the late 1960s and expresses a fear that 'the planetary crisis of population, and the development of automation, and new manipulatory techniques in communication, leave the way open for, among other things, neo-Nietzschean and crypto-Nietzschean politics, gentle only in their language'.[114] His trepidation about these developments was certainly warranted. And yet, O'Brien also suggests that the path to the kind of democratic socialist future that he desires, with its basis in the 'idea of human brotherhood', 'requires us to be more, not less, *suspicious* about humanity, intelligence, responsibility, kinship, compassion as well as about disguised forms of cruelty and contempt'.[115] His role models for this kind of inquiry are Marx and also, ironically, Nietzsche, that other 'master of suspicion', whose 'suspecting glance' gives the published lectures their title.

As he looks back on Yeats's writing from the tail end of the modernist period, what O'Brien cannot deny, despite his best efforts, is the status that Nietzsche's texts had achieved: the philosopher 'inscribed his name in the list of classics', according to Sloterdijk, because his books are able to 'survive their interpretations', so that just when they seem to be exhausted, they manage to enrich their readers in 'the most surprising way'.[116] In the early years of the century, as the modernist period was getting underway, Shaw, Yeats, and Joyce had each enlisted Nietzsche in his own way to forge competing myths of the modern artist. In his philosophy, they found distilled into striking images and metaphors a devastating critique of bourgeois social norms, Christian or slave morality, indulgent sentimentality, nationalistic zeal, and aesthetic conventionalism – in short, all manner of modern illusions, including the abiding artifices of Western thought. But where Shaw and Yeats each drew on this cache of tropes to articulate his own mythos of the future, which verged on a form of visionary mysticism or dark utopianism, Joyce could be said to have turned his own 'suspecting glance' toward Nietzschean language in order to come to terms with the modernist cliché of the heroic artist, as well as to confront the oppressive forces of metrocolonial modernity. In the process, by appropriating this language, they each explored the potentiality of an Irish modernism that can also be said to imagine worlds at a critical distance from historical realities in order to breach a dimension that would otherwise remain out of sight, a dimension that raises persistent questions about what should be considered possible, necessary, or desirable. Or, to put this another way, these Irish modernists respond to Nietzschean provocations with their own array of provocative images, metaphors, and myths, which repeatedly traverse the borderlands between art and society, aesthetics and politics. This is not to suggest that the success of these writers owes some unrepayable debt to the philosopher: his provocative generosity did not seek to incur such liabilities, but instead, as Sloterdijk has it, worked 'to generate dissensus, which is to say competition'.[117] It is to affirm, then, that the writings of these Irish modernists have attained the status of classics themselves.

Notes

1 'Debate on Mountjoy Executions', Dáil Éireann Debate, 8 December 1922, www.oireachtas.ie/en/debates/debate/dail/1922-12-08/9/. Accessed 15 May 2021.
2 Friedrich Nietzsche, *Beyond Good and Evil*, Helen Zimmern (trans.) (New York: Macmillan, 1907), p. 145.
3 Allan Megill, *Prophets of Extremity: Nietzsche, Heidegger, Foucault, Derrida* (Berkeley: University of California Press, 1987), p. 82.
4 See Nicholas Allen, 'Yeats, Spengler, and *A Vision* after Empire', in Richard Begam and Michael Moses (eds), *Modernism and Colonialism: British and Irish Literature, 1899–1939* (Durham: Duke University Press, 2007), pp. 209–25.
5 Bernard Shaw, 'Preface: the Infidel Half Century', in Bernard Shaw, *Back to Methuselah: A Metabiological Pentateuch* (New York: Brentano's, 1921), p. x.
6 W.B. Yeats to Olivia Shakespear, 24 July 1934, in Allan Wade (ed.), *The Letters of W.B. Yeats* (London: Rupert Hart-Davis, 1954), p. 825.
7 W.B. Yeats, *The Collected Works of W.B. Yeats, Volume XIV: A Vision: The Revised 1937 Version*, Catherine E. Paul and Margaret Mills Harper (eds) (New York: Scribner, 2015), p. 37.
8 By the end of the month, on a blank page facing the first question from 28 January, Yeats had linked his own Phase Seventeen to that of Nietzsche and Cuchulain: 'Ego of 17 goes to 12 because the fourth back has similar aim in search'. Asking 'why ugliness at 12', Yeats received as his response a line drawn to 'hatred of self', which thus seemed to reflect on all those associated with the phase, indeed the entire contemporary era encompassed by the phase. This association became increasingly significant for Yeats, who questioned further, 'If Nietzsche belongs to phase 12 is his thought characteristic of this epoch', to which George responded succinctly, if cryptically, 'Forerunner', going on to

clarify, of 'this epoch'. George Mills Harper, *The Making of Yeats's* A Vision: *A Study of the Automatic Script, Volume 2* (Carbondale: Southern Illinois University Press, 1987), p. 4.
9   Ibid., p. 28.
10 W.B. Yeats, 'The Phases of the Moon', in W.B. Yeats, *Wild Swans at Coole* (New York: Macmillan, 1919), p. 92.
11 W.B. Yeats, *The Collected Works of W.B. Yeats, Volume XIII: A Vision: The Original 1925 Version*, Catherine E. Paul and Margaret Mills Harper (eds) (New York: Scribner, 2013), p. 52.
12 Ibid., p. 52.
13 Friedrich Nietzsche, *Thus Spake Zarathustra: A Book for All or None*, Alexander Tille (trans.) (New York: Macmillan, 1986), p. 2.
14 Stanley Rosen, *The Mask of Enlightenment: Nietzsche's Zarathustra* (New Haven: Yale University Press, 2014), p. 88.
15 See, for instance, Frances Nesbitt Oppel, *Yeats and Nietzsche: Mask and Tragedy, 1902–1910* (Charlottesville: University of Virginia Press, 1987); Otto Bohlmann, *Yeats and Nietzsche: An Exploration of Major Nietzschean Echoes in the Writings of William Butler Yeats* (New York: Springer, 1982), pp. 130–36; Richard Ellman, *The Identity of Yeats* (Oxford: Oxford University Press, 1964), pp. 84–89.
16 Yeats, *A Vision: The Original 1925 Version*, p. 53.
17 Ibid., p. 53.
18 Robert Gooding-Williams, *Zarathustra's Dionysian Modernism* (Palo Alto: Stanford University Press, 2001), p. 31.
19 Yeats, *A Vision: The Original 1925 Version*, p. 53. Denis Donoghue claims that what follows is virtually a transcription from *Thus Spake Zarathustra*, Part 2, 'On Self-Overcoming'; Yeats is aligning himself with Nietzsche's understanding of the highest and hardest solitude as expressed most fully in the book. *William Butler Yeats* (New York: Viking Press, 1971), p. 107.
20 Ibid., p. 53.
21 Ibid., p. 53.
22 Ibid., p. 90.
23 Nietzsche, *Zarathustra*, p. 198.
24 Ibid., p. 202.
25 Yeats, *A Vision: The Original 1925 Version*, p. 93.
26 Gooding-Williams, *Zarathustra's Dionysian Modernism*, p. 206.
27 But the German philosopher, insofar as his 'doctrine of Eternal Recurrence' teaches that such a new emotion is caught up in a continual process of becoming, rather than being, 'almost' belongs to Gyre Eleven.
28 Yeats senses this counter-movement has already many of his modernist compeers, writers such as 'Mr Ezra Pound, Mr Eliot, Mr Joyce, Signor Pirandello' who integrate a new strangeness into literary language or who undermine logical thought with associative techniques. Yeats connects this revolution of the word with political revolution, which is possible for the last time in Phase Twenty-Three, as men experience the same kind of

technical inspiration in affairs of state, 'the doing of this or that not because one would, or should but because one can' (Yeats, *A Vision: The Original 1925 Version*, p. 175).
29 Ibid., p. 176.
30 Ibid., p. 176.
31 Ibid., p. 177.
32 Friedrich Nietzsche, *A Genealogy of Morals*, William A. Haussmann (trans.) (New York: Macmillan, 1897), pp. 8, 45, 4.
33 Ibid., p. 129.
34 Ibid., p. 8.
35 Yeats, *A Vision: The Original 1925 Version*, p. 176.
36 Nietzsche, *A Genealogy*, p. 20.
37 Yeats, *A Vision: The Original 1925 Version*, p. 176.
38 Ibid., p. 177.
39 Bernard Shaw, *Man and Superman: A Comedy and a Philosophy* (New York: Brentano's, 1905), p. 196.
40 Shaw, 'Preface', p. x.
41 Ibid., p. lxxix.
42 Nietzsche, *Beyond Good and Evil*, pp. 192–93.
43 Ibid., p. 195.
44 Ibid., pp. 195–96.
45 Shaw, 'Preface', p. lxxix.
46 Bernard Shaw, *Back to Methuselah: A Metabiological Pentateuch* (New York: Brentano's, 1921), p. 77.
47 Shaw, 'Preface', p. viii.
48 Ibid., p. xix.
49 Ibid., p. lx.
50 Shaw, *Back to Methuselah*, p. 92.
51 Shaw, 'Preface', p. xix.
52 Ibid., p. xc.
53 Ibid., p. xci.
54 Ibid., p. xcii.
55 Ibid., p. c.
56 Shaw, *Back to Methuselah*, p. 26.
57 Ibid., p. 78.
58 Ibid., p. 92.
59 Ibid., p. 77.
60 Ibid., p. 109.
61 Ibid., p. 108.
62 Ibid., p. 157.
63 Ibid., p. 210.
64 Ibid., p. 175.
65 Ibid., p. 219.
66 Ibid., p. 206.
67 Ibid., p. 203.

68 Bernard Shaw, 'Preface: First Aid to Critics', in Bernard Shaw, *John Bull's Other Island; and Major Barbara* (New York: Brentano's, 1907), p. 152.
69 Friedrich Nietzsche, *The Joyful Wisdom*, Thomas Common (trans.) (Edinburgh: T.N. Foulis, 1910), p. 65.
70 Nietzsche, *A Genealogy*, p. 58.
71 For more on Nietzsche's biopolitical prescience, see Roberto Esposito's *Bíos: Biopolitics and Philosophy*, Timothy Campbell (trans.) (Minneapolis: University of Minnesota Press, 2008), pp. 87–109.
72 Shaw, *Back to Methuselah*, p. 235.
73 Nietzsche, *Zarathustra*, p. 432.
74 Shaw, *Back to Methuselah*, p. 241.
75 Friedrich Nietzsche, *Twilight of the Idols*, Thomas Common (trans.) (London: H. Henry, 1896), p. 178.
76 Ibid., p. 163.
77 Shaw, *Back to Methuselah*, p. 290.
78 Ibid., p. 248.
79 Bernard Shaw, *Too True to Be Good; Village Wooing; On the Rocks* (London: Constable, 1934), p. 143.
80 Shaw, *Back to Methuselah*, p. 298.
81 Daniel Conway, *Nietzsche and the Political* (New York: Routledge, 2005), p. 3.
82 See Richard Brown, *James Joyce and Sexuality* (Cambridge: Cambridge University Press, 1988); Mary Lowe-Evans, *Crimes Against Fecundity: Joyce and Population Control* (Syracuse: Syracuse University Press, 1989).
83 Enda Duffy, 'Interesting States: Birthing and the Nation in "Oxen of the Sun"', in Kimberly J. Devlin and Marilyn Reizbaum (eds), Ulysses: *En-Gendered Perspectives: Eighteen New Essays on the Episodes* (Columbia: University of South Carolina Press, 1999), pp. 210–28.
84 Ibid., p. 218.
85 Ibid., p. 222.
86 James Joyce, *Ulysses* (London: Egoist, 1922), p. 375.
87 Duffy, 'Interesting States', p. 223.
88 Joyce, *Ulysses*, p. 375.
89 Ibid., p. 375.
90 Ibid., p. 375.
91 Ibid., p. 402.
92 Geoffrey Hartman, *Criticism in the Wilderness: the Study of Literature Today* (New Haven: Yale University Press, 2007), p. 134.
93 Joyce, *Ulysses*, p. 402.
94 Qtd in Geoffrey Gilbert, 'Introduction', in Thomas Robert Malthus, *An Essay on the Principle of Population* (Oxford: Oxford University Press, 1999), p. xx.
95 Thomas Carlyle, 'Reminiscences of My Irish Journey in 1849', in John P. Harrington (ed.), *The English Traveller in Ireland: Accounts of Ireland and the Irish through Five Centuries* (Dublin: Wolfhound, 1991), p. 261.

96 Andrew Gibson, '"Let All Malthusiasts Go Hang": Joyce's "Oxen of the Sun" and the Economists', *Literature & History* 10:2 (November 2001), 71.
97 Ibid., 72.
98 Ibid., 72.
99 Joyce, *Ulysses*, p. 402.
100 Ibid., p. 403.
101 Nietzsche, *Zarathustra*, p. 42.
102 Joyce, *Ulysses*, p. 375.
103 John Burt Foster Jr., *Heirs to Dionysus: A Nietzschean Current in Literary Modernism* (Princeton: Princeton, 1981), p. 30.
104 Paul van Caspel has pointed out Joyce's 'melkest' should be 'melktest' in the German. See 'Annotations to the Annotations of *Annotations*', *James Joyce Literary Supplement* 6:2 (Fall 1992), 14.
105 Hartman, *Criticism*, p. 134.
106 Nietzsche, *Zarathustra*, p. 42.
107 Joyce, *Ulysses*, p. 403.
108 Ibid., p. 34.
109 Ibid., p. 403.
110 Ibid., p. 403.
111 Peter Sloterdijk, *Nietzsche Apostle* (Los Angeles: Semiotext(e), 2013), p. 7.
112 Conor Cruise O'Brien, *The Suspecting Glance* (London: Faber & Faber, 2015), pp. 67, 68.
113 Conor Cruise O'Brien, 'Nietzsche and the Machiavellian Schism', in *The Suspecting Glance*, p. 52.
114 O'Brien, *The Suspecting Glance*, p. 90.
115 Ibid., pp. 89–90.
116 Peter Sloterdijk, *Thinker on Stage: Nietzsche's Materialism* (Minneapolis: University of Minnesota, 1989), pp. 68, 3.
117 Sloterdijk, *Nietzsche*, p. 62.

Index

Note: Nietzsche's individual writings can be found under 'works'

Abbey Theatre 80, 129, 132–37
   see also Irish Literary Theatre; Irish National Dramatic Society
Anglo-Irish Ascendancy 46, 94, 108, 111–14, 137
Aquinas, Thomas 155–56, 167
   Summa Theologiae 155
Aristotle 118, 167
Arnold, Matthew 2
   Study of Celtic Literature, The 83, 107–8, 113
Ascheim, Steven 49
Auden, W.H. 225

Barry, (Father) William Francis
   Heralds of Revolt 151–52
Bax, Belfort 84
Beaumont, Francis 258–59
Becker, Wolfgang
   Nietzsche Cult, The 196
Begam, Richard 179
Bell, Michael 11, 15
Best, Richard 103
Bildung 149, 154–55, 161, 170–71, 185
Blake, William 92, 95, 243–44
blond beast 18, 96, 203–4, 228–29
Bloom, Harold 14, 52
Bourdieu, Pierre 14, 26, 167
Brandes, George 6, 8, 17, 183
Brown, Richard 257
Butler, Samuel 62–63, 84, 249
   Evolution, Old and New 63
   Luck or Cunning? 63

Caesar 75, 77–79
Carlyle, Thomas 152, 261–63
Casanova, Pascale 26, 46
   World Republic of Letters, The 26–29, 31
Casement, (Sir) Roger 212, 219
Castle, Gregory 161
Catholic Church 12, 81–83, 159–61
   influence in Ireland 111–13, 168–69, 174, 197
Catholicism 111–13, 146–49, 151–53, 159–60, 164, 181
Cheng, Vincent 172
Childs, Donald 105
Clarke, Austin 215–16
   Penny in the Clouds 215
Cleary, Joe 5
Cole, (Rev) R. Lee 213
colonialism 12, 26–27, 147, 169, 217
Colum, Padraic 148–50
Common, Thomas 43, 207, 222
   Nietzsche as Critic, Philosopher, Poet and Prophet 123–32
conscience 54, 93, 95, 159–60, 167–68, 171–78, 185
   bad 2–4, 34, 148, 163–65, 169–71, 174–76, 180, 184, 244
   national 5, 30, 32–33, 75–83, 132, 137–38, 147, 153, 186, 235
Conway, Daniel 49, 68, 256
Cosgrave, W.T. 235
cosmopolitanism 25, 29–31, 132, 197–98, 221
Cousins, James 200
   Sold 92
Cousins, Margaret 200
Creative Evolution 35, 237, 247–55
Cromwell, William 75, 77–78, 169
Cullingford, Elizabeth 105, 126
cultural capital 3–4, 8, 14, 20, 27, 94, 149, 162, 167–68, 180–81

cultural distinction 14, 94, 136–38, 162–63, 221, 266
cultural production 4, 14, 27–28, 133, 151, 183
Curran, (Rev) Stanislaus 218

Dana: An Irish Magazine of Independent Thought 31, 150, 152
Danto, Arthur 205, 223
Darwin, Charles 68, 220, 254
   Origin of Species 62
   see also evolutionary theory
Davidson, John 43
Davis, Thomas 214–17
Deane, Seamus 154
Delany, (Rev) William 152, 213
Deleuze, Gilles 100–1
de Man, Paul 14–15
Derrida, Jacques 15, 194
   Spurs 223
Doggett, Rob 119, 133
Dostoevsky, Fyodor
   Brothers Karamazov 205
Duffy, Charles Gavan 199, 262
Duffy, Enda 257–58
Duhamel, George
   Civilization, 1914–1917 225

Eagle and the Serpent, The 24, 42, 44, 78, 207
Eagleton, Terry 12
Eastlake, Allan
   Oneida Community, The 75
Egerton, George (Mary Chavelita Dunne) 6–10, 21–22, 201
   Discords 6, 21
     'Regeneration of Two, The' 8–9, 261
   Keynotes 6
     'Cross Line, A' 7–8
     'Now Spring Has Come' 8
     'Spell of the White Elf, The' 8
Eglinton, John (William Patrick Magee) 26–31, 150, 157
   'Nationalism Drama and Contemporary Life' 29
   'Way of Understanding Nietzsche, A' 31, 150–51, 179, 183
   'What Should Be the Subjects of National Drama?' 26
Ellis, Havelock 23–24, 43

Ellmann, Richard 102, 146, 148–49, 258
Euckens, Rudolph Christoph 222
eugenics 45, 49, 57, 68–69, 72–74, 77, 80–82, 107–8, 138, 172, 237, 255–56, 261–62
Everard, (Sir) Nugent 218
evolutionary theory 43–44, 54–58, 60–68, 75–76, 85, 220, 247–48
   Darwinian 44, 56–57, 61–63, 67–68, 113, 244, 249
   Lamarckian 44, 61–63, 173, 250
   see also Darwin, Charles

Fabian Society 42–43, 46, 48, 73
   see also socialism
Fanon, Frantz 171
Fay, Frank 92, 118
Fitzgerald, T.H. 199
Fletcher, John 258–59
folklore 5, 26–27, 104–5
Förster-Nietzsche, Elisabeth 17, 196
Foster Jr., John Burt
   Heirs to Dionysus 10, 263
Foster, Roy 111, 112, 133, 136
France, Anatole 160
Frazer, J.G.
   Golden Bough, The 250
Frazier, Adrian 102–3, 105
futurity 12–13, 35, 100, 126, 211, 227–29, 235–37, 250, 253, 256–66
   of human race 15, 46, 50–51, 54–56, 59–60, 64, 85, 186, 239–44, 246–47
   of Irish culture 25, 82, 101, 109, 171, 178–80, 186

Gabler, Hans Walter 178
gender 7–8, 116–17, 181
   masculinity 9, 96, 116, 118, 122, 149, 180, 200, 260
generosity 33, 47, 98–102, 114–17, 123–29, 137, 240, 266
Gibson, Andrew 262
   Joyce's Revenge 170
Goethe, Johann Wolfgang von 52, 68, 77–78, 248
Gogarty, Oliver St. John 148, 177–79
Gonne, Maude 110–13, 216
'good Europeans' 196–98, 206, 221, 248, 252

Gooding-Williams, Robert 12, 99, 171, 176, 241, 243
Granville-Barker, Harley 59, 110
Gregory, Augusta 26, 92–93, 96–97, 135
   Cuchulain of Muirtheme 103, 115
   Gods and Fighting Men 124, 127
   Poets and Dreamers 103–4
Grein, John T. 24
Grierson, (Sir) Herbert J.C. 134
Griffith, Arthur 179, 199–200, 201
Gwynn, Denis 215–16

Hales, Sean 235
Halévy, Daniel
   Life of Friedrich Nietzsche, The (*La vie de Frédéric Nietzsche*) 34, 193, 196
Hamsun, Knut 6, 8
Hansson, Ola 6
   Young Ofeg's Ditties 22
Hardy, Thomas 207–8
Hartman, Geoffrey 182, 261
Higgins, Kathleen 210
Holyroyd, Michael 46
Hone, Joseph 196
   'Nietzsche and War' 208–9
Horniman, Annie 110, 136
Howes, Marjorie 94, 105, 112, 217

Ibsen, Henrik 6, 16, 20, 25, 29–30, 48, 148–49, 167
   Doll's House, A 146
   Enemy of Society, An 158
   Ghosts 24
   Hedda Gabler 8
   Peer Gynt 28, 125
individualism 16–17, 19, 24, 42, 111, 147, 162, 181–83, 240, 266–67
Irish Literary Theatre 93–94, 109, 152
   see also Abbey Theatre
Irish National Dramatic Society 32, 80, 92, 94
   see also Abbey Theatre
Irish National Theatre Society 102, 149
Irish Women's Suffrage League 200

Jameson, Violet
   'Nietzsche and Women' 200–1
Jeffrey, Keith 211–12
Johnson, Thomas 235
Joyce, James 28–29, 33–34, 82–83, 146–49, 153–86, 268
   'Holy Office, The' 149
   'Ireland: Island of Saints and Sages' 169
   'Painful Case, A' 161–63
   'Portrait of the Artist, A' 150
   Portrait of the Artist as a Young Man, A 30, 34, 81, 163–78
   Stephen Hero 33, 153–61
   Ulysses 1–5, 34, 35, 168, 176–86, 237, 256–66
Joyce, Simon 162, 183

Kaufmann, Walter 160–61, 210
Kennedy, J.M.
   Quintessence of Nietzsche, The 199
Kettle, Thomas 34, 151–53, 193–207, 211, 215–24, 268–69
   Battle Songs for the Irish Brigades 221
   'Catholicism and Modern Literature' 152, 157
   Day's Burden, The 198
   'Europe against the Barbarians' 202–6
   'Introduction' to *The Life of Friedrich Nietzsche* 193–97
   'Is Peace Possible?' 201–2
   Ways of War, The 222–24
Kofman, Sara 194
Kornhaber, David 84

Law-book of Manu 130–31
Lawrence, D.H. 10
Lewis, Pericles 82, 172
Lindberg, Kathryn
   Reading Pound Reading 11
Literary Ideals in Ireland 26–30
Lowe-Evans, Mary 257
Lukács, György 16

Mahaffy, (Professor) J.P. 215–16
Malory, (Sir) Thomas 258
Malthus, Thomas
   Essays on the Principle of Population 261–62
Malthusians 257, 261–62
Mann, Thomas 10
Martyn, Edward 26, 93
May, Keith
   Nietzsche and Modern Literature 10
Mencken, H.L. 52
Milroy, Sean 235

Mitchel, John
  Jail Journal 199–200, 211, 214, 216
modernity 12–13, 64, 79, 149
  European 6, 169
  in Ireland 3, 6, 12, 30–31, 149
Moore, George 28, 150, 196
Moore, Gregory
  Nietzsche, Biology, and Metaphor 56
Moore, Thomas 167–68
morality 7–9, 43–44, 53–59, 78, 137, 155, 175
  Christian 23, 43, 58, 84, 114, 228
  master (noble) 18, 117, 124–28, 159, 244–46
  slave 18, 79, 112, 124–28, 130–31, 150–51, 170
Morel, Benedict 16
Morris, William 92, 95
Moses, Michael Valdez 120, 122, 180
myths 1, 5, 177–78, 227, 237, 243–44, 250, 266–68
  Irish 5, 95, 114, 123–26, 128, 168
  new 13, 180, 195, 236, 247, 266
  Scandinavian 120, 126

Napoleon (Bonaparte) 8, 77–79, 183, 252–53
nationalism 27, 80, 169, 172, 186, 221, 242, 248–53
  cultural 2, 5, 28–30, 105, 110, 114, 149–51, 157
  Irish 12, 81–82, 94, 134, 168, 178–78, 197–200, 214–19, 256–58
  see also propaganda; ressentiment
Nehemas, Alexander 194
neo-paganism 9, 148, 178–80, 236, 259, 266
Nesbitt Oppel, Frances 102
New Age, The 207
New Life Fellowship 42–43
nihilism 160–61, 180, 236–38, 241, 245, 266
Nordau, Max 30, 157–58, 179, 193–95
  Degeneration (Entartung) 15–24, 50, 158
Norris, Margot
  Beasts of the Modern Imagination 11
North, Michael 114
Notes for Good Europeans 207
Noyes, John Humphrey 75

O'Brien, Conor Cruise 107, 137, 267
  Suspecting Glance, The 267–68
O'Grady, Standish
  History of Ireland 114
O'Keefe, (Rev) P. 220–21
Ó Máille, Pádraic 235
Orage, Alfred
  Friedrich Nietzsche: the Dionysian Spirit of the Age 207

parody 4, 13–14, 180–82, 204, 258–59, 262–63
Pater, Walter 160
Pearse, Patrick 211, 215–16
philistinism 8, 14, 16, 22, 27, 35, 221
propaganda 15–16, 57, 74, 94, 130–32, 147, 195, 202–9, 212–17, 226–28, 238
  nationalist 29, 94
  see also nationalism
prophecy 107, 184, 226, 243–50

Quinn, John 92, 96–97, 123, 124

Rabaté, Jean-Michel 183
race 71, 82, 106–14, 171–73
Rahilly, A.J.
  'Gospel of the Superman, The' 219–20
Redmond, John 198, 202, 206, 211–12
Ree, Paul 43
ressentiment 70–71, 81, 129, 147, 151, 154, 168–72, 184–86, 216, 267
  nationalist 81–82, 147, 168–69, 186
  see also nationalism
Roberts, George 146, 148–49
Rosen, Stanley 241
Russell, George (Æ) 26–30, 122, 136
  'Nationalism and Cosmopolitanism' 30

Said, Edward 171
Schopenhauer, Arthur 58–59, 220
Shaw, George Bernard 3, 32, 42–85, 92, 173, 207, 222, 268
  Arms and the Man 51
  Back to Methuselah 35, 50, 237, 247–56
    'As Far as Thought Can Reach' 253–56
    'Gospel of the Brothers, The' 250–51

'Thing Happens, The' 250–51
'Tragedy of an Elderly Gentlemen,
  The' 251–52
'Degenerate's View of Nordau, A'
  19–21
Fabian Essays in Socialism 55
Getting Married 257
John Bull's Other Island 47, 80–83
Major Barbara 84, 252
Man and Superman 32, 42–43, 45,
  48, 49–79, 85, 250
'Don Juan in Hell' 32, 60–69
'Epistle Dedicatory' 51–53, 58,
  61, 84
'Revolutionist's Handbook' 57,
  72–79
On the Rocks 255, 267
Perfect Wagnerite, The 126
Quintessence of Ibsenism, The 20,
  23, 48
reviews of Nietzsche 22–25, 42, 45,
  55
Socialism for Millionaires 70
Widowers Houses 24
You Can Never Tell 55
Sheehy-Skiffington, Frank 200
Sheehy-Skiffington, Hanna 200
Sinn Féin 133–34, 178–79, 199, 211,
  215
Sloterdijk, Peter 13–14, 16, 47, 100–3,
  162, 176–77, 182, 266–69
socialism 47–49, 55, 69–77, 84–85, 95,
  163, 195
  Fabian 23–24, 32, 42, 47–49, 55, 79,
    247, 255, 257
  see also Fabian Society
Solomon, Robert 210
Spencer, Herbert 44, 54–57, 61, 67, 77,
  220
Spengler, Arthur 237
Steele, Tom 162
Stone, Dan
  Breeding Supermen 68
Strindberg, August 6–8
Stutfield, Hugh
  'Tommyrotics' 21, 179
Symons, Arthur 93
  'Nietzsche on Tragedy' 120
Synge, J.M. 135
  Playboy of the Western World, The
    105, 133

taste 8, 14, 16, 19–20, 92–93, 113,
  129–30, 162, 221
Tille, Alexander 44–45, 54
transvaluation 9, 18–19, 45, 56, 82,
  100, 169, 218, 229
Trebitsch, Siegfried 42

Übermensch 1, 3, 7, 69–73, 98, 100–2,
  107, 146–49, 154, 161–62,
  180–85, 248, 254–57, 265–66
  adaptation of 32–33, 49–50, 73
  evolutionary ideal of 18, 64–66
  indeterminacy of 13, 15
  insanity of 151, 153
  mythos of 236, 241, 266
Unwin, Fisher 24

Valente, Joseph 116
von Harnack, Adolph 222

Wagner, Richard 22, 28–29, 65, 120,
  125–26
  Ring of the Nibelung, The 125
wars
  Anglo-Irish war 237, 256–57
  First World War 201–30, 236–37,
    250, 257
  Irish Civil War 35, 237
Webb, Beatrice 52
Webb, Sidney 52
Wells, H.G. 208
Weston, Jessie
  From Ritual to Romance 250
White, Richard 101
Wilde, Lady Jane
  Ancient Legends of Ireland 103
Wilde, Oscar 5, 20–22, 46, 179
  'Decay of Lying, The' 21
will to power 13, 65–67, 99–102, 110,
  112, 126–28, 157, 166, 209,
  224, 249
Woolf, Leonard 225
works
  Antichrist, The 1, 65, 112, 130, 177
  Beyond Good and Evil 48, 124–25,
    127, 174, 197, 248
  Birth of Tragedy 119–22
  Dawn of Day, The 24, 151
  Ecce Homo 47, 199
  Genealogy of Morals, A 18, 24–25,
    43, 54–55, 78, 108–9, 128,

163–66, 172–74, 178, 201, 246, 253
'First Essay' 150
'Second Essay' 66
'Third Essay' 165
Human, All Too Human 31, 199
Joyful Wisdom, The 15, 156, 199
Thus Spake Zarathustra 13–15, 51, 61, 65–67, 96–100, 160–62, 174–76, 182, 193–94, 223, 230, 240–42, 259–61
'Back-Worlds-Men' 102
'Of Delights and Passions' 263–64
'Of Giving Virtue' 101
'Of the Famous Wise Men' 103, 105

Yeats, George 238
Yeats, W.B. 3, 5, 10, 25, 28, 32–33, 92–138, 173, 215, 268
'Canonical Book, A' 103
'Celtic Element in Literature, The' 107, 120–21
Celtic Twilight, The 104
Countess Cathleen, The 93, 105–6, 215
'Dramatic Movement, The' 129
Estrangement 137
Fairy and Folk Tales of the Irish Peasantry 104
'First Principles' 31, 113, 129, 131
Golden Helmet, The 134–35
Green Helmet, The 135
'Irish Literary Theatre, 1900, The' 109
King's Threshold, The 33, 94, 100–6, 110
'Leda and the Swan' 244
'Note on National Drama, A' 28, 125
On Baile's Strand 95, 114–20, 132
'On Being Asked for a War Poem' 226
On the Boiler 267
'Phases of the Moon' 226, 238–39
'Second Coming, The' 225–30, 244
Vision, A 35, 225, 237–46, 267
Where There Is Nothing 33, 92, 95–99

EU authorised representative for GPSR:
Easy Access System Europe, Mustamäe tee 50,
10621 Tallinn, Estonia
gpsr.requests@easproject.com

www.ingramcontent.com/pod-product-compliance
Lightning Source LLC
Chambersburg PA
CBHW051604230426
43668CB00013B/1978